Mass Media Unleashed

Mass Media Unleashed

How Washington Policymakers Shortchanged the American Public

Carl R. Ramey

ROWMAN & LITTLEFIELD PUBLISHERS, INC.
Lanham • *Boulder* • *New York* • *Toronto* • *Plymouth, UK*

ROWMAN & LITTLEFIELD PUBLISHERS, INC.

Published in the United States of America
by Rowman & Littlefield Publishers, Inc.
A wholly owned subsidiary of The Rowman & Littlefield Publishing Group, Inc.
4501 Forbes Boulevard, Suite 200, Lanham, Maryland 20706
www.rowmanlittlefield.com

Estover Road, Plymouth PL6 7PY, United Kingdom

British Library Cataloguing in Publication Information Available

Library of Congress Cataloging-in-Publication Data
Ramey, Carl R., 1941-
  Mass media unleashed : how Washington policymakers shortchanged the
American public / Carl R. Ramey.
     p. cm.
  Includes bibliographical references and index.
  ISBN-13: 978-0-7425-5569-3 (cloth : alk. paper)
  ISBN-10: 0-7425-5569-0 (cloth : alk. paper)
  ISBN-13: 978-0-7425-5570-9 (pbk. : alk. paper)
  ISBN-10: 0-7425-5570-4 (pbk. : alk. paper)
  1. Mass media policy—United States. 2. Broadcasting policy—United
States. I. Title.
  P92.U5R36 2007
  302.230973—dc22

                        2007008397

Printed in the United States of America

♾™ The paper used in this publication meets the minimum requirements
of American National Standard for Information Sciences—Permanence of
Paper for Printed Library Materials, ANSI/NISO Z39.48-1992.

To Karen, Mark, and Christian
For Amelia, Avi, and Niall

Contents

Preface

Modern mass media pulsate through the veins of contemporary society, 24/7. They are the relentless lifeblood of American democracy, feeding the nation with essential news and information of its business, politics, and culture. But they are also active carriers for some of the ailments and excesses of American society—heightened commercialism; sound-bite politics; faster-paced, less reflective lifestyles; and a general coarsening of many everyday experiences.

Despite media's capacity to uplift as well as sap America's spirit, most people take it for granted. While everyone enjoys being a media critic, hardly anyone acts on those instincts. Parents that decry the depiction of excessive violence notoriously fail to supervise their own children's television viewing. Despite federal legislation designed to assist worried parents by requiring a "V-chip" (that allows them to block programs they deem objectionable) to be installed in TV sets, far more parents continue to place separate TV sets in their children's bedrooms, effectively ceding control to their offspring.[1] The Federal Communications Commission has long required broadcast stations to solicit public comment on their performance, but the procedures go virtually unused. We live in an age of instant messaging and endless connectivity, yet specific complaints from individual listeners, viewers, or readers remain minuscule.

This is not likely to change. Despite what some media activists see as a recent breakthrough in public participation on media issues,[2]

waiting for the general public to rise up and express widespread dissatisfaction in any palpable form is about as fruitless as waiting for
Godot. What we are beginning to see, however, is a major shift in the
viewing and reading habits of the American public. Audiences for traditional media (print and broadcast) are not only shrinking, they are
migrating to alternative media—pay services, the Internet, and a host
of new audio and video devices allowing consumers to select what
they want, when and where they want it. This new media world is
also marked by fierce marketplace competition, further intensifying
the fragmentation of mass audiences. The availability of more
sources catering to the more personalized tastes of increasingly seg-
mented audiences has had a profound impact on both the content
and use of mass media. Even though an occasional television program can equal the entertainment value of any mass medium, the
dominant form of programming on network television today is lower
cost, serviceable material that tends to be more voyeuristic than value
raising, more celebrity-obsessed than character building, more formulaic than risk taking. Similarly, the quality and reliability of much
of our news and information continue to decline—with competing
twenty-four-hour electronic news services demonstrating every day
how it is possible to receive less with more. In response, audiences
are expressing their dissatisfaction or disenchantment by devoting
less undivided attention to mainstream media or seeking alternatives
in emerging or more specialized media. Whether these trends, standing alone, constitute a crisis in American mass media is debatable.
Less uncertain is that key policy decisions near the end of the twentieth century have robbed America of a promising start to the twenty-
first century.

Most modern texts examining mass media and society focus on the
failures of our dominant media institutions to better serve the American public and the specific business practices that have contributed to
such failures. Or they explore the relationship of media and society
through the more nuanced lens of the social scientist examining cause
and effect. This book touches some of those same bases but concentrates on the making of government policy and its impact on American mass media. The policymaking I refer to is the ongoing process by
which a myriad of media-specific rules, regulations, and policies are
crafted, revised, and applied by government officials. The policymakers are members of Congress who write the laws and those officials of
the executive branch, starting with the White House and including key

administrative agencies—principally, the Federal Communications Commission, the Federal Trade Commission, and the Department of Justice—who not only administer the laws passed by Congress but devise their own rules and policies.

While all mass media businesses are controlled by certain common laws and policies—antitrust, libel, copyright, unfair trade, and deceptive advertising—the electronic media have been most directly influenced from the beginning by government policymaking, starting with the need to obtain a federal license just to operate. Indeed, today's electronic media are largely the product of a string of public policy decisions stretching back nearly eighty years. Let there be no doubt, mass media policymaking is not some esoteric exercise carried out by cloistered, narrowly focused bureaucrats having little impact on what the public hears and sees. In fact, it is just the opposite. More than any other external force, policymaking determines who can own our most popular mass media and how they can operate.

Modern mass media are not severable from American society. Rather, they are inextricably bound up with our political, cultural, and economic life. No modern nation, in fact, has been forged without exerting a strong influence on the development of media. Mass media policymaking can be viewed as both a macro- and microprocess. While this book generally focuses on the latter—specifically, the direct influence of broadcast regulation or antitrust enforcement on the media business—it is worth noting that the whole social milieu in which mass media operate can be regarded as a form of indirect, ongoing, macro-policymaking. As Paul Starr demonstrates in his recent history of modern media, our media system results as much from broad-based political choices (the essence of public policymaking) as it does from technology and commercial enterprise.[3]

Today's mass media remain an evolving amalgamation of the social, political, and economic forces shaping American culture. If contemporary mass media are seen as failing American society, there is no single party or institution that should shoulder all the blame. I reject the age-old and tiresome line of criticism that blames only broadcasters and publishers for all the shortcomings of mass media. The usual supposition accompanying such criticism is that if only we could rid ourselves of greedy, capitalistic owners, irresponsible managers, and biased messengers, mass media would somehow be magically transformed into the kind of print, broadcast, and cyberspace service envisioned by its critics. If only it were so simple.

In this book, I have chosen to focus a major share of the blame on policymakers. The reasons are fairly straightforward. First, despite the pivotal role policymakers have historically played in the development of American mass media, scant attention is usually given to their direct influence. Second, at this advanced stage of mass media development, policymakers possess the best, most realistic means for redirecting resources and charting a new course that will better serve the American public.

In the pages that follow, I cast a spotlight on the last three decades and the first few years of the new century, a period characterized by rapid technological advances and a vastly expanded mass media marketplace. These years have also been marked, however, by a series of public policy failures. At the core has been the near total unleashing of commercial broadcasting—by the removal or relaxation of numerous regulatory standards—without also building a better financed, less commercialized public broadcast system. Public policy during these years has been propelled almost exclusively by an abiding faith in the marketplace that failed to recognize that even the most vibrant form of commercial competition will not meet all public needs in a diverse, complex, open democracy. Betting that commercial competition and deregulation would produce the same or better public services as the old regulatory regime was failure enough. It was compounded by a corresponding neglect of the noncommercial realm. Simply put, America deserves better not only from its mass media but from its mass media policymakers.

Some thirty-five years ago, two successive takeover attempts of ABC—the first by International Telephone and Telegraph, the second, within months, by the reclusive billionaire Howard Hughes—provided my baptism in the swirling waters of mass media policymaking. As a lawyer fresh out of law school and working for ABC's communications firm in Washington, D.C., I also found myself in a Senate hearing room months later, listening to the fiery senator from Rhode Island, John O. Pastore, scold the television networks (then, only ABC, NBC, and CBS) for abuses in program content. It was my first brush with television violence, a subject of unique intensity in the late 1960s—when violence was filling America's streets as well as its TV screens—and an issue that has continued to confound policymakers ever since.[4] From these early years to the writing of this book, I have never ceased to be intrigued, discouraged, buoyed, and disappointed by the mass media policymaking process.

Social responsibility of media is an issue as old as media. While new problems may appear to be popping up everywhere, most of the major media problems we face today have been debated since the very beginning. The issue of journalistic standards has been with us since colonial days. The issue of televised violence and its impact on children dates at least to the early 1950s. Concerns about commercialization can be traced to the formative years of radio in the 1920s. And, the perceived dangers of mass media operating as a big business are certainly not new—they are merely magnified as new markets erupt and then evolve so rapidly.

Another thing that has not changed is that when the public and policymakers complain about the media—as they often do—they usually grouse about specific content that would be impossible to regulate without running afoul of constitutional protections. For instance, they point to the violence, sex, sleaze, and dumbed-down content of entertainment programming or the frothy, freakish, and fast pace quality of news programming.[5] Knowing that they could never cleanse media content in a way that would fully satisfy either their personal tastes or the constant cries of media critics, many lawmakers and government regulators still persist in devoting their principal policymaking energies to such topics. But the time has come to recognize the utter futility of government rules designed to regulate the qualitative nature of broadcast content. Despite what some would say has been a half-century of unmitigated violence on television, America is a less violent society today than it was at other periods of our history when television did not exist.[6] And, despite long-standing fears that television entertainment would contribute to an overall deterioration of cultural taste, there is no demonstrable evidence that this has happened. Equally important, even if such content matters could be legally regulated in the electronic media (the usual target), any effort to do so would fail—unless such regulation was likewise extended to newspapers, magazines, video games, music lyrics, DVDs, movies, and everything on the worldwide web. Simply posing the dilemma suggests finding answers elsewhere.

Mass media—radio, television, newspapers, magazines, and the Internet—play an inescapable and profound role in the life of every American, from the professional or elitist who regards anything for the armies of people somehow degrading, to the philistine perceived too obtuse to even have a view. Even as the nature of mass media has started to change—from large, centralized operations of the past to more fast-paced, tailored distribution mechanisms of today—their overall influence on American society broadens and deepens. Mass media connect and reflect our political, economic, and cultural systems as never before. As sociologist Todd Gitlin puts it, the torrent of contemporary media is "an accompaniment *to* life that has become a central experience *of* life."[7]

A central finding of this book is that there are few business practices that can or should be changed by regulatory fiat. Rather, both the application and use of media technology must remain primarily dependent on the natural forces of the marketplace. As such, practical alternatives for reform are drastically limited. We can look backward, urging reinstatement of policies and practices from before deregulatory days, but that has been the cry of media reformers for years—with no success. We can charge ahead, demanding the divestiture of stations and the imposition of mandatory program requirements in certain prescribed categories. But such schemes are likewise doomed to failure. There are just too many practical and political hurdles to overcome—given the rapidly changing levels of competitive service and consumer choice found in today's commercial media market.

Nevertheless, remedies are available to bring contemporary mass media policymaking more in line with contemporary mass media conditions and societal needs. The public policy failures of recent years can still be turned into public policy successes. All that is required is recognition that the current system is broken and the will to fashion an adequate replacement. Absent a fundamental shift leading to major changes in the current system, American mass media policy is doomed to remain adrift, clinging to theories of the past that no longer assure adequate levels of public service.

Inaction or delay will not only confirm past failures but sidetrack public policy at a particularly crucial juncture. Whether mass media policy remains stuck in neutral, backtracks to policies of the past, or, as suggested here, is routed in an entirely new direction, there is no stopping the impending "train wreck" in the marketplace. Longstanding business models in electronic media are beginning to unravel, brought on by the way consumers use cable, satellite, and the Internet (including the many personal devices linked to those services). A marketplace increasingly dependent on subscription-based, on-demand information and entertainment is becoming increasingly less relevant to an eighty-year-old "public trusteeship" system that policymakers continue to pretend is the best prescription for today's electronic media. If policymakers want a mass media policy more consonant with evolving business practices and consumer habits, they must act now—not years from now.

PLAN FOR THE BOOK (AND FOR ACTION)

The path followed in this book is the usual one: a brief initial sketch of relevant history leading to contemporary developments, which are then examined in greater detail in order to highlight the gaps in public service that have been opened further by years of deregulation. It departs, however, from texts traveling similar ground in at least two distinct ways. First, it is a detailed account of the policymaking process in a nontechnical style, allowing readers with no background in law or communications to easily grasp the longstanding interplay between the laws Washington policymakers adopt and the myriad mass media the American public actually use on a daily basis. Second, because the current regulatory system has become dysfunctional, it develops a drastically different reform package that advocates tearing up the old and writing an entirely new policy script. While the general subject is mass media, my emphasis is on electronic media because they remain our most popular and continue to be the only ones directly regulated by Washington policymakers.

Despite the ubiquitous nature of mass media, Americans hardly ever pause and reflect on how such media indelibly impact society at large. However, no social order, especially one as complex, open, and dynamic as contemporary America, can function without a responsive media system molded to the conditions and needs of its citizens. That is why *Mass Media Unleashed* opens with a brief examination of the evolving nature of mass communication and how the first vestiges of print and electronic mass media emerged out of America's early history. Chapter 1 also serves as a short prologue for the more detailed policy discussions to follow, illustrating how the first and most fundamental principles of public policy grew out of social conditions and constitutional protections unique to American life.

Chapter 2 shows how government regulation and the business of broadcasting are conducted today, first identifying the actual policymakers and then highlighting the key laws and policies they enforce. Chapter 3 then emphasizes how, beginning in the mid-1970s and continuing to the present, deregulation (or the dismantling of previous standards) has been the driving public policy force, fueled by significant changes in business and ideology and eventually exalted to a binding rule of the road by the most sweeping change in communications legislation in more than sixty years.

After establishing a framework and historical context for how mass media policy is created, and how it has changed course so dramatically in recent years, the middle of the book concentrates on how today's media marketplace has been unalterably transformed by technology, evolving industry practices, and changing audience patterns (chapter 4). It also includes an examination of the roles mass media are expected to perform in a democratic society, followed by a detailed assessment of their actual performance in the current deregulatory era (chapters 5 and 6). In a democratic society, mass media are both a mirror of the diverse public they serve and an outlet for the depiction of diverse views, differing ethnic backgrounds, and distinct creative talents that constitute the culture. In our system, government can promote such functions but it can neither command nor choreograph their performance. It is a delicate balancing act that has been at the core of regulatory policy from the beginning but has been abandoned and rendered unworkable in the modern era. That is why my concluding chapters (7 and 8) argue for an entirely new approach. If the habits of the American viewing and listening public had not splintered in many new directions, if the commercial media marketplace had not been transformed in such fundamental ways (producing vastly more outlets with far less public service), and if the essential functions of mass media in a democratic society were being met by new and alternative services, there would be little reason to tamper with the current, eighty-year-old system. But the overwhelming tide of deregulation, the vastly altered business arrangements, the shifting of cultural habits, and the poor performance of commercial media, described in chapters 3–6, all dictate pursuing the fundamental change in direction outlined in the last two chapters.

The torrent of media now flowing over the American landscape comes in many new forms—delivering our news, information, and entertainment over the air, cable, satellite, wireless, and cyberspace. In an age where we can read a newspaper on an unplugged laptop at Starbucks and watch news headlines or entertainment snippets on cell phones and iPods, it becomes increasingly difficult, as a practical matter, and far less sustainable, as a policy matter, to continue to perceive and regulate commercial broadcasting in ways that differ drastically from how we perceive and regulate other commercial media (cable, satellite, wireless, and the Internet) that also enter our "private" spaces and use wires or electronic impulses that pass over or through "public" spaces. Bear in mind, the newspaper you are able to read online, while sitting in Starbuck's, is only available because, like broadcasting, its content is accessed over America's "airwaves" (different frequencies and technology, yes, but the same electronic spectrum nevertheless).

With our timeworn theories of broadcast regulation fatally shredded by the stark realities of the contemporary media landscape, it is time to recognize that the current system is broken and must be replaced. Accordingly, chapters 7 and 8 not only elaborate upon the failures of our current system but recommend the construction of an entirely new one. Instead of rehashing policies of the past, my plan calls for elimination of all remaining nontechnical regulation of commercial broadcasting, in exchange for better funding and improved regulation of public broadcasting (without additional government appropriations or new taxes), accompanied by more rigorous, regular, and expanded monitoring of commercial broadcasting under the antitrust laws. Even as another round of broadcast deregulation is under way in Washington—with federal regulators considering further relaxation of broadcast ownership standards, and vested and special interest groups of all persuasions pushing in conflicting directions[8]—only a cockeyed optimist would predict a definitive outcome. Like a recurring political or international crisis, broadcast deregulation is always on the table and always unresolved. A principal reason is that despite all the grunts and groans of the varied interests wrestling with the issues, there is very little to connect broadcast ownership standards to public service goals—given the deteriorating state of regulatory accountability and the irreversible state of the commercial audio and video marketplace recounted in chapters 3–6. That is why chapter 8 calls for a new plan of action. Instead of policymakers continuing to pretend that regulatory accountability of commercial broadcasting can be achieved or restored by tinkering with what remains of a few broadcast competition rules (focused on who owns what broadcast stations and where), they should look to other, more targeted, more achievable, ways of ensuring minimal levels of public service. In my view, placing a new emphasis on public broadcasting represents our last, best hope of ensuring that we continue to have an over-the-air service that is free, local, and dedicated to serving Americans as citizens, not just consumers.

1

The Rise of
American Mass Media

Stories of the evolution of mass communication, the beginnings of a free press, and the genesis of government regulation of electronic media have been told often and need not be repeated in any great detail. Rather, these opening chapters will merely highlight anew those early episodes in order to help set the stage for evaluating the conditions and public policies that shape American mass media at the start of the twenty-first century. I begin by briefly recounting some of the key social forces basic to the growth of all mass media and then providing a more detailed look at the distinct structural arrangements that sustain electronic media.

THE MEANS OF MASS COMMUNICATION

The foundation for mass communication can be traced to the birth of an alphabet to produce writing that could "store" knowledge. With the subsequent invention of the printing press near the middle of the fifteenth century, a new path to modernity was opened. The form of mass communication we recognize today first began to take shape in Europe and the developed part of the United States during the middle of the nineteenth century. It was propelled by advances in paper production, printing press methods, and the invention of the telegraph, all vastly changing the way information could be conveyed. Telegraphy

separated communication from transportation, allowing messages to
be transmitted instantaneously rather than carried from one point to
another by foot, horse, rail, or ship.

Until fairly recently, mass communication could be defined by
three principal characteristics: (1) it was directed toward relatively
large, heterogeneous, and anonymous audiences; (2) it was transmitted for general public consumption, often timed to reach the largest
possible audience simultaneously; and (3) it was delivered by a relatively complex organization involving considerable expense.[1] While
these basic characteristics still define many traditional media, modern
technology has spawned new and alternative media forms that are re-
defining what constitutes mass communication. For instance, is Matt
Drudge, who "publishes" a tabloid-type gossip sheet on his website,
without a complex organization and without great expense, a mass
communicator? Drudge, in fact, may reach far more people more
quickly than many traditional mass media outlets. Even what constitutes "mass" is now being redefined, as many established media organizations purposely seek highly homogenous audiences fragmented into discrete demographic groups. Also, whereas the standard
definition of *mass communication* would have previously mentioned
minimal or no contact (interaction) between sender and receivers,
this, too, is changing. Advances in technology and the blurring of media methods have introduced new levels of interactivity, not only to
the Internet but to broadcasting and cable. And, as the Matt Drudge
example suggests, it is now possible for individual citizens to create
their own communication "medium" instantly available to everyone
on the worldwide web. Requiring little expense and employing widely
available software programs, these web logs (or "blogs") are turning
traditional notions of mass communication upside down—producing
media *of* (instead of *for*) masses where anyone, professional or ama-
teur, young or old, can spout personal musings or post instant reactions on virtually any topic, light or serious.[2]

SOCIAL CONDITIONS THAT PAVED THE WAY
FOR EARLY MASS MEDIA

Mass media are born of the political and cultural conditions and institutions of the time. Technology and economics may be vital to their
gestation, but they take their place in society by responding to and

serving the political and social conditions and institutions that already exist. It is not surprising, therefore, that many of the key events in the early history of American mass media can be traced to a largely haphazard fusion of social, economic, and political forces. As Irving Fang notes, "An inseparable connection has always existed between the tools of communication and the social fabric. Throughout history they have been developed together in an intertwined, mutual cause and effect relationship, each giving impetus to the other."[3] For example, the rise of journalism paralleled the rise of capitalism, and printing itself was one of the earliest forms of mass production. Because many early printers in England and America were primarily businessmen, the early fight for press freedom in England arose not just from political causes—it was stirred also by the trade demands of London printers who sought to pursue wealth without state interference.

While important democratic principles were implanted during colonial times, many democratic rights were not established until years later. Leaders in business, government, and the arts through the last half of the eighteenth century and the first half of the nineteenth century were largely an "elite" class who by good fortune or enormous personal struggle were educated and cultured in a way that clearly stood above the rest of society. But, following the Civil War, this started to change. For one thing, the electorate was broadened as restrictions on voting gradually eroded (although it was not until 1920 that women obtained the right to vote and many years later that African Americans were afforded protections to ensure the same right).

The suffrage movement was, in turn, a major impetus to the spread of free popular education—something that was not fully established until the last half of the nineteenth century. Education for all children at public expense, combined with a land grant movement that made even a college degree more available, helped spread the basic tools of literacy to a broader public. During these same years, between the end of the Civil War and the start of the twentieth century, industrialization and mechanization began to sweep over America with dramatic results. Rails linked and expanded the nation, bringing citizens closer together but with the ability to move about more freely. Factories blossomed wherever vital resources could be found. Steam power replaced water power and electricity, and the internal combustion engine replaced steam.

An elaborate system of mass production and mass distribution also began to envelop the country. And, to succeed, mass production and distribution needed a form of inexpensive mass salesmanship. When the tools and techniques of manufacturing were finally able to produce mass quantities of goods more efficiently and inexpensively, better methods of marketing the new stream of goods became essential. The marriage of advertising and mass media was, in a sense, a natural, blending the need to expand the sale of products and services with the need to generate sufficient revenue to support an independently viable media business.

These social and economic developments also contributed to the greater clustering of people in urban environments—arriving from farms and foreign soils. Rapid urbanization, in fact, produced a larger, ready-made audience for mass media—easier to reach and more inclined to seek out entertainment and information. With citizens acquiring more mobility, greater individual liberty, and improved skills with which to use outlets of information and entertainment during newly acquired leisure time, the role of modern mass media was firmly established.

THE BIRTH OF MASS CIRCULATION NEWSPAPERS

The emergence of representative government and the unshackling of the British monocracy in America unleashed a political, economic, and social revolution that provided fertile ground for a form of mass communication that appealed to a broader public with new powers of participation. Print media, and later audio and visual media, became a critical source of education, political dialogue, and the sharing of cultural values and experiences.

The earliest "newspapers" were more like what we would call newsletters today. Political pamphlets and leaflets circulated separately and often surreptitiously because political content was rigorously controlled by colonial authorities. As the American Revolution unfolded, partisan or "party" papers began to appear. Such papers blatantly took one side or the other relating to the revolution and the formation of a new government. They promoted a set of views or individuals who subscribed to such views. At the same time, a thriving mercantile press focusing on business and shipping also emerged. Not only were America's earliest papers starkly partisan or designed for a specialized audience, they were expensive, by the standards of the time, generally beyond the means of the average person.

The Industrial Revolution, starting in England but expanding rapidly to Western Europe and then to the American colonies, transformed all societies in its wake. Agricultural economies became industrial economies. A massive shift in population from the countryside to new or enlarged urban communities also took place— bringing people together to a degree not previously experienced in Western society. Overall, the transformation brought new choices and new freedoms but also produced new city-related miseries— conditions especially ripe for new modes of communication.

Although newspapers had started to lose some of their partisan nature and elite appeal near the end of the colonial period, the most profound change was the birth of the "penny press" in 1833, ushering in the modern era of journalism. In that year, Benjamin Day launched the *New York Sun* under the ambitious masthead "It Shines for All." Unlike most papers of the day, it was not sold by subscription but was hawked on city sidewalks and offered for the remarkably low price of one cent (when most other New York City papers were selling for six cents a copy). Equally important, Day's *Sun* shined its light not so much on "all" but on New York's growing immigrant population and its emerging middle class, purposely eschewing the commercial and political elite. It was a new form of "popular" journalism, focused more on scandal, crime, and human interest stories than the business and political news of the day. By attracting a wider, more generalized audience, Day's *Sun* was also able to expand newspaper advertising on a bolder, larger scale, something that was essential to selling papers at a bargain price. Affordable to all, the penny press spiked the growth of newspapers in America, increasing circulation and expanding availability to the "masses."

Shortly after the birth of the penny press, the newspaper business was transformed further by the introduction of the telegraph. Whereas news from one part of the country might have previously taken days or weeks to reach a newspaper published in New York, it could now get there from almost anywhere in a single day. More fundamentally, the telegraph changed the way information moved through society. Previously, a message had to be transported by human voice (within earshot, literally) or written down and carried by foot or horse over great distances. Now, it could be carried hundreds or thousands of miles by wire in a matter of seconds. The telegraph greatly improved news gathering and distribution—allowing news and information to not only travel faster and farther but to new places. It also led to the first wired news service (the Associated Press) in 1848.

The telephone (growing out of telegraphic technology) added a dramatic new dimension and drew us one step closer to creating the electronic media we know today. Indeed, in a harbinger of the future, some early telephonic hookups were used to deliver live music, church services, and political speeches to targeted audiences and locations. This was a form of point-to-point communication, first as wireless telegraphy and then as wireless telephony. Broadcasting, of course, when it arrived, would transmit information and entertainment from one point to many points, simultaneously.

EARLY STIRRINGS OF FREEDOM OF THE PRESS

Open, political discourse was not something that flowed naturally or easily from man's ability to set movable type and distribute content to a large public audience. Rather, the publication of commentary critical of governmental institutions and public figures was a right that had to be earned by courageous editors and publishers. The first newspaper in America, Benjamin Harris's 1690 *Publick Occurrences, Both Forreign and Domestick*, was, in fact, shut down after only one issue when it criticized colonial and European dignitaries. This was possible because, under English laws that had been transplanted to colonial America, Harris was not a "licensed" printer.

John Cambell's *Boston News-Letter* escaped the quick fate of Harris's *Publick Occurrences* but only because, when it was first published in 1704, it was "by authority" of the colonial government. Everything he wrote was submitted to local authorities before it was printed. Not surprisingly, it was fairly dull, featuring relatively safe foreign news, reprints of articles from England, government announcements, and shipping news. A few years later, however, as licensing laws started to fade, James Franklin began publishing his *New England Courant*, the only Boston paper among three at the time that was published without "authority." The *Courant* was popular and controversial, landing Franklin in jail at one point when he criticized the Massachusetts governor. When his troubles continued to mount, he installed his younger brother, Benjamin, as nominal publisher. Ben Franklin, of course, subsequently moved to Philadelphia, where, before his illustrious public career, he established a print shop and, in 1729, took over a failing newspaper, which he renamed the *Pennsylvania Gazette*. In 1731, Franklin articulated an early rationale for freedom of the press in an editorial in the *Gazette* he called "An Apology for Printers." It was prompted by criticism the *Gazette* had received for an advertisement promoting a sea voyage that stated "no black gowns" would be admitted. The reference was taken as a slur against the clergy. In his editorial "Apology," Franklin wrote:

> The opinions of men are almost as various as their faces. . . . If all printers were determined not to print anything till they were sure it would offend no body, there would be very little printed.[4]

Newspapers also faced other government restraints. Colonial laws against seditious libel made it illegal to print derogatory or potentially inflammatory remarks about the government or government officials. But a milestone in press freedom occurred in 1735 with the trial of John Peter Zenger, publisher of the *New York Weekly*, a paper prone to highlighting the failings of New York's royal governor. When Zenger accused the governor of, among other things, stealing land, soldiers under the governor's command burned copies of Zenger's paper. Although most of what Zenger published was true, the law of seditious libel made any criticism (true or not) of the government and its agents illegal. During Zenger's trial, his lawyer argued that no matter what the law said, it ought to be permissible for a newspaper to publish the truth. Although the trial judge ruled Zenger's lawyer out of order, the jury in the case ignored the letter of the law, finding Zenger not guilty. While the First Amendment was not ratified until fifty years later, the Zenger case helped formulate an abiding principle that has profoundly affected the American press ever since—a principle that says the press is cloaked with an inherent right to publish the truth about government actions and officials.

But even the First Amendment, with its powerful recitation that Congress "shall make no law . . . abridging the freedom of speech, or the press," did not end the struggle. Only eight years after ratifying the First Amendment, Congress, responding to an echo from its recent colonial past, passed the infamous Alien and Sedition Acts of 1798, making it illegal to write, publish, or print "any false, scandalous and malicious writing" about the president, Congress, or the new federal government. Highly unpopular, the Alien and Sedition Acts were abruptly ended after only two years.[5]

By the time broadcasting was born a century later, a certain freedom of expression was generally acknowledged to have passed to the new

medium as a result of traditions established by print media. The original version of the landmark Communications Act, in fact, explicitly
stated:

> Nothing in this [law] shall be understood or construed to give the Fed-
> eral Communications Commission the power of censorship over radio
> communications or signals transmitted by any radio station, and no reg-
> ulation or condition shall be promulgated or fixed by the Federal Com-
> munications Commission which shall interfere with the right of free
> speech by means of radio communication.

The words ring so clearly that one could easily conclude that Congress
intended to banish government regulation of any broadcast content.
The reality, of course, has been far different. While broadcasters have
generally been free of government actions that might constitute a
prior restraint of speech, they have not escaped after-the-fact governmental oversight of some of their programming. Indeed, because
broadcast stations face potentially punitive government actions for
certain programming deficiencies or excesses, their First Amendment
rights have always been more restricted than those traditionally enjoyed by America's print media.

THE START OF THE ELECTRONIC AGE

As the nineteenth century closed with improvements continuing in
telegraphy and telephony, the twentieth century opened with explosive advancements in radio. While early pioneers viewed radio as an
evolutionary device to enhance point-to-point communication (and
its first practical applications were, indeed, for ship-to-ship and ship-
to-shore communication) it soon became evident that radio would be
more of a revolutionary device, capable of transmitting voices and
music at great distances to large numbers of people. It would, in fact,
become an entirely new medium of mass communication, one that
would explode in popularity just as American society was entering the
modern era. Unlike newspapers and magazines, electronic media arrived at a time when a large, well-educated, more engaged middle
class, more urban than rural, had already reached full flower.

The earliest legislation to deal with radio was the Wireless Ship Act
of 1910, requiring the installation of wireless apparatus on seagoing
vessels carrying fifty or more passengers. Two years later, prompted by

the sinking of the *Titanic*, Congress passed the Radio Act of 1912, the government's initial effort to actually license radio. The 1912 law required, for the first time, every radio station to secure a license from the secretary of commerce and labor. It did not, however, give the secretary any discretionary power to make new rules and regulations. In particular, he was given no power to specify the frequency, transmitting power, or hours of operation of any broadcast station.

That shortcoming proved to be fatal. After station KDKA, Pittsburgh, introduced modulated voice broadcasting in 1920, similar stations began popping up elsewhere. In 1921, Herbert Hoover, the incumbent commerce and labor secretary, designated two distinct wavelengths for private broadcasting. Stations were allowed to operate on whichever they chose. But when Hoover subsequently tried to limit and not renew a license, the courts declared that he had no such discretion—ruling that he must, in effect, give a license to anyone who demanded one.[6]

The path to chaos was laid. Broadcasters were on their own in terms of adhering to power, height, and frequency. They operated on any frequency and during any hour of the day they chose. Some stations increased their power, jumped frequencies, and changed hours of operation at will in a frenzied effort to enlarge their coverage and achieve competitive advantage. While some radio operators entered into private agreements to control the increasingly intolerable interference, others refused to do so. In deliberate cutthroat fashion, some broadcasters attempted to drown out the signals of lower-powered stations. Francis Chase Jr., in his informal history of broadcasting, characterized conditions at the time:

> Chaos road the airwaves, pandemonium filled every loud-speaker and the twentieth century Tower of Babel was made in the image of the antenna towers of some thousand broadcasters who, like the Kilkenny cats, were about to eat each other up.[7]

THE FIRST CALL FOR FEDERAL LICENSING OF BROADCASTING

The Radio Act of 1927 arose out of this national bedlam—when the industry, especially manufacturers of radio sets, pleaded for relief. In what might be called the critical compromise of radio history, a new law restored order and permitted the industry to grow and prosper. But the Radio Act of 1927 also effectively made broadcast media separate from rather than equal to print media. It did so by establishing the fundamental principle that broadcasters would be permitted to *use* but not *own* the frequencies on which they operate. Ownership was to remain in the public domain, with broadcasters assigned the role of caretakers for an important national resource, the airwaves.[8]

In the frantic early days of radio, when broadcast buccaneers battled more responsible operators for any advantage, some radio pioneers even asserted permanent "squatters' rights" to the frequencies they were using. But Congress sought to thwart such claims at any early stage.[9] Later, when crafting a final legislative package, it permanently preempted the issue by declaring that it would

> maintain government control . . . over all channels of interstate and foreign radio transmission; and . . . provide for the use of such channels, *but not the ownership thereof*, by persons for limited periods of time, under licenses granted by federal authority.[10]

In one further crucial step that continues to vex the industry, the Federal Communications Commission (FCC), Congress, and the courts, the Radio Act of 1927, borrowing from earlier legislation regulating transportation, mandated that the standard for awarding licenses would be whether such action was in the "public interest, convenience or necessity." On those five words have hung eight decades of tension-filled regulatory history.

COMMERCIALS TO THE RESCUE

The transition from limited-circulation newspapers intended only for partisan or special interests to low-cost newspapers reaching larger, more generalized audiences was made possible, in no small part, by the simultaneous growth of the marketing and advertising business. To reach a broader audience, newspapers adopted a less controversial, less confrontational style of reporting. Advertising helped these early newspapers break free of a system long subsidized by wealthy partisans and special interests. As sociologists Croteau and Hoynes remind us, "There is, in fact, good reason to believe that the historical roots of what we now refer to as 'objectivity' in journalism lie in the process of commercialization, whereby the news industry developed a new non-partisan framework for reporting news."[11]

When broadcasting took its halting first steps in the early 1920s, it was thought by RCA, GE, Westinghouse, and other manufacturers that the sale of radio equipment would provide the requisite economic base for the medium. Reflecting this view, David Sarnoff, the general manager of RCA, described the newly formed NBC as a "nonprofit" organization. It would be supported by annual contributions derived from the manufacturing and sale of equipment. Proposals were also advanced to finance early radio stations by a system of "endorsements" funded by public-spirited citizens. Other schemes envisioned municipal financing and voluntary subscriptions by listeners. Many in the academic community fought hard for broadcasting to remain noncommercial and modeled on broadcasting systems beginning to take shape in Britain and Canada.

It was a genuine dilemma. Unlike other mass media at the time—newspapers, magazines, and the nascent motion picture industry—the "product" of broadcasting was transmitted over public airwaves and available to anyone with the necessary equipment. There was no ready means to extract a point-of-sale payment. And, although advertising had developed as a major revenue source for print media, the idea of direct appeals for products and services over the airwaves into people's homes was still unsettling. The First Annual Radio Conference called by Secretary Hoover,[12] in fact, passed a resolution condemning direct sales talks, and Hoover himself viewed the prospect with "alarm." "It is inconceivable," he remarked, "that we should allow so great a possibility for service, for news, for entertainment, for education . . . to be drowned in advertising chatter."[13] Equipment manufacturers thought broadcast advertising debased the medium, while various trade journals railed against the practice.

But something had to give. The business was starting to mushroom and the public was increasingly fascinated with the new medium. Although fleeting references to direct government ownership had been heard at the outset (it was a notion particularly pushed by the navy after it had been allowed to take over all U.S. radio stations during World War I)[14] it was an idea that never took hold. Far stronger was the gravitational pull of the free enterprise system, deeply engrained in the nation's fabric by the early twentieth century. In fact, Secretary Hoover, despite his reservation about direct appeal advertising, remained an ardent believer in free enterprise and did not favor

government operation or even want much direct government regulation. His promotion of four national radio conferences that became
the overture to the 1927 Radio Act was really intended to push the industry to better self-regulate.[15]

AT&T, already dominant in the business of renting equipment to
people to communicate over the telephone, also operated one of the
nation's pioneer radio stations, WEAF, in New York City. Initially,
AT&T perceived a radio studio and transmitting equipment as something that could be leased to business interests and others under a system called "toll broadcasting." Although the general concept failed,
out of it grew the first broadcast commercial. When, in 1922, WEAF
sold a block of time to the Queensboro Corporation, a Long Island
real estate firm, to extol the virtues of apartment living, a system of
broadcast advertising was hatched. And, of course, the rest is history.
Direct advertising of products and services became the sole support of
broadcasting, shooting commercial messages up and down the radio
dial—first like a pellet gun but, ultimately, more like a scattergun.

MASS MEDIA IN A POSTMODERN WORLD[16]

Mass media are the ubiquitous filter through which a democratic society molds its identity—learning about its history and culture, ob-
serving the experiences and customs of others, and collecting ideas
and information on emerging trends and unfolding public issues.
This trait was thought to be particularly strong in electronic media. As
recounted by Professor Starr:

> The promise of broadcasting, even more than earlier media, was to make
> culture accessible to all, to enable the electorate to become better in-
> formed, to put people instantaneously in touch with the news of the
> world. Here was a new, buzzing and booming sphere, an updated means
> of forming public opinion and public taste appropriately scaled to the
> age of mass democracy.[17]

Four score and more years later, the promise of broadcasting (along
with its media cousins) is still being debated. What can no longer be
disputed, however, is that mass media in contemporary America are
mostly mature businesses reaching audiences that, at once, are more
approachable yet difficult to reach, more diverse yet still in need of
common services. At no time in our history has mass communication

been distributed to mass audiences more quickly and more efficiently. Americans tend to forget that the instantaneous communication we now enjoy (when the president can speak to all Americans—indeed, most of the world—instantaneously and events far and wide can be covered live and continuously) is of relatively recent origin. Seventy-five years ago a "whistle-stop" tour was a necessity, not a novelty. The methods of communication we now enjoy are not only a vast improvement, they are increasingly vital to modern democracy. To appreciate this fact, one need only imagine for a second the frustration, panic, and utter chaos that would immediately ensue if all traditional media outlets were somehow shut down. Americans need to be connected and they need to be responsibly informed. These needs, one might say, are the new "inalienable rights" of Americans at the start of the twenty-first century.

In a complex, fast-paced world of specialized tasks and shrinking distances, the ties between a person and his or her next-door neighbor may be less important than those that bind that person to his or her own profession, hobbies, or tastes. As some of the social bonds of the traditional community weaken—especially in intensely developed metropolitan areas—mass media represent one element of the social structure still capable of creating a new set of common interests and experiences. They allow millions to respond to the newest fad or expression, feel the same thrill or anxiety brought on by compelling events, or just revel in the same heroes and celebrities. Not too long ago, when only three national television networks were able to command more than 90 percent of the prime-time audience, such shared experiences were common. In the 1960s and 1970s, most Americans did not have cable or video recorders, so they watched a program like "All in the Family" (which premiered in 1971) in a familial way—in other words, at the same time, as a common Saturday night gathering experience. And they might later discuss that episode over coffee with coworkers on Monday morning.

This sort of informal bonding experience is largely a thing of the past. But the need for television and other media to provide Americans with common cultural and other experiences remains. We are "connected" like never before—tethered to our cell phones, pocket-size computers, pagers, and faxes—but also increasingly "disconnected" from one another. Walking down the street, up an escalator, or into a theater or store while conversing on the telephone or checking one's e-mail messages is hardly connecting with the outside world.

The cruel irony for American democracy is that, given these more liberating tools of communication, we have chosen, as a society, to turn more inward—spending more time watching mindless entertainment shows, playing computer games, or surfing anonymously over the web. At a time when we need a greater sense of community to survive the complexities and strains of modern life, we are spending more hours at home or on the job becoming less, rather than more, directly engaged. Americans vote less, turn out for town and community meetings in smaller numbers, and, all the while, wallow in greater distrust of government and the social structure around them.[18] Perhaps an even more profound development is a growing tendency to also look inward about politics. An increasing number of Americans, for instance, are selecting where to live, what books to read, and what radio and television programs and personalities to follow based primarily on political views and attitudes. It is as if the planned communities or distinct urban neighborhoods so many people choose to live in are being replicated in a new walled attitude pervading people's minds.[19] While the nation has been sharply splintered along political lines before—most recently in the 1930s and 1960s—the polarization has never reverberated so clearly and widely in our mass media.

The traditional bias long associated with the editorial pages of newspapers has found many new media homes. Leading radio personalities preach almost exclusively to their political flock, advocacy books written by political activists are intended to soothe partisans mainly by blasting the opposition, websites appear almost instantaneously either to comfort or inflame political passions on unfolding issues, and television programs, even entire networks, unabashedly appeal to audiences who, it is said, are seeking an alternative to the unbalanced and unfair coverage of news and information on other programs and networks. However, if we continue to stir this pot, allowing one's own strong personal convictions to be turned into abhorrence for the convictions of others, the prospect for an engaging civil dialogue on important public issues will be dimmed even further.

At the same time, it is worth noting that, even as critics decry the body blows to media diversity delivered by burgeoning consolidation,[20] we are today a far more diverse nation than just a single generation ago. The Hispanic and Asian populations have grown to rival the African American population in ways that are evident across the land—by workers in the fields and factories of rural America and by entrepreneurs running small businesses in larger towns and cities. Where and how we live adds to such diversity—with a recent influx into some cities beginning to resemble a previous one-way flight from cities to suburbs. Where we go to school, where we work, and where we retire have all changed in recent decades by the greatly expanded choices offered by institutions, businesses, and communities, which are themselves more diversified or specialized. Even the dominant social track one was expected to follow—education, job, marriage, and children, all in seamless succession—has long been shattered, allowing people more life choices on a more free-form timetable.

And media choice and accessibility have literally exploded. There are, counting those serving the Hispanic community, three times the number of national TV networks now than existed in the 1960s, and the choices of channels via cable and satellite number in the hundreds. Modern bookstores, specialty magazines, and the worldwide web create choices that are almost limitless. Our cup runneth over, but the question must still be asked: at what price? Is there a social cost in moving to a world where not only the distribution of information is highly fragmentized but its use is increasingly personalized? Will specialized media best positioned to serve vital public services become both less accessible and more expensive to those most in need?

In a leading case decided in 1973 in which I had a very minor role, the U.S. Supreme Court declared that "for better or worse, editing is what editors are for; and editing is selection and choice of material."[21] The comment was made in the context of a claimed right of unfettered access to the broadcast medium by persons and groups who sought to use radio and television without editorial control by broadcast licensees. Today, voices are again being raised in support of communications technology that will allow citizens to access information without having such information filtered through (or edited by) mainstream mass media. To some, getting one's news and information (or latest rumor) without the aid of traditional media is viewed as a liberating experience.

But is it? Imagine for a moment a world without the traditional media that prepare, edit, and "filter" information to the American public. No radio or television—via cable or satellite, or over the air—and no daily or weekly newspapers. And no weekly or monthly newsmagazines. Indeed, no MSNBC.com, CNN.com, or other leading Internet news and information websites because, of course, all of those streaming news services are prepared and edited by traditional mass media enterprises. Information and news reports would still be available—from random leaflets on the street to burgeoning armies of bloggers and podcasters on the Internet—but it would be totally scattered, haphazard, and unvarnished, arising from sources whose credibility was neither established nor easily checked. In the end, will we be made more free or more vulnerable?

We already know that the Internet is an abundant source of misinformation and rumor. But the problem is larger, owing to the very nature and structure of communication via the Internet. If mainstream media with their professional editors were to disappear—or, more likely, substantially recede from prominence and use—we would not be able to turn to reliable alternatives in cyberspace. To date, the Internet emphasizes unmediated communication, allowing self-appointed opinion makers to reach decisions and promulgate viewpoints without the intervention of editors. While supporters of direct democracy may revel in the possibilities of eliminating the "middleman" in our public dialogue, those who favor our existing representative democracy may view such developments with alarm. Not only do traditional media gather, edit, and assemble the profusion of information washing over us every day in a usable, convenient format, but, equally important, they filter popular passions and base prejudices that often accompany mass rule. If all our democracy needed to make fair and deliberate decisions was the introduction of direct voting, we could base everything on public opinion polls—until all homes had Internet access and then we could submit every issue to every household.

Our culture and democracy are not served merely by an endless flow of information. Having more unstructured media outlets pumping more information into the system has not made us a more informed society. More than ever, we need access to information that allows us to make sense out of the raw data. In short, we still need structured, institutional mass media to serve the critical role of conduit—both filtered and sometimes unfiltered—of events, ideas, trends, and public issues.

Until "alternative" media change enough to perform this role, traditional, organized mass media will remain the indispensable ingredient of a representative democracy. They reach virtually everyone and provide an astonishing amount of entertainment and a breathless array of news, opinion, information, and cultural events in real time and with state-of-the-art technical skill. They have, in no small way, contributed positively to the American way of life and our high standard of living. But they also portray and likely contribute to the foibles and failures of contemporary society.

2

Government Regulation and the Business of Broadcasting

Broadcasting is nearly ninety years old, and the statutory framework under which it operates is nearly eighty years old. But because the social, economic, and political environment in which broadcasting exists is constantly changing, our view of the role and influence of broadcasting likewise keeps changing. Is broadcasting drowning in commercial messages—producing more with diminishing effect—or is it just another business in a broad societal sea of commercialism? After all, our children now read books wrapped in covers supplied by cereal companies or Nike and attend schools that rent space on school property to pitch products and services. Is broadcasting dragging America into the gutter with coarse language, excessive violence, and overly sexual themes, or is it still uniquely sensitive to public tastes— when compared to movies, music, magazines, video games, and the Internet? Is the overly hyped, fast pace of most broadcast content unique to the medium, or is it just part of faster lifestyles generally, where speed and superficiality often replace reflection? And, more directly relevant to the democratic process, is broadcasting perverting contemporary politics and elections by presenting candidates like packaged goods, or is the real perversion politicians and their handlers who attempt to orchestrate the media with "feel-good" themes, calculated "sound bites," and message campaigns conveyed on "background" only?

The answer to these and similar questions will, of course, depend upon one's own social, economic, and political views—adding yet another dimension to the linkage of media and contemporary American society. Some of these themes will be developed in later chapters. At this point, I'll lay some preliminary groundwork, showing how today's electronic media are regulated and the relationships they have developed to conduct business.

REGULATION OF ELECTRONIC MEDIA

The United States has the most extensive, multilayered broadcasting system in the world. Thousands of licensed broadcast stations and hundreds of broadcast and cable networks span the nation, bringing local, regional, and national service to towns from Miami to Juneau and New York to Honolulu. Equally relevant, an intricate web of public policies has evolved to oversee the system.

The Policymaking Apparatus

The policymaking process that has helped shape American media is almost as old as the nation. Well before the rise of mass-appeal newspapers in the nineteenth century and the birth of broadcasting in the twentieth century, laws had been written to preserve freedom of speech and promote the circulation of information. Not only did the federal Constitution guarantee free speech, but a separate clause recognized copyright protection for creative material, effectively encouraging investment in print media (and, of course, all subsequent media). And, since the eighteenth century, federal postal laws have been used to partially subsidize the publishing business—offering favorable mailing rates for certain printed material.

Because radio and television signals cross state lines as easily as migratory birds, direct regulation of broadcasting has always been the exclusive province of the federal government, under the interstate commerce clause. Public policy for electronic media is set by federal laws enacted by Congress and administered by the Federal Communications Commission (FCC), an independent government agency directly responsible to Congress. The FCC is directed by five commissioners appointed by the president and confirmed by the Senate for five-year terms. The president designates one of the commissioners to serve as chairperson. Only three commissioners may be members of the same political party.

Accordingly, America's principal mass media policymakers are the 535 elected members of Congress and the five political appointees sitting on the FCC. Collectively, they have the exclusive power to write the laws and enforce the rules and policies that govern electronic media. Congress influences policy in several different ways. In the most direct and permanent way, it writes and amends all federal statutes affecting mass media, including those that dictate the size, authority, and responsibilities of the FCC. But it also exercises continuing influence over mass media policy by conducting special investigations of specific issues, holding periodic oversight hearings on FCC activities, and approving (or disapproving) the FCC's annual budget. There is also periodic, fairly persistent informal contact between members of Congress (and their staffs) and FCC officials (and their staffs). These exchanges occur in written correspondence, telephone (or e-mail) inquiries, and face-to-face meetings. When congressional voices are raised on such topics as broadcast indecency, budget cuts, reorganization of the FCC, or even potential changes to a particular rule or policy, the FCC listens. When those voices emanate from the chairperson or a senior member of the respective commerce and appropriation committees (and their key subcommittees) in the Senate or House of Representatives, the FCC listens more intently.

At the FCC, policy is set by the five-member commission appointed by the president and approved by the Senate, especially by the chairperson who directs the agency's agenda, serves as the principal spokesperson for the commission (to the press and before Congress), and selects most top staff officials. Each commissioner maintains his or her own staff of experts, all of whom play an active role in FCC policymaking. Ongoing responsibility for the administration and enforcement of relevant rules and policies—including the process for considering any changes to such rules and policies—falls to the scores of officials who head and run the Media Bureau, which regulates broadcasting as well as cable and satellite services, and the Enforcement Bureau, which undertakes individual enforcement actions when rules or policies have been violated.

To the foregoing pivotal policymakers, one must add numerous officials in other government agencies such as the Federal Trade Commission, the U.S. Department of Justice (in particular, its Antitrust Division), and the U.S. Copyright Office. Any one of these specialized agencies or departments can take individual actions having a direct impact on mass media businesses. Finally, with its power to pick who will lead the FCC and other crucial federal agencies, the White House exerts a singular influence over mass media policymaking. The president not only nominates or appoints key officials and retains unique authority to push or veto specific communications legislation, he or she sets the overall tone or distinct ideological bent of the executive branch of government.[1] This is reflected in both the substance of new policies pursued and the vigor with which preexisting policies are enforced.

The Laws and Policies Governing Broadcasting Today

In early 2005, there were 13,517 radio stations and 1,745 television stations in the United States. Of the radio stations, 4,761 were operating on the AM band and 8,756 were operating on the FM band (2,551 of which were "educational"). Of the television stations, 1,366 were commercial (both UHF and VHF) and 379 were "educational." In addition, thousands of secondary facilities help bring broadcasting to every nook and cranny of America—8,371 "translators" and "boosters" that do nothing but rebroadcast the signals of other stations (FM or TV) and 2,670 low-power TV stations—for a grand total of 26,303 broadcast stations.[2]

All of these stations are directly licensed by the FCC and governed by a set of administrative regulations flowing from authority reposed in the Communications Act (passed in 1934 but much amended since). At the heart of this regulatory regime is the FCC's power to assign specific frequencies and to impose technical requirements necessary to prevent interference between stations. This is the "traffic cop" role universally acknowledged to be the FCC's most fundamental responsibility. It is reflected in a vast array of technical standards that determine the precise location of all broadcast stations, the frequencies on which they may operate, the hours they are allowed to operate, the amount of power they are allowed to transmit over assigned frequencies, the exact height at which they are allowed to place a transmitting antenna, and (in conjunction with the Federal Aviation Administration) the height, lighting, and painting of the transmitting towers or support structures used to broadcast.

More broadly, the FCC is required to examine every application that comes before it—whether the application proposes to build, modify, renew, or sell a broadcast station—to determine if the specific proposal would serve the "public interest, convenience or necessity" (those five pesky words long emblazed in the Communications Act). Periodically, the FCC also conducts public hearings to consider the adoption, modification, or deletion of various rules and policies designed to define a broadcast station's operation in the "public interest." Finally, on a case-by-case basis, the FCC considers complaints filed against broadcast stations that raise issues relevant to compliance with specific rules, regulations, or policies.

As explained in chapter 1, the First Amendment and Section 326 of the Communications Act generally prohibit the FCC from censoring broadcast content and from interfering with freedom of expression in broadcasting. For this reason, there are no FCC policies on the dissemination of news and information, artistic standards, music formats, the nature of products advertised, or anything to do with program quality. Individual radio and TV stations are responsible for selecting everything they broadcast—news, sports, opinion, entertainment, and all commercial messages. The FCC will not entertain or investigate a complaint that, instead of invoking a specific agency rule or policy, attempts to focus solely on editorial discretion—for example, matters touching on the choice, taste, and timing of programming, the subjective quality of program material, or the particular amount and orientation of specific content.

While academic literature, the popular press, and congressional debate going back more than fifty years overflow with concerns about the portrayal of violence on television, this is a subject that, owing to conflicting concerns about censorship, remains unregulated. The closest Congress has come to direct regulation was a measure enacted in 1990 that would have given broadcasters an exemption under the antitrust laws to develop common standards for self-regulating portrayals of violence[3] and six years later a law requiring TV sets with screens thirteen inches or larger to be equipped with so-called V-chip technology (this, along with a rating system created by the television industry, allows parents to program their TV sets to block the display of TV programming they regard as harmful to their children).

Because broadcasting arose out of conditions and traditions differ-ent from print media, there are, however, a few rules that do directly affect program content. They fall into three principal categories:

1. *Political Broadcasting.* When a qualified candidate for public of-fice has been permitted to use a particular broadcast station, the Communications Act requires that station to "afford equal op-portunities to all other such candidates" competing for the same office. A variety of FCC rules and exceptions have grown up around this basic statutory mandate. A separate provision af-fords candidates for federal elective office (Congress or the presidency) an affirmative right of access to certain broadcast facilities—the only such access obligation imposed on any mass medium.
2. *Children's Television Programming.* Under the Communications Act and FCC rules, every TV station is required to serve the specific educational and informational needs of children. The standards, among other things, effectively establish a three-hour weekly minimum amount of programming that each station must de-vote to programming specifically designed to serve the needs of children. The rules also set discrete, numerical limits on the amount of advertising that may be placed in TV programs that are specifically aimed at children twelve years of age and under.
3. *Obscenity* and *Indecency.* Separate provisions of federal law (reposing in the criminal code, not the Communications Act) di-rectly ban "obscene" speech on broadcast stations and severely restrict (but do not ban outright) what is termed "indecent" speech.

A Potpourri of Policies from a Nearly Bygone Regulatory Era

Despite nearly three decades of deregulation, a number of other policies and rules remain that affect programming content in less in-trusive but nevertheless varying ways. For example, there are rules re-garding certain on-air contests conducted by broadcast stations, rules restricting the broadcasting of false information concerning a crime or catastrophe ("broadcast hoaxes"), rules relating to the airing of tele-phone conversations, and rules governing the advertising of certain games of chance.

From the start, the Communications Act and FCC rules have also contained a provision requiring radio and TV stations to identify the sponsorship of certain broadcast content—from the briefest ads to the longest programs. The concept is that if someone pays for something being broadcast, the public is entitled to know the identity of that "sponsor" or financial source. The permutations of this basic rule are many and varied, covering not only products and services but circumstances where films, records, talent, and scripts are supplied in connection with political programs or programs discussing controversial issues.[4] In the wake of the TV quiz show scandals of the 1950s and widespread reports at about the same time of undercover payments to radio disc jockeys to promote certain records or artists, this section of the law was amended to outlaw rigged contests and to ban a practice known as "payola." The first prohibits anyone from seeking to influence, prearrange, or predetermine the outcome of broadcast contests involving knowledge, skill, or chance. The second prohibits undisclosed payments made to broadcast station personnel to influence what is broadcast or played on the air.[5]

Other than in programs designed for children twelve and under, the FCC no longer regulates the amount of advertising that may be broadcast and leaves issues concerning false or deceptive advertising claims primarily to the Federal Trade Commission. With respect to particular products, federal law singles out and prohibits the broadcast advertising of cigarettes, "little cigars," and chewing tobacco. Although controversy has long raged over alcoholic beverages, and a former broadcast industry code restricted their advertising, there is no federal law prohibiting broadcast advertising of any kind of alcoholic beverage, including "hard liquor."

Finally, it should be noted that FCC rules are especially designed to encourage public participation in the broadcast licensing process. On the surface, these rules appear substantial. All broadcast stations must maintain a file with key information concerning both station operations and the licensing process that must be regularly available for public inspection at a reasonably convenient location. If one were to peruse a properly maintained public file, they would find, among other things, a straightforward description of how members of the public can file complaints with the FCC concerning various matters. They would also discover that whenever a station requests the renewal of its license or the sale of its business, members of the public can ask that the request be blocked or modified by filing what is called a "petition to deny."

Restrictions on the Ownership of Media Properties

Another major way the FCC has long regulated the broadcast industry is by imposing certain structural constraints—rules and policies specifically targeted to determine who can own and control what and where. Also known as multiple and cross-ownership rules, these regulations flow from the FCC's authority to distribute broadcast licenses fairly and equitably throughout the nation and its long-held belief that broadcasting must remain a competitive service whose facilities are spread among as many diverse and different owners as possible.

As a result, various rules have been adopted to limit the total number of radio stations and the total number of TV stations that one person or commonly controlled corporate entity may own in the same city or local media market ("local" ownership restrictions). Similar rules previously limited the overall total number of radio and TV stations one party could own regardless of location ("national" ownership restrictions). However, as a result of the 1996 Telecommunications Act, there is no longer any national ownership restriction in radio, and the remaining restriction in television only addresses the total number of television households (expressed in the form of a percentage) one entity may reach.

Separate rules currently restrict the common ownership of a daily newspaper and a broadcast station serving the same market area. And, the FCC has long restricted (although recently relaxed) the combined number of radio and TV stations that could be owned and controlled by the same party or entity in the same local broadcast market. Starting in the late 1980s, the FCC developed policies governing the relationships (short of outright ownership) one broadcast station owner can have with another station owner in the same market—for example, one radio station taking over certain business, program, or advertising arrangements of another radio station that it does not own, under what have been called "local marketing," "joint sales," or "time brokerage" agreements.

—⁂—

This brief overview of the existing regulatory regime ends with a note about FCC enforcement powers. The FCC's ultimate power rests with its ability to deny or dismiss a pending application or, in a truly egregious case, to conduct a formal evidentiary hearing before an administrative judge, the required statutory step before the agency may revoke a license previously granted. However, such remedies, extremely rare in the past, have become virtually moribund. More typically, if the FCC finds wrongdoing or has serious questions about a station's compliance with a specific rule, it will investigate the matter and assess a "forfeiture" or monetary fine for any misconduct.

THE BUSINESS SIDE OF BROADCASTING

To better understand how broadcasting is regulated, it is useful to look at how the business of broadcasting is conducted. The FCC issues licenses only to individual stations; it does not license television, radio, or cable networks. However, because all major national broadcast networks (ABC, CBS, NBC, and Fox) own local stations, it has been possible for the FCC to write rules and enforce policies directed to local stations that also directly impact some of the business arrangements of national networks. For instance, FCC rules limit the ability of a local station to enter into an affiliation agreement with a national network if that network does not allow the local affiliate some veto power over the carriage of some network programming.

The way broadcast stations are licensed assumes a business conducted on a local basis by independent station owners. The prevailing regulatory policy, in fact, presupposes that local stations are best able to serve the specialized needs and interests of local audiences. Yet, the entertainment part of the broadcast business, by far the predominate part, originates from New York, Hollywood, and a few other major production centers.

Programming on a typical "local" radio station, whether in the largest city or smallest town, is likely to consist of music and features or news and talk. The music is recorded and supplied by record companies (all located elsewhere) and the feature material (news, sports, weather, traffic, or lifestyle) usually originates from a combination of sources (local, network, and specialized). With the availability of satellite-distributed program services, even the smallest local radio station can air a music format with a professional disc jockey located elsewhere, interspersed with news, traffic, and weather obtained from specialized services, also located elsewhere.

Programming on a typical local television station follows a similar pattern, with a few important distinctions. With the number of national networks expanding from only three in the 1960s (ABC, CBS, and NBC) to at least seven at the start of the twenty-first century (ABC, CBS, NBC, Fox, Pax TV, The CW, and My Network TV) plus the Spanish-language networks, Univision and Telemundo, most local TV stations are affiliated with a network that provides significant and, in the case of the major networks, substantial amounts of entertainment and information on a daily basis. In those time periods not filled by network-supplied programming, the typical local TV station airs entertainment, game and talk shows that are purchased from national syndicators and other nonlocal distributors of such program material. Some major market stations (and most stations affiliated with major networks) fill significant segments of the day with locally produced news programming. On the other hand, some stations—particularly those lacking an affiliation with a major network—devote virtually no time to news.

Overall, the structure of today's broadcasting business can be divided into four main groups:

1. *Local Stations*

These come in various sizes and audience reach, based on the power, tower height, and frequency specified in a station's federal license. In general, local radio stations offer more specialized, more local programming, heavily dependent on local advertising. In contrast, local television stations typically reach larger audiences covering larger areas and offer more generalized programming, dependent on a combination of local and national or regional advertising.

2. *Group Owners of Stations*

These range from the heavyweights, like Clear Channel Broadcasting Corporation, owning more than twelve hundred radio stations scattered over the entire nation, or CBS, owning just the biggest radio and TV stations in the biggest markets; to the mediumweights, like Gannett or Sinclair Broadcasting, owning scores of stations in both large and medium-size markets; to the bantamweights, like a single family, owning just a handful of radio stations in the smallest markets.

3. Networks of Stations

Both radio and television stations are served by various network organizations. For these purposes, a network is a national distribution service supplying a partial or nearly full schedule of ongoing programming to affiliated stations (mostly nonowned) in all fifty states. In radio, some networks exist merely to distribute a news service, a discrete program format to affiliated stations,[6] or just the individual programs of a popular talk-show host or celebrity. On the other hand, "turnkey" networks provide round-the-clock music coverage, allowing local radio stations to be fully automated, sometimes staffing just a single engineer to provide certain local inserts.

In television, it is important to distinguish between the major, full-service national networks (ABC, CBS, NBC, and Fox) and the secondary, limited-service networks (The CW, My Network TV, and PaxNet). In addition, two specialty national networks, Univision and Telemundo, feed Spanish-language programming to local Hispanic stations. National television networks either produce their own news and entertainment programming—directly or through a co-owned Hollywood production company—or acquire such programming from the broader production community.

Even though the over-the-air television network business has survived for nearly sixty years and has undergone significant expansion in the last two decades, it is a business model under stress. Competition from hundreds of cable and satellite networks and the growing fragmentation of the video audience has certainly taken its toll. Also chipping at its foundation is a developing strain of bad blood between network companies and their affiliated stations. A relationship long fraught with inherent tension has recently taken on the feel of a genuine fight. As summarized by Bill Carter of the *New York Times*, "Regulatory changes, increased competition, technological advances and consolidation of power by the networks and big station owners, have gradually pushed networks and their affiliates all the way to opposite corners of the ring."[7] Skyrocketing programming costs and a dated business arrangement in which networks still pay many affiliated stations to broadcast their programming (not the reverse) have further strained the relationship.

4. Program Suppliers for Stations

Program suppliers (more commonly called "syndicators") are companies or ventures that produce and sell individual programs (or a series of programs) to individual stations, usually on a market-by-market basis. Radio syndicators, typically owned by the major networks or large group owners, supply stations with special, one-time events or the daily program offerings of such nationally known radio personalities as Rush Limbaugh, Howard Stern, and Dr. Laura Schlessinger. In television, discrete entertainment, lifestyle, or children's features are usually syndicated in a package of self-contained individual programs (thirty minutes or one-hour in length). They are categorized as either "off-network," meaning that they initially aired on a TV network and are being offered as "reruns" (such as "Seinfeld"), or as "first-run," meaning that they were not previously shown elsewhere and are being offered as syndicated "originals" (such as "Jeopardy," "Oprah," and "Live with Regis and Kelly"). Syndicators also sell Hollywood films and various nonentertainment program material to national networks and local stations.

—⁂—

A discussion of the structure of broadcasting must also include cable and satellite television—the delivery systems that supply most Americans with their television programming. Even though cable television is regulated in discrete categories by the FCC, it is not licensed by the federal government in the same way that broadcasting is licensed. Instead, before a cable system is allowed to string its wires and cable over, under, and around public property, it must first enter into a franchise agreement with a local government. This franchise agreement defines the relationship between the system and the local community, covering key operational aspects of the business.

Some cable operators "originate" their own programming, supplying local news, advertising, and certain specialized services (such as public or government access channels mandated by local franchising authorities). But the vast bulk of cable programming is composed of the carriage or "retransmission" by cable systems of over-the-air broadcast stations and a host of diverse cable "channels" that either repackage broadcast television programs or offer discrete, new program services tailored to specialty rather than general audiences. In the former category are such cable channels as A&E, Nickelodeon, USA Network, TBS, and TV Land. In the latter are such cable channels as MTV, BET, HGTV, ESPN, the Golf Network, twenty-four-hour music video and shopping channels, the Weather Channel, and the Travel

Network. Supplementing these are the twenty-four-hour news, business, and public service channels such as CNN, CNN Headline News, MSNBC, CNBC, Fox News Channel, and C-Span.

Most of the major cable channels are owned in whole or part by large cable companies or other news and entertainment companies. It takes enormous financial resources to launch and sustain a cable service and, equally important, it takes special expertise and leverage to reach agreements with the ever-shrinking number of large multiple system operators who own and control the majority of local cable systems spanning the country. Typically, cable-created channels are packaged with over-the-air television stations and then sold to subscribers as an "expanded basic" or "standard" cable service. For an additional fee, most cable systems offer "premium" channels such as HBO, Showtime, and Cinemax. Many systems also offer "pay-per-view" services, allowing customers to order recent feature films, sporting events, concerts, and other special events based on a one-time fee.

The development of "geostationary" satellites[8] in the 1970s that so dramatically spiked the growth of cable in the 1980s—giving cable the ability to provide its own multichannel programming—finally gave birth in the 1990s to direct broadcast satellite (DBS) systems. DBS competes with cable by offering the same or similar channels of programming. But it reaches subscribers' homes with a direct satellite feed, not over wired cable lines. Although launched in the 1980s, DBS did not begin to make significant competitive inroads until the early 1990s, when, owing to improved technology, more powerful satellites and much smaller subscriber receiving dishes were introduced. The major disadvantage DBS previously experienced in competing with cable—its inability to deliver local television stations to subscribers—has been largely eliminated by recent changes in copyright law and steady improvements in technology.

THE SEPARATE STRUCTURE OF PUBLIC BROADCASTING

The Early Struggle for Policy Recognition

Just as commercial radio was springing from the chaotic 1920s, another flank of broadcasting was emerging. Some of the first broadcast stations had been licensed to universities where experiments in science and engineering laboratories had spurred radio's development.

Although mostly noncommercial, these early "educational" AM stations held the same kind of license as a commercial station—because, at the time, no policy distinction existed between commercial and noncommercial operation. Despite vigorous efforts to stem the rising tide of commercialism by an eclectic group of activists and reformers, the country moved forward with commercial radio in a lead role and noncommercial radio as little more than a bit player. In fact, during this period, despite a promising beginning, many of the original AM stations supported by educational institutions eventually disappeared for lack of funding.

However, even without reliable funding or supportive government policy, noncommercial radio somehow survived and was later joined by noncommercial television. In 1945, when the FCC decided to allocate discrete channels for FM radio, it also announced a new policy directly supportive of public broadcasting. It specifically "reserved" the lower portion of the new FM band—88 MHz to 92 MHz—for educational use.[9] Putting aside the fact that radio sets capable of receiving FM signals were not yet widely available, this was still an important beginning. Indeed, most public radio stations today broadcast on those FM channels originally "reserved" in 1945.

In television, like FM radio (but unlike AM radio), specific channels or frequencies are assigned for use in specific communities in what is called a "Table of Allotments." At the start, only a limited number of channels were assigned for television on the very high frequency (VHF) band. When television grew rapidly and the pressure increased to assign frequencies beyond the original VHF channels (2–13), the FCC, in 1948, imposed a freeze on allocations to allow time to study the problem. Its historic decision four years later (the famous *Sixth Report and Order*) ushered in a new era of American television. It did so by expanding the number of TV channels nearly sevenfold, adding seventy new channels in the ultra high frequency (UHF) band to the original twelve channels in the VHF band. The decision not only represented a dramatic expansion of television service in general, it, for the first time, specifically reserved scores of channels for the exclusive use by noncommercial educational television stations in designated local communities.[10] From these origins, public broadcasting has become a well established if fiscally challenged component of America's mass media.

Public Broadcasting Turns an Important Corner

In the beginning, public television (originally labeled "educational television" or "ETV") was viewed as a promising tool for educating and uplifting the general public. There was, however, little consensus on how it should operate or how much government support was necessary and appropriate. Still, many educational institutions rushed to become licensees, often viewing ETV as little more than an advanced audiovisual aid for schools and colleges. Without much funding or experience necessary to produce creative, appealing programming, many of these early efforts tended to be low-budget lectures or panel discussions. In partial response, a group of stations formed National Educational Television (NET), a cooperative service designed to help ETV stations develop and share quality programming. Although NET offered stations a few hours of improved programming, the distribution system was crude—relying principally on mail service to deliver prerecorded programs from one station to another. Not until 1969 was regular national interconnection established.

Like public television, public radio had its roots in education. As noted, a few colleges and universities played an important role in developing radio technology. Once the medium was established, many more simply became radio station operators. Typically, these stations were used as adjuncts to broadcasting curricula or as student activities. Indeed, even into the late 1960s, most of these stations were low-powered, low-budget, limited-schedule operations virtually inaudible to the general public. In fact, many operated with no full-time paid professional staff.[11]

A major turning point for public broadcasting occurred in 1967. In that year, the Carnegie Foundation, a nonprofit organization, formed the Carnegie Commission to explore the problems and potential of educational television. Believing that ETV was vastly underutilized, the Carnegie Commission recommended that a national "corporation for *public* television" be established. The conceptual and language shift from "educational" to "public" was intentional. Seeing untapped potential, the Carnegie Commission wanted "public" stations to offer a broader cultural and informational service for the general public—an alternative to what was generally available on commercial television but a major step up from the dull, more limited fare featured on many ETV stations at the time. The Carnegie Commission was also hopeful that better funded, more broadly based "public" TV stations could better serve local needs.

In a remarkable confluence of disparate, partisan interests and stellar public policymaking, the Carnegie Commission's recommendations were largely translated into legislation within less than a year of being made public. The Public Broadcasting Act of 1967 created the Corporation for Public Broadcasting (CPB), whose principal role was to funnel money appropriated by Congress for public broadcasting to organizations operating public stations (both television and radio). The 1967 act cemented a critical cornerstone for future development but did not establish a permanent level or formula for funding.

Implied but not specifically prescribed by the 1967 act was the necessity of a better organizational structure in public broadcasting. This led first to the formation in 1969 of the Public Broadcasting System (PBS), a national organization of local public television stations, followed in 1970 by the formation of National Public Radio (NPR), a similar organization of local radio stations. Today, PBS is a national distribution network that, instead of producing its own programming, facilitates the sharing of programming among member stations. Most of the programming is produced by leading public stations in major metropolitan centers or acquired from other sources such as the Children's Television Workshop and the British Broadcasting Corporation.

Because the 1967 act started out as an effort to reform public television at a time when public radio was struggling, radio might not have been included except for some feverish, last-minute maneuvering.[12] But radio overcame the threat and, in the end, benefited greatly from inclusion. For instance, in order to be eligible for federal funds under the new scheme, public stations were required to meet a number of performance standards imposed by CPB that, ultimately, helped lift public radio from mediocrity and broaden its public appeal. Especially instrumental in this transformation was the creation of NPR, which today exemplifies excellence in radio. NPR not only interconnects noncommercial stations throughout the nation, it (unlike PBS) produces programs for member stations—typically, representing about 20 percent of their daily schedule, including highly acclaimed morning and afternoon news programs.[13]

3

The Rising Tide of Deregulation

It started as a mere trickle in the mid-1970s and was first called "reregulation." A few years later, following the 1980 election of President Ronald Reagan, it broadened into a major stream and was renamed "deregulation." Then, in what can only be called a sea change, it rose to the level of established national policy in the Telecommunications Act of 1996. Like the swollen Mississippi River in springtime, the tide of deregulation has been building to a perilous crest ever since. Now flowing freely over the entire media landscape, deregulation has led to a flood of changes in how broadcasting and other mass media serve American society. While widely promoted as a way to expand competition and create better services, unbridled broadcast deregulation also contributes to increased fragmentation of media sources and greater reliance on subscription services.

America at the start of the twenty-first century is a nation with extraordinary resources but facing great challenges. The same characterization describes contemporary American media. If one were to use statistics as a brush, two totally different pictures could be painted. In the one, always drawn by existing media conglomerates but just as eagerly sketched by some Washington policymakers, our vision is filled with an ever-expanding number of media outlets offering unlimited choices to all facets of the American public. Another picture, usually drawn by media critics, gives us a less rosy view, where darkening clouds of dwindling diversity produce homogenized views stretched over multiple media platforms, all colored with the same corporate logo.

Neither picture, of course, is complete. Each reflects a certain reality while also containing certain distortions. What is clear, however, is that by the time the deregulation movement reached full flower (and the marketplace changes it helped cultivate became deeply entrenched), we had passed the point where we could simple rely on or merely adjust the existing policy framework to achieve longstanding regulatory objectives. On the contrary, what this and all succeeding chapters attempt to show is that drastically changed circumstances require drastically changed thinking in developing a new policy framework.

THE PRE-1980 PERIOD
OF CONTEMPORARY REGULATION

The first four decades of broadcast regulation—starting with the Communications Act of 1934 and continuing into the early 1970s—were characterized by dynamic policymaking. After some initial skirmishing over its authority, the FCC quickly became a powerful force in deciding not only who would broadcast but how those given broadcast licenses should perform.[1] Starting with exclusive dominion over all technical matters, the FCC's authority gradually expanded to include a wide array of both structural and content-related matters. Indeed, the breadth of programming, advertising, and operational rules promulgated by regulators by the early 1970s would stun many observers today.

Also near the end of this period, consumer and activist groups were routinely agitating for change and forcing FCC action. The turbulent 1960s and early 1970s, in fact, gave rise to the direct involvement of public interest groups in broadcast proceedings, a development that was particularly instrumental in shaping a number of new FCC policies. Among the most prominent were those (1) requiring broadcast stations to follow a unique set of equal employment opportunity procedures, (2) imposing special rules for children's television programming, and (3) extending the "fairness doctrine" (a policy prescribing the treatment of controversial issues of public importance) to broadcast advertising. With an increasingly aggressive citizen's movement pushing for more restrictions in an already heavily regulated environment,[2] it was almost inevitable that one would start to hear refrains of regulatory overkill. Eventually, even government officials began to question the new and increasingly intricate web of regulation imposed on broadcasters.

The earliest deregulatory steps focused on the least controversial subjects: discarding outdated rules, eliminating unnecessary paperwork, and generally seeking to simplify and streamline some of the FCC's more complex or burdensome regulations. At this stage, the effort was viewed as little more than minor tinkering with an otherwise sound regulatory system. In the spring of 1972, the FCC announced the formation of a three-member "Reregulation Task Force." At the start, the objective was to unburden broadcasters and lighten the FCC's administrative load. For example, by the late 1970s and early 1980s, virtually everyone agreed that a few Byzantine procedures had gotten out of hand. One of those was "ascertainment," a process whereby every time a broadcaster—from the smallest AM radio station to the largest VHF television station—filed an application for renewal (then, every three years) or sought to build or buy a station, it was required to (a) conduct a detailed public opinion survey of the general public and (b) interview a bevy of community leaders in nineteen enumerated categories cutting across virtually all cross-sections of the community.[3] The goal of this mandatory exercise was to "ascertain" separately from members of the general public and community leaders what each group viewed as the leading problems or most important issues facing the local community where the station operated. Survey results were then tabulated and explained in written exhibits. Even more important, each application was required to include a detailed narrative description of the specific programs the station proposed to broadcast to address the major problems and issues identified in the surveys.

As one might imagine, because broadcast stations at the time genuinely feared license renewal problems, they tended to file inordinate amounts of material. The exercise became a massive paper chase with stations seeking comfort in the sheer volume of their filings. On the other hand, each new level of detail only produced more pitfalls for applicants. Objectors had more to exploit and the FCC faced escalating delays and other administrative burdens. No wonder the FCC and broadcast stations alike sought a return to a simpler, more streamlined approach.

While "ascertainment" stands out as regulatory activism gone amok, it is well to remember the viselike grip held by the FCC over so many other station activities during these years. In addition to rules affording political candidates special privileges (which remain today), radio and television stations faced a number of other standards designed specifically to measure their performance on a recurring basis. These included "processing guidelines" (that, in practice, operated as rules) requiring broadcast stations to make written commitments concerning minimal levels of "news," "public affairs," and certain other "nonentertainment" programming. They were expressed as percentages for a typical broadcast week—for example, x percent devoted to news, y percent devoted to public affairs, and z percent devoted to all other nonentertainment programming. Stations were also expected to specify the number of public service announcements (PSAs) they would broadcast in a typical week. On top of this, the FCC required stations to set the maximum amount of commercial matter—expressed in the form of total minutes—they would broadcast in a given hour. To ensure that its guidelines were being met, the FCC pursued a "promise versus performance" policy in which broadcast stations were effectively graded on their performance in these critical programming categories. This was enforced by comparing a station's actual performance as shown in a current application—namely, the specific amounts devoted to news, public affairs, and advertising—with its promise in a previous application. A passing grade ensured speedy renewal. A failing grade ensured deferred action that, unless resolved to the FCC's satisfaction, could snowball into formal proceedings that would potentially threaten a broadcaster's license to operate.

In these same pre-1980 years, all broadcast stations were required to, among other things, file annual financial reports, annual ownership reports, annual employment reports, and, in the case of TV stations, annual programming reports. They were also required to prepare annual listings of problems and needs of their local community, keep and maintain (for public inspection) detailed program logs, and advise the FCC of any "substantial" change in the accuracy of their ongoing representations relating to programming and commercial matters (including a brief explanation of the reasons for any such change). Finally, broadcasters were required to comply with the "fairness doctrine."[4] That policy imposed two additional programming and operational responsibilities on all broadcast stations: (1) an affirmative obligation to cover certain controversial issues of public importance affecting their local community and (2) a corresponding requirement to present representative and contrasting viewpoints on the controversial issues they elected to cover.

Against this backdrop, the first rumblings of serious deregulation were beginning to roll over Washington. What started as an uncontroversial effort to reregulate overly burdensome procedures and reduce unduly complex guidelines ultimately became a more sweeping and fundamental reform movement that continues to reign at the start of the twenty-first century.

As the 1970s came to an end, some members of Congress entered the fray—promising a "basement to attic" review of communications legislation.[5] This, it should be emphasized, was more than twenty years before the great rewrite of 1996. As action heated up in Congress and continued to capture the attention of the FCC, the nature of the deregulation debate also started to change. The push to deregulate became more ideological, propelled by a widening belief that government should play a more limited role in national life. Reliance on the marketplace instead of governmental intervention to control private economic behavior and ensure public service became an increasingly popular view.

THE POST-1980 PERIOD

Although the deregulatory trend continued through the single-term presidency of Jimmy Carter in the late 1970s, it found a new kindred spirit and a more focused political agenda with the election of Ronald Reagan in 1980. By early 1981, the deregulation tide was well under way.[6] It started with radio and quickly spread to its video sibling.

The first substantial deregulatory action by the FCC was to drop all community ascertainment procedures for radio. Shortly thereafter, it eliminated guidelines for news, public affairs, and other nonentertainment programming. In addition, radio stations were relieved of all commercial time guidelines and the obligation to maintain program logs. Once it was decided that radio broadcasters would no longer be held accountable under such guidelines and procedures, it was possible for the FCC to cut its multipage renewal application down to a mere "postcard." Three years later, in 1984, similar actions were taken to deregulate television.[7]

Also, in the mid-1980s, the FCC clipped what it called regulatory "underbrush" from its federal yard, eliminating a number of policies and minor rules that it said were no longer warranted or required by the public interest. These included policies covering such matters as audience ratings, conflicts of interest—stemming from a broadcaster's private business activities—concert promotion announcements (again, where a broadcaster's private business interests might be implicated), and false, misleading, and deceptive commercials.[8]

A number of other events coalesced during this period to put a different face on deregulation, setting in motion a dramatic upheaval of the broadcasting business that continues today. First, the FCC eliminated what was called its "antitrafficking" rule. This rule required anyone acquiring a broadcast station to hold and operate the station for at least three years.[9] For decades, the rule had been thought to be commensurate with the notion that broadcast stations were ingrained with special public service responsibilities—responsibilities that could only be met if a station was owned for a sufficient period of time. Second, in a further streamlining of the application process, the FCC eliminated the need for applicants to supply personal financial statements or written commitments from financial institutions in order to demonstrate their financial qualifications to acquire and operate a broadcast station.[10] Taken together, these actions made it much easier to trade and flip broadcast stations at will. With no "holding period," broadcast stations could be acquired with maximum flexibility to sell out or bail out quickly, either to take profits or to avoid losses. It was a major step in making a broadcast station more like any other commodity.

Overlapping these actions, the FCC also began loosening structural regulations to allow media companies to acquire more stations. For the better part of four decades, starting with the 1940s and ending in the 1970s, ownership of broadcast stations was severely limited, with a single party restricted to only three, five, or seven stations nationwide in each service (AM, FM, and TV, respectively). The breakthrough to double digits and beyond did not occur until 1984 when the FCC raised the overall station limits from seven, seven, or seven to twelve, twelve, or twelve.[11] As the 1980s drew to a close, a perception grew—fed, of course, by broadcast lobbyists—that the radio industry was unduly saturated with stations and in need of a marketplace stimulus. In response, the FCC raised the national radio limits to eighteen AM stations and eighteen FM stations (in 1992) and then to twenty AM stations and twenty FM stations (in 1994).

The most significant deregulatory action during this period involving content was elimination of the "fairness doctrine."[12] Long opposed by most leading broadcast groups as a restriction on their First Amendment rights, but just as vigorously championed by public advocacy groups as a vital shield against those who might limit minority or less popular views, the doctrine ultimately fell when the FCC decided that it was no longer necessary in a more vibrant mass media marketplace.

Another noteworthy development in the post-1980 period was the removal of various network rules—regulations which had limited the ability of the major TV networks (ABC, CBS, and NBC) to acquire ownership interests in television "reruns" and "first-run" syndicated programming, as well as their ability to engage in general syndication or to exhibit on their own networks all the shows they were able to produce themselves. Originally designed to ensure that the TV networks did not wield excessive power in the television programming market, the rules also had the effect of prohibiting the common ownership of a national television network and a major Hollywood production company. When these rules were eliminated in the mid-1990s, the reaction was almost immediate. Disney (owner of Walt Disney, Buena Vista, and Touchstone Films) acquired ABC, and Viacom (owner of Paramount Pictures) acquired CBS. Fox, not in existence when the rules were imposed, had been allowed to combine its Hollywood production business (Twentieth Century Fox) with its TV network business much earlier.

As this period ends and we approach the long-promised major "rewrite" of the Communications Act, special note should be made of one policy moving against the deregulatory tide. Although the FCC had taken the first steps to oversee children's programming on television during the 1970s and 1980s, it was Congress, in 1990, that enacted legislation mandating limits on advertising in children's programming and affirmatively requiring television licensees to serve the special educational and informational needs of children.[13] Several years later, under a Democratic chairman (Reed Hundt) who viewed broadcasting with far more suspicion than awe, the FCC added weight to these standards by effectively requiring television stations to broadcast three hours of children's programming each week.[14]

THE TELECOMMUNICATIONS ACT OF 1996:
UNDERMINING THE "PUBLIC INTEREST" STANDARD

Even as deregulation was seeping into virtually every corner of FCC policymaking, Congress initially reacted with only a mixture of limited measures and failed proposals. Then, in the mid-1990s, certain interests coalesced. Conservative leaders in Congress, long committed to a deregulatory agenda, joined forces with a Democratic administration that wanted to stimulate jobs in telecommunications and spur further technological advances in information services. The prevailing view, with nary a dissenting word, was that a strong deregulatory legislative package would usher in a brand new world where competition would be king. In the telecommunications sphere, the hope was that long-distance telephone companies would provide local telephone service and the regional or local telephone providers would enter the long-distance business. Cable television would provide telephone service and a host of interactive applications. Existing players would invade each other's territory, and many new players would join in the competitive games. For the public, this would mean more jobs—in a vastly expanded telecommunications sector—and lower consumer prices with better and more innovative services.

The legislative promise, however, was never as explicit or sweeping when addressing electronic media. To be sure, deregulation of cable television was viewed as fostering competition because cable operators could move into areas dominated by others, but broadcasting seemed to benefit simply by all the movement elsewhere. If Congress could stir competition in other sectors, why not loosen the regulatory reins on broadcasting as well? While radio's weakened economic health in the early 1990s and new competitive threats supposedly faced by television from foreign media interests were factors often cited by industry leaders, broadcasting basically sailed in on the rising tide of deregulation that was already overtaking telecommunications. But unlike telecommunications, where policymakers promised lower prices and more innovative services, there was no specific, demonstrable policy analysis underlying deregulation of broadcasting. If Congress thought deregulation of radio and television would introduce more and varied public service programming or less blatant commercialism, for example, it did so in virtual silence.

Instead, Congress simply alluded to changes in the audio and video marketplace—such as more outlets and heightened competition—as sufficient justification for regulatory reform. With no affirmative policy goals in mind, Congress altered the regulatory framework simply to correspond to what it perceived to be new marketplace realities.[15] As the House Commerce Committee observed, in words that could have been written by industry proponents (and probably were):

> . . . these market developments require substantial deregulation of local station ownership and greater reliance on marketplace forces to assure vigorous competition and diversity. Permitting common ownership of stations will promote the public interest by harnessing operating efficiencies of commonly owned facilities, thereby increasing competition and diversity.[16]

Incredibly, this little slice of legislative history seems to conclude, rather unabashedly, that striking rules to permit fewer parties to control more properties will actually stir competition and enhance diversity. In sum, not only was the policy analysis underlying broadcast deregulation in the 1996 act surprisingly superficial, it rested on a shockingly unproven premise.

Interestingly, the only specific effort to focus on new program services or renewed public service responsibilities as a justification for broadcast deregulation came about shortly after the 1996 law was passed. It took the form of a broad-based Advisory Committee on Public Interest Obligations of Digital Television Broadcasters established by the Clinton-Gore administration to explore ways broadcasters might better serve the public interest in the digital age. Known as the Gore Commission, this adjunct study of public policy had been ignited by the only real light shone on television broadcasting in the waning days of the legislative debates. Up to that point, broadcasting, and especially television, drew little public attention in the wider controversies that focused primarily on telecommunications matters. But, near the end, the entire legislative package was threatened when the award of digital channels to existing television stations suddenly erupted into public view.[17] Because inauguration of digital television required a transition period during which television stations would use both analog and digital technologies—to avoid denying service to consumers not yet equipped to receive the new digital signals—the FCC proposed granting all incumbent analog television stations a second channel on which they could start digital broadcasting. Although it was generally accepted that one of the two channels would be returned to the government once the transition was completed, the controversy centered on whether incumbent television broadcasters should "pay" for the "second" channel—either by making a direct payment to the U.S. Treasury or by being bound to new standards of public service.

The posing of this question at the very end of a two-year, massive overhaul of communications law was, in fact, the closest Congress ever came to debating the specific public policy implications of broadcast deregulation. The issue finally broached was whether a new regulatory era should be launched before ensuring some direct benefit or level of improved service to the public. But it never became a serious debate. Instead, and typical of many Washington legislative debates, it degenerated into last-minute grandstanding by some policymakers— such as then Senate majority leader Robert Dole and FCC chairman Reed Hundt—who characterized the assignment of digital channels to incumbent broadcasters as a "giveaway" of monumental proportions. Broadcast lobbyists, meanwhile, attacked any proposals to pay for the channels as an inequitable and harmful tax on the airwaves.

The positions of the leading players not only missed the mark but were drawn in such extremes as to almost ensure that no meaningful deliberative dialogue would take place. Those screaming "giveaway" and attaching astronomical and unproven dollar values on the new digital channels failed to acknowledge the realities of transitioning the American public from a deeply embedded analog system to an entirely new digital system. Often, they pursued an agenda directly antagonistic to the existing broadcast system, even if it meant its total unraveling in favor of promised advances by those from the computer or wireless worlds. On the other hand, broadcast lobbyists and those sympathetic to their cause wanted to use the digital channels with a free hand—the better to battle more competitive conditions. In the end, the FCC was authorized to issue the digital channels and Congress attached neither a monetary nor a public service obligation.

When positions are drawn in this fashion, it frustrates the discussion of other issues and alternatives, absent strong leadership by policymakers with a determined vision of their own. Sadly, such leadership and vision were missing in the debate over the 1996 act. The effort to deregulate electronic media floated along on the tide of telecommunications deregulation and was hardly noticed—until the very end. And, even then, the debate centered on a tortured and twisted analysis of digital technology—not the future direction of American broadcasting.

It could have been different. The push to loosen broadcast regulatory restraints and to launch the digital era in television—the major changes affecting broadcasting in the 1996 act—could have provided an opportunity to reassess communications policy on a broader scale. Instead of framing the debate over whether the government was engaged in a public giveaway or poised to tax the airwaves, the issue could have focused on establishing entirely new core principles to guide mass media policy. Certainly the massive transition contemplated, with its many technical possibilities and expanded service opportunities, should have had policymakers questioning whether it was time to reexamine an outdated public trusteeship model. What do we as a nation expect and want from our electronic media? Is it just increased outlets and facilities? Is it assurance that there will be continued free access to certain basic services in an increasingly subscription-based marketplace? Is it a minimal threshold of defined public service that must be performed by every licensed station? Or have we reached the point where, as a society, such comprehensive regulation is no longer necessary or productive, with reliance on the marketplace being more efficient and reliable in serving most Americans? These are all valid and timely questions—but all are lost in the sometimes nearly mindless rush to deregulate.

SPECIFIC BROADCAST POLICY ISSUES ADDRESSED IN THE 1996 ACT

Beyond resolving the digital channel issue, the 1996 act established a new high-water mark in broadcast deregulation. The FCC had already discarded numerous standards and key monitoring tools which had been used to measure a broadcast station's overall performance. It had also moved aggressively to relax its ownership regulations. Congress, on the other hand, had taken only piecemeal actions prior to the 1996 act. In stages, it had nearly tripled the length of a broadcast license[18] and, for the first time, authorized the FCC to award certain broadcast licenses by public auction.

But the 1996 act brought broadcast deregulation to a crest never before imagined. It not only ripped away longstanding structural standards but laid down an unmistakable ideological message. In the words of the House Commerce Committee, Congress "chooses to depart from the traditional notions of broadcast regulation and rely more on competitive market forces." And to underscore this overriding message, Congress did not just change the rules. It ordered the FCC to work harder to keep the tide of deregulation rolling.

Among the most drastic ownership changes was complete elimination of the benchmarks that had previously determined the total number of radio or TV stations any one person or company could own. Before the 1996 act, FCC regulations set a national ownership limit of twenty FM, twenty AM, and twelve TV stations. After the 1996 act, there was no limit whatsoever on the number of broadcast stations one party could own. On the separate issue of how large a national audience one company could reach with an unlimited number of individual radio or TV stations, Congress placed no limit on radio but, in the case of television, established a 35 percent limit on the number of TV households a single operator could reach. Earlier, the FCC had created its own limit of 25 percent. Accordingly, following the 1996 act, a large media company could own as many TV stations as it wished, as long as the total TV households reached by those stations did not exceed 35 percent of all TV households in the United States.

When it turned to local ownership standards—those geared to individual markets—Congress greatly increased the number of radio stations a single party could own. Whereas FCC rules at the time permitted one party to own only two AM and two FM stations in a single market, the 1996 act raised the total per market to anywhere between five and eight radio stations—the range varying with the total number of stations serving a particular market. While Congress did not change the FCC rule on ownership of local TV stations (at the time, only one per market), it did order the FCC to conduct an administrative proceeding to determine whether its rule restricting one party from owning more than one TV station in a local market should be retained, modified, or eliminated.

Finally, in what amounted to a clarion signal that all remaining remnants of the old regulatory regime should be in play, Congress instructed the FCC to keep reviewing all of its remaining ownership rules—minimally, *every two years*.[19] This bizarre paean to the virtues of the marketplace is called the biennial review process. It puts the FCC in a position where it must engage in a nearly perpetual reexamination of its ownership rules—specifically, holding public proceedings, issuing reports, defending the inevitable court appeals of any decisions, and then starting all over again. When one considers the usual length of time to conduct serious administrative rule makings, resolve substantive issues, and obtain complete judicial review, it is obvious that this mandated process, at best, invites hasty policymaking. Far worse, on a substantive level, it smacks of force-fed policymaking. Congress sounds reveille, and the FCC must fall into formation!

The 1996 act deregulated broadcast licensing in other fundamental ways. Historically, public participation in FCC application proceedings (e.g., those involving the renewal of a license or the transfer of station ownership) takes place when "interested"[20] parties file written petitions with the FCC seeking denial of a particular application. While such petitions rarely result in the outright denial of an application, they do allow for a public airing of certain questions, sometimes leading to changes in or conditions to a given transaction. This *general* process was unchanged by the 1996 act.

A crucial related process, however, was changed. Up to that point, the real threat to an existing station's continued right to broadcast could be traced to a provision that allowed any other party to file a "competing" application when the operating station filed its regular application for renewal. This was called an "overfiling," since the new party was effectively applying for the same technical facilities as the incumbent broadcaster. In theory, a station could lose its very right to broadcast as a result of such "overfilings." Under rules in place prior to the 1996 act, the FCC was required to consider both the license renewal application and the competing application of the "newcomer" in an evidentiary hearing (administrative trial) whose main purpose was to compare the two proposals. Because longstanding FCC practice usually tilted the scale in favor of the incumbent—if its past record of public service met minimal standards—"overfilings" were seldom used and rarely successful. Nevertheless, the very threat of such filings was enough to cause most broadcasters to commit to a respectable level of public service—without a demonstrable record of ongoing public service, they faced the real risk of losing their license to someone who merely promised to operate the station better.

This durable regulatory scheme was shut down by the 1996 act. Instead of a potentially competitive renewal process, we now have a two-step renewal procedure that does not allow for competing applications. In all renewal situations, including those where a petition to deny is filed (the only formal remedy still available), the FCC must grant the renewal application if it finds that the station has: (1) served the public interest; (2) committed no serious violations of FCC rules or the Communications Act; and (3) committed no other violations which, taken together, would constitute a "pattern of abuse."[21] If the FCC is unable to make this type of finding, it must impose sanctions or, in the most egregious circumstances, set the renewal application for evidentiary hearing. In making such determinations, the FCC is specifically forbidden by the 1996 act from considering whether the public interest would be better served by anyone other than the renewal applicant. Only after the FCC has undertaken these elaborate procedures and reached the almost unheard decision of stripping a station of its license can it accept and consider applications by others to operate on the same channel or frequency.

Understandably, the broadcast industry had been quietly lobbying for this type of relief for years. Its inclusion in the 1996 act meant that the most serious risk of being in the broadcast business—the threatened loss of one's license to someone else seeking the same facility—had been stripped from the law. Henceforth, new entrants choosing to buy and sell broadcast properties like pork bellies or existing license holders electing to deemphasize the service aspect of broadcasting could do so with impunity. The threat of overfilings had been lifted and new procedures for license revocation had become so convoluted and difficult that any pursuit of this remaining remedy was almost guaranteed to fail. When juxtaposed against a prevailing deregulatory environment where most enforcement is uninspired, at best, the threat of losing a broadcast license under these revised standards is about as great as a hurricane in Helsinki.

THE POST–1996 ACT PERIOD

The message of the 1996 act could not have been clearer. Congress not only enacted more generous broadcast rules of its own, it assured the ascendancy of the deregulatory tide by ordering the FCC to conduct more administrative proceedings to review virtually all remaining ownership rules. With few exceptions, the years after the 1996 act have been characterized by more deregulatory measures, followed by more deregulatory proposals.

Even a less conservative, mostly centrist, two-term administration headed by William Jefferson Clinton and Albert Gore that had installed the first African-American chairman at the FCC (William

Kennard) was unwilling or unable to stem the deregulatory tide. Following the election of George W. Bush in 2000, a new (and second African American) FCC chairman (Michael Powell) made it abundantly clear that as the agency soared into the twenty-first century it would be on the wings of marketplace forces, not government initiatives.

As soon as the 1996 act was signed, business deals were struck that both tested and stretched the new standards. Almost immediately there was pressure to lift the 35 percent national audience cap imposed on owners of television stations by large media companies who wanted not just more stations (the numerical limit having already been lifted) but greater national reach. Others pushed the FCC to allow one company to own more than one TV station in more local markets (in 1999, the FCC had increased the limit to two, but only in the largest markets and only where certain conditions were met). At the same time, efforts persisted to achieve relaxation or elimination of the rule prohibiting common ownership of broadcast stations and daily newspapers in the same market.

UNDERCURRENTS STIRRING THE DEREGULATORY TIDE

A regulated industry always believes it is being regulated unfairly or unduly. It has been so in broadcasting ever since the industry itself pleaded for government regulation to end the frequency wars in the early days of radio. So it is not surprising that national broadcast associations and leading group owners continue to plea for regulatory relief. If not always uniformly calling for the same type of relief, the industry—whether united or divided—has at least been persistently consistent in pressing for some form of deregulation.[22]

As explained, the deregulatory drift started rather modestly in the early 1970s when industry cries for relief were actually matched by a growing concern within government that certain forms of regulation had become too burdensome. When, a few years later, the streamlining of some procedures led to calls for the total uprooting of many long-established rules, a full-fledged regulatory reform movement was under way. It was kindled and continues to be sustained by several related developments.

1. Changing Ideology in National Politics

Just as the first batch of "reregulatory" ingredients was beginning to brew at the FCC, the nation's political life was jarred by the presidential election of 1980, a remarkable turning point in the dominant national political ideology. A consensus effort to replace outdated rules with more streamlined procedures designed to lighten the load on broadcasters and regulators was about to become more serious and sweeping.

Although strains of more limited government had been punctuating political debate for several years, it was the election of Ronald Reagan in 1980 that provided real ideological fuel for the drive to deregulate. Reducing government and trusting the marketplace was a goal enthusiastically endorsed by President Reagan's new FCC chairman, Mark Fowler. Fowler, in fact, quickly became the Reagan administration's lead cheerleader when he suggested that a television set was nothing more than a "toaster-with-pictures." Whether Mr. Fowler really meant what he said, his metaphor crystallized the notion that the broadcasting business differed little from the consumer product business. And, if that were so, there was no need to interpret the public interest standard of the Communications Act as demanding specific accountability for public service. Rather, like the electrical appliance business, one could depend upon marketplace competition and consumer demand to achieve the requisite level of consumer satisfaction. This was a sharp turn for policymakers, and the debate "electrified" by Fowler's toaster remark continues to influence the discussion more than two decades later.

Even when expressed less vividly, Fowler's view has become increasingly prevalent among policymakers, serving as a vital underpinning for the continued deregulation of broadcast, cable, and satellite media. It developed renewed strength with the ascendancy of the national Republican Party in 1994, was the major force behind the deregulatory measures contained in the 1996 act, and remains the principal rationale supporting efforts to further deregulate commercial media.

2. Changing Ideology in Appellate Courts

Broadcast deregulation has been assisted in no small part by a perceptible shift in the personal political philosophy of those sitting on federal appellate courts. Starting with the Nixon administration in the late 1960s and continuing for nearly twenty-five years until the election of Bill Clinton in 1992, judicial appointments were made against the backdrop of an ascending political view favoring more limited government over proactive regulation.[23] Although this tendency obviously was not reflected in all appellate court appointments, it was strong enough and widespread enough to eventually be reflected in judicial decision making.[24]

No attempt will be made here to trace or label the conservative or liberal tendencies of sitting appellate court judges or to even contend that one political persuasion (liberal or conservative) necessarily translates into decision making that is either regulatory or deregulatory on particular issues. But certain facts and trends are obvious. First, FCC decisions are appealable only to a U.S. Circuit Court of Appeals, the level of the federal judiciary just below the U.S. Supreme Court. Second, the U.S. Court of Appeals for the District of Columbia Circuit (referred to as the D.C. Circuit) is generally regarded as the most important appellate court for federal administrative law overall and FCC matters in particular. Indeed, by law certain FCC decisions must be appealed to the D.C. Circuit and by longstanding practice most other FCC decisions are reviewed by that court.

Third, it is fair to say that during the 1960s and 1970s, the D.C. Circuit was dominated by judges who engaged in active oversight of FCC adjudicatory and rule-making decisions.[25] Judges David Bazelon, Skelly Wright, and Harold Leventhal, the lions of the court at the time, "were all products of Post-War liberalism. Each graduated from law school during the New Deal, served in the Roosevelt or Truman Administration, and was placed on the bench by a Democratic president."[26] While attributing any particular regulatory theory to such judicial luminaries might be difficult, it can be safely said that their background hardly caused them to view government intervention as a last resort. Judges Wright and Bazelon, in particular, "were famous for engaging in aggressive judicial protection of the rights of minority groups."[27] Moreover, during these years, the D.C. Circuit famously championed the rights of broadcast audiences and special interest groups, giving them, for the first time, specific "standing" to participate in FCC proceedings.[28]

Fourth, during this period, decisions of the D.C. Circuit were just as likely to be critical of the FCC for not doing enough to protect the rights of minorities or the general public as they were to be critical

of the FCC for overstepping its bounds. On matters such as oversee-
ing program format changes or enforcing the fairness doctrine, the
D.C. Circuit often took a more expansive view of the FCC's authority than did the agency itself. For example, beginning in 1970, in a
series of cases involving broadcast station sales, the D.C. Circuit
gradually developed a set of criteria for determining when the "public interest" standard required the FCC to hold a hearing to review
proposed changes in the entertainment formats of radio stations—
despite the FCC's own reluctance to review such matters. It is almost
inconceivable that judges sitting on the court today would be as
proactive in forcing the FCC's hand, especially on a matter involving
content.

The changed nature of the D.C. Circuit's influence on FCC policymaking is likewise illustrated in the area of equal employment opportunity (EEO) enforcement. In 1968, the FCC declared that any
broadcast station discriminating against employees or potential employees on the basis of race, color, sex, national origin, or religion
would not be operating in the "public interest."[29] Several years later,
the U.S. Supreme Court acknowledged that the FCC had a responsibility to assure that diverse views, including minority views, are reflected in programming and included in programming decisions.[30] At
about the same time, in a string of cases, the D.C. Circuit began
adding weight to the FCC's EEO role. In one, the court required the
FCC to make certain specific additional inquiries of broadcast stations
that did not satisfy threshold EEO standards.[31] In another, the court
ruled that the FCC was required to hold a hearing on a license renewal
application where there was a "pattern of inconsistencies and mis-
statements that marked the licensee's communications . . . with the
FCC" on EEO matters.[32] In sum, beginning in the late 1960s and continuing for nearly two decades, the FCC's regulatory role in this area
was more frequently applauded than scorned by the influential D.C.
Circuit. In some cases, the court even called for specific strengthening
or refinement of the agency's EEO policies.[33]

But flash forward to the 1990s and a far different picture begins to
emerge. The judicial mainstays who sometimes went out of their way
to support policies designed to assist minorities have long since left
the bench. They have been replaced by a group of justices generally regarded as having a more conservative, less government-interventionist
bent—and, given the chance, they are poised to demonstrate that different approach.

Which brings us to 1998. In that year, an unusual, long-running broadcast renewal case raising several different issues was transformed into a full frontal attack on the FCC's EEO procedures when it reached the D.C. Circuit.[34] In a surprise ruling, the court found those procedures unconstitutional—essentially the same procedures that it had implicitly approved (even encouraged) on numerous earlier occasions. Thereafter, in 2000, the FCC adopted revised procedures thought to be responsive to the court's concerns. However, in a further decision announced the following year, the D.C. Circuit again found parts of the FCC's procedures unconstitutional, sending the agency's entire EEO program into a tailspin.[35] In December 2001, the FCC announced yet another effort to establish EEO rules for broadcast stations that would pass muster with a determined D.C. Circuit. The area, however, remains muddled in the wake of those court decisions because, if nothing else, they removed much of the steam from the FCC's longstanding EEO enforcement program. Although some observers attribute the D.C. Circuit's turnabout on this issue solely to the U.S. Supreme Court's 1995 *Adarand*[36] decision dealing with race-based preference programs—programs far different than the latest FCC procedures emphasizing recruitment techniques and eschewing numerical goals—it is foolhardy to ignore one simple fact. Over the years, the political leanings of judges on the D.C. Circuit Court had changed, just as the dominant political ideology of the Washington regulatory scene had changed.

The shifting ideology of the D.C. Circuit was also being felt in the FCC's approach to media ownership. A 2001 report in the *New York Times* summarized the change: "In a marked departure from decades of Supreme Court opinions . . . the agency [FCC] and the appeals court [D.C. Circuit] have become significantly more sympathetic to the free-speech rights of corporations and more skeptical of the role of government in promoting diversity in mass media."[37] After many years of judicial activism in other areas, "the federal judges in the Washington court [D.C. Circuit] have indicated a deep skepticism that government-imposed limits on media ownership will effectively promote diversity on the airwaves."[38]

The D.C. Circuit's assault on FCC media ownership rules is illustrated by two key decisions. In the first, the court, in early 2001, struck down the FCC's horizontal cable ownership rule—which imposed a 20 percent limit on the number of cable subscribers a single cable owner could serve—as being in excess of the FCC's authority;

and, in the same decision, it ruled that the FCC's separate vertical integration rule—which imposed limits on the number of cable channels a cable operator could carry if it had an ownership interest in
such channels—violated the First Amendment.[39] Less than a year
later, in February 2002, the D.C. Circuit ordered the FCC to recon-
sider its decision to retain the 35 percent national television ownership cap and struck down entirely the FCC's ownership rule that
banned the common ownership of cable systems and TV stations in
the same local market.[40] The case is noteworthy not only for dismantling one and severely weakening another plank in the FCC's
longstanding media ownership platform; it also stands out as a remarkable piece of conservative-leaning, pro-marketplace judicial policymaking. It centered on the provision in the 1996 act that requires
the FCC to review its media ownership rules on a biennial basis to
determine whether such rules remain necessary. As interpreted by the
D.C. Circuit, this biennial-review mandate was more than a genuine
reexamination and gradual updating of policy. On the contrary, it
was more like a set of congressional marching orders "to continue
the process of deregulation." Expressing frustration with the FCC's
announced intention to follow a more gradual approach, the court
sharply opined that the "mandate of [the biennial-review provision]
might better be likened to Farragut's order at the Battle of Mobile Bay
('Damn the torpedoes! Full speed ahead')."[41]

3. Influence of Modern Lobbying

Lobbying of Congress and administrative agencies such as the FCC
is a time-honored tradition that is not only permissible but essential
in a representative democracy.[42] Policymakers need to know the positions of those affected by government policy and, in turn, policy advocates have a right to advise the government of the positions they either support or oppose. That being said, there are inherent dangers in
the level and manner with which modern lobbying is practiced. In
2005, the *Washington Post* reported that the number of registered lobbyists in Washington, D.C., had nearly doubled—just since 2000.[43]
Many of these are former lawmakers or high-ranking government
aides exiting offices on Capitol Hill or federal agencies for high-
paying jobs on the "outside." In the meantime, the nature of the role
has changed. Whereas in the past lobbying was largely reactive, fend-
ing off specific proposals advanced by government policymakers that

might hurt private interests, the process is often highly proactive to-day. As the same *Washington Post* report remarked, "With pro-business officials running the executive and legislative branches, companies are [now] hiring well-placed lobbyists to go on the offensive and find ways to profit from"[44] specific changes in government rules (changes sometimes drafted with the help of lobbyists or their experts). If nothing else, this burst of lobbying activity exacerbates an already uneven balance between those with resources and those without resources.

As the importance of some FCC decisions has risen, so too has the importance of lobbying to influence those decisions. The lobbying I refer to is access to the FCC and other parts of the government that interact with the FCC—access that permits someone, either directly or on behalf of someone else, to get their viewpoint before policymakers (by supplying information or perspective). While usually not considered lobbying in the strictest sense, the most obvious way to get one's views on media issues before the FCC is to file a written petition requesting that the FCC initiate action on a matter within its authority. An easier way is to submit comments that either support or oppose FCC action on proposals that are already under consideration in a public inquiry or rule-making proceeding. Such proceedings are the principal means by which the FCC both formulates and changes policy.

But written comments by diverse individuals and groups on public proposals is only the beginning of FCC policymaking, and hence, FCC lobbying. Lobbying by advocates with a stake in the outcome of a proceeding often begins in earnest after the public comments have been filed. This typically takes the form of direct oral (sometimes written) presentations to individual policymakers—FCC commissioners, their key staff assistants, and other officials (political appointees or career public servants) who manage the branches of the agency. If there is no public rule-making proceeding and the issue is instead centered on an application or petition for action by one or more individual parties, the lobbying may actually start with some form of direct contact even before the application or other request for action is filed. Although lobbying usually continues right up to the point of an agency decision, special rules sometimes place greater restrictions on such unilateral contacts after the application or other request is filed.

Lobbying at the FCC can be limited to one issue or one transaction—or it can be continuous, covering a host of evolving issues. For those specializing in the latter—usually larger companies with recurring business before the agency—lobbying becomes more structured, detailed, and institutionalized. It might start with having a full-time lobbyist or group of lobbyists on staff or in one's employ in Washington, D.C. Disney (ABC), Fox, GE (NBC), Viacom (CBS), and Time Warner all have paid representatives in Washington who routinely track media issues before the FCC and Congress. It is their job to ensure that the interests and perspectives of their companies are well ventilated on those issues. The largest media companies also employ outside communications counsel and government relations specialists to assist in their overall lobbying effort. Smaller media companies may rely on Washington-based trade associations such as the National Association of Broadcasters or the Association of America's Public Television Stations.

Lobbying on mass media issues is also routinely conducted by those not directly engaged in the broadcast business, such as consumer or public interest groups. These range from those who champion the special interests of children, minorities, women, labor, or the handicapped, to those who perform a broader watchdog role such as the Media Access Project, a longstanding activist group that either on its own or in concert with other organizations participates in virtually all major policy decisions affecting broadcasting and cable. In addition, because many broadcast issues have an impact on nonbroadcast businesses—such as newspaper publishing, consumer electronics, cable and satellite services, and wireless telecommunications—these nonbroadcast interests are also frequently engaged in lobbying mass media policymakers.

Whether it is simply maintaining a visible, ongoing presence where policymakers work and gather or periodically treating key government contacts to an informal lunch, effective lobbying requires having people on the ground in Washington. Organizations with their own professional staff and independent resources are also able to sponsor or participate in special events such as industry meetings, conventions, and ceremonial dinners frequently attended by government policymakers (often as invited guests of those organizations). The biggest media companies have one more advantage. They can offer government officials unique opportunities to attend high-profile concerts, sporting events, movie premiers, and other alluring entertainment features which they either control or promote.

Since the key to successful lobbying by any party on any issue is developing relationships that provide ready access, it is no secret that those with the best and largest resources usually succeed to the greatest extent. In the lobbying world, success is not defined just by winning but also by achieving ongoing and meaningful access even if one's position on a given issue is not ultimately favored. No one company or lobbyist, no matter how big or influential, always prevails, simply because the environment they play in is almost always complicated by the presence of numerous conflicting political and practical pressures. Nevertheless, the larger media groups with entrenched lobbying operations hold distinct advantages. They have the full-time staff or paid outside consultants to build and maintain relationships and, when necessary, to deploy resources rapidly.

Although the FCC is an "independent" body in our bureaucratic system, whose members and key staffers are political appointees of the party controlling the executive branch of government,[45] it is Congress, the legislative branch, that has the most direct and abiding influence over the agency. Congress enacts the laws that the FCC implements, it confirms members of the commission who have been nominated by the president, and, through the appropriations process, it controls the FCC's purse strings. Because the FCC must listen to and carefully weigh the concerns of important members of Congress, effective lobbying on major media issues usually entails separate, coordinated efforts on Capitol Hill. Whether the intent is to initiate or halt FCC action, developing relationships and building access to key legislators is often a crucial element in influencing media policy. To illustrate, the broadcast industry lobby worked diligently and directly with key legislators to bring about many of the mass media provisions of the 1996 act and, in an especially quick show of force, public and commercial broadcasters, working together, obtained a targeted provision in appropriations legislation for fiscal year 2001 that had the effect of slowing down and severely restricting an FCC initiative—backed by the Clinton administration—designed to establish a widespread, community-based regime of low-powered FM radio stations.

Because the institution is larger, more powerful, and deals with issues that touch every American and every business, gaining meaningful access to policymakers in Congress is far more difficult than gaining access to policymakers at the FCC. Despite the towering and persistent presence of the TV networks and national trade associations, it is still relatively easy for individuals, small groups, and less connected special interests to obtain a "hearing" before the FCC. Written comments may be submitted, telephone or e-mail inquiries initiated, even in-person meetings arranged with someone involved in the

FCC decision-making process—all without extraordinary resources. On the other hand, it is almost certain that no meaningful connections will occur between those who make policy and those who seek to influence it in Congress, unless ample external resources have been brought to bear—namely, money and power. Everyone connected with the legislative process—whether elected to make (or working to influence) policy—knows that it is extremely unlikely that anyone will be heard on a matter of substance unless they are either a powerful public figure or have made a significant political contribution (usually both). Ernest ("Fritz") Hollings of South Carolina, upon his retirement from the Senate in 2004, recounted his experience this way: "I've got to get money, money, money, money. And I only listen to people who give me money." Expounding further on what's wrong with Congress today, he added that "with the shortage of time and everything else, you've got to listen to the $1,000 givers. I mean no individual is corrupt, but the body has been corrupted."[46] Even if one assumes that real corruption remains rare, there is no doubt that the system heavily favors those with the resources to raise and spend substantial amounts of money. And the media business—with its large organizations, active trade associations, well-paid lobbyists, and hordes of consultants—commands unique abilities to do both. Mainstream mass media, like all other well-heeled business interests, ensure organizing political action committees, helping arrange campaign fund-raising functions, and facilitating thousands of individual campaign donations. But they also stand in the unrivaled position of being able to, in fact, grant "access" to those they seek to influence. As one congressional communications expert observes, "Members of Congress are completely and totally dependent on the media . . . when the head of Viacom [CBS] is lobbying, saying loosen [media ownership] regulations and at the same time we're going to give you coverage—whether this is a conflict of interest or not, it's impossible not to see the connection."[47]

In short, for mass media and members of Congress, "access" is a two-way street. Smart politicians use media to convey their message and gain or ensure visibility. Savvy media types with special interests to pursue know that political contributions to their own elected representatives and other influential public officials can help ensure the type of access that is the essence of successful lobbying. Sprinkling campaign contributions on the two major political parties and key members of Congress—usually those sitting on the commerce committees in the House and Senate, but any other committee or sub-committee affecting media issues at any given time—is commonplace among major media companies, their lobbyists, and lawyers.

Another related way mass media increase their access to members of Congress is by engaging in "grassroots lobbying." While also practiced by other media, it is especially effective in the broadcast business. Since all members of Congress represent states or districts that are the home of powerful media interests—from the news centers of New York and Los Angeles to the local stations that populate the plains of Kansas and Nebraska—there is a symbiotic relationship that arises naturally between members of Congress and their media constituents. Members want easy and favorable access to the media outlets in their districts (to convey their views and facilitate reelection) and broadcast stations want regular access to members whose districts fall in their coverage areas (to better report the news). Equally important, however, if these grassroots relationships are carefully nurtured, they can, over time, ensure better access to policymakers on issues broadcasters regard as crucial to their business.

Eddie Fritts, the enterprising head of the National Association of Broadcasters for more than two decades before his retirement in 2005, explained how his group systematically built fifty state broadcast associations into grassroots machines:

> Every election, you have 50 or so new members in every Congress. You have to do more education of members on your industry. You have to make sure local broadcasters go see them, introduce them to the staffs, show them around [local radio and TV] stations and talk about what broadcasters do.

According to Gordon Hastings of the Broadcast Foundation, Fritts made broadcasters understand that they are in a position to exert the "ultimate lobbying presence because . . . lobbying . . . is done right in the legislator's home constituency."[48]

None of this is particularly startling or new. What is new, however, is the pervasiveness with which the fundraising and lobbying game is played. As Andrew Jay Schwartzman, head of the influential Media Access Project, observes:

> The nature of Washington and the nature of the independent agencies [like the FCC] has changed because of money and politics. . . . The Congressional oversight role has changed from an occasional review of

agencies to [the] micromanagement of an agency on a day-to-day basis, fueled by campaign contributions and political influence.[49]

On issues from multiple ownership to alternate uses of the electronic spectrum, members of Congress today yield more readily to the special pleas of influential contributors to intercede on their behalf before the FCC.[50] As a result, the process has become more blatantly political and increasingly tilted toward those with greater reach and deeper financial resources. Public interest voices—not only organizations proudly wearing that label but policymakers still placing paramount importance on service to the public—have been muted in the rising tide of deregulation.

While there are still many at the FCC and on Capitol Hill who try to put the public interest first and see themselves as serving the public at large, money and politics certainly get in the way. Canny members of Congress have always taken a strong interest in broadcasting, alternately sucking up to local media to enhance their reelection prospects while also bashing media to curry favor with voters sensitive to media excesses. In the past, such grandstanding might have seemed relatively harmless. Today, the voices we hear are often more partisan, reflecting either a new regulatory ideology or the influence of campaign contributions from regulated industries, or both. How else can one explain such a dramatic shift in policy when, for instance, the chairmanship of the powerful House Commerce Committee changed following the 2000 elections? When Thomas J. Bliley, Republican of Virginia, chaired that committee in the 1990s, he maintained a distinctly friendly regulatory posture toward AT&T and other long-distance carriers. However, as soon as Bliley retired and the chairmanship was assumed by W. J. "Billy" Tauzin in 2001, a member of the same party from Louisiana, Tauzin introduced legislation that favored local telephone carriers in providing long-distance Internet service (a position heatedly opposed by Bliley's long-distance constituents).[51]

4. Wall Street Trumps Main Street

At one time, broadcasting and cable television were quaintly referred to as mom-and-pop businesses, implying that they were typically family or locally owned. Indeed, when only a few years ago network and other large media companies were all limited to just seven TV or FM radio stations, there was plenty of room for smaller, family-owned enterprises. Outside the largest markets that was, in fact, the norm.

That condition has been relegated to the graveyard of historical memory after only two decades of deregulation. Today, even in medium and smaller markets, one is more likely to find mass media owners of an entirely different breed. Not only are the companies that own broadcast stations, cable systems, and daily newspapers likely to be larger and more centralized (the absolute antithesis of the mom-and-pop image), they are likely to be publicly owned, at least in part, and increasingly beholden to Wall Street rather than Main Street.

In the past, only the largest network companies and a few newspaper chains with broadcasting interests were publicly owned. Now, the universe of publicly traded media stocks takes in companies big and small, extending well beyond the easily identifiable broadcasting giants. It is not just Disney-ABC, Viacom-CBS, or Time Warner that are public, it is lesser-known companies such as Sinclair, Belo, Emmis, Insight Communications, Media General, and the relatively new radio behemoth, Clear Channel. This trend toward public ownership of electronic and related media is yet another undercurrent of deregulation —effectively, both a cause and an effect of that movement.

The oldest surviving publicly traded broadcast companies (CBS, NBC, and ABC) had a long tradition of public service cultivated in a regulatory environment that demanded more tangible accountability. Today, not only do these old media tigers have new stripes, they have been joined by a handful of new media conglomerates and other significant players whose outlook is decidedly different. A new perspective pervades, occasioned by analysts from Wall Street who survey the performance of media players almost daily, constantly beating the drum for "shareholder value." Instead of programming for the public —generating advertising profits by meeting public tastes—the new imperative is meeting the periodic and ongoing expectations of Wall Street analysts. To be sure, these companies still want to be perceived as leaders of the entertainment or news business, but more and more they are focused on asset value.

It is a malady that affects virtually all business today. A company goes public or creates a sensational splash in a new business sector and almost immediately it is met with demands from investors and analysts for steady earnings, increased cash flow, or other forms of perceived growth. With stock analysts constantly seeking growth in stock values and public companies required to file quarterly reports to the federal Securities and

Exchange Commission, it is easy to see how this new Wall Street mentality has put most public media companies at the mercy of quarterly
reports—a system in which analysts review reports, predict performance
for ensuing quarters, and cause media management to become fixated
on meeting those estimates.[52] Rather than focusing on the big, long-term
picture, planning and nurturing programming, many of these media
companies become too wrapped up in a short-term planning and execution cycle directed at impressing (or at least not disappointing) investors and analysts. The always candid if mercurial Ted Turner makes
the point this way: "When the ownership of these firms passes to people
under pressure to show quick financial results . . . the corporate emphasis instantly shifts from taking risks to taking profits. When that happens,
quality suffers, localism suffers, and democracy itself suffers. . . . Top
managers in these huge media conglomerates run their companies for
the short term. After we sold Turner Broadcasting to Time Warner, we
came under such earnings pressure that we had to cut our promotion
budget every year at CNN to make our [quarterly] numbers."[53] Jack
Fuller, then head of the Tribune Company, described a similar pressure
after his company (a major broadcaster and leading newspaper publisher) acquired the Times-Mirror chain in 2000. Because the purchase
had "created certain expectations" among Tribune's investors, Fuller acknowledged that if those expectations were not met, "the consequences
would be a fairly significant drop in the stock price, which would put
enormous pressure on everyone." The result, Fuller concluded, would be
"to crunch" (meaning cut back, invest less).[54] Fuller's prognostication
was right on the money. Near the end of 2006, investors and money
managers holding influential blocks of Tribune's stock (and unhappy
with its performance) were pushing Tribune's management to not only
trim operations but to restructure the entire enterprise.

The new Wall Street mentality fits neatly with the deregulatory tide
where receding accountability exposes a more sweeping, wide-open
marketplace. Broadcasting has always been a business; now it can be
a business like any other business, measuring performance solely on
shareholder value unencumbered by standards that might look to
public service.

—⁂—

Clearly, deregulation grew out of a changing political environment
and has been pushed to a fare-thee-well by an opportunistic media in-

dustry. But we must also recognize that some form of deregulation was both inevitable and essential. In the brief interval between the first introduction of the deregulatory refrain in the late 1970s and its appearance as a complete symphony of fully formed policies in the late 1990s, cable television exploded, satellite service became a major competitive force, digital began to overtake analog, and the Internet grew from infancy to adulthood. These changes, standing alone, were sufficient to prompt a comprehensive reassessment of the existing, long-embedded regulatory regime.[55]

But the gathering forces at the time demanded more than a simple choice between less regulation and more regulation. They required a fundamental change in the type of regulation and the underlying policy goals. Sadly, when the issue finally reached the corridors of legislative power to be enshrined in the Telecommunications Act of 1996, deregulation was uncritically accepted as the new, prevailing political philosophy. There was, it seemed, neither time nor need for a searching reexamination of what might be best for the American public—other than encouraging a competitive marketplace. Indeed, after hearing the drumbeat of deregulation for so long, from political allies and industry lobbyists, trusting the marketplace became a powerful tonic for Washington policymakers. At the same time, gradual changes in the federal judiciary, the growing influence of the Wall Street community, the increased prominence of Washington "think tanks" promoting a more conservative agenda, and a one-dimensional trade press that quickly picked up and waved the deregulation banner for a grateful industry,[56] all contributed to a major change in the policymaking climate.

Massive changes in the media business, accelerating just as deregulation was being launched, have produced a vastly different media milieu that, at least on the surface, made deregulation the right ideological wave to catch. As industry reports and FCC decisions were quick to catalog, the escalating number of media outlets fueled by advancing technology not only confirmed the wisdom of deregulation but demanded its continuation. It was the classic numbers game—more media outlets in more places presumably translating into more and better service for the American public. With such startling persuasive numbers, growing every day, the march was on, almost like a crusade, to use such numbers to justify relaxing structural regulations and weakening procedural protections—without any serious debate about the effects on society or American democracy. In sum, the most glaring failure of public policy during the twenty-five-year period covered by this chapter was the relentless determination to tear down (or fatally chip away at) the existing system of regulation without recognizing the need to build a replacement system with new and different safeguards—the primary topic of chapters 7 and 8.

4

Today's Media Marketplace

Years of deregulation and rapid advances in technology have produced a vastly altered mass media marketplace. In earlier times, three television networks dominated the national scene and a legion of powerful, locally owned radio and television stations stood tall in their own markets. Now, a handful of media conglomerates cover the country with multiple platforms and control huge clusters of local media properties. In the pages that follow, I start with a thumbnail sketch of the myriad branches now being spread over the mass media landscape by five leading media giants. This leads to a broader description of the changing nature of the broadcast business and some of the general trends impacting all mass media at the start of the twenty-first century.

THE NEW MASTERS OF MASS MEDIA

My narrative begins with a snapshot of how America's leading media companies looked at the beginning of 2006. The purpose is to depict general trends, not attempt a comprehensive listing. Indeed, since the underlying facts are changing so rapidly, any further designs on the data would be pointless.

The mass media enterprises dominating the deregulatory era differ remarkably from their predecessors. This is plainly evident in the

multifarious activities that mark today's five leading media companies: CBS-Viacom; NBC-GE; ABC-Disney; Fox News Corporation; and
Time Warner.

1. *CBS* has had a dominant presence from the earliest days of
   broadcasting. Today, in addition to owning the CBS television
   network and more than two hundred radio and TV stations scattered throughout the country, it is part of the vast Viacom-CBS
   empire that also owns a 50 percent interest in a second over-the-
   air television network (The CW) and a host of cable and satellite
   network services—MTV, VH1, Showtime, Nickelodeon, Comedy
   Central, CMT, Sundance Channel, The Movie Channel, Spike TV,
   and BET. It is also a major producer of television shows and,
   through its King World affiliate, syndicates two of the most popular nonnetwork programs in history, "Wheel of Fortune" and
   "Jeopardy," to hundreds of individual stations around the country. Its ownership of the Hollywood colossus Paramount Pictures gives CBS-Viacom heavyweight status in the motion picture
   industry. In other entertainment venues, Viacom operates theme
   parks, controls theater chains worldwide, owns Blockbuster
   video stores, runs various Internet businesses, and publishes
   books under such well-known houses as Simon & Schuster and
   Pocket Books. To round out the picture, CBS syndicates news
   and other radio programming to thousands of local stations
   and, with or through Viacom, holds exclusive advertising rights
   on buses, subways, trains, kiosks, and billboards in major metropolitan markets throughout the nation.[1]
2. *NBC* can also trace its beginnings to the early days of broadcasting, having been formed by one of the first giants of the business, the Radio Corporation of America (RCA). Today, of course,
   it is owned by General Electric (GE) and, as such, is part of a corporate behemoth of a different sort. The vast manufacturing and
   commercial holdings of GE produced annual revenues of $134
   billion in 2003, far more than any of the other media giants.[2]
   NBC, like CBS, not only owns key television stations in many
   major markets, it owns and operates the NBC television network
   and a leading Spanish-language TV network (Telemundo) and
   has a significant minority interest in a third national TV network
   (PaxNet). It also owns wholly (or with other media companies)
   a variety of cable television network services such as CNBC,

MSNBC, A&E, The History Channel, AMC, and Bravo. Until recently, NBC was the only major TV network that did not also own a major Hollywood film company. That gap was filled, however, in 2004 when NBC-GE acquired control of the massive Universal Studies complex from Vivendi Universal. That transaction also added the USA and Sci-Fi cable networks, as well as Universal Parks and Resorts, to NBC holdings.

3. *ABC*, the third of the "original" major television networks that dominated prime-time television in the 1970s, achieved media conglomerate status in 1996 when it was acquired by the Walt Disney Company. Now, ABC-Disney owns and operates the ABC television network and a number of key radio and television stations in the largest, most important markets. They also own, in whole or in part, a plethora of national network services available via cable or satellite that serve vastly different cultural interests: ABC Family, The Disney Channel, SoapNet, ESPN, ESPN2, ABC Radio Networks, ESPN Radio, Radio Disney, A&E, The History Channel, Lifetime, and "E" Entertainment. On the production side, ABC-Disney is a major force in both television (Buena Vista, ABC Entertainment) and motion pictures (Walt Disney Pictures, Touchstone Pictures, Miramax Film Corporation). The world, of course, has long been familiar with Disney's massive and highly popular theme parks located in California, Florida, and Europe. It is now being introduced to other Disney "family-oriented" ventures such as cruise lines, Broadway productions (*Beauty and the Beast* and *The Lion King* in New York's revamped Times Square area), and hundreds of retail stores and catalogues, all selling merchandise, teaching aids, and films highlighting Disney characters or projects. Less known but still important are ABC-Disney's interests in publishing (Walt Disney and Hyperion Books, *Disney Magazine*, *ESPN* magazine) and music (Walt Disney Records, Hollywood Records). Finally, Disney's expanding presence on the Internet is evident in a wide variety of sites: ABC.com, ABCNews.com, Disney Online, Disney.com, Family.com, ESPN.Sportzone.com, NFL.com, NBA.com, NASCAR.com, and toysmart.com, among others.

4. *Fox*, the fourth and newest of the so-called major networks, is owned by Rupert Murdoch, whose holdings flow from the Australian media giant News Corporation. Starting with newspaper properties down under, News Corporation, in a very short

period of time, came to dominate the newspaper business in England—from ownership of the staid *London Times* to the sensationalistic *Sun* and *News of the World*. It also dominates satellite television services worldwide with vast holdings in Asia, Europe, Latin America, and Australia, including BskyB and STAR TV. In this country, this brash upstart has, within recent years, acquired the legendary Hollywood studio Twentieth Century Fox and successfully launched a new national television network to challenge the former "big three." The foundation for the new network was a bunch of strong major-market "independent" television stations acquired from Metromedia in the mid-1980s. Now, Fox owns scores of big-market television stations, operates a major television network with hundreds of affiliated stations, and, in 2006, launched a secondary network (My Network TV) with a separate set of affiliated stations. It also owns and programs the cable and satellite network services FX, FMC, and the Fox News Channel. More important, perhaps, Fox has begun to rival Disney's ESPN in the distribution of sports programming by acquiring a number of regional sports network services throughout the country. In print, Fox and News Corporation own the *New York Post*—in a city where, with generous FCC waivers, they have also been allowed to own two TV stations— *TV Guide* magazine, the *Weekly Standard* (a conservative-leaning national newsmagazine), and one of the world's leading book publishers, HarperCollins. The Fox empire was given a major boost in late 2003 when the FCC approved its acquisition of a controlling interest in DirecTV, whose fourteen million satellite subscribers make Fox the second largest multichannel (cable and satellite) video program distributor in the nation. Fox had long been the dominant or sole provider of satellite television service throughout most of the rest of the world. Now it is the largest domestic satellite provider as well. Finally, in 2005, News Corporation began laying the groundwork for its own Internet portal which would, unlike existing portal giants Yahoo! and Google, own most of its own content (derived, obviously, from Fox's other media assets). It announced the acquisition of Intermix, the parent of MySpace, a social networking site highly popular with younger users, and Scout, a leading college sports site. At the time, it was reported that, with those acquisitions, News Corporation websites would draw an aggregate fifty million unique visitors a month, the sixth-largest audience on the world-wide web.[3]

5. *Time Warner*, the fifth giant domestic media player, owns a 50 percent interest in one of the "minor" TV networks (The CW, owned jointly with CBS) but is decidedly major in all other respects. It is, in fact, the largest media company in the world, forged from some of the oldest and newest mass media activities. With America Online, CompuServe, Netscape, and AOL Instant Messaging under its corporate umbrella, Time Warner casts one of the largest and most powerful shadows over the Internet user world. Even if The CW is a relative neophyte in the national network business, Time Warner dominates television in other critical ways. Its premium assets include ownership of HBO, TBS, TNT, Cartoon Network, CNN, Headline News, and Turner Classic Movies. The power and influence of Time Warner is further enhanced by being the second largest provider of cable television systems in the nation—all of which carry the aforementioned services. Indeed, as a content producer for media, Time Warner's role is unparalleled. In movies and records it has been a worldwide leader for years. It runs the Warner Bros. and New Line Hollywood movie studios and owns more than forty different music labels producing CDs, tapes, and DVDs sold here and around the world. Its ownership of two Hollywood movie studios and the related Castle Rock production company also make Time Warner one of the largest producers of domestic television programming. If possible, Time Warner's dominance is even more striking in the world of print—from which its reputation and influence first sprung. It owns more than sixty magazines, including such popular and powerful fare as *Sports Illustrated*, *Money*, *Fortune*, *Time*, and *People*. Its eminent media domain also includes books; in addition to Warner Books, it owns Little, Brown and Company, Time-Life Books, and the Book-of-the-Month Club (with Bertelsmann).

These five companies dominate contemporary American media in ways never before seen.[4] In the past, we had major television networks, major Hollywood studios, major cable operators, and major print publishers dominating their respective realms. Now we have them all combined under the same corporate tent, a continuous, multi-ring circus of separate but centrally choreographed media acts.

No one should doubt that these new media masters operate from a uniquely commanding position. But it would be wrong to suggest that they have become so dominant as to push aside or render inconsequential other, less integrated media companies. Not only should we expect more changes (even some breakups) involving the current Big Five, we should keep an eye on the continuing, in some cases, growing, influence of other media heavyweights. For example, Comcast, the cable giant, has annual revenues that rival or exceed those of three of the Big Five, and the New York Times Company, the Washington Post Company, Gannett, Cox, Dow Jones, and that old-time publishing behemoth, the Hearst Company, continue to exercise vigorous editorial voices, even if they do not rank at the top of the heap based on the size of their assets or revenue. And, on the horizon, there are still others having both significant influence and the potential to replace one of the Big Five. In this category are burgeoning telecommunications companies such as AT&T and Verizon and the existing giants of the Internet world: Google, Yahoo!, and Microsoft. In short, despite some troubling signs, the future shape of the media world may not be as settled or bleak as some critics would have us believe.

THE STATE OF RADIO TODAY

Today's radio sure ain't your daddy's radio. A medium once the very essence of local Americana has become a series of dots and clusters on the national map all connected and controlled by a few large corporate enterprises. A medium once thought to embrace broader community interests is now principally viewed by its large corporate owners as an opportunistic way to cater to advertisers. "I'm in business to sell automobiles, or tamales, or toothpaste or whatever," says Lowry Mays, patriarch of America's largest radio group.[5] For Mays, advertisers rule. "Our customers want to sell products," he notes. "We sell their products."[6]

Obviously, the music played by today's radio stations has changed. So too has the role of local personalities and the influence of national networks (both diminished). But these changes are natural and necessary. A medium based on popular tastes must evolve with changes in popular culture. Whether it satisfies your taste or not, hip-hop, which enjoys widespread popularity among younger, more urban audiences, is as relevant today as swing music or the Motown sound were to earlier generations. On the other hand, changes in the on-air packaging and nonentertainment message of today's radio have altered the basic character of the medium.

Radio has been a remarkably resilient industry. It grew out of seeds initially planted by wireless telegraphy in the early twentieth century and has since survived the onslaught of television and the coming of the Internet. At the start of the twenty-first century, radio remains the most portable and personal of our electronic media, reaching virtually every populated corner of the earth.

One of the main reasons radio survived television is that the invention of the transistor made radio fully portable at about the same time television was invading America's living rooms. Radio was no longer housebound but could be taken anywhere. Another major reason is that discrete format programming came on the scene just as drama, situation comedies, game shows, musical variety, and soap operas—genres that had been invented on radio—were finding a new home on television. In radio's early heyday, most successful stations were "full-service," reaching broad audiences with a wide variety of program features. Today, this aspect of radio has been turned upside down. Although the total number of radio stations has vastly increased since the ascendancy of television, nearly all of them now follow a distinct, narrow program format—a type of consistent programming that adheres to a prescribed formula or set pattern designed to create a recognizable sound or personality. From the smallest town, with minimal competition, to the biggest city, with a beehive of competition, it is likely that virtually all of the more than ten thousand commercial radio stations across America will be identified by a distinguishable narrowcasting format. Adult contemporary (AC), country, news/talk, album-oriented rock (AOR), adult standards, Spanish and ethnic, contemporary hit radio (CHR), oldies, religious, and urban contemporary are some of the leading program formats of today's radio.[7] Despite repeated promises by the nascent super radio groups that deregulation would not only cut costs and improve efficiencies but would also produce new and varied services, the leading formats today are nearly identical to the leading formats ten or twenty years ago when deregulation was first gaining momentum.[8] In fact, no new major radio format has emerged in decades. What we have seen, if anything, has been minor nibbling at the edges of existing formats, not the creation of new program formats. Instead of something original and creative, modern radio has merely produced more and finer slices from the same format pie—usually nothing more than repackaging music under different names and gimmicks such as Music of the '70s and '80s, Jammin' Oldies, or Jack (a "format" that seeks to mix music from multiple formats, like putting one's CD player or iPod on shuffle).[9]

Programming competition in radio has become a battle among existing or reshaped formats, not one that produces any real new program "product." With as many as eight stations (usually the most powerful, and hence, leading ones) controlled by the same party in a given market, much of the "competition" among formats occurs within the same corporate family. If only eight or ten leading formats draw the lion's share of the audience in most large markets, is it any wonder that a corporate owner holding the maximum number of eight stations in that market necessarily competes with itself?

In a recent analysis prepared by BIA Financial Network, a diversified consulting company serving the broadcast industry, it was noted that, on a national basis, the top five format categories (AC, CHR, country, urban, and news) garner more than half (51.4 percent) of all radio listening.[10] Indeed, the top ten formats—which add rock, AOR/classic rock, Spanish, oldies, and EZ/beautiful music—pick off nearly 85 percent of the total audience. What this demonstrates is that the format categories that dominated the radio scene in preconsolidation days are even stronger today, creating an environment that is less rather than more conducive to innovation and expanded program choice.

The Washington, D.C., market, the ninth largest, typifies the state of contemporary radio. In 1996, before the impact of the Telecommunications Act, ten major radio owners operated in the market. In 2001, only five years later, that number had been cut in half.[11] And the top three (Infinity/CBS, Clear Channel, and ABC) generated nearly 70 percent of the total radio revenue in the market.[12] Moreover, the array of program formats in 2001 was remarkably similar to those available in 1996.[13] Of the estimated fifty-five radio stations that served the greater Washington metropolitan area in mid-2001, forty-eight followed a music, news/talk/sports, religious, or ethnic format and two followed a business format (generally, a variation on the news/talk format). The only genuine alternatives in the market—in 1996 and 2001—were three public radio stations, a small progressive station owned by the University of Maryland, and an independent facility operated by the Pacifica Foundation, all five of which are noncommercial.[14]

The record is worse on the news and information front. Again, the promise of those attempting to rationalize deregulation on the grounds that the public would reap a news and information benefit has proven largely illusory. If commercial radio has become a better, broader supplier of news and information in the wake of deregulation it is only in the self-indulgent eyes of those continuing to spread deregulatory fever. On the other hand, only a Luddite would expect all commercial radio stations to program the same diet of news and information typical of radio's "golden age." With so many stations within reach of most listeners, and the choices from other media continuing to mushroom, radio's role as a news and information medium has changed. The days when every single radio station was expected to adhere to a set percentage of news, public affairs, and other kinds of nonentertainment programming in order to qualify for a license are long since past. The proliferation of news and talk formats, complemented by the increased availability of public radio, renders that approach obsolete.

The real problem with radio news today is not that fewer stations offer it but that it is highly marginalized on stations that do. It was not surprising that news staffs shrunk dramatically as the super radio groups acquired market clusters and consolidated operations.[15] Nor was it surprising that industry downsizing left untold numbers of radio stations temporarily exposed in the immediate aftermath of the 11 September 2001 terrorist attacks on New York and Washington. In some cases, radio was reduced to simulcasting CNN's audio feed while delivering "maudlin expressions of sorrow by clueless deejays," according to Washington Post columnist Marc Fisher.[16] But the role of radio as a news and information medium is being downgraded in ways that go beyond cutbacks in staff and resources. If a station is not operating in a news/talk format—and that represents approximately 90 percent of all stations—it is likely that news is viewed, at best, as something to be woven into the music format with minimal interruption. Even stations that continue to originate their own news or carry national news from a network typically do so in capsule-news style. Today, instead of a full five-minute or longer regularly scheduled newscast, once common in radio, one is more likely to hear a few brief headlines wrapped around commercial content that may run longer than the news. Condensed news delivered in rapid-fire fashion that flies by as quick as or quicker than a commercial break fits perfectly with the "more music, less talk" epithet that characterizes so many modern formats.

News stories, if and when aired, are typically read verbatim from wire services or loosely cribbed from local newspapers. As the Project for Excellence in Journalism found in its 2006 *State of the News Media* report, "Most local radio stations offer virtually nothing in the way of reporters in the field." Stations may still favor local stories, but local reporting, the actual gathering of news and telling of community stories, is just not the way of today's radio.

Compounding these traits, many local stations now "outsource" the news, not to traditional networks like ABC but to new, more adaptive suppliers like Metro Networks, a service that started by offering traffic reports. It now provides news "sound bites" to more than a thousand local stations from a centralized location in Phoenix designed so that "it sound[s] to the listener as if the newscaster works at their local station."[17] According to Metro Networks' senior vice president, music stations that take its newscasts usually choose what he calls "the 'one breath' stories—five to seven stories delivered rapid-fire in one minute. 'If it takes more than one breath to deliver the story, it's too long.'"[18]

While news/talk stations obviously supply more news and information, they too have succumbed to format pressure, producing and presenting news according to the same rigid "format clock" used on music stations (where program content is preset for every minute of each hour). On stations categorized as "all-news," this often results in the repetitive airing of the same bare-bones news summaries interspersed with traffic, weather, and sports in the same systematic order. On stations featuring a longer form of "talk," a set pattern of another sort is usually followed. Whether it is a local host attempting to titillate or a national personality like Rush Limbaugh pushing a political agenda, the idea of most "long-form" radio talk today is to command attention by being edgy or controversial, not informational.

If they are not being edgy or controversial, sometimes they are faking being edgy or controversial. For example, one nationally syndicated radio talk program enjoying a certain temporary notoriety in the early 2000s was the "Phil Hendrie Show." As summarized by the *New York Times*, Phil Hendrie spent three hours every weekday pulling off the longest-running phone prank in history.[19] Maintaining a "deep faith in the witlessness of AM talk radio's hard-core listeners and their profound capacity for unrelieved humorlessness and unreflective anger,"[20] the show thrived on Hendrie's ability to impersonate bogus "guests" who, in masterful ventriloquist fashion, would be called upon to "address" controversial issues in a way that inevitably enraged callers who apparently did not understand the charade being performed.

With so many stations in so many local communities, radio still retains the capacity to act as an outlet for diverse expressions of music, culture, and information—stimulating and reflecting a wide range of minority, artistic, and even radical points of view. But, with the possible exception of "shock jocks" like Howard Stern and others who use the lewd and tasteless as a form of entertainment, you will not find much community-defining, individualistic content on mainline stations served up by media conglomerates. No, challenging and different views or alternative forms of entertainment are usually relegated to certain public radio stations or the smaller, independently owned properties that still survive.[21]

What one typically finds on the larger, "super group" owned stations is much more homogenized and formulaic. Although updated formats have emerged around more contemporary music, the formula and presentation often produces a result more mind-numbing than engaging. Except for the musical style of songs played, one format is likely to sound much like another—especially when engineered by the same owner using the same audience research consultants and managerial talent to simultaneously program up to eight "competing" radio stations in the same local market. And, from market to market across the country one encounters the same music selections, played in the same order by the same style disc jockey, all wrapped around the same endlessly repetitive slogans such as "more music, less talk."

Scanning your radio dial is like strolling the corridors of your local shopping mall—the basic and most popular formats are all on display, just like the assortment of popular stores and restaurants one finds at a typical shopping mall. Go from one city to the next and you will find the same kinds of stations on the radio dial in the same way you find the same kinds of stores in shopping malls. The result, in radio and retailing, is more homogenization than diversity, more uniformity than individuality. Instead of picking up a distinct flavor of each community, you get more sameness from market to market. Operating multiple stations in the same area with common managerial and sales personnel may produce cost and operational efficiencies, but it drains the market of viewpoint and creative diversity.

Adding to the homogenization of radio from market to market is the trend of the super groups to spread their talent and material over multiple platforms. Imagine driving through a small town in Maryland or a medium-size city in New Mexico and listening to an "oldies" format on a local AM station. Since a specialized format is unlikely to take root in a community with only a handful of radio stations, you quickly realize that the sound you are hearing, consisting of highly polished announcers and professionally produced features of special interest to an older adult audience, is originating from elsewhere. The local station is, in fact, transmitting an entire program schedule produced in Los Angeles or New York and distributed via satellite. It is a modern form of network radio bringing quality programming to stations that could not afford to supply the same programming themselves. Typically, the local station is largely automated, using a computer device that inserts local commercials and an occasional public service announcement.

Now imagine that you are driving through a small town in Indiana or a medium-size city in Idaho and you hear a distinctly different sound—also professionally produced but with a live disc jockey conducting interviews and spouting hometown homilies. It sounds good and it sounds local. In today's radio, if you encounter something that sounds so good and polished (with celebrity interviews and other feature material) in a modest-sized community, there is a good chance that the "local" part is faked. Using a practice called "voice-tracking," today's radio giants are able to "pipe popular out-of-town personalities from bigger markets to smaller ones, customizing their programs to make it sound as if the DJs are actually local residents."[22] The same disc jockey sitting in San Diego may assume multiple identities as a "local" radio personality in a number of other, distant communities. Contemporary radio technology, drawing upon computer systems and digitalized music, permits a disc jockey at one location to package as much as five hours of programming in less than one hour, which can then be linked by a high-speed digital network to multiple locations around the country. The station in Boise taking programming produced in San Diego might also import entire disc jockey shifts from other production centers, resulting in a "virtual" station programmed elsewhere but interspersed with a few local tidbits supplied by non-air personnel in Boise.

All of this, of course, allows the large media owner to spread its best talent over multiple outlets, while also exercising more centralized control over specific formats. By drawing upon the same pool of talent and sharing logos and promotional material, a great number of stations under common ownership can be manufactured from the same "cookie cutter," creating a similar product in both small and large markets. Playlists, promotional announcements, even station contests are dictated from a distant, yet centralized location. In the end, the greatest appeal and utility of this approach is that it allows the super groups to sell national format brands on a broader scale in more diverse places while reaching the same demographics—exactly what is sought by big national advertisers. Not everyone in radio believes this trend is wise or viable over the long term. It saves money and helps maintain tight control. The question remains, however, whether instilling a discipline in the operation of a radio station that resembles the formula for running a McDonald's will, over time, build audiences and maintain local flavor and loyalty. Will radio remain something more than a slick package purposely wrapped for advertisers? If not, will it gradually lose relevance as other technologies such as satellite radio and hand-held music storage systems, also highly mobile, begin to take hold? Satellite radio offers hundreds of nationally produced, distinct entertainment and information audio "formats," while new devices like the tiny iPod sold by Apple Computer contain a "hard drive" capable of storing and programming thousands of music selections that can be carried anywhere, anytime. The iPod, in fact, joins laptops and sophisticated cell phones (and their progeny) as the latest mobile method for obtaining not just music but information and banter off the Internet. Today, enterprising individuals as well as some mainline broadcasters are posting "podcasts"—compact, programlike segments consisting of music, personal ramblings, interviews, or the like—on their websites for downloading to this newest generation of listening devices.

While radio as an industry remains relatively strong, it also seems to be at another crossroads.[23] When radio needed to specialize in order to survive television, it did so and entered a new era of prosperity. The question today is whether specialization as now practiced will begin to undermine that success. We know, from its long and varied history, that radio has a unique capacity to change and evolve quickly when faced with changes in technology and culture. Must it, can it, transition into something else one more time?

THE STATE OF TELEVISION TODAY

Unlike radio, today's television still resembles yesterday's television—
at least on the surface. Local stations affiliated with a few leading national networks still dominate, and programs (entertainment and
news) continue to be offered in the same discrete thirty-minute or
sixty-minute segments that mostly conform to tried-and-true genres.
But scratch the surface, and changes abound—in the mode of delivery,
the size and type of company delivering the product, the content and
packaging of the product, the size and composition of the audience,
and, most profoundly, the overall number of competitive services
available.

Most of these changes result from a combination of factors. Some,
such as cable (with a boost from satellite) becoming the leading delivery system, result from advances in technology and improvements
in marketing. Technology and marketing also account for the dramatic increase in the sheer number of television services, from a mere
handful three decades ago to hundreds today. Other changes, such as
shrinking and aging audiences for traditional network programming,
may be attributable not only to expanding markets (producing more
outlets offering more alternatives) but to shifting lifestyles, especially
among younger viewers. A few changes can be linked to specific deregulatory measures. For instance, recall that in the 1996 Telecommunications Act, Congress raised the national TV ownership cap, removed
the overall limit on the total number of stations that could be owned,
and ordered the FCC to reexamine its local TV ownership rules. In
subsequent and separate steps, the FCC relaxed its "duopoly" rule to
permit ownership of more than one TV station in a single market and
eliminated rules that had restricted the ability of the major TV networks to produce and syndicate their own programming. The industry reaction was nearly instantaneous. Disney purchased ABC. Viacom, parent company of a Hollywood studio competing with Disney,
purchased CBS. Time Warner, parent company of yet another Hollywood studio, created its own mini-TV network, the WB (which has
since been merged with UPN and renamed The CW). Then, in a second wave of activity, Viacom-CBS, Fox, and several other big operators
purchased more local TV stations, mostly in large markets. Finally, following modifications to the dual network rule, Viacom-CBS was allowed to acquire the UPN television network (since merged with the

WB and renamed The CW), and NBC purchased Telemundo, a lead-ing Spanish-language network.

If you are a media giant specializing in consolidation, you are no doubt convinced that becoming bigger and stronger is good—good for business and good for the public. If you are a key policymaker—a member of Congress who voted for the 1996 act or one of a string of FCC officials who pushed an activist deregulatory agenda over the past two decades—you proudly point to the expanded number of me-dia outlets as contributing to the public good. In what has become a ritual policy dance in Washington, decision makers periodically sur-vey the media marketplace in order to declare that a rapidly expanded number of outlets justifies further deregulatory actions. Ironically, as soon as one deregulatory action is taken, industry representatives are before policymakers again, arguing that the consolidation already having taken place—which created bigger and more nimble competi-tors controlling expanded numbers of outlets—actually justifies fur-ther consolidation. For those exhorting this view, counting the sheer number of outlets intentionally masks the importance of counting the number of owners or assessing the nature and influence of different media outlets. In the real marketplace, a hundred suburban dailies do not begin to match the power of the *New York Times* any more than a UHF station in metropolitan Washington, D.C., licensed to Manassas, Virginia, can match the power of NBC's VHF station in the heart of the nation's capital.

Other than a vague promise that merging and expanding opera-tions will enhance overall service, neither policymakers nor consol-idators offer much satisfaction. Indeed, when pressed to spell out the public good resulting from consolidation, consolidators usually ex-plain how they can use all of their new media toys to build better packages for advertisers and improve their negotiating power in deal-ing with suppliers. For example, citing package deals and cost effi-ciencies for advertisers, Mel Karmazin, then president of Viacom (CBS), put it this way in 2002: "Not only can we give [advertisers] tel-evision, but we can also give them radio and outdoors [billboards]."[24] Similarly, when Disney acquired the Fox Family cable network in 2001 it candidly described its business strategy as being able to spread program costs over several venues (each producing separate advertis-ing dollars) and being able to combine sales to advertisers across an array of different TV properties. Perfectly legitimate and prudent business objectives—by Viacom and Disney—but not readily translatable into any tangible public benefits.

There is no question that large media companies with multiple platforms find it much easier to cross-promote different services and spread programming content over different venues. Consider the 2001 release of the first Harry Potter movie (*Harry Potter and the Sorcerer's Stone*) by Warner Bros., the Hollywood pillar of the Time Warner empire. Subscribers to America Online, the company's Internet service, were led to various links featuring the movie, including those highlighting Harry Potter merchandise that Time Warner licensed and sold. Moviefone, which the company also owns, promoted and sold tickets. The magazine branch of the company, which publishes *Time, People, Fortune, Sports Illustrated,* and *Entertainment Weekly,* contained advertisements, contests, and various feature stories about the movie. Warner Bros. advertised the movie on Time Warner's many cable systems and networks. Warner Music Group produced the soundtrack for the movie and sold CDs and tapes. As summarized by Ken Auletta in the *New Yorker,* "No communications company touches as many consumers, or controls so many interlocking pieces."[25]

Although the efforts of others may pale in comparison to the unique cross-promotional buzzsaw of Time Warner, all of the super media groups employ similar strategies. Incessant cross-promotion and recycling of content may increase revenues, even contribute to our consumer-oriented economy, but it does nothing to enhance, vary, or expand the message communicated to the public. What the public, in fact, gets is the same message, more often and in more places. When NBC produces a news story that airs on its "Nightly News" (on the NBC television network) but then repeats the same identical report, within the same twenty-four-hour period, on cable channels CNBC and MSNBC and finally on "The Today Show" the next morning, the public gets more chances to see the same thing, but it is still the same thing. When a prime-time show aired by a major network is quickly re-aired on a cable channel owned by the same company or posted on the Internet for downloading to laptops, video iPods, or mobile phones, a similar conclusion can be drawn. Although these expanded distribution methods may result in reaching a slightly different, marginally larger audience, the content remains recycled. It provides the media company an efficient way to spread the cost of such material and, in the case of full-length programs, an opportunity to sell a different set of commercials. It offers the public a different viewing opportunity—but only of the same material.

Not only are TV networks today seeking ways to control costs by spreading content over multiple platforms, they are exhibiting programs that are cheaper to produce. To meet the challenge of rising program costs, "reality" shows, celebrity-based contests, and "soft" news programs now crowd out sitcoms and dramas, once the proud staple of prime-time television. Although all major networks have contributed to the explosion of prime-time reality (a trend started on MTV and in Europe), one network in particular, Fox, has found a way to be the boldest, if not the best, exponent of the genre. In what might be branded Fox Schlock, epitomizing the sleaziest, cheapest form of entertainment, Fox has not only staged a legal TV marriage to a millionaire that failed before it could be consummated, it scheduled and promptly cancelled a program called "The Chamber"—in which contestants were strapped into a chair, sealed in a box, and forced to endure a series of tortures that included being shocked by electrical impulses. It also hatched a celebrity boxing match between notorious has-beens and counter-programmed against the 2002 Winter Olympics with something called the "Glutton Bowl: The World's Greatest Eating Contest," a program the *Washington Post* described as involving "40 large men with 40 large appetites participat[ing] in an eating contest featuring such delicacies as 'bowls of mayonnaise' and 'sticks of butter.'"[26] Demonstrating that its search for new lows knows no bounds, Fox, in early 2005, broadcast "Who's Your Daddy?," a reality series that featured a contestant who turned out to be a one-time actress in a soft pornographic film, trying to identify her birth father in a quest for $100,000.

If this were not enough, public affairs, cultural programming, and hard news documentaries have virtually disappeared from commercial television. This state of affairs is not only the result of more intense competition, it is rooted in government policymaking decisions beginning in the 1980s. Two decades of deregulation did more than just relax ownership standards. It also greatly diminished broadcaster accountability. As described in chapter 3, most of the programming and advertising standards that once governed broadcasting have been removed and, just as important, the legal procedures for challenging a broadcaster's performance have been so weakened that license renewal has become a perfunctory, virtually automatic process. If anything still holds networks and some station groups back from further reductions in news and other public service programming, it is the fear of a regulatory backlash. In other words, they no longer fear regulatory difficulties or challenges; instead, they fear that any further programming cutbacks or excesses could be used against them to halt or slow down the long-running engine of deregulation.

In this new environment, with regular public affairs limited to a few longstanding Sunday morning news interview shows such as "Meet the Press" and hard-hitting news documentaries relegated to memory, what the public gets are newsmagazine shows like "60 Minutes" and "Dateline" that have survived only because they still make money. Even these shows have turned to lighter themes and current cultural fixations in order to continue to attract an audience advertisers will buy. News divisions that were once a proud and prominent part of broadcast-dominated companies are now little cogs in huge media and entertainment conglomerates. They must produce profits on their own just like any other division or operation. Part of this, as noted, is the absence of any regulatory accountability. Just as important, however, is the competitive explosion in the video news business, exemplified by the proliferation of twenty-four-hour news channels on cable and satellite and the spread of real-time news sources over the Internet. With so many additional sources available around the clock, the traditional network newscasts have had to adjust. Part of that adjustment, as we have seen, involves spreading and sharing content, talent, and other resources among different news outlets owned by the same parties. But traditional network newscasts have also altered their focus. Important news of the day is still the principal ingredient. The rest, however, is increasingly gorged with consumer news you can use, the latest medical news affecting the elderly, the young, or, more likely, the baby boom generation, capped with coverage of the latest celebrity trial or political scandal.

The picture in local television news is not any brighter. Like national TV news, local TV news today must sell or fail—a harsh business equation that is no longer influenced by regulatory concerns. While many local stations in larger markets are broadcasting more news than ever, other stations are dropping news entirely. Many of the stations abandoning news—or those never initiating news—operate either as independents or as affiliates of secondary networks such as The CW, My Network TV, or PaxNet; others, however, are affiliates of the leading networks.[27] In fact, the size of market or kind of station matters little these days. The only determinant is whether the news can be sustained as a standalone program segment. That is why some stations in major markets can successfully run three hours of local news in the early evening and other stations have never launched or are shutting down news operations. The bottom-line reason is the same in both instances. A three-hour news block on one station only stands out because it serves as a distinct profit center (laden with commercial slots that are in high demand). At the same time, a half-hour newscast on another station may not sell enough advertising to cover the operating costs of the program.

Local television news, in particular, has been widely criticized for being highly superficial, excessively exploitive, and unduly concentrated on crimes, fires, and accidents. Even the best local TV stations persist in following insignificant events with "great pictures" or live-on-the-scene "standups" by young reporters that, although breathtakingly labeled "breaking news," are, in reality, nothing more than the routine ebb and flow of daily life. And, like their network brethren, local TV stations today increasingly focus on "news you can use" such as consumer reports, health tips, and shopping trends, including the latest gadget. During designated months of the year when audience ratings are taken, such features tend toward the most shocking or eye catching.

Almost anywhere you look, "soft" news—defined by one researcher as consisting of "routine crime, accident, and disaster stories, along with celebrity stories and other fluff"—has taken over like crabgrass. After analyzing more than five thousand television, newspaper, and newsmagazine stories, Thomas E. Patterson, a professor of government and the press at Harvard's Kennedy School of Government, found that soft material had grown from less than 35 percent of the total in 1980 to about 50 percent in 2000.[28] Whether this "softer" approach drives audiences away or helps hold those who might be overwhelmed or annoyed by more serious content,[29] the evidence is mounting that audiences for broadcast news are diminishing. A June 2000 study by the Pew Research Center for the People and the Press reports that regular viewership to network news dropped by one-half since 1993, from 60 percent to 30 percent. While the number of American adults watching local television news also dropped, from 77 percent in 1993 to 64 percent in 1998, it is noteworthy that far more Americans watch local TV news than network news—the brand specializing in the "softest," most sensationalistic material.[30]

The laserlike focus on the bottom line that typifies today's television is perhaps best illustrated by examining the number and quality of commercial messages that are broadcast. In order to maintain profit margins in an exceedingly competitive environment, television networks and stations have taken to not only selling more advertising time but airing more commercial announcements of questionable quality. This is not, I assure readers, one of those screeds against all commercialism.[31] It is, however, a cautionary note that a medium struggling with fragmenting audiences and fewer advertising dollars spread among more outlets may be in danger of resorting to practices that can only exacerbate those trends.

With no accountability to the government or any self-regulatory body,[32] the broadcast industry seems poised as never before to pursue any means necessary to uphold profit margins. For viewers already awash in excessive commercialism in virtually all phases of daily life, one must wonder whether a limit is in sight—one where, faced with longer and more excruciating commercial interruptions, they will seek greater relief in pay services or digital recording devices that permit the skipping of commercials. For the moment, however, commercial clutter on broadcast television shows no signs of dissipating. A study released in 2004 by MindShare, a leading advertising buying agency, showed that TV clutter—defined as commercials, promotional announcements, and public service announcements—is at an all-time high. On all four major networks, clutter exceeds or approaches fifteen minutes per hour in prime time.[33] Another study by the American Association of Advertising Agencies that included all-day parts also found commercial clutter at record levels.[34]

Efforts to extract more advertising dollars out of the broadcast business have led to practices that would have caused outrage just a few years ago. Absent any real accountability and pressured to meet more demanding budget targets, stations have closed their eyes or held their noses to accept commercial endorsements and paid programming for products and services they know are borderline just to improve the bottom line. Paid programs or program-length commercials that push beauty treatments, exercise paraphernalia, weight-loss products, or the latest "miracle" (untested) drug fill the unsold airtime of many local stations—airtime that is no longer confined to the graveyard hours between midnight and 6:00 a.m. And, in 2001 it was revealed that some network-owned television stations (and a few others) had been using a high-tech device called the "Time Machine" to speed up the action of some sports and network programming in order to squeeze in an extra spot announcement. The device was able to compress the programming content in a way that was imperceptible to most viewers but allowed for the extra commercial time. Finally, television today is much more likely to feature commercials that are especially engineered to sound louder than the surrounding program content. The FCC, which formerly had policies targeting such practices, tossed in the towel on this fight more than two decades ago.

Of course, the urge to sell everything in sight is not limited to television. Commercial television merely stands out in a society where advertising seeps into nearly every facet of daily life. Pop-up ads blink, beep, and move across the computer screen to the point of distraction. Advertising in the classroom is now as common as chalk and erasers, and every athlete and coach in every major sport from junior high to the pros wears merchandise that promotes a product. Advertising messages stream in unsolicited on our telephones, and then, when calls are placed for services we actually want, we are greeted by automated voicemail systems that seek to sell us something even while directing our call. Open the Sunday newspaper and behold an accordion of advertising messages in assorted sizes and colors. Board a bus, attend a ball game, or enter a movie theater and be surrounded by cascading sales pitches. A sign of our times has become the essence of our times.

A Concluding Word on Television Today

From the foregoing, one might conclude that the television business model is broken, brought to this state of disrepair by its own poor practices and escalating competitive pressures. Far from it. At least, not yet. Broadcast television, certainly network television, is in a state of decline—if measured only by eroding audience shares. On the other hand, it seems far too early to crown cable (or the Internet) as the new visual champ. Although most American homes (approximately 85 percent) install cable boxes or satellite dishes to watch television, those delivery systems still rely heavily on programming originated by over-the-air television—obtained either from local stations they are allowed to "retransmit" in whole or from syndication companies that sell them "reruns" of individual programs originally aired on over-the-air networks. Moreover, even the most successful cable channels draw only a small fraction of the total TV audience.

Those ready to bury over-the-air television (and the chorus of voices chanting this theme has been building steadily in recent years) arrive at this position with little regard for history. As any student of media should know, newspapers survived television, movies adjusted to television, and radio, which started near the beginning of the twentieth century, has now, after eighty years, shifted into yet another position of strength at the beginning of the twenty-first century. The evidence remains unconvincing that declining audience shares and the fragmentation of viewers to competing media will alone spell the death knell of traditional television. Yes, television (network and local) will change, perhaps dramatically in the coming decades, but it will survive. It may eventually become primarily a video-on-demand ("a la carte") pay service and it may, in the future, be viewed almost as frequently over computer screens and small portable devices as standard TV sets, but it will survive.

Although audience shares for TV networks and local stations have fallen significantly over the past three decades, the fragmented media environment contributing to such declines has not produced a new winner, capable of knocking broadcast television off its leadership perch. It still commands the largest share of the audience and it still stands out as a unique and efficient method for advertising many-mass market products and services. And, despite the proliferation of small, portable devices allowing viewers to record, retrieve, and replay whatever they want wherever they want it, most Americans continue to watch television on big screens in the comfort of their homes. We also need to be leery of cries from network owners that the network business is suddenly dying and will not survive under the same economic model. Not only are such pleas generally advanced to support further deregulation, they ignore the long history of television networking—a business that, standing alone, has rarely been consistently profitable for all major players.[35] No serious observer doubts that the network business has changed—owing to shifting relationships, the migration of audiences and advertisers to alternative media, and rising programming costs—but those factors miss a key point. Network companies have always been successful businesses, overall, by combining the operation of their networks with the ownership of key local stations in the largest and most lucrative TV markets (a side of the business they have been allowed to expand manyfold under deregulation). They have done this not just to extend their existing dominance or better control their own destinies—exemplary business objectives, to be sure—they have done so because operating margins at most major market stations (generally in the 25 percent to 35 percent range) are the envy of virtually every other business in America. The television network business we have long known is both changing and branching out in new directions. That process will persist. But some combination of key local outlets linked to powerful media parents will continue to dominate the television business.

The rise of the media conglomerates highlighted at the beginning of this chapter should tell us something else about the state of contemporary television: it is no longer just a broadcast television world. It is a wider world constructed of many new visual and content-based platforms. The companies providing broadcast television have changed and continue to evolve in size and in composition. For example, it is no longer relevant to look at ABC and just measure its share of the traditional prime-time network audience. You must look at the wider Disney empire of which it is now an integral part. Disney-ABC not only strives for audience share for its shows on the ABC television network, it simultaneously picks up audience on ESPN, SoapNet, ABC Family, and Lifetime cable networks. At the same time, it reaches audiences with releases from Walt Disney Pictures or Miramax Films and competes for the leisure time of Americans by operating massive theme parks, producing Broadway shows, and publishing popular books and magazines. Disney-ABC also operates retail stores and taps into the Internet with a highly diverse online stream of products and services. By early 2006, ABC and other major TV networks had announced that they would, for the first time, offer on-demand, near-instant replays of some of their most popular shows— over the Internet for downloading to both stationary and portable devices. Yet another platform on which to operate. Such developments foreshadow a repositioning of broadcast television, not a death spiral.

OTHER TRENDS IMPACTING TODAY'S MEDIA MARKETPLACE

The changes in radio and television are only part of the picture. The state of mass media in this country is also deeply affected by key technological developments and shifting audience habits. Consolidation and its twin sister concentration dominate contemporary discussions of mass media. But important social and regulatory consequences also flow from six other discrete trends: digitalization, convergence/interactivity, fragmentation, globalization, and the continuing expansion of new media forms such as satellite broadcasting and the Internet.

1. Digitalization

The future of mass media is digital. Those who do not embrace that technology will not survive. The only legitimate debate is when and how all elements of the radio, television, and cable businesses will fully convert to the technology that already dominates the Internet and satellite worlds.

Broadcasting, which sends signals through the air, and cable television, which sends signals through encased coaxial or fiber-optic wires, distribute most of their programming to the American public by analog, not digital, means. The gradual conversion of broadcasting and cable to digital technology is one of the most significant ongoing developments in mass media. Broadcast stations and cable systems use digital equipment for many of their operations, but the signals they transmit to reach the public remain almost entirely analog.

The analog technique in broadcasting involves imposing an electronic pattern on the center frequency of a station's channel (its "carrier" wave) that is similar or "analogous" to the wave pattern of the original information—for example, the sound or picture captured by a microphone or camera. The result of such electrically induced variations (at the outset and along the path) is a radio wave containing patterned variations analogous to the original sound or picture. In contrast, digital processing of sound and pictures first involves encoding the wave patterns of the original image and sound into a series of numerical symbols that represent the original wave patterns but are not analogous to them. Rather, digital encoding reduces all forms of information to numbers for transmission. This binary code, in fact, consists of only two digits, usually written simply as "0" and "1." As such, all sound and picture content is broken down into strings of zeros and ones. To retrieve or receive information transmitted digitally, it is necessary to decode the numerical information by converting it back to what it originally represented—specifically, video, audio, or data. A digital signal is still sent out or broadcast in a wave form, but it is transformed into a digital configuration prior to being modulated. At the reception end, it must be converted back into analog form for listeners and viewers to perceive something beyond what was actually transmitted, a string of zeroes and ones.

Digitalized signals improve quality and flexibility. As long as the numerical code in the signal can be received (usually a factor of power and distance) by someone's radio or TV set, it is free of the distortions caused by interference long plaguing analog signals. Significantly, digital signals do not lose quality when they are repeatedly processed by being recorded, relayed, or otherwise manipulated. In fact, each copy of a digitally encoded piece of sound or video is equivalent in quality to the original. The immense flexibility of a digital signal stems from the fact that it can be taken apart and reassembled or pieced together with other material, with the reassembled parts being indistinguishable in the new "whole."

Because digitally processed signals occupy more space than comparable signals in analog form, practical applications in broadcasting were initially limited. However, with major advances in compression technology in the 1990s it eventually became possible to transmit multiple programs (even combined with data) in the same-size channel required for a single analog signal. Starting with the flexibility that is possible once content is converted into digital form, compression allows a medium to eliminate all information not essential to a particular communication. In turn, this frees more space for increased amounts of other content. The explosive growth in channel capacity on cable systems and satellite services is directly attributable to being able to compress a digital signal in this fashion. It is also what will enable conventional terrestrial TV stations to eventually broadcast multiple digital signals (along with some nonprogramming data) over the same 6-MHz-size channel that TV stations use today to broadcast a single analog signal.

Although the term "HDTV," or high-definition television, is still used interchangeably with digital television, there is a major distinction. Digital television (or DTV) is television broadcast in digital mode, whether it uses 480 or 1,080 lines of resolution. HDTV does not yet have an official, all-encompassing definition but generally refers to the form of DTV that uses at least 720 lines of resolution or the maximum 1,080.[36] When the FCC adopted a digital television standard in 1996 and later awarded a new, second channel to all existing TV stations to inaugurate DTV service, it did not require that TV stations broadcast in HDTV. Rather, it said they would comply if they commenced DTV service by broadcasting at least one signal in digital form that matched the resolution level of their preexisting analog signal.

The process of converting local television stations from analog to digital commenced in the late 1990s and is ongoing. Although analog stations embraced digital techniques to handle different phases of TV production fairly early, the process of constructing new technical facilities in order to broadcast a fully separate over-the-air digital channel has moved more slowly. This is not surprising. With virtually all Americans watching television on analog sets, a quick conversion was impossible without most sets fading to black. Moreover, facing large build-out expenditures and many uncertainties about the transition, most TV stations favored a go-slow approach at the outset. On top of this, the FCC established a ten-year period before one of the two channels had to be returned to the government and, shortly thereafter, Congress effectively extended the period indefinitely by providing that no channels were required to be returned until 85 percent of a given station's viewers are able to receive the digital signal either over the air or via satellite or cable.

The transition from analog to digital involves much more than revamping local television stations. It requires big adjustments by the cable industry that delivers TV stations to most American homes, rapid technological advances by the consumer electronics industry that designs and builds TV sets, major marketing improvements by the retail industry that sells TV sets, and, finally, crucial protections for content providers—such as production companies and artists (writers, actors, and composers)—who hold valuable copyrights to material that, in a digital television world, will be especially vulnerable to easy duplication and unauthorized distribution. While the FCC clearly placed too much reliance on the marketplace to resolve these many conflicting yet interrelated interests, the practical problems and financial stakes almost ensured there would be no quick or easy resolution. Nevertheless, the FCC's early reluctance to accept a broader responsibility for implementing the digital transition was a significant failure of public policy. Six years into the transition, Edward J. Markey, ranking Democrat on the House Telecommunications Subcommittee, declared that "our digital policy is a mess, and in the absence of the federal government intervening with a comprehensive policy, the American consumer is unlikely to ever receive the full benefits of the digital revolution."[37] Whether one accepts or rejects this indictment, there is little doubt that stronger, more consistent policy leadership from the start would have moved us much closer, more quickly to the full realization of this sweeping technological change.

Not until 2006—ten years into the transition—did Congress remove any lingering uncertainty about the timing of the switch to digital. On 1 February 2006, it passed a law that, among other things, sets 9 February 2009 as the outside date when television stations must stop broadcasting in analog and begin broadcasting exclusively in digital. Analog television sets still in use at that time will only be capable of receiving digital programming (either directly over-the-air or via a cable or satellite provider) if they are connected to a special converter box—which consumers must purchase separately to change digital broadcasts into an analog format.

There is, therefore, no turning back. The television industry is moving inexorably to digital just as all other transmission industries are moving to digital. Once analog channels disappear, the real possibilities for digital television will emerge. Not only will we experience better pictures and surround sound—especially when offered in a high-definition format—we will begin to see a new style of news and entertainment. This will involve much more than simply splitting the digital channel of one station into separate services. The greater flexibility and manipulability of digital will kindle more innovation in the content and visual presentation of entertainment programs, sports, and commercials, leading to more dramatic special effects and different kinds of enhancements. It will also generate new activities centered on the TV set—such as interactive contests and broader, more sophisticated methods of audience participation.

The digital revolution in broadcast radio has taken a different, somewhat easier—although not necessarily faster—path. At the outset, the policy and technical questions focused on whether AM and FM stations, like TV, would be assigned an extra, temporary frequency —to be effective until enough digital radio receivers had been produced and sold—or whether they would be able to generate a digital signal over their existing frequency, while continuing to broadcast in analog. By early 2005, it appeared that the preferred transition would involve a "hybrid" operation using "in-band, on-channel" (IBOC) technology. IBOC refers to a method of sending a digital radio signal centered on the same frequency as an AM or FM station's present frequency. The system is called a hybrid because it is neither fully analog nor fully digital. New receivers being developed are expected to incorporate both modes of reception, having the capacity of switching automatically to the analog signal if the digital signal cannot be decoded or is lost by the receiver. In the meantime, hybrid operation allows all existing radio sets to receive the analog (nondigital) signal. Hundreds of stations throughout the country have received interim authorizations to broadcast in this mode, even as the technology is still being refined. IBOC digital radio is expected to provide near-CD quality reception for FM stations and improve the reception of AM stations to equal that of today's FM analog reception.

2. Convergence

A term conceptualizing intermedia technological developments and relationships is *convergence*. It refers to the blurring of functional lines between discrete media and related forms of communication (radio, television, cable, computers, e-mail, wireless devices, motion pictures, and print) which, some futurists predict, will eventually lead to their coming together in a single, compatible, and interchangeable instrument—usually thought to be a television set, computer, or some more sophisticated, yet to be developed, Dick Tracy–like device. Another term associated with this general concept is *multimedia*, or the blending of more than one medium (speech, music, video, text, and data) into an integrated, commonly controlled environment.

On one level, convergence is already a visible success. Walls that previously separated the broadcasting, cable, computer, and telecommunications businesses have started to fall. Telephone companies (landline and wireless) are beginning to offer video and audio (to television sets and cell phones) and cable companies are beginning to offer telephone service. Both offer high-speed, broadband access to the Internet. Smart boxes found in homes today increasingly combine technologies and software that are common to the telephone, cable, and computer businesses. But the walls have not fallen completely, and no one yet is in a position to control the only line into the house that would connect and operate a single, fully compatible, all-purpose media device that could be carried and used anywhere.

Nor is the public necessarily ready for the level of convergence propounded by some futurists. A lot has been written in recent years about the "500-channel universe," the "information superhighway," and the interlinking of devices and methods of communication. Still, the promise of convergence, interactivity, and multimedia continues to dash ahead of the reality. The television set is still used to watch entertainment, and the computer is still used primarily to process information and communicate on an individual rather than mass media basis. There is no one all-purpose device through which people engage in a dizzying array of multimedia experiences. Even though people, especially the young, increasingly multitask, they still perceive and use television as one type of device and the computer as another. And they do not yet regularly watch sitcoms on their Palm™ Pilots or BlackBerrys—even though the latest iPod does display video and some cell phones are capable of picking up tidbits of news and information.

As such, it seems likely that people will continue to have and use different devices for different functions even if at some point in the future they are more closely linked. People will use a computer to search, browse, learn, and communicate. They will use the convenience and privacy of a mobile device to make calls, send e-mails, receive text messages, and, occasionally, watch video or pick up the latest news and sports, when outside the home. And, they will turn to bigger, flatter television sets for entertainment and sports when broadcast in high definition. Despite giddy predictions of a seamless world that will blend all communication activities, there is little evidence that people want one machine to do everything.

3. Fragmentation

One of the factors often trumpeted in support of deregulation and consolidation is that the mass audience for broadcasting is fragmenting into tiny pieces, enhancing diversity and stirring competition in a way that, proponents and some policymakers say, validates more deregulation and further consolidation. Whether such claims can be sustained, there is no denying that the audience for virtually all media is in a state of continual fragmentation. Walk into a modern bookstore and survey thousands of specialized books and magazines, scan the radio dial and sample scores of formulaic music stations, pick up your cable or satellite remote and surf hundreds of channels, or, for sources of information and amusement knowing no limits, just go online. You have entered the world of fragmentation. Audiences for mass media are being broken down and spread out over more niche-oriented, specialized sources than ever before. Fragmentation has cut into the readership of many mass appeal publications, changed the focus and marketing of motion pictures, and, most dramatically, reduced the size of television network audiences from a combined audience share of more than 90 percent in the 1970s to less than 50 percent today. Ironically, one of the ways national television networks have dealt with this is to stir the fragmentation process further by creating or buying "competitive" channels or networks and then displaying their program product on different outlets at different times. In the past, television networks would have been paranoid about losing viewers for the original and exclusive run of a show. Today, only 20 percent or less of the nation's viewers may see one airing, leaving a lot of audience to be reached with repeat showings on the same or different media platforms not a month or year later, but right now.

Fragmentation, of course, is not a new phenomenon. It has been part of the history of mass media for most of the last century. Long before national television networks dominated the scene, national radio networks and mass appeal magazines such as *Life, Look,* and the *Saturday Evening Post* held sway. Then, with the advent of television drawing the audience in new directions, radio became less of a national medium and more of a local service offering distinct, specialized formats. The success of television also changed the focus of motion pictures and cut into the influence and popularity of the national, mass-appeal magazines, giving rise to more specialized, demographically oriented movies and publications. In fact, television has remained a general-appeal mass medium the longest, swimming along in a broad stream while, for decades, competitive mass media have had to navigate narrower tributaries in order to attract audiences. Now, however, fragmentation has come to television. From a single set in the living room tuned to one of only three channels, video choices have exploded. Multiple sets are now scattered among many rooms and connected to cable or satellite services offering hundreds of channels. Simultaneously, viewer choices have been expanded and personalized by videocassette recorders, digital video disc players, personal video recorders, personal computers, and fully portable, wireless video devices. This proliferation of services and equipment translates into smaller television audiences for specific stations, networks, and cable services leading, inevitably, to increased fragmentation of the overall video audience.

Historically, such changes have resulted in adjustments but no fundamental alteration of the broad media landscape. New forms have arisen and existing forms have been reshaped and restyled to avoid extinction. The audience has been dispersed but remained relatively steady. Have we, however, arrived at a more defining moment in the history of mass media? Will burgeoning choice and individual selection finally produce a more engaged audience so fragmented along so many lines that "mainstream media" will start to sound like an oxymoron?

Certainly, the outlines of a new model for viewing television and gathering information are beginning to take shape. Set-top boxes displayed by cable systems and satellite services have become more and more computerlike, allowing increased amounts of program material to be viewed on demand or retrieved, stored, and viewed later. On the Internet, agile users can pick and choose their news and information from diverse, less-edited sources that may more closely reflect their own interests or preconceived attitudes. On some satellite news services available in Europe you can press a button to divide the TV picture into eight separate screens, each showing a different news or feature item. Press again to select the screen you wish to have enlarged for viewing. Unsatisfied, press again and go back to the eight screens and pick something else.

A new rush at the turn of the century to upgrade distribution systems—via cable lines, telephone lines, and set-top boxes—strongly suggests that the push to engage the audience in some viable form of interactivity continues. Whether characterized as broadband communication or just television on demand, the choice offered viewers will continue to expand, and with such choice will come more fragmentation. If cable companies, satellite services, or telephone operators can store vast arrays of program material—old films, replays of current series, or special features on health, cooking, or golf—on giant servers linked to sophisticated set-top boxes in the home, the process of fragmentation will reach new heights. If, at the same time, Internet-based technology allows more viewers to pick their own news, entertainment, and sports instead of relying on prepackaged versions offered by traditional video channels (cable, satellite, or over-the-air), the basic television viewing experience will be transformed. Instead of sitting down and viewing scheduled shows that are simultaneously transmitted to millions, individuals will be able to build their own personalized program schedules and retrieve only news stories that match their own tastes and predilections. The value of this transformation to individual consumers (in choice and convenience) is obvious. The value to society at large is more complicated.

The challenge for policymakers is deciding where fragmentation is leading us as a democratic society. Is it, ultimately, a liberating trend fulfilling the utopian dream of individual choice amidst a cornucopia of information? Certainly proponents of deregulation have long relied upon advancing technology and expanded choice as one of the overriding rationalizations for removing standards. Or is escalating fragmentation ultimately defeating, setting many, if not most, Americans adrift in an uncharted, choppy sea of unfiltered and largely indecipherable information? The difficulty, of course, is that there is evidence of both likely outcomes.

A democratic society benefits when its citizens have more independent access to more information. Audiences are empowered in ways never before imagined, with the ability to choose whatever they want from whatever source at whatever time. Some might argue that liberating individuals and groups in this fashion is actually the antidote to media consolidation and centralized media control. Instead of a few large media conglomerates establishing the news agenda and making the entertainment choices for a mass audience, an increasingly fragmented public finds its own tailored satisfaction from an endless stream of specialized information and entertainment. On the other hand, this path is not without risks.

First, a greater diffusion of media could, ultimately, instill more confusion than confidence among vast segments of the public. There is still no proof that most viewers are both able and willing to navigate a boundless sea of information and entertainment on their own. If they are not, the balance of power and influence in mass communication might eventually tilt more in favor of (not away from) the leading media companies. While we have always had only a few leading sources of information and entertainment, it is certainly possible that a more fragmented media environment may actually enhance the role and influence of the few surviving national newspapers, magazines, and television networks.

Second, it is noteworthy that the multifarious program services offered by cable or satellite, as well as the many alternative sources of information available on the Internet or in specialized publications, are almost all national in origin and outlook. Local governments and communities need responsive, proactive media as much as the U.S. population at large needs responsible national media. Yet coverage of state legislatures, city and county councils, and individual neighborhoods and communities is already overshadowed by broadcast news reports that focus on news clips from national and regional services. An audience more reliant on sources and outlets that supply only nonlocal news drives another stake in the heart of localism (already vastly weakened by years of broadcast deregulation). It is possible, of course, that, over time, some new form of local media will evolve in cyberspace, using "blogger-style" technology and software. If it does, will it still be enough?

Third, a fragmented media environment potentially leads to a more fragmented society, with fewer people sharing the same common experiences. To date, however, it is revealing that despite hundreds of channels to choose from, most Americans continue to watch only a few leading ones on a regular basis—30 percent watch five or fewer channels and 33 percent watch six to twelve channels.[38] This general pattern also occurs in the use of popular websites. Either the choice is too overwhelming or it is just too easy to stay with familiar sources.

Fourth, and perhaps most important, while greater access to customized information and entertainment may liberate and uplift many in society, it may also leave many others behind, creating an even greater knowledge and experience gap between members of different social and economic classes. Communications theorists have even given this notion a name, the "knowledge-gap hypothesis."[39] It is not just the cost and availability of mass media delivery systems (e.g., cable, pay cable, satellite, set-top boxes, computers, printers, and broadband servers) that contribute to this gap, it is the fact that most mass media information is oriented to the middle class and more affluent in our society because they represent the largest groups that advertisers and pay services seek to reach. A further fragmented commercial media in this country will likely exacerbate this trend, orienting more entertainment and information to the tastes and interests of such groups, to the detriment of less advantaged groups.

If American society migrates to new technologies prematurely—technologies that require skills, initiative, and financial resources beyond those necessary to use traditional media—the less educated, less affluent, and less able will have less access and a lesser role. One media scholar, Gerald Sussman, observes that the advent of "corporate driven technological change," combined with deregulation have "enabled the privileged and business strata to segregate themselves in terms of access to communication services, with fewer trickle-down subsidies going to the working class."[40] It is only slightly ironic that while the penny press ushered in the era of affordable media for the masses in the first half of the nineteenth century, we are seeing the first significant trends in the opposite direction, at the start of the twenty-first century. Most newspapers can still be purchased for cents (twenty-five, fifty, or seventy-five) and radio and television are available to virtually everyone. At the same time, personal computers, personal video recorders, online services (with or without a high-capacity modem), assorted handheld devices, and various satellite services (video and audio) are only available to those able to afford significant equipment purchases and sizable ongoing monthly charges.

Another risk along the road to greater fragmentation arises from the new ways information is gathered and disseminated. Recent technical advances undoubtedly produce expanded amounts of increasingly customized, interactive information and entertainment at breakneck speed. But the amount and speed make it increasingly difficult to assess the veracity of information available online or disseminated by rapid-fire, edit-on-the-fly, 24/7 news services. Affordable, portable TV cameras, cell phone camcorders, digital editing technology, satellite transmissions from almost anywhere, combined with "blogging," "podcasting," and webvideo sites like YouTube on the Internet make it possible for anyone (professional or man-on-the-street) to be cast in the role of mini producer of media content. Policymakers eager to champion new technology that expands consumer choice to the point where we decrease our dependency on traditional media sources also need to assess these potential negative side effects.

Until the introduction of the Internet and the vast array of niche services available by satellite, Americans received most of their entertainment and information through traditional media sources that acted as a filter for or editor of the material offered. A local station, national network, or daily newspaper selected the entertainment presented and edited the news and information offered. They still do, of course. But for the more venturesome consumer, it is now possible to select one's own brand of entertainment and information—customized to one's own needs and interests—or to roam over channels and cyberspace collecting bits and pieces at random. To the technically savvy and highly skilled, this may be a liberating, highly satisfactory experience. To others, probably most Americans, the disorder and disarray of cyberspace and the continuous surfing of satellite niche channels may prove frustrating and unrewarding.

Americans need more than the click of a mouse to pierce the fog of information overflow; they need familiar, trusted sources to perform an editorial role. Machines and software programmers can categorize and index information pegged to key words and phrases but that is only a rudimentary selection function. Self-appointed individuals (bloggers and podcasters) can package information inexpensively on a website but they have no accountability—in either the marketplace or journalism. As one prominent blogger, Markos Moulitsas of the Daily Kos, so graphically explains: "I don't plan on doing any original reporting—screw that."[41] In short, we still need someone to gather, edit, and report information, subject to peer review, and someone with sufficient resources and credibility to challenge big government, big business, and other major institutions.

Gossip, rumor, and just plain unfounded news items can be spread faster and farther than ever. Individuals and groups with little concern or responsibility for accuracy are able to create mischief and injustice for targeted individuals. While miscreants actually intending to spread socially destructive misinformation are few, there remain plenty of individuals and groups unskilled or uninterested in following the fundamental principles of journalism practiced by mainstream news media. In light of these risks and developments, it is not surprising that the most recognizable and used news and information outlets on the Internet are AOL.com, Yahoo.com, MSNBC.com, CNN.com, and New York Times digital, all familiar news and information brands.[42] More than ever, we need good, strong, credible, and accountable mass media to lead us out of the disjointed, unedited "mass of porridge" frequently served up on the Internet.

4. Globalization

While the term *globalization* conjures up many, sometimes competing, notions covering a host of complicated issues, it is discussed here strictly in a mass media context. The enormous size and breadth of today's media giants produce footprints everywhere in the world. All of the domestic powerhouses have outlets and relationships in virtually any place on the planet where movies or TV reach local residents. A few of the global media players—Bertelsmann and Sony—are based in Europe or Japan but likewise produce for the rest of the world. To media researcher and critic Robert W. McChesney, this transformation of the corporate media system into a global commercial media market represents a form of "cultural imperialism" in which media giants, most of whom are U.S.-owned or -based, are "inculcating the world's people with western consumer values and undermining traditional cultures."[43] McChesney and other critics of cultural imperialism paint with a very broad brush, usually leaving only a thin first coat of an argument.[44]

American media companies have long dominated the international syndication business, supplying television programs not only to developed nations in Europe, South America, and the Far East but to many third world nations as well. Out of a concern that the images and values depicted in such American programs might damage local cultures and also with a view toward protecting their own local production enterprises, authorities in those countries have periodically imposed specific program import restrictions targeting American content. This tension has existed for years and was especially pronounced when, in the past, American television and movies held far greater sway over video production and technology in Europe and elsewhere.

Today, even though the technology and production gap between the United States and many developed nations has narrowed, the issues persist. One of the reasons is that power and influence have been concentrated in just a few dominant media companies—most of them U.S.-based—that, with the help of advances in technology, are able to spread their program offerings more widely and more rapidly. Satellite and Internet services put CNN and BBC World in reach of anyone with a TV set or computer almost instantly. Even entertainment channels like MTV are distributed worldwide in various regional- and country-specific versions, such as MTV Europe, MTV Asia, MTV India, and MTV Japan. And, larger media companies with more control and direct ownership of greater amounts of program content are able to strike more syndication deals with more countries spanning the globe. Although characterizing such developments as cultural imperialism is a vast overstatement, there is no doubt that advanced technology and widespread dissemination of American programming by larger and more powerful companies adds a certain new dimension to media globalization—what communications scholar James Lull calls "communication connectivity."[45] In Lull's words, "We live today in an ever-increasingly hyper-interconnected world, a 'global ecumene' of communicative interactions and exchanges that stimulates profound cultural transformations and realignments."

Notwithstanding such provocative labels as "cultural imperialism," there is no evidence of American policies specifically designed to influence cultures abroad by use of privately owned American media— even though some antiglobalists would undoubtedly interpret some foreign policy actions as having that ultimate effect. There is also a dearth of evidence that the exportation of television programming and other media content by private companies is actually intended by producers or distributors to spread American influence or values or to force any particular images on others. If that were the case, far more programming would be specifically produced and written for discrete foreign audiences. As it is, most exported programming is programming originally made and shown to Americans, not with the purpose of influencing other cultures. The power or influence these media conglomerates or transnational companies seek is economic—they simply want to extend their markets and generate added revenues.

The usual concern expressed by critics is that Western countries, particularly the United States, will, through these powerful transnational media companies, monopolize the mass communications of other countries, damaging their economic well-being and cultural identity. The menace of American popular culture trampling on the national habits, attitudes, beliefs, and tastes of other populaces is a notion that still exists in many parts of the world. But there is little evidence it is growing or uniformly held. Although cheap imports from America may fill the airways in countries that have not yet developed a production capability of their own, the appetite for American programming is likely to diminish as that condition begins to change. More developed and advanced countries are far more likely to both push and prefer their own programming—even while expressing a lingering fascination with product from the United States. Yes, countries around the world have had and continue to have a large appetite for American television and film product—but that does not mean they are ready to abandon their own culture, any more than Americans who prefer Japanese cars are likely to exalt Japanese business acumen over American business enterprise. Quotas and import restrictions have been a factor, but the urge to experience one's own familiar culture in movies and TV is ultimately stronger. When American media conglomerates like Disney, Time Warner, and Viacom start producing "local" versions of their branded content (such as MTV Japan or CNN in Turkish) they are recognizing the importance of building on, not trampling, local cultures. If, as appears to be the case, this trend reflects the reality that it is easier for American companies to sell advertising in such programs, it likewise demonstrates that advertising is most effective when it remains parochial in nature. Finally, the international trade in television programming is becoming less and less of a one-way street. Among the leading, non-American, worldwide media conglomerates are: Sony (Japanese); Bertelsmann (German); Univision (largely Mexican); and BBC World (British). In addition, successful TV shows launched in Europe, such as "Who Wants to Be a Millionaire," "Survivor," and "Big Brother," have been imported to America and molded into local versions elsewhere around the world.

Another unproven assumption of the cultural imperialism thesis is that American programming is all bad. It certainly has appeal or it would not be so popular in so many places. While programming originated in the United States reflects many American experiences, ideas, habits, trends, and attitudes, not all of these are negative. The best of Disney's children's programming can be a positive influence for children and parents everywhere. Other programs reflect the workings and benefits of an open society, if only by implication, as well as respect for the rule of law and the role of women and minorities. Although there are risks that messages and images will be misconstrued —a risk inherent to a free and open society anywhere—there can be no doubt that satellite and Internet transmissions have opened up and extended a dialogue and connection among different people around the world. If some continue to bemoan that such "technological togetherness [has] not created the human bonds that were promised" but instead has made the world a less understanding, less tolerant place,[46] others will say wait. It takes time and experience for some nations and people to assimilate the sort of information flow that has been common in the developed nations of the West.

Finally, media globalization cannot be stopped, in any event. As James Lull says, "Nations, cultures, economies, corporations, social movements, and the rest" really have few good choices, they "must either integrate into the global scene, ignore, or disconnect from it"— and ignoring or disconnecting from the global stage, for nations and media, is ultimately self-destructive.[47] Cultural groups and national societies do not simply imitate other cultures. Even if they are influenced in some nonpassive fashion, they still absorb the images and messages from other cultures through the prisms of their own experiences and social conditions.

5. Satellite Broadcasting

After struggling as a secondary service for many years, direct-to-the-home satellite television became a significant competitive force by the turn of the century. Better business practices combined with improved technology—digital compression, more powerful and better-performing satellites in the sky, and much smaller receiving dishes on earth—have finally made satellite television a direct competitor to cable television. Today, the number of subscribers served by satellite television exceeds the number of subscribers served by all but the largest cable system operator. In early 2005, the two satellite television services, DirecTV and EchoStar, had 14.4 million and 11.2 million subscribers, respectively. Only Comcast Cable (the largest multichannel video provider, with 21.5 million subscribers) and Time Warner Cable (the fourth largest, with 10.9 million subscribers) had comparable numbers.[48] With recent changes in the law allowing satellite services to retransmit local television stations, the typical offerings of satellite television are nearly identical to those available on modern cable systems.

On the other hand, satellite radio can be regarded as both a new method of distribution and a new type of service. In 1997, the FCC earmarked a discrete portion of the nation's radio spectrum for "digital audio radio satellite service." Using frequencies much higher and different than conventional, terrestrial radio, two companies, Sirius Satellite Radio and XM Satellite Radio, launched limited service in late 2001 and early 2002. Each company provides a subscription-based service offering more than 120 channels of commercial-free music, comedy, sports, news, and information—all delivered directly from satellites to cars, homes, or palm-sized mobile receivers anywhere in the continental United States. Other than a monthly fee, the only precondition to receiving the service is that one's car, home, or portable radio must be equipped with a special receiver. Some observers are tantalized by the prospects of satellite radio offering the first real alternative to standard radio. Others see it as carving out little more than a niche market. Much depends upon satellite radio's ability to offer program features that continue to distinguish it from what is available on traditional, terrestrial radio—such as an abundance of commercial-free material, more uninhibited or ribald personalities like Howard Stern (who jumped from broadcast radio to satellite radio in 2006), and a full array of major league sporting events (e.g., not one, but all major league baseball games played everyday). By the end of

2005, satellite radio was approaching seven million subscribers, a mere fraction of the more than two hundred million listeners that still tune in to terrestrial radio. Whether the gap will narrow measurably in the foreseeable future depends on satellite radio's ability to build upon its distinct features and, correspondingly, terrestrial radio's ability to find answers to its recent audience losses, minor overall but especially significant among teenagers and those eighteen to twenty-four years old.

6. The Internet

The first question to ask about the Internet, particularly the world-wide web, is whether it is an entirely new medium of mass communication. It deals in text, audio, and video, combining those attributes in a way that both resembles and differs from traditional mass media. Although it originally sprang from the noncommercial realm—a government-sponsored computing network in which most content was free—it has now blossomed into a full-fledged commercial cauldron. Whether measured by subscriptions paid to access the Internet, the myriad commercial enterprises that use the medium to conduct business, or just the unrelenting burst of banners, catchy graphics, and moving icons that inevitably greet users, the Internet is now a dedicated commercial or promotional venture in virtually all of its contemporary applications and services. Even the "free" search engines that lead users to vast pools of information are versatile vehicles for marketing products and gathering information on users. The Internet may be a mold-breaking new medium but, as with all that came before it, somebody has to pay—and if not the government, that usually means users.

In the beginning, the Internet was a wild frontier, with many experts doubting the sustainability of ventures like Amazon.com, eBay, or Yahoo!. The thought was that since anyone could start a website, virtually all Internet entities were vulnerable to having their businesses stolen by copycats. It has not happened. The companies that began to control people's online time a few years ago—America Online, Yahoo!, Microsoft, and Google—are in an even more commanding position today. Moreover, pioneering e-commerce companies such as Amazon and eBay continue to dominate. Businesses and users have settled into familiar patterns. Obviously, people still surf for various needs but, increasingly, with the novelty gone, and for sheer convenience, people tend to return to the same sites for the same functions. They surf when they want something new. New sites and businesses still continue to appear, but increasingly they fill niches as the established Internet giants become bigger and stronger.

Since one of the largest entities navigating people over the Internet (America Online) is an integral part of the world's largest media company (Time Warner), it should come as no surprise that media functions and services on the Internet are dominated by established print or broadcast media organizations. One can certainly find new players performing media functions—such as Matt Drudge and a few prominent, independent bloggers. But it is the "old media" firms that still command people's time on the Internet. In 2005, it was reported that eighteen of the top twenty online destinations for current events (and other global news) were owned or controlled by established print or broadcast news organizations. The other two (Yahoo! News and Google News) are services of the two most entrenched Internet giants.[49]

Table 4.1. Top Twenty Current Events and Global News Sites (June 2005)

Company	Unique Visitors (in millions)
Yahoo! News	24.9
MSNBC	23.8
CNN	21.4
AOL News (owned by Time Warner)	17.4
Gannett Newspapers (excluding *USA Today*)	11.4
NYTimes.com	11.2
Internet Broadcasting (websites for broadcasters)	10.9
Knight-Ridder Digital	9.9
Tribune Newspapers	9.0
USAToday.com	8.6
WashingtonPost.com	8.5
ABC News Digital	7.7
Google News	7.2
Hearst Newspapers Digital	6.9
World Now (websites for broadcasters)	6.2
Fox News	6.0
CBS News	5.9
BBC News	5.1
Advance Internet (websites for print publications)	4.5
McClatchy Newspapers	3.6

In a remarkably short period of time, the Internet has evolved from the exclusive province of academics, government specialists, and random computer geeks to become a mass-consumer resource and communication tool available to millions. Estimates of Internet use vary wildly, but some reports suggest that nearly 75 percent of adult Americans were online in 2005 (at home, at work, or at other locations).[50] Ten years earlier, only about 9 percent of Americans were online. When we add the vast numbers of children who now grow up with Internet access in their homes and schools, it is evident that Internet use now rivals other communications media. Equally significant, broadband connections to the Internet were approaching 40 percent of U.S. homes by early 2005—spurring faster, more diverse uses of the Internet. With the capacity to deliver millions of bits per second, broadband services make it easier to offer multiple channels of video, audio, and computer data simultaneously.

If the Internet is not yet a distinct mass medium in the all-encompassing traditional sense, it surely is a medium *of* masses—a multipurpose public forum for gathering information, conducting business, passing documents, corresponding with friends and colleagues, hooking up, playing games, joining in conversation, raising funds, organizing protests, and providing music, pictures, videos, and other entertainment that can be downloaded to iPods, laptops, cell phones, and other handheld devices (in addition to stationary PCs). It is distinctly different than broadcasting, print, or movies—even as it increasingly performs many of the same functions.[51] Whether the Internet will become more dominated by mainstream media businesses, whether traditional media rooted in print or broadcast will transition most of their operations to the Internet, or whether cyberspace-centric businesses like Google and Yahoo! will eventually become the new masters of mass media, the media world we have known will never be the same.

The Internet, of course, raises a host of important policy issues that go well beyond this modest discussion—matters such as personal privacy, websites displaying obscene or indecent material accessible to children, and illegal scams using computer technology. Overshadowing all of these, of course, is the broader public policy question of which, if any, of these and other activities can and should be regulated in any fashion. What I am concerned about here, however, is simply how the Internet fits into the general mass media milieu that, from a public policy perspective, helps grease the wheels of a complex, changing society. Will the Internet ultimately enhance both personal lives and society at large? Will it become just as ubiquitous as the telephone and television, accessible to all? Or will it draw people into more subgroups, magnifying instead of reducing the demographic and cultural dividing lines of society? Although those with the resources and ability to tap the potential of the Internet and other new media may be enriched, those unable to do so may be left with only a dwindling supply of media sources requiring neither user fees nor technical savvy.[52]

A Few Closing Thoughts on Today's Media Marketplace

Years of deregulation, coupled with improvements in technology, have drastically altered the nature of the mass media marketplace. Eroding structural regulations have led directly to massive consolidation while reduced broadcaster accountability has unleashed business practices that, as never before, exalt private corporate interests over the public's interest. Whether measured in terms of program diversity, local service, the quality and quantity of news and information, or just the general level of entertainment programming, it would be absurd to declare deregulation and its most visible progeny, consolidation, a public service success. No doubt some costs have been saved and some efficiencies achieved. And, as a matter of sheer numbers, the country has far more media outlets than ever before. But none of this translates into any discernible on-air, public service benefit.

It should be remembered, however, that broadcasting has always been much more of an entertainment business than a news and information business (in marked contrast to newspapers). Those who decry the current trends in radio and television should not ignore this fact. In the early years of television, nightly network newscasts were limited to fifteen minutes, and the earliest version of "The Today Show" on NBC was hosted by a nonnews personality, Dave Garroway, who regularly interacted with a star chimpanzee (J. Fred Muggs) assigned to the show. The current version of the "Today" program may be extremely "soft" around the edges, but none of its regular personalities are animals.

If viewed solely as an issue of economic competition, the easing of regulatory restraints and the dropping of ownership standards are positive steps, creating opportunities for growth and profit. As broadcasting companies are transformed into larger media conglomerates, spreading their wings over the sources of content as well as the means of production and distribution, they gain financial leverage, increase returns, and expand control over their interlocked properties. But, as the rest of this book makes clear, it is incumbent on policymakers to assess these developments from a broader perspective. For too long they have assumed, without demonstrable evidence and after decades of history teaching just the opposite, that policies that stir vigorous marketplace competition also pay discrete public service dividends.

Even though the marketplace changes and other trends mentioned in this chapter should not, and cannot, be halted, or altered, the underlying policy framework can, and must, be changed. It is totally unrealistic to think that existing policies and methods can continue to work in such a vastly different and still evolving environment.

5

Mass Media in Modern Society

Mass media should be playing a starring role in America's contemporary social drama. Instead, some of the most visible trends at the start of the twenty-first century suggest a less prominent, even fading role—especially in fulfilling the functions media are expected to perform in a highly diverse, open society. The reasons stem from changes in the regulatory environment, changes in the lifestyles of the American public, and, ultimately, changes in the way mass media strive to connect with audiences today. In this and the following chapter the focus is less on the regulatory environment and more on changes in lifestyles and media performance. I start, however, by highlighting the major roles usually assigned to mass media in a democracy.

SPECIFIC FUNCTIONS ATTRIBUTED TO MEDIA IN A DEMOCRATIC SOCIETY

The standard formula for this kind of discussion is that a lively and open debate on political issues generated by mass media equals a vibrant, open democracy. However, since an open, democratic society operates on many different levels of discourse and experience, the enumeration of media functions that follows is purposely more expansive.[1]

1. *Supplying Information, Discussion, and Debate on Public Affairs.*
   First and foremost, mass media are the vital link between the
   government and its citizens and citizens and the outside world.
   No democratic system can function properly without a certain
   level of trust between the government and the represented, and
   trust is built upon an open exchange of information subject to
   debate and discussion. Without it, the act of voting and other
   forms of participating are made hollow. Because mass media are
   the "major vehicle for communication between governors and
   [the] governed," they bear a special responsibility "to convey to
   voters a considerable volume of accurate, policy-relevant information about politics in as impartial a manner as possible."[2] In
   their case study of the American electorate during the 1996 elections, Kenneth Dautrich and Thomas Hartley spell out this responsibility: "transmitting current information, educating the
   public, monitoring the activities of government, verifying the accuracy of public officials' statements, and encouraging the public to become interested and participate in politics."[3]

2. *Acting as Watchdog Over Government Officials and Activities, in Order to Safeguard the Rights of Individuals.* This is perhaps the most
   commonly cited and easily understood of the functions of mass
   media in a democratic society. A strong and independent press
   can monitor government more closely than individuals can, ex-
   posing the errors and abuses of public officials and facilitating
   political dissent. The watchdog role should, of course, also include monitoring other sources of power in American society.
   Three cases from contemporary life illustrate the need for vigi-
   lant media conducting independent investigations: (1) the failure of government intelligence leading to the terrorist attacks on
   11 September 2001; (2) the priest sex scandal in the American
   Catholic Church which had been misrepresented and mishan-
   dled for years by church hierarchy until it began to unravel in
   2002; and (3) the corporate and Wall Street abuses that went virtually uncovered during the stock market exuberance of the
   1990s. As Dean Thomas Kunkel reminds us, "Public institutions
   try desperately to suppress information—from the public and
   from each other. If we [the mass media] don't keep them honest, no one will."[4] While the watchdog function is usually associated with guarding against abuses of power, there is an important correlative role that, when performed, also protects the

public welfare. We all know that mass society needs mass media to supply information in times of crisis—ranging from a serious weather threat to a surprise terrorist attack. But a large, complex, and technologically dependent society also needs mass media to supply a steady flow of credible information on important recurring matters posing a different level of risk. For instance, problems such as environmental pollution, dangers to our food supply, the risks of certain drugs, and misconduct in the delivery of healthcare services would be impossible to address without widespread public access to credible, relevant information.

3. *Expressing the Culture.* A democratic society is sustained by the passing of values and ideas from generation to generation. Mass media—from the most popular, commercial forms to the most esoteric, edifying forms—are the most prominent and prolific conveyors of the messages, portrayals, beliefs, and behaviors that constitute the culture. As Straubhaar and LaRose point out, "Today the media have assumed the role of storytellers, teachers, and even parents."[5] Whether the topic is serious or superficial, the medium public television or comic books, Americans look to media for concepts, stories, and drama (real and fictional) that help them better understand who they are. At the highest level, media help teach us about our diversity, our interests and tastes, our common traditions, our standards of conduct.

4. *Supplying Entertainment.* All healthy societies require a rich diet of entertainment or diversion. From Shakespeare to Sinatra or high art to low comedy and everything in between, television, radio, newspapers, magazines, and movies entertain and divert America. That it could be done better, as most critics charge, is beside the point. It still needs to be done. Mass media tell stories and spread information, with the capacity to not only entertain but occasionally uplift.

5. *Linking Buyers and Sellers of Goods and Services.* The media business, having become much bigger and more consolidated in recent years, is still much smaller than many of the businesses it serves—the retailers who advertise in local newspapers or the automobile and banking companies that advertise on radio or television. Some commentators, of course, decry the very act of commercialism in the media and blame many of its excesses and failures on this factor.[6] But such rants rarely come with any practical alternatives. The possibility that commercial vices may

sometimes engulf creative and journalistic efforts aside, the advertising of goods and services undoubtedly fuels the general economy by better connecting sellers with buyers.

6. *Maintaining Financial Independence and Avoiding the Undue Pressures of Special Interests.* This is more a basic objective than fundamental role. But it is axiomatic that without financial independence—derived almost exclusively from the commercial advertising that some critics delight in vilifying—media businesses would be hard pressed to perform essential functions. Certainly not as a watchdog of government abuse or excess. Certainly not as a provider of diverse information, discussion, and debate featuring multiple voices on public affairs. The *New York Times*, the nation's most influential source of news and information, remains such, it must be remembered, because of the financial independence it derives from those splashy, sometimes exotic, but always crass commercial advertisements that literally envelop the stories and news articles that contribute to our democracy. To those who would prefer that our newspaper, television, radio, magazine, and Internet businesses be supported by some other means, let them show us what those means would be—and at what cost to our pocketbooks and independence.

—ɯ—

This simple cataloging of the specific functions attributed to mass media in a democratic society should remind us that, without mass media, our lives would be vastly different. Obviously, our basic forms of entertainment would disappear. More important, our sense of self and what it means to be an American would change. There would be no opportunity to reflect on or benefit from the experiences of anyone other than those we came in direct contact with. Our sense of security and safety would also change. Our awareness and participation in politics would change. Our discussions of public issues, as well as sports and entertainment, would change. Although large blocks of time would be freed up to interact with those we do not meet on a daily basis, how enriching would that time be, overall, if we had no newspapers, magazines, television, radio, or motion pictures to both enjoy and provide context for such interaction?

All this suggests is that mass media in a democracy are more than a public fountain spraying weighty ideas and information in ways that influence public debate. They are also the common carriers of the culture. The larger, more complicated our society becomes, the more critical it becomes for modern media to perform all of the foregoing roles.

MASS MEDIA AND CONTEMPORARY LIFESTYLES: A MARRIAGE OF CONVENIENCE?

Mass media neither produce nor perfectly reflect social reality. Rather, what we typically see and hear are bits and pieces of ideas, sounds, images, beliefs, and behaviors, all selectively conveyed by reporters, writers, producers, and actors of varying skill. Some of these symbolic, fleeting fragments may resemble our surroundings but others may not. Over time, this flow of mass media messages may detect and portray general social trends or changing tastes. It may even help chart new directions. Television, in particular, regularly disseminates or depicts values, attitudes, fashions, thoughts, and lifestyles—in programs and in commercials. Who would argue, for instance, that Bart Simpson does not more nearly reflect the attitudes of America's youth in the early 2000s than Beaver Cleaver or the Fonz from an earlier television era?

Disputes over the exact social role played by modern media have reverberated through academia for years. Do they, as some media critics have long charged, primarily parrot the beliefs and values of the elite classes of society including, in particular, the media establishment?[7] More fundamentally, do media alter the societies they occupy or do they merely reflect those societies? Despite the strong opinion and loose assumptions these questions usually trigger, simple, definitive answers are lacking. Mass media may popularize expressions, influence fashions, or even open eyes with new information or experiences. But, media messages rarely induce specific behavioral reactions or change preset attitudes. Media content is far more likely to harden, confirm, or slightly modify attitudes than change them. We know, for example, that people can learn from television, but how they learn and absorb something will be influenced by the totality of their media experiences, their own level of knowledge and conviction on a topic, and a whole network of interpersonal relationships (friends, relatives, coworkers, organizational ties, etc.).

Most media criticism focuses on how mass media are perceived to influence society.[8] Little, if any, attention is paid to any influence flowing in the opposite direction. Nevertheless, there can be little doubt that events and trends in society have had and continue to have a significant impact on mass media content. Indeed, it could not be otherwise—especially in the electronic media where programming must satisfy not only popular tastes but commercial advertisers. It is a simple formula: if a program fails to attract sufficient viewers or listeners, it will also fail to enlist advertisers to support that program. It is for this reason that those who believe everything would be right if only we could exercise more control over the media messenger are so wrong. Breaking up media combinations, reinstating rules and policies of a bygone era, or threatening new initiatives focused on media performance will neither improve the quality of advertiser-supported media nor turn the American public into more focused, more serious media users. Such measures could, of course, produce hours ofmandated public service programming. But they could not produce programming that the public would watch or that advertisers would support.

The Innate Bond Between Electronic Media and American Society

The connective relationship of mass society with mass media is most pronounced during times of national stress or great adventure. In its early years, radio was the powerful medium that Franklin D. Roosevelt used to help bind and heal a troubled nation. In his first inaugural address, FDR's calming voice was carried into the homes of millions of Americans as he assured them that "the only thing [they] had to fear was fear itself." Later, Roosevelt's fireside chats helped comfort the nation as it fought off the ravages of the Great Depression and faced the early years of World War II.

Anyone who lived though the early years of America's space program, leading to Neil Armstrong's walk on the moon, or the assassination of President John F. Kennedy, when the nation mourned together over a fitfully long weekend in 1963, will readily appreciate the bonding effect of broadcasting during certain momentous events. For those of more tender years, events like the Persian Gulf War of 1990 or the death of Princess Diana of Great Britain in 1997 may have invoked similar feelings. Most recently, the terrorist attacks that struck New York City and Washington, D.C., nearly simultaneously on 11

September 2001 again reminded us of the crucial role the electronic media play in providing some level of comfort to all citizens in the most troubling of times. Especially in the early hours and days of a crisis, seeing and hearing familiar media personalities as they relay crucial unfolding events is reassuring, or at least highly preferable to the alternatives: widespread pandemonium (in the absence of any instantaneous, live media reporting by established journalistic enterprises) or widespread suspicion (with the only information coming from jittery government spokespersons). In short, no open society can successfully navigate the troubled waters of a national threat or impending disaster without a free and credible media.

The bond that Americans have with their local newspaper and broadcast stations is longstanding. It is integral to the American system and experience. Affordable newspapers with a more generalized orientation arose in the early nineteenth century to give all Americans, not just elite Americans, a regular source of news and information. When radio appeared a generation later, it was not just an instant success in major metropolitan areas. Right from the start, it also popped up in small college towns, rural America, and newly emerging suburban areas. Lee DeForest, the self-styled "father of radio," was eager to proclaim this first electronic mass medium as a special social elixir:

> Radio has kept the wanderer home at nights, it has brightened the gloom of separation and shortened the long hours of loneliness. It is a comforting companion to the shut-in; it soothes the pain of the suffering. It brings counsel to the housewife, information to the farmer, entertainment and gaiety to the young. On silent wings it flies to the forgotten corners where mails are uncertain and few, where the cheer of kindly voices comes only through the head-phones, where music is never heard . . .[9]

A more contemporary voice ascribes a similar, if less grandiose, role to television: "Television is our common cultural ground," notes media critic Charles Paul Freund. "It is the only thing most Americans know and experience more or less together, and whatever is next on the list is small beer compared to it."[10]

Television, newspapers, radio, magazines, movies, and the worldwide web all connect and add context to our lives. They entertain us and provide a shared cultural awareness. Other than work or sleep, most Americans spend more time watching, listening, reading, or connecting with some form of media than they expend on any other concentrated activity. Indeed, as Croteau and Hoynes point out, some

even "argue that [mass] media have become the dominant social institution in contemporary society, supplanting the influence of older
institutions such as the educational system and religion."[11]

Media Traits Tracking Societal Traits

Covering historic news events and illuminating contentious political issues are certainly among the highest media functions. But the
real spice and flavor of electronic mass media is more frequently
found in the vastly greater number of daily hours devoted to entertainment. From "Seinfeld," "The Simpsons," or the latest dose of
"reality" programming on network television, to "shock" radio and
round-the-clock pumping and preening on MTV, radio and television
are the most common conveyors of American culture—absorbing and
mimicking the varied trends and traits that characterize contemporary
habits and lifestyles.

Although complaints about the adverse impact of mass entertainment are as old as silent movies, there is little question that American
society and popular media have evolved on nearly parallel tracks.
Whereas the typical entertainment program of the 1950s was more es-
capist and less intrusive, matching the tamer lifestyles of that decade,
today's typical program is more hard-hitting, more in tune with contemporary lifestyles. Any "reality" gap that might have existed between what is seen on television or heard on radio and what is hap-
pening in American society on a day-to-day basis has vanished. The
day's events are now reported in real time and unvarnished, and much
of our entertainment has become just as permissive, fast-paced, and
varied as what American audiences routinely experience at work, in
school, or on the street.

For instance, our perception and acceptance of sexual matters has
changed dramatically in recent decades. With popular television
shows now bearing such provocative titles as "Sex and the City" and
"Desperate Housewives" and the content of these and similar shows
more than matching the promise of their descriptive labels, it is obvious how far we have come from the days when TV network standards
flatly prohibited "gratuitous sexual references—implicit or explicit"
(ABC program standards, 1970s) and a now-defunct industry code
opined that "material with sexual connotations, shall not be treated
exploitatively or irresponsibly, but with sensitivity: Costuming and
movements of all performers shall be handled in a similar fashion"

(Television Code, National Association of Broadcasters, January 1980).

Today, American society is awash in sexual content or connotation—most of which is just as accessible and far more graphic than what is generally found in electronic media. Complaints targeting coarse programming on radio or television usually ignore the widespread availability of more ribald material offered by pay cable, motion pictures, video games, magazines, music lyrics, and the Internet. The sexual revolution that made America a more promiscuous nation grew out of the turbulent 1960s, when forces stronger and more integral than mass media were stirring the pot and producing profound changes in the way Americans view their government and each other. As a result, the way sexual conduct and relationships are portrayed in the media today and the openness with which sexually suggestive products are regularly advertised are not necessarily at the forefront of social behavior and belief. Indeed, since television, in particular, is usually the medium most sensitive to public reaction and advertiser pressure, one could legitimately conclude that much of the sexual content seen on television and heard on radio differs little from what is already widely available in the commercial marketplace or otherwise part of most people's lives.

In another sense, mass media help contribute to the altered perceptions Americans have of one another, just as the social conditions helping form those perceptions undergo transformation. Whereas women were often portrayed in sitcoms of the 1950s and early 1960s as relatively helpless, dependent housewives, modern sitcoms paint a more textured and layered woman's role that better conforms to modern life—from working housewife to single mom to strong professional (married or not). In a similar vein, whereas minorities were often portrayed in the cruelest stereotypical manner in the early years of radio and television, such portrayals have virtually disappeared from mainstream broadcasting. It is worth noting, however, that not until the rise of the civil rights movement in the 1960s did racial stereotypes really begin to evaporate in the broadcast media. Now, of course, minorities and all Americans benefit from the more enlightened depiction of minority actors in different roles and characterizations.[12] Whether the mass media led or, more likely, caught up with such societal changes, the worst stereotyping of the past has been eliminated.

One of the things these examples illustrate is that American mass media, at the start of the twenty-first century, stand as a nearly perfect symbol of contemporary American mass culture. What we applaud in today's mass media—the sheer volume and speed of information flow, an updated, more progressive view of women and minorities, and the breadth of artistic achievement—are also strengths of American culture. Conversely, what we criticize in today's media—excessive commercialism, an obsession with celebrities, a coarsening of message, and a quicker pace geared to shorter attention spans—are also traits that permeate the underlying culture.

A Fixation on the Famous and Notorious

Mass media have a unique ability to confer status or notoriety on persons, issues, or movements. In turn, the American public has a seemingly insatiable appetite to read, listen, or watch whatever personality or event is placed under a media microscope. Hardly any medium or person escapes the phenomenon. It is embedded in the culture and found almost everywhere you look.

For instance, look first at contemporary magazines. Some center on a single celebrity—such as Oprah Winfrey or Martha Stewart (whose celebrity status was not even dimmed by time spent in jail). Virtually all feature celebrities on covers or in other prominent positions to stimulate circulation. Even venerable newsmagazines such as *Time* and *Newsweek* have waded into these waters by emphasizing lifestyle features over hard news. For example, in 2001, *Time* magazine inaugurated a five-part series devoted to profiling "America's Best" in entertainment, the arts, and other fields, featuring movie star Julia Roberts as its lead "cover girl." In 2005, *Time* published a "special" issue listing the world's most influential people. The list ranged from Presidents Bush and Clinton, to teenage professional basketball star LeBron James, to the Halo Trinity, a video game. Of course, magazines like *People* and *Us* (two of the most popular overall) make no pretense of being anything but fixated on the famous and notorious.

Look next at the typical chain-operated bookstore. One of the first things you will notice is that the celebrity chase is also rampant in the world of hardbacks and soft covers. Shelves and displays are littered with "books" by all sorts of public figures ranging from politics and arts to cooking and sports. Many are written by people other than their purported authors. It's called ghostwriting (not fraud) and it's common in the literary world. Books that once would have been advertised "by [celebrity figure] with [ghostwriter]," are now frequently merchandised as "by [celebrity]." The deceit is magnified as the celebrity alone hits the talk show circuit to promote the book.

While celebrity and lifestyle features have long held a prominent place in American newspapers, the emergence of *USA Today* greatly raised the celebrity-seeking tendency of daily newspapers. Celebrity-related pictures and stories now commonly appear on the front pages, whereas in the past they were more typically relegated to the style or entertainment sections. The renewed popularity of the tabloid format by some metropolitan dailies fits perfectly with the tabloid style, emphasizing the visual and sensational.

Twenty-five years ago, "Entertainment Tonight" ("ET") legitimatized celebrity news as a daily genre on television, spawning numerous copycat competitors.[13] Today, America's television screens are filled with flickering images of "ET" almost around the clock. "Access Hollywood" is currently "ET"'s strongest competition, but daily versions of "Inside Edition," "The Insider," and "Extra" appear on many over-the-air stations as well. On cable, one can find other celebrity-based features such as "E News Daily," "Celebrity Profile," and "True Hollywood Story"—all standard fare on the "E" channel—and "Hollywood Lives and Legends" on American Movie Classics. Not celebrity news, but still heavily steeped in celebrity guests and happenings are such popular syndicated TV programs as "Live with Regis and Kelly."

The emphasis on celebrity status in our culture goes beyond an obsession with the lives and activities of public figures. It is also found in the growing tendency to rate and rank virtually everything. Magazines, newspapers, and TV shows have, for years, reviewed and ranked the "best of" movies, shows, cars, or stars. And opinion polls offer their own brand of rankings on almost everything under the sun. But we have taken this exercise to new heights (or lows) in the last few years. The highest-grossing movies (hence the most popular) over the weekend are now routinely reported as "news" in Monday morning newspapers and on Monday morning radio and television programs. A "top 10," "top 25," or "top 100" list is now what garners the greatest media attention and, in turn, gives the person, thing, or entity being ranked the greatest credibility. Once-proud universities now maneuver for cherished position in yearly magazine rankings along with listings of the best preschools. The best doctors, lawyers, chefs, and hairdressers are tallied in the latest lifestyle magazine, leaving the vast hordes of those not placed in the media spotlight to wallow in their obvious lack of credibility. About the only groups to have escaped a "best of" list conferring celebrity status are priests and police officers. It is probably only a matter of time.

Once published and relentlessly publicized, it is hard to put such lists in proper perspective or subject them to appropriate scrutiny. They are on public view for all to see and almost always afford the featured person or thing some degree of status and credibility. If someone is mentioned or appears enough in the media, that person is clearly viewed differently, even by those who knew the person before their moment in the spotlight. The media's tendency and society's willingness to gauge credibility and status by how well someone is known can be just as invasive and negative as it is fawning and positive. While most published lists are cast as "best of" and not "worst of"—for obvious reasons of public interest and potential liability— the public and media easily revel in celebrity figures that are more notorious than admirable. Sports, entertainment, and politics produce many unfavorable portraits of public figures—but celebrity figures nonetheless.

Our emphasis on celebrity status goes beyond just famous or infamous people, affecting the way we increasingly approve or view anything —movies, restaurants, neighborhoods, services, clothes, and products of infinite variety. We look for confirmation in a published list or media exposure before giving anything credibility—exalting the status attributed to something by others over our own self-examination and independent judgment. What is the "buzz," we want to know? Are people talking about something before we pass judgment or accept, acknowledge, or use? Is it trendy?

Frank Rich, writing in the *New York Times* on Memorial Day weekend in 2001, observed that Hollywood research had confirmed that a far larger percentage of the public knew about *Pearl Harbor*, the motion picture, opening that holiday weekend than they knew about Pearl Harbor, the historical event. He continued:

> In the American marketplace of ideas, product recognition rules, and so this weekend's most prevalent tribute to those who fought and died for our country will be the lines for Disney's three-hour salute to the Greatest Generation. Pearl Harbor may have been a day which was supposed to live in infamy, but the infamy of 1941 is no match for the fame conferred by publicity in 2001.[14]

For years, critics and social scientists have argued that a "cult of celebrity" can undermine respect for individuality and potentially erode other values. Some even suggest that superficiality and sensationalism contribute to the diminution of moral judgments and a general breakdown in authority and virtue.[15] I doubt whether the level of fixation I comment on here is that deleterious. Fame and celebrity status is not unique to contemporary life. Celebrities or exalted figures have always been part of developed societies.[16] What has changed is the speed with which fame can be created and spread and the more intimate feeling modern media can engender between the famous and the fan. I do not suggest that the images and symbols exalting celebrities in today's mass media will necessarily transform audiences into unthinking robots or hopeless introverts. Rather, what I fear is that this incessant emphasis on the famous and notorious will transform the mass media experience, so vital to a vibrant, self-governing society, into a more shallow, superficial, increasingly useless experience for many Americans.

The Loss of Reflection

An obsession with people or things popularized by media attention or published rankings solidifies a society in which style not only sells, but wins. We become accustomed to looking for and accepting rankings and snapshot judgments on matters that could benefit from more study or independent thought. I call this a loss of reflection, a process by which parts of American culture are being simultaneously speeded up and "dumbed down." Everything is "cool" (or not) depending on how it is perceived. Life is so speeded up that, increasingly, there is little time for anything not immediately visible or disposable with a quick comment or judgment.

Not only does this turn life upside down, ensuring that style often trumps substance, but the loss of reflection makes us a less serious, less engaged society that, in turn, impairs the effectiveness of our democratic system. If we ignore this trend or cast it aside as merely one of the unfortunate side effects of our high-tech, fast-paced business and private lives, the impact could be profound and long-lasting. Left unchecked, it will accelerate negative strains already apparent in our media and culture, making education more difficult and daily life more challenging and, ultimately, less satisfying.

We did not lower standards or become more superficial by suddenly shifting into reverse. We have been heading in the same unmistakable direction for years. And, with evidence of accelerated lifestyles and an eroding attention span permeating mass media daily, it seems unlikely these tendencies will be turned around anytime soon. The loss of reflection in a society increasingly given to fast-talking, fast-acting multitasking is both confirmed and magnified by contemporary mass media. The glibness and premium placed on quick action seeping into so many social encounters is already deeply ingrained in modern media, especially broadcasting. Because commercial media cater to younger demographics—teenagers, young adults, and, most broadly, those eighteen to forty-nine years old—themes and styles (in both entertainment and advertising) are carefully chosen to reflect those target audiences. Motion pictures tilt toward action-adventure because it is thought to be more attractive to a more impatient new generation of ticket buyers. Likewise, television programming typically caters to a younger target audience that favors a quicker, steady stream of action—looking to being entertained without being entertained *and* absorbed. Even public affairs and talk shows depend more upon fast-paced theatricality than thoughtful dialogue and reflection. Despite scores of news and information services operating twenty-four hours a day, seven days a week, nuance and complexity almost always give way to glibness and brevity. As critic Tom Shales observes, the typical TV talk show today finds the host "utter[ing] Pavlovian prompts" and guests spitting out "programmed responses." Genuine conversation and anecdotes are discouraged since, as Shales notes, they just "take too much time."[17] The best known experts in politics and the social sciences are no longer those who think the deepest but those who know how to condense their answers to thirty seconds or deliver the best sound bites.

In radio, stations are highly formulaic, offering niche services typically favoring superficial pace over thoughtful reflection. Usually, listeners are fed music of only one genre by highly generic disc jockeys. Any interruption for news and information is kept to a bare minimum. Even when stations elect something less bland, it is rarely more reflective. More than likely, it is live banter by announcers hoping to "get in your face" by suggestive, titillating remarks. Indeed, in many cases, "talk" radio has become audience-baiting radio, purposely intended to stir controversy or to shock by dialogue that is both real and fabricated.[18] Or it has become agenda-setting radio with hosts more dedicated to spewing their own views than listening to or absorbing the views of others.

Daily newspapers have not only become more colorful and sprightly, they have added special features, even special editions, designed to attract more youthful, action-oriented readers who have been drifting away to other, speedier, more convenient sources of information. Starting in 2002, major metropolitan dailies in New York, Chicago, Philadelphia, and Washington, D.C., began experimenting with shorter, hipper, youth-oriented tabloids to draw this audience back.[19] At the same time, some of the more sedate newspapers of Europe, or broadsheets, as they are often called, have started publishing slimmer, down-sized, less-serious tabloid editions in order to attract younger readers with material better tailored to more youthful lifestyles.[20] In some cases, compact, more "readable" formats have completely replaced the old broadsheets. As one editor of the venerable *Times* of London explained, the change results in "less stories, more headlines," because "we're in an Internet age, a headline age."[21] In late 2005, the *Los Angeles Times*, America's fourth-largest daily newspaper, announced that it would henceforth emphasize shorter stories, increase coverage of celebrities, and introduce a special subscription package that would include only the Friday through Sunday editions (hoping to win back busy readers, at least on weekends).[22]

Many magazines have also adopted glitz over content for busy and less reflective readers. Some have become nearly all visual with no literary pretense whatsoever. Yes, we still have *Atlantic Monthly*, the *New Yorker*, and the *National Review* serving small elite audiences, but most magazines today (whether mass circulation or specialty) are more celebrity conscious than cerebral. For example, men's magazines like *Maxim*, *Stuff*, and *FHM* "are unapologetically formatted for people who do not read." An official of *Stuff* magazine proclaims, "What we do is more like movies than traditional magazines." "We are utterly of the moment and utterly disposable."[23] Similarly, the editor of *Maxim* boasts, "Our readers [mainly young men] are busier today than they will ever be in their lives; they have shorter attention spans than any previous generation; they are chronically over-stimulated and easily bored." And, the editors of *Rolling Stone*, once known for reflective, long-form articles, now sing the same sad tune: "People just don't have much time to read." As they explain, "Back when *Rolling Stone* was publishing [those] seven-thousand word stories, there was no CNN, no Internet."[24]

If Americans are spending less time with serious newspapers and meaty magazines, it is hardly surprising that they also have a diminished appetite for book-length material. Indeed, a 2004 survey by the National Endowment for the Arts found that less than half of the adult population now reads for pleasure. Young adults between the ages of eighteen and thirty-four, once ranked as the most active reader group, is now the least active, dropping 28 percent since 1982.[25] There is even evidence that people spend more time learning *about* books then they do reading books. They scan print reviews, watch or listen to interviews of authors on radio and television, or tune in to celebrities like Oprah Winfrey who regularly trumpet their favorite books. Just as often, they surf the Internet for random tidbits about books and authors, a process that almost always favors speed over reflection. As Philip Roth, America's literary lion puts it, there has been a "sea change" in American culture from serious fiction to "the screen." "First, the movie screen, then the computer," Roth says. "The human mind prefers the screen."[26]

One would assume, from listening to radio, watching television, or even perusing certain daily newspapers, that audiences do not want to be bothered with anything but capsule news and information—and even then only with material tending more toward amusement or fascination than understanding. Virtually all commercial radio news, even news distributed by national networks, has been reduced to little more than headlines. A three-minute newscast, *with* commercial interruptions, is relatively long on most radio stations. Television news, still presented mostly in half-hour or longer segments, also follows a similar up-tempo, short-story style.[27] Even with more air time, TV favors softer, personality-oriented news when it is not covering crime and human tragedy. The talking heads and in-depth pieces are left to public stations.

Despite the time-worn assumption that if only our popular media were to provide more thoughtful, longer forms of news and information, they would be eagerly embraced by a waiting audience, there is no credible evidence to support this claim.[28] Instead, modern society and today's popular media seem increasingly wedded to a faster-pace, less reflective approach. It is the 24/7 attitude that sweeps over life, business, and most media content. Little time is left for engaging others or using media sources in any serious, thoughtful way.[29] Being "connected" and "in touch" is a constant in both our business and private lives. And technology keeps pushing the process to new limits. It started with facsimile machines, then voicemail, pagers, cell phones, e-mail, portable PCs, and, most recently, versatile handheld devices performing multiple functions. You must not only stay in touch, you must respond quickly as well. In the end, you spend more time processing—connecting, checking, reviewing, and then replying quickly—and less time in reflecting on the substance of the subject being covered.

It is difficult envisioning a reversal of this trend. If anything, mass media seem more committed than ever to reaching a younger audience. And the audience they are targeting has grown up with MTV and the Internet. Nonstop action facilitated by fast and crimped speech or writing are the stuff these electronic environs are made of. Short-hand, sloppy writing, in fact, is accepted in Internet communication as the norm—because getting the message communicated quickly seems more important than crafting something that would reflect more careful thought. Instead of considering what to say, many people send e-mail messages where their thoughts just drool out onto the screen. The point-and-click technique that has become the very hallmark of the Internet actually accentuates using shortcuts to navigate and communicate. Today's craving for rapid-fire communication has even produced a whole new Internet lexicon—where, for example, the opening query "Are you there?" comes out *AYT*, or where online chat room participants are asked to identify themselves with *A/S/L*, for age, sex, and location.[30] When the communication is text messaging on a tiny handheld device, abbreviated, less reflective speech becomes essential.

Another reason for this breezy, less focused approach to life on the Internet is that many users today, especially young users, combine online time with other activities. In fact, a particularly dexterous youthful media practitioner may be engaged in TV viewing, e-mailing, Internet surfing, and telephoning all in the same sitting—a multitasking grand slam.[31] On the other hand, kids who send instant messages to friends while watching music videos while doing their homework are likely to be more tuned into the multimedia world than focused on their studies.

Multitasking, of course, is also practiced by older Americans. What urban dweller has not witnessed someone hailing a cab, making a purchase, approaching a bank teller, or descending an escalator while also carrying on a cell-phone conversation? Or seen someone attempting to unobtrusively check e-mail messages on a handheld device while sitting in a private meeting or attending a public event? Now, with the advent of miniature-screen, handheld video receivers and four-minute versions of some popular programs, it is possible to pass the time commuting, taking one's lunch break, or standing in line at Starbucks while getting a quick video fix.

But speed and ease of accessing data may have a cost—if the process of information gathering is valued over the process of deliberation, if breadth is substituted for depth, and if the prepackaged arguments of others are, for speed and convenience, too often favored over one's own. Ask today's teachers or other professionals who emphasize research and writing and they will acknowledge that computer technology is beginning to shape the thinking skills of youthful writers. Increasingly, the first recourse for most students, as well as young journalists or lawyers, is the Internet—for virtually any kind of information. They are able to make more connections, sift more data, and generate work product far more quickly than previous generations. But, again, at what cost? Is the quality of information comparable to what is available in print? More important, is the thinking process diluted? While subscription-based sources such as Nexis offer a higher-quality, better organized research tool than the "free," largely disorganized web, they still encourage quick responses that can lack the context or nuance of more deliberative research. As Bernard Cooperman notes, "The Web is designed for the masses. It never presents students with classically constructed arguments, just facts and pictures."[32]

Another, somewhat different interlacing of contemporary lifestyle and mass media experience is found in cable's great success story, MTV. Today, MTV reaches about 350 million households in 140 countries, nearly 80 million alone in the United States. MTV is an instantly recognizable brand that stands for young and cool around the world. As *USA Today* reported on MTV's twentieth anniversary in 2001, this specialty network "has a lock on the coveted demographic, ages twelve to twenty-four. The way this age group looks, talks, acts and consumes material goods is molded by the clothes, music and attitudes aired on MTV's programming and youth-slanted commercials."[33] And, the way MTV ensures that the way this age group looks, talks, and acts on television reflects real lifestyles is to conduct its own continuous, sophisticated research on the changing habits and tastes of its target audience.

One of the signature characteristics of MTV is a fast-paced, action-filled, glossy approach—whether the material is music, fashion, dialogue, or even the occasional serious issue. There is, in fact, a "classic MTV technique of quick-cutting and color-drenched imagery" combined with a "whole bag of [other] tricks."[34] With Hollywood movies now being made by former MTV music video directors, no one should be surprised that the teen culture born and bred on MTV is increasingly infiltrating the movie industry. The effects have also been evident on over-the-air broadcasting. At the start, local stations and network services simply offered their own music video shows. Later, network television began featuring dramas that mimicked MTV's pattern of quick-cut editing with integral music. TV historian Tim Brooks notes that "beyond the literal aping of MTV, you have fast-paced shows" such as youth-oriented police dramas that typically "do things fast and furious."[35] The most often-cited example of this is "Miami Vice," a highly popular mid-1980s network show which set long-lasting trends in fashion and storytelling on television. Other, more recent shows like "Gilmore Girls" on The CW are purposely shot to achieve a dizzying pace. Targeting teenagers, "Gilmore Girls" emphasizes fast talking and frequent walking from place to place while deemphasizing "close-ups" (which, of course, slow things down). And, producers of "West Wing," with a more mature audience than "Gilmore Girls," reportedly found another reason to speed up the dialogue: if actors are portrayed talking faster the audience will think that people who talk faster are somehow smarter.[36] Even a family drama like NBC's "American Dream," a rare success story for this genre in the early 2000s, typically included as many as seventy-five scene changes in a single one-hour episode, a frantic pace compared to the forty scene changes that might have accompanied similar dramas in the past.[37] Although the program was set in the 1960s and covered serious issues like the Vietnam War and racial discrimination, the actual pacing of the show was more attuned to TV viewers who grew up with MTV.

If, as seems likely, future television and cable channels are able to offer greater audience interactivity, the foregoing trends will become even more pronounced. Younger, developing generations who have grown up with such techniques and mastered multitasking will most easily adapt to the full promise and impact of media interactivity. With more rather than less distractions, all moving at rapid speeds across our lives and culture, the temporary loss of reflection we have already experienced threatens to become a more permanent condition.

The United States has become a 24/7, less reflective society following a series of social upheavals, all of which strongly influence how we use and absorb mass media. The United States has the longest workday and workweek in the developed world.[38] Dual working parent households, single-parent families, suburbanization, longer commuter distances and times, and failing institutions have all contributed.

Weekends that are just as overscheduled as workdays and stores and services that never shut down both fit the pattern and further stimulate the activity level. And, the power of the Internet and other mass media to keep us surfing, chatting, and buying without limits just keeps everything churning—at breakneck speed. Commerce on the Internet, in fact, is often so fast-paced that not only does communication suffer, ethics suffer. To some business ethicists, the sheer speed of the activity is largely to blame. "One of the problems is that ethics implies deliberation," notes Dennis Moberg, director of Markkula Center for Applied Ethics at Santa Clara University. It connotes "periods of contemplation and deliberation, and working through a moral calculus." Precious time exists for "navel gazing" when everyone is "moving @ Internet speed." Adds Kirk Hanson, a senior lecturer in ethics at Stanford University, it's not that ethically challenged people are "evil . . . just that in the rush, a lot of things just don't get reflected upon."[39]

Working Americans seem to compress more activities into the same number of daylight hours and are then heard to complain about a lack of time. With more available information, greater disposal incomes, and higher levels of education, one's schedule of activities and experiences is expanded. So we speed up, multitask, cut corners. Technology, producing more devices and outlets, both frees us and enslaves us. Mass media, as the messenger of this new cultural course, adopts and enforces the same trends. We work, move, and even relax at home in a culture of interruption—because we are so connected, all the time. Connectivity without either time or disposition to synthesize the cascade of information is, ultimately, less productive and less satisfying.

Broadcasting, the Internet, and many of today's newspapers and magazines are uniquely geared to a fast-paced, ephemeral experience. The presumed need for immediacy (often eschewing editing or oversight) and the competitive fear of being rejected by a fast-clicking, channel-changing, headline-reading, picture-oriented audience inevitably pushes contemplation into the corner. Confronting more time pressures in their daily lives and overwhelmed by the constant rush of information, is it any wonder that many Americans, especially younger ones, seem to have adopted the same transience of attention and reflection? The computer mouse and television remote have become the tools of our impatience and eroding contemplation. Alvin Toffler, the guru of "third wave information technology," captured this dilemma more than two decades ago:

New information reaches us and we are forced to revise our image-file continuously at a faster and faster rate. . . . This speedup of image processing inside us means that images grow more and more temporary. Throwaway art, one-shot sitcoms, Polaroid snapshots, Xerox copies, and disposable graphics pop up and vanish. Ideas, beliefs and attitudes sky-rocket into consciousness, are challenged, defied, and suddenly fade into nowhere-ness.[40]

There is, it should be noted, nothing revolutionary about a stepped-up pace of activity. Society has historically advanced by achieving greater speed in production, transportation, and communication. The sense of greater speed today comes, no doubt, from greater urbanization —where rapid movement is essential to many activities or lifestyles. It is magnified by the onslaught of personal gadgets and devices that appear so quickly and spread through society so rapidly. It simply takes less time today for inventions that affect daily lives to become widely used in daily lives. Then, when you add thousands of media outlets flooding our consciousness with endless content, the sense of speed is nearly palpable. As sociologist Todd Gitlin observes, "The most widespread, most consequential speed-up of our time is the onrush of images—the speed at which they zip throughout the world, the speed at which they give way to more of the same, the tempo at which they move."[41] Paraphrasing Gitlin, how fast can this montage go without leaving reflection (he says "perception") behind?[42] A more superficial society soaked by a relentless stream of media sounds and images runs the risk of becoming just that—more superficial and more overwhelmed. If one is swimming against the same unremitting tide most waking hours, little time is left for real dialogue, real connection, or meaningful participation in civic and social affairs.

Recent surveys point to a decline in the types of activities that lend cohesion and efficiency to a culture. Fewer people joining community organizations or turning out for elections are usually cited.[43] This tendency arrives in American society just as we are inundated with expanded information and improved technology allowing, even encouraging, a more personalized, private media experience. This could be a particularly unhealthy confluence. An increasingly apathetic, less engaged citizenry increases the possibility that a more controlling, less responsive government might emerge. A representative democracy requires thought and patience, if only to get through the often lengthy, unwieldy deliberative process. Modern media such as twenty-four-hour, continuous news services and the Internet invite instant thinking, often specializing in unfiltered information and opinion. They operate at breakneck speed and in a competitive environment which puts a premium on reducing complex thoughts and provocative ideas to the most simplistic, succinct form possible.

Pointing to the loss of deliberation (a close cousin of reflection) attributable to Internet usage and contemporary "talk radio," Benjamin R. Barber warns of "unmediated communication." The immediacy of the Internet is not only "a democratic virtue . . . it is also a democratic vice, because unmediated conversation can be undisciplined, prejudiced, private, polarizing, and unproductive."[44] "Talk radio," he says, represents a particular warning sign. "Calling itself 'democratic,' it actually encourages immoderate views, divisiveness, impulsive [nonreflective] rhetoric, and foolishness. The unmediated exchange of violent prejudices does nothing for conversation and still less for democracy."[45] Exchanging or collecting thoughts in cyberspace, participating in rant and rave radio, or just watching one's favorite cable news channel is far more likely to fuel partisanship than stir real debate or serious reflection. Out of the cacophony of voices and images propelled by today's mass media, it is the most shrill, opinionated, and fast talking that is most likely to achieve greatest prominence. Slower-talking, more equivocal, more reflective persons need not apply.

One final reflection is apropos of this section. If, as many critics claim, mass media are largely to blame for the foregoing trends, why do the more serious media outlets—and there are many—not attract more stable audiences, catching at least a few of the readers and viewers retreating from the pabulum increasingly served by commercial broadcasting, popular magazines, and jazzed-up newspapers? Part of the problem is that, even as we are threatened from the outside world as never before, we live in a society where the dominant lifestyles have become less compatible with the mission of more serious newspapers, magazines, and broadcast journalism. Is it reasonable, therefore, in light of such developments, to expect our popular mass media, so dependent upon the vagaries of popular tastes, to become more serious and reflective when, at the dawn of the twenty-first century, most American citizens read less, move faster, and pause to reflect less?

6

Evaluating Mass Media Performance in a Deregulatory Era

Deregulation—the dominant public policy theme for the past twenty-five years—is premised on the theory that stimulating economic competition in the marketplace will produce source and content diversity better than that produced by government regulation. That is a point worth emphasizing. We did not start down the deregulatory road expecting to arrive at a new media wasteland. Rather, the overwhelming public policy objective—wrapped in an ascending regulatory philosophy, stirred by shifting political winds, and capped by a grandiose legislative initiative—was to stimulate greater competition leading to better overall service to the American public.

Before critiquing the electronic media's actual performance in specific categories, it may be useful to highlight anew the vastly different regulatory stage designed by policymakers. Today, with most performance standards abandoned, license renewal reduced to a postcard mailed in once every eight years, public participation minimized, and the threat of a "competing offer" for one's license finally gone, a new regulatory order reigns. By removing basic standards and eliminating serious challenges, deregulation has simply eviscerated any remaining licensee accountability. A broadcast station today worries about its bottom line but fears not its ability to keep its license to operate. At the same time, the FCC has become a largely toothless agency— aggressively enforcing only broadcast indecency (still banned by criminal statute) and a few technical rules. With individual policymakers

willing to halt the drumbeat of deregulation being about as rare as a
Puccini devotee at a rap concert, the effects were highly predictable.
They included:

1. An overall *increase* in the volume and variety of media outlets
   available to the public—specifically, larger total numbers of FM radio stations, AM radio stations, UHF television stations, over-the-
   air television networks, cable and satellite channels, Internet websites, and specialty or suburban newspapers ("competition").
2. An overall *decrease* in the number of owners of radio, television,
   and daily newspaper properties, especially in many local markets ("consolidation").
3. The emergence of a few dominant media conglomerates spanning
   many media and media-related businesses, resulting in more centralized control of divergent media services ("concentration").
4. The survival of a few failing media properties by virtue of sales,
   mergers, or joint operational arrangements previously disallowed.
5. The achievement of certain operational efficiencies and cost savings by media businesses allowed to own and manage multiple
   outlets serving the same general market.
6. An increased level of commercialism infecting virtually all media.
7. The increased fragmentation of audiences both within one
   medium and over a much broader media landscape.
8. A decreased emphasis on or total abandonment of news and
   public affairs by an increasing number of broadcast stations,
   combined with a heightened focus by virtually all stations on
   lighter, more entertainment-oriented features that sell better in a
   more competitive, fragmented media environment.

Some of these trends were expected, even promised. Some result directly from government policymaking. Others are the inevitable consequence of maturing businesses facing more competition and evolving
technology. Some are even positive, reinforcing what media in a democratic society are capable of doing and competitive businesses in a
capitalistic economy must do. On balance, however, it is hard to assess
these changed conditions objectively and conclude that the combined
effect of altered public policy and restructured markets has produced a
media more responsive to public needs or more conducive to public
dialogue. Whether stirred by changes in public policy, technology, or,
more broadly, tremors throughout the whole social order, they collec-

tively show how mass media in the twenty-first century are either less inclined or less able to fulfill some of the vital roles they assumed (or were presumed to have assumed) during the twentieth century.

CONCENTRATION

The concentration of power in electronic media and its potential influence on media performance are not new issues—they have been around for years, starting with the forced breakup of NBC's two national radio networks in the early 1940s.[1] Similarly, flash back to the late 1960s and behold how regulatory authorities reacted to the prospect of a major broadcaster being compromised merely by association with certain nonbroadcast interests. In rapid succession, a proposed merger between ABC and International Telephone and Telegraph floundered on regulatory and antitrust grounds before failing and, just a few months later, a hostile takeover of ABC by the notorious recluse Howard Hughes was thwarted. In both cases, concerns were expressed that the news operations of a national network and its local stations not come under the potentially negative influence of conflicting business interests—whether in the hands of a transnational corporation or a mysterious mogul.

One might have thought that the massive, step-by-step deregulation of electronic media in more recent years, at a time when technology was transforming the information business and combinations of previously unknown size and shape were being formed, would have given rise to similar questions. It has not. Indeed, media mergers far larger than anything faced in the 1940s or 1960s are approved today without any examination whatsoever of the impact such business arrangements might have on the news function or the broader marketplace of ideas. As a result, we have far larger companies engaged in more diverse media activities. If, like General Electric (NBC), they also own vast nonbroadcast interests and hold billion-dollar government contracts, no questions are asked. Whereas in the past, broadcast, movies, music, and other media activities were controlled by a distinct and separate set of players, at the start of the twenty-first century all major commercial networks, all major Hollywood studios, most leading newsmagazines, most leading television and radio stations in the biggest markets, most leading cable and satellite program services (including all the twenty-four-hour news services), most recorded music sold in the United States, many leading book publishers, and a host of prominent websites and Internet news services are all in the hands of the Big Five media conglomerates described in chapter 4.

That being said, a brief clarification is still in order. When critics speak of consolidation and concentration in the media business, they usually draw an image of a few giants gobbling up everything and stifling all competition. Actual marketplace facts, however, produce a more nuanced landscape. In some cases—such as local radio—concentration has indeed greatly reduced competition, certainly among over-the-air stations. But that is only part of the picture. Those local clusters owned by a few national radio companies now face competition from two satellite radio companies that each supply more than two hundred separate channels of music, news, information, and lifestyle programming. They also face an audio explosion of nearly limitless proportions from the Internet and an ever-expanding universe of more mobile, more versatile listening and recording devices. None of this competition existed in preregulatory days.

In television, some competitors in some local markets have also been allowed to combine forces, significantly reducing competition. But, it also needs to be pointed out that in virtually every local television market (big and small) the number of stations operating has increased substantially since the late 1970s. And, like radio stations, all of these television stations face competition from two satellite services that now supply over two hundred video channels each. They also face competition from cable systems and, increasingly, telephone companies, which pump hundreds of video services into their markets. Most of this competition did not exist in preregulatory days.

Even in the newspaper business, where most cities support only one daily paper, digital and satellite technology now make it possible for readers to get leading national newspapers—such as *USA Today*, the *Wall Street Journal*, and the *New York Times*—from boxes on the street or couriers in their local neighborhood. Or they can turn to a growing number of suburban or specialty newspapers. Still curious, they can read daily newspapers from almost everywhere, online.

The point is, we have a concentration problem, but it is not necessarily manifested in a reduced number of competitive sources—at least in any across-the-board fashion. What we really have—amongst an otherwise competitive market—are a few giant companies that have been able to combine far-flung media operations on a national basis, as never before, and an unprecedented clustering of media outlets under common ownership in many local markets.

On the other hand, when deregulatory advocates argue that broadcasting is not as concentrated as many other American businesses—noting, for example, that the biggest radio operator owns only about 10 percent of the total number of radio stations nationwide—they conveniently ignore three obvious points. First, the greatest degree of concentration has occurred on the local level where one or two radio operators often own all the dominant stations and garner the lion's share of audience and revenues. Not quite the monopoly position of the local utility company, but the envy of most other businesses nevertheless. Second, broadcasting is not like the automobile or banking business. Its product is speech (visual and audio content) that Americans use and need in ways that differ greatly from how they use and need banks and cars. Third, although one media conglomerate may only control a relatively small percentage of the total number of stations nationwide, the remaining stations (nationally and in key markets) are either controlled by another media conglomerate or they are far less significant—because they are located in smaller markets (reaching fewer people) or because they are confined to nonpremium frequencies (reaching fewer places with less influence).

Another justification for media combinations proffered by merger proponents and eagerly adopted by many policymakers is the prospect that media businesses will achieve operational efficiencies and cost savings. It is the classic justification that has long supported consolidation in virtually all business enterprises. While the separate but related notion that combined operations will also produce vast "synergies" may no longer be highlighted—given some very public, large failures under this banner (such as AOL/Time Warner and Vivendi/Universal)—there is no question that an operator can cut costs and achieve certain efficiencies by combining media activities on either a nationwide or local market basis. The public benefit from such corporate savings, however, is less clear. If cost savings result in staff reductions affecting the production of news and informational programming, the public gains nothing. Even if a failing station is saved by allowing it to be combined with a more profitable, successful operator, the public benefit is marginal. Spectrum that was not being used efficiently or effectively is placed in the hands of a competitor instead of being relinquished for some other nonbroadcast purpose that could more directly benefit a larger segment of the public. That the "surviving" station might now produce a newscast or similar program with the assistance of its more successful competitor (now owner) is not a very persuasive argument. Very few markets really need an additional, copycat newscast. Finally, using public policy to save failing stations is much more difficult to justify at a time when all television stations will have, and some radio stations may have, the ability to broadcast multiple channels of programming over their new digital signals.

Mass media concentration—addressed here and in chapter 4—has been the most visible, readily quantifiable development in the deregulatory era. Less obvious but just as crucial for the American public have been the cascading consequences in such areas as diversity, public service programming, commercialism, conflicts of interest, standards of journalism, and the electoral process. To complete this preliminary grading of mass media in the deregulatory era, one would also need to consider those topics.

DIVERSITY

Diversity has been a bedrock principle of communications policy almost from the beginning. It is usually linked with competition. Indeed, most mass media policymaking today proceeds from an assumption that fostering competition in the provision of media services will ultimately enhance diversity—first, in producing a greater number and variety of outlets, and, second, in producing a greater number and variety of formats, ideas, sources, and perspectives. Without question, the overall number and variety of media outlets today exceed anything available at any time in history. Some even complain of media overload. Despite the great tide of deregulation leading to massive consolidation of ownership, we remain awash in the sheer number of media outlets. Most of this new growth, however, is in nonlocal media—*national* television networks, *national* cable and satellite services, *national* magazines (specialty and general), *national* newspapers (*USA Today*, the *New York Times*, and the *Wall Street Journal*), and *national* (indeed, international) Internet services. In local markets, one is more likely to find fewer daily newspapers and fewer owners of electronic media—even in circumstances where the total number of outlets remains relatively stable. What has changed are government policies that now allow media businesses to either acquire more competitive properties or to combine the operations of newspapers or stations that previously operated independently.

The notion that media ownership in concentrated form produces diverse, conflicting views is intuitively open to suspicion. But, there is also no precise proof that media pluralism equals impartiality and overall balance. We instinctively know that a greater number of out-lets and a more plentiful supply of competitive owners are more likely to produce more diversity than can be produced with fewer outlets and fewer owners, we just do not know how and to what degree. Moreover, concentrated ownership and control is not always antithet-ical to content diversity. A giant radio company with tentacles in vir-tually all entertainment and information businesses and owning as many as eight stations in a given market will obviously program dif-ferent music on most of its local stations. It might even offer conflict-ing or "competing" news/talk formats (one liberal, one conservative), as long as each attracts a sufficient audience and is profitable. And, on the national level, it is possible for multimedia conglomerates to own and control over-the-air, satellite, and cable networks which, collec-tively, represent a relatively diverse array of news and entertainment product.

Nonetheless, the process of consolidation inevitably leads to some sanitization and homogenization of content. Even if they do not in-tentionally exclude ideas or stifle some creative expression, there is a tendency for all large, multifaceted companies to take a similar view and approach on most matters. The "corporate voice" is subtle but of-ten the only voice heard or acted upon. As companies grow larger and amass more and different media interests, they tend to exclude any-thing with limited commercial potential or incapable of benefiting the corporate whole. In this environment, alternative media voices without the same resources—such as independent producers, minor-ity owners, and nonformat-driven radio entrepreneurs—find it diffi-cult to survive, emerge, or be heard. This is not to suggest that large media companies are any different than many other institutions in America. It is understandable when national television networks favor the entertainment product produced by the Hollywood studios they own. Or, once committed to a particular program or talent, they wish to spread it over additional media platforms under their control. Sim-ilarly, with a bunch of different media businesses under the same cor-porate umbrella, it only makes bottom-line sense to use one to pro-mote another. Yet, when a large multimedia company spreads the same content and talent over different outlets and expends significant energy in figuring out how to maximize the common use of such assets, the consumer public loses an opportunity to be exposed to different content and different creative talent in each different outlet.

This homogenization and assimilation of voices has progressed the furthest in radio. With one operator able to control as many as eight radio stations in one large market, instead of competitive voices the public gets one consolidated entity in which the programming, sales, and even engineering skills of all participants are combined into a single effort to achieve *collective* success. The operation is naturally focused on manipulating the many pieces to control the overall market, not to succeed with one single station. In fact, operating a large cluster of local radio stations not only allows the operator to control the largest slice of advertising revenues in the market but to package some of the program formats in a way that allows the operator to "control" a certain demographic group—such as adult males, male teens, or all teens. In turn, the operator gains greater leverage with advertisers who need to reach that target group. But it does not stop there. If you are a contemporary radio giant you are thinking of controlling more than just one market. You operate on a regional and national basis for the purpose of coordinating and assimilating your efforts on a much larger scale. You are not only in the radio station business, you are in the outdoor or billboard advertising business, the TV business and, possibly, the concert and entertainment promotion business. To bring some of these elements together you are also likely to be in the program syndication business—owning regional services that supply "local" weather and traffic not only to your own stations but to hundreds of competitive stations as well. In a similar vein, you probably have contracts with major league talent allowing you to package professional "dj shows" and to syndicate the programs of leading talk show personalities to radio stations anywhere in the country (whether owned by you or not). The synergy that media consolidators often allude to may facilitate efficiencies in operation and the cross-pollination of business interests, but it rarely, if ever, contributes to creativity and performance in either entertainment or journalism. In fact, amassing large, disparate media activities under one big corporate tent is more likely to stifle creativity and enterprise, introducing inherent conflicts that run counter to independent thought and action.

These companies, of course, argue strenuously that despite their vast scope of activities they still operate in highly competitive markets and, more significantly, provide the public with needed diversity. The diversity they usually point to, however, is, at best, nothing more than the superficial sort that existed prior to consolidation. If eight radio stations in a single market but under a common owner follow eight separate program formats, it is probable that the same stations under separate ownership followed a comparable number of distinct program formats (allowing for a few "overlaps" in either case). If one owner controls eight radio stations in a single market, it is reasonable to assume that the program formats followed by each will be among the most popular formats followed anywhere. It is also highly unlikely that any one of those stations will adopt a distinctly alternative format designed to "counter-program" against that owner's more popular or mainstream formats (which might have been the case in preconsolidation days). Indeed, if one company controls the lion's share of the overall audience, it can then strive to control larger portions of the various subcategories of the audience, such as the total news/talk audience. While, in the past, two or three operators might have competed in the same market segment, seeking to push the other out of the format, now the dominant operator's objective is to develop synergy between different "products" within the same cluster or subset of stations in the market. For example, an operator with a news/talk cluster in a particular market will want to ensure that each station in the cluster is different yet complementary. Finally, if a large company controls many formats and employs standardized playlists, you naturally have fewer decision makers or risk takers in making programming choices, even if some local autonomy is permitted.

In television, if one national network is allowed to own or, alternatively, strike a partial ownership arrangement with, another national network (such as CBS and UPN; NBC and Telemundo; and NBC and PaxNet) or with a cable network (such as ABC and ESPN; NBC and USA; CBS and MTV; and Fox and FX Channel), it is safe to conclude that they will share and coordinate program product, resources, and program scheduling to an extent unheard of or simply impossible prior to any such combination. If a local television station, under new, more relaxed duopoly rules, operates a second television station in the same local market, it can be expected that the two stations will combine operations, resulting in the reduction and sharing of staff as well as the sharing and coordination of program material.

The most obvious marker of the digital, deregulatory age is the amount of media content. More content, to be sure. More diverse

content, not necessarily. The long-touted five-hundred-channel universe may be approaching its numerical goal on some cable systems
but not without a lot of duplication. Instead of one HBO channel, we
now have eight or ten HBO channels; instead of one shopping, news,
or sports channel, we now have multiple, largely duplicative shopping, news, and sports channels. More diverse, less duplicative content
is available, but mostly in less popular, less affordable media outlets
that existed prior to deregulation.

Diversity in the broadcast media may have suffered its most serious
setback when the deregulatory tide washed away the fairness doctrine
in the mid-1980s. In radio, the impact was particularly immediate and
conspicuous. Freed of any obligation to present contrasting viewpoints
on controversial issues, stations not only devoted less time to public issues, many of them began broadcasting daily blocks of conservative
talk programs, one after another. Once they had formed this day-long
parade of personalities pushing partisan positions—featuring such
right-wing luminaries as Rush Limbaugh, Sean Hannity, Michael Sav-
age, Oliver North, G. Gordon Liddy, and Bill O'Reilly—these stations
simply abandoned any pretense of balance and viewpoint diversity.
Right-wing talk radio, of course, is only one example of a vast array of
contemporary programs, cable channels, and websites that cater to the
special tastes and distinct viewpoints of certain target groups. While
such outlets may succeed in matching media more precisely to the specific tastes and interests of individual listeners and viewers, there remains a decidedly negative side to this trend. Talk programs or even entire news channels skewed toward the interests and biases of targeted,
largely homogeneous audiences are also capable of inhibiting diversity
by harboring more divisiveness.

PUBLIC SERVICE PROGRAMMING

More competitive markets and increased consumer choice have done
nothing to enhance public service programming by commercial
broadcasters. Instead, national networks and local stations uniformly
emphasize less serious news while scheduling fewer programs containing weighty information, enriching entertainment, or uplifting
cultural experiences. Although consumers can purchase cable and
satellite services offering hundreds of channels, including ones devoted to news and information, most of these reach relatively small

audiences and rarely offer anything beyond the simple tracking of daily news stories. Once viewed as a genuine breakthrough in broadcast journalism, nonstop news services like MSNBC, CNN, and the Fox News Channel have either grown "softer"—hiring well-coifed, lookalike anchors and emphasizing human interest stories—or have become "harder," featuring celebrity hosts with unmistakable attitude. Using fast-talking, edgy anchors who can put guests on the spot is just one of the techniques honed in this genre. In short, while more outlets theoretically produce more programming choices, serious public issue or information programming vital to an open democracy is becoming harder to find in commercial broadcasting. The only discernible growth has been in a few niche pay services presenting news and information more as fast-paced entertainment than no-nonsense journalism.

Similar trends are evident on the local level. While some local TV stations broadcast more news—usually the market leaders featuring large blocks of news in the morning and early evening—many stations, not able to sustain a profitable news operation and no longer faced with any regulatory consequences, simply broadcast no news at all. And, the local news the public does get usually involves little more than run-of-the-mill reporting of daily events. In-depth documentaries requiring independent gathering of hard news, never a centerpiece of broadcast journalism, no longer warrant even the occasional sidebar treatment. Rather, more typically, local stations dispense a carefully concocted mix of daily headlines, weather, and sports, interspersed with lifestyle features and breathless remote reports shamelessly hyped by studio anchors as "breaking news." Television, in particular, has turned the term *breaking news*—which, in the past, might have meant something of importance—into nothing more than a stock lead-in phrase to introduce whatever crime or accident scene can be captured live via minicams and satellite feeds during a regularly scheduled newscast. Increasingly, the most distinctive feature of local TV news is its production style—fast-paced, attention-grabbing stories presented by personality-tested, professionally dressed anchors performing on high-tech sets, all under the watchful eye of an outside "news consultant." Nothing is allowed to interrupt the brisk pace or breezy style. If information beyond a headline is needed, today's viewers are simply referred to a station's website.

It would be wrong to presume that mass media in earlier times presented news and information in a more serious, insightful manner.

The history of mass media is too filled with periods and incidents of sensationalistic, personality-focused coverage to make that case. Nevertheless, there is little doubt that, in recent decades, all media— magazines, newspapers, broadcasting, and now the Internet—have tilted more to news of celebrities, personal tragedy, misdeeds, or personal failings of public figures while deemphasizing coverage of government and policy. The Project for Excellence in Journalism conducted a study of the front pages of two newspapers (the *New York Times* and the *Los Angeles Times*), the content of nightly news programs on ABC, CBS, and NBC, and featured stories in *Time* and *Newsweek* magazines. They found that from 1977 to 1997 the number of stories about government dropped from one in three to one in five, while the number of stories about celebrities rose from one in every fifty stories to one in every fourteen. Fewer than one in ten stories concerned the combined topics of education, the economy, foreign affairs, the military, national security, politics, or social welfare. More than half of the stories did, however, focus on lifestyle, consumerism, health, or celebrity entertainment.[2]

Only deregulatory zealots believe that more intense competition in the news and information business leads to higher quality and more diverse news and information. If the deregulatory period tells us anything, it is that more intense competition leads to more imitation and less innovation, more fluff and less serious treatment of issues, and, above all, more, not less, focus on the bottom line (to beat off all the extra competitors).

COMMERCIALISM

Another trend accentuated by heightened competition is increased commercialism. It is not surprising that as media companies have become larger and more diverse, they have sought more opportunities to finance their expanded operations. And, faced with both shrinking audiences and migrating advertising dollars (to other entertainment sources), mainline media have increasingly sold more advertising space using less quality control.

Deregulation of electronic media, which removed meaningful accountability, certainly has contributed to this trend. It has made it much easier for station owners and network companies to view their businesses as serving advertisers instead of audiences—although the two goals have never been mutually exclusive. The new mindset is that if you consolidate operations—by owning two national networks, two local TV stations, or a bundle of radio stations—you not only save costs but can provide advertisers with a more targeted, comprehensive solution to their needs. Large, multifaceted business operations almost always create a strong corporate culture in which finding ways to enhance their products for customers is a paramount objective. In a deregulatory environment, the captains of that corporate culture are given more latitude to regard advertisers as their primary customers. As a result, the signs are everywhere that commercial broadcasting is a changed business, with more emphasis on finding ways to better serve advertisers than audiences.

We have already discussed the virtual disappearance of programming with limited commercial appeal. Another clear sign is the general, overall increase in the amount of commercial matter and promotional clutter in radio and television. Commercial breaks in both entertainment and news programming are not only more frequent but longer. As reported in chapter 4, nonprogram material on the major TV networks has risen to the point where it fills about fifteen minutes of each prime-time hour. In contrast, under the television industry's self-regulatory code in effect until 1984, the standard was nine and one-half minutes per hour. While comparable figures are not available for radio, there is no doubt that many talk stations today broadcast twenty minutes or more of commercials per hour. A decade ago the average would have been closer to one-half that figure. Another difference is that radio stations today often use what the industry calls "stop sets," those dreaded breaks when the music or talk stops and the audience is greeted with eight, ten, or even fifteen minutes of commercials, one right after another. Not long ago, such breaks might have lasted only one or two minutes. Now, when the radio announcer says, "We'll be right back," there might be enough time to run an errand, or even a mile. In a 2002 airing of the 1999 movie *Notting Hill*, starring Julia Roberts and Hugh Grant, ABC stretched this feature film (with a running time of two hours and four minutes) to fill an entire three-hour prime-time period, and they did it twice in the same week. In short, nearly an entire hour of ABC's three hours of prime-time programming on each night was devoted to commercial and promotional material—perhaps more, if the network made any editorial cuts in the movie.

Another sign of soaring commercialism can be found in the commercials themselves—for products and services that in an earlier era would have been banned by self-regulatory measures. Some of this simply reflects more permissive or tolerant strains spreading through the culture. Some is the result of sour economic conditions that made broadcasters in the late 1990s and early 2000s more willing to sell products previously rejected or shunned. Nevertheless, radio and TV stations today are littered with commercials for personal products, health remedies,[3] and questionable financial schemes that would never have found their way into mainstream media in the past. The numerous "herb"-based products intended to enhance one's sexual drive heard on radio stations today—especially on sports talk shows appealing to male listeners—are the twenty-first-century equivalent of the "snake-oil" medicinal remedies that scandalized the early days of radio.

Another sign can be found in the increased willingness of media companies to accept "product placements"—where an advertiser, instead of purchasing a discreet commercial announcement, pays for a mention or use of his product or service that is incorporated into the script or visual portion of a program or movie. The current form of product placement might be better termed "product integration," since the idea is to interweave the commercial and programming content without the audience actually realizing what constitutes the sales pitch. As summarized by *Time* magazine in the summer of 2001:

> Products are becoming part of the show, be it the Taco Bell that's a site of a 'murder' investigation on a new reality show or an SUV used in a TV-staged transcontinental race. . . . This summer, on Fox's *Murder in Small Town X*, 10 contestants will solve a murder mystery in a Maine town peopled by actors and well stocked with Nokia phones, Jeeps and Taco Bell's grilled stuffed burritos. On ABC's *The Runner* . . . a contestant will travel the country, trying to elude capture by viewers who will compete for a growing pot of cash, while driving cars, using ATM cards and scarfing the fast food of yet to be signed patrons. 'The runner lives in the real world, just like you and I', says ABC sales president Mike Shaw. 'If the runner eats lunch at McDonald's in Cincinnati, or shops at Sears, that's all very natural.'[4]

Another version is called "branded entertainment," where not only is a product displayed or mentioned casually, it is intentionally woven into the script and made an integral part of characterizations developed by the program. Advertisers on TV soap operas are no longer content to have their product used by an actor or prominently displayed on the set. Now they want writers to develop script lines specifically designed to include and promote the product in a positive way—for example, building a plot around a certain cosmetic or piece of jewelry.

If these new tactics make it increasingly difficult to know where the commercial stops and the program begins, consider that video technology companies today are able to seamlessly insert modern images of products into the video footage of vintage programs, use the image and voice of a deceased John Wayne in contemporary beer commercials, and even change the sign in a sports stadium or outdoor billboard to depict the image of a paid advertiser during the television broadcast of an event. Digitally inserted ads that, for example, appear painted on signs behind home plate in a baseball game but "really" exist only on the TV screen even have a new name—"virtual ads." Princeton Video Image, a New Jersey firm that developed the sophisticated computer program that makes a yellow line appear on the TV screen as the first-down marker during football games, now offers technology that "will digitally insert products into any show, live or taped, as many times and in as many places as a client [advertiser] desires."[5]

These trends come amidst intensifying concerns in the broadcast industry about how the national networks can retain the bulk of key corporate advertising budgets despite a diminishing share of the overall audience. With hundreds of channels available at the flick of a remote control and personal video recorders making traditional commercials increasingly easy to avoid, advertisers are eager to find different ways to reach the largest number of viewers. Layered on top of this are heightened competitive pressures, which not only continue to send major broadcast companies down the consolidation road but out searching for potentially new business models. Have they reached the limit of what the public will tolerate in blatant commercialism? Will disguised commercial messages that do not interrupt programming be an answer? Will product placements ultimately lead to more direct advertiser control, harking back to earlier broadcast days when a single advertiser purchased and sponsored an entire program—such as the "Kraft Television Theatre" or the "Colgate Comedy Hour"— sharing creative design and other decision making with the broadcast producer?[6] Or will an overly saturated, advertising-supported system gradually give way to an a la carte system where the consuming public makes direct payments for individual, commercial-free programs?

There is little doubt that, without modification or abatement, the level of commercialism will become self-defeating. Broadcasting, unlike print media, is unable to just add pages to accommodate more advertising without necessarily reducing noncommercial content. Rather, in broadcasting, there is a simple, direct relationship—add five minutes of commercial material and delete five minutes of news or entertainment programming. At a certain point, therefore, large segments of the public will be driven away by the increased level and length of broadcast interruptions. Many will migrate to pay services on cable and satellite that offer uninterrupted program features or purchase digital devices capable of stripping out or skipping over commercial messages.

CONFLICTS OF INTEREST

Given the complexity of American society and the critical roles played by mass media, it is not difficult to imagine certain risks in allowing unfettered concentration. We have already touched upon the threat to diversity if the number of independent antagonistic viewpoints is quelled. Another risk is found in business conflicts that can chill the aggressive presentation of important viewpoints. As media giants expand, the conflicts they encounter in disseminating news and information will increase. Having more vested interests in multilinked, far-flung enterprises makes it increasingly difficult for even the most earnest, upstanding media company to avoid stepping on its own interests in reporting news and delivering entertainment and cultural experiences.

National television networks naturally favor program product and talent from the studios, syndicators, and distributors that they own. Large cable companies have long been accused of favoring the cable program services in which they have a direct financial interest. And, early morning and late night talk shows on TV networks routinely feature a parade of celebrities promoting programs, movies, books, and other projects in which the host network often has its own vested interest. Some of this is harmless, even valid promotion for an upcoming movie, news program, or entertainment feature on the same network. On the other hand, some early morning or late night fluff raises legitimate conflict-of-interest questions where, for example, a movie or book is reviewed and it is not made apparent to viewers that the movie or book is produced or published by an affiliated company of the network. More serious conflicts arise when news gatherers and reporters—on the local or national level—are placed in a position of biting the hand that feeds a corporate parent or affiliate. Will reporters in such positions aggressively pursue issues relating to the safety of products produced by other divisions within the same corporate family? Will they openly discuss newsworthy problems affecting other entertainment-based enterprises in which the media company is engaged? And will they report on a questionable environmental record of a corporate parent? For example, how can NBC report fairly and objectively on computer giant Microsoft as long as Microsoft is a major partner of NBC in such ventures as MSNBC and MSNBC.com? Similarly, if a mass media empire like News Corporation routinely takes positions and shapes agenda in prominent outlets like the *New York Post* (a daily newspaper) and the *Weekly Standard* (a weekly, national newsmagazine) how can it maintain its "objectivity" on the Fox News Channel—a news service blatantly self-promoted as "fair and balanced"?

Shortly after Disney acquired ABC, several incidents surfaced to demonstrate that Disney was not likely to let a principle such as news integrity interfere when something as precious as Disney's carefully honed family image was at stake. In one such incident a news investigation of pedophilia and lax security at theme parks, including Walt Disney World, by reporter Brian Ross, was ordered killed by ABC News executives when the potential embarrassment to ABC's corporate parent was apparent. As Neil Hickey points out in the *Columbia Journalism Review*, "Such tensions between TV investigators and their bosses are the inevitable byproduct of the wave of consolidations that swept the industry starting in the mid-1980s."[7] He also quotes long-time TV producer Av Westin: "Michael Eisner [then Disney-ABC], Jack Welch [then GE-NBC], Mel Karmazin [then Viacom-CBS], and Rupert Murdoch [News Corporation-Fox] need never worry that a story done by their news divisions is going to rip the lid off their company, because the guys down below are not going to ok it."[8]

Conflicts of interest, of course, permeate virtually all businesses and societal institutions. Some, like the corporate and Wall Street scandals of the early 2000s, can directly impact the lives and wealth of individuals. In the mass media business, conflicts range from those that are borderline innocuous to those so dangerous that they threaten basic journalistic or creative integrity. A media company, understandably, does not want to broadcast or print something that will denigrate key advertisers, its own performance, or its primary business interests. Media companies that pull their punches in covering a sports franchise because they own the team, own the stadium, hire the announcers, or broadcast the games is one thing. It is quite another when a newspaper or broadcast station avoids a public issue or purposely slants its coverage of an issue because of conflicting business interests. Whether the result of a conscious mandate from corporate headquarters or, as more likely, the reflexive actions of editors and reporters who are generally aware of conflicts and have learned to avoid them as a calculated career move, not covering or not treating such issues surely adds to the distrust and cynicism of the American public toward mass media. More important, allowing one's vast interests and business agenda to affect coverage of public issues strikes at the very heart of the mass media role in a democratic society—presenting vital, fair, and accurate information.

STANDARDS OF JOURNALISM

The effects and changes discussed to this point also contribute collectively to the general erosion of journalistic standards. The concentration of media ownership leading to fewer independent voices in given markets; staff reductions resulting in fewer people to gather and report the news; more intense competitive pressures leading to excesses in advertising; far-ranging business activities of multidimensional companies creating both real and perceived conflicts; and the general "softening" of news and feature stories, all contribute to a vastly different journalistic environment. Thomas Kunkel, dean of the Philip Merrill College of Journalism at the University of Maryland, posits the policy conundrum this way: "In theory, today's media environment should be a godsend for consumers, and in terms of entertainment and sheer access to information, it has been. But the promise of a robust new day in journalism hasn't materialized. Here, if anything, the media frenzy actually has been counterproductive, with competition across the spectrum having become so intense that costs are pared at every turn, and nothing costs more than good journalism."[9]

Journalistic traditions and standards remain relatively strong in this country despite the turmoil caused by years of deregulation, media mergers, and fluctuating economic conditions. Because, with few exceptions, American media are profit-driven, private businesses, it has always been unrealistic to expect a pristine, total separation of the news function from the sales and advertising function. Even though most news media earn their keep by taking paid advertisements from companies they may have to report on, respectable media constantly strive to keep their advertising and editorial staffs apart. Newspapers, with their much larger focus on news and information, have been able to maintain this separation somewhat better than their broadcast brethren. But in the age of consolidation, with increased pressure on media companies to leverage advertisers and spread operational costs over multimedia platforms, this tension has been pushed up a notch even at highly established, big-city daily newspapers. Steven Proctor, deputy managing editor for sports and features at the *Baltimore Sun*, is quoted by Sharyn Vane in a recent issue of the *American Journalism Review*. He says:

> It used to be if you had a newspaper in town, you were able to make a steady profit. Now, like so many other things in the world, newspapers are more at the whim of the opinions of Wall Street analysts. There's a lot more pressure to increase the profit margin of the paper, and so that has led to a lot more interplay between the newsroom and the business side of the newspaper.[10]

Newspapers and magazines, for example, routinely publish "supplements" edited to blend in with the paper or magazine but whose purpose is blatantly commercial.[11] Television stations insert "health-line" features in their newscasts that are largely produced by local medical centers featuring their own healthcare staff. Radio stations air sixty-second "programs" that "bring listeners the very latest medical news from . . . the world's finest health care institutions."[12] Because such "programs" are offered free of charge one must presume such "fine" healthcare centers are dispensing something other than medicine to their "client" radio stations around the country. Both radio and television stations frequently devote discrete half-hour segments to people and products that are packaged exactly like news and information but are nothing more than thirty-minute commercials. In one of the most common, a medical doctor fields soft-ball, scripted questions from paid talent (usually unaffiliated with the station) designed solely to tout the "cure-all" properties of a product personally hawked by the presumed medical professional. Other, less offensive examples include newspapers preparing special sections on weddings, remodeling, and gardening that are little more than a showcase for advertisements and "do-it-yourself" stories generated by merchants selling those products or services.[13]

To date, the typical media response to shrinking audiences and readership has been to become softer, lighter, and shorter. It is, however, an uphill fight. Even as newspapers add more color, feature better graphics, and offer a larger window into the lifestyles of the rich and famous, they continue to lose overall readership, especially younger readers, many of whom are increasingly distracted or apathetic.[14] Even as broadcast and cable channels offer more headline-style news, superficial fluff centered on personalities, and highly condensed bits of information designed for people on the run, a new generation is either tuning out more frequently or finding alternatives on the Internet. This has not, however, stopped news services from trying. CNN, ABC, and CBS each announced in early 2002 that they were aggressively trying to lower the median age of their viewers by better designing news for young audiences. CBS, for example, inaugurated news segments for its MTV and VH1 cable networks and began supervising a newscast on its Black Entertainment Network. CNN, on the other hand, totally revamped one of its news channels to appeal to younger viewers.

> [CNN's] Headline News completed a makeover last summer [2001] that is intended to attract the busy, multi-tasking younger viewers perceived as wanting the news delivered fast and furiously. They also want to have fun. To underscore the point, the revamped Headline News promoted its debut with commercials featuring Moby, the D.J. and singer, and New Order, the alternative pop band.
>
> People should enjoy watching and the anchors are having as much fun as the audience, said Teya Ryan, general manager of CNN Headline News.[15]

These tendencies, while widely reported and a favorite topic of media critics, remain largely anecdotal. The nature and extent of such trends may well depend on one's definition of news, as well as one's perception of what role the media should perform in contemporary society. Nonetheless, certain facts are real and indisputable: (1) audiences for daily newspapers and television news have been dwindling;[16] (2) competition from other news and information sources has caused mainstream news media to make certain adjustments to hold audiences and readers, especially younger ones; and (3) changes in American society continue to impact how media are used. Not only is the computer generation finding ways to customize the news and information they wish to receive, they are adopting lifestyles that leave less time for curling up with an evening paper or watching network television news at a set hour. In fact, since most newspapers arrive only in the morning, when responsibilities for family and work are the greatest, it is increasingly unlikely that younger consumers will embrace the reading and viewing habits of older generations. Life in the fast lane is no cliché to working couples with young children or to virtually anyone else living in major metropolitan areas where available time is effectively compressed by longer commuting times and longer hours at work.

Is it any wonder that our journalistic outlets sometimes become a mirror image of a fast-paced society obsessed with celebrity status and pecuniary pursuits? Newsreaders and anchors who are paid and paraded as celebrities and news organizations that emphasize profits over everything else naturally have a strong influence on the ultimate journalistic product. An approach to news reporting once abhorred as a phenomenon found only in local television news—the "if it bleeds it leads" syndrome, where stories emphasizing personal tragedy push out the "hard" news of the day—has graduated to mainstream national networks. Morning "talk" shows on NBC, CBS, and ABC, always heavily weighted toward entertainment and human interest, have tipped the balance even further in recent years. Such shows often lead and dwell excessively not on national news stories but on stories of human tragedy, personal failings (sometimes triumph), or just the bizarre. They overflow with celebrity features, live musical performances, and interviews with personalities that unabashedly cross-promote entertainment programs appearing in prime time. Even nightly network news is softer. Reacting to competition from cable and the Internet, the showcase evening news broadcasts of ABC, NBC, and CBS are generally faster paced, more sprightly packaged, and filled with announcements cross-promoting the news on other platforms. And, despite an increase in their overall numbers and frequency, network newsmagazines have become more like *People* magaine than hard-charging news documentaries. Don Hewitt, the creator of "60 Minutes," recently observed that

the copycat progeny of his show have become little more than "pro-
motable nonsense."[17]

> As ratings sink even further, the TV news magazines, worried that their
> eye candy isn't emotionally satisfying, try to pluck heartstrings with
> clichés and hype. A recent *Prime-time Thursday* report on a baby born to
> a woman in a coma called the story "emotional and amazing," "full of
> astonishments," "a journey of discovery," "wonderful," "truly extraordi-
> nary," "amazing," "magical," "rewarding," "remarkable," and "almost
> unheard of."
> A [program] form that spins and twists to disguise its own emptiness
> —this is the definition of decadence.[18]

Of course, even if the hard news product of the major networks
is not what it used to be, we now have CNN, MSNBC, CNBC, The
Fox News Channel, and a host of other cable and Internet services
that offer news twenty-four hours a day, seven days a week. Some
might say we have reached news nirvana. Not exactly. A closer look
confirms that we are a long way from the promised land where television news is the constant, uplifting oracle of American democracy. In the first place, these "alternative" video news channels are
little more than niche services, reaching only a fraction of the audience reached by the major broadcast networks. Second, filling the
screen with endless news and information does not produce a fine
new harvest of solid journalism. More often, the type of 24/7 competition engaged in by these services results in news and information being spread so thin that it actually cheapens the national
news product. When studio anchors and remote-location announcers are forced to fill airtime and talk constantly about things and
events that are either breaking or highly fragmentary, you get bab-
ble, not bright commentary based on knowledge and a moment of
reflection. It takes time to figure out the rudimentary elements of
any major news story. Journalism's standing suffers when a twenty-
four-hour news service is so desperate to tell the story—any breaking story—that its reporters are forced to report before they have
been able to gather and digest the key facts. This form of television
news has almost no patience. Talking heads talk to themselves and
others live, on the air, making much of it up as they go along. The
perfunctory, often confusing nature of news coverage on these cable
channels was aptly characterized by Alessandra Stanley in the *New
York Times*:

Facts, half-truths and passionately tendentious opinions get tumbled together on screen like laundry in an industrial dryer—without the softeners of fact-checking or reflection.[19]

For those wanting even breezier, uninhibited content, there is the Internet, where, in the hands of some cyberspace "journalists," solid sources and researched stories have obviously become secondary to fun and salaciousness. From the Drudge Report, an online rumor mill that occasionally produces tantalizing tidbits for mainstream media, to news programs featuring anchors in full undress, evidence abounds of the unique clash of new media and contemporary culture. For example, one of the newest niche services offered in 2002 was a website news program that was also available as a pay-per-view TV program featuring nude newsreaders. The TV program version was described on their website as follows:

Naked News TV is a news infotainment television program featuring an all-nude female cast who deliver both the serious and lighter side of the news. The show is bright, energetic and fast-paced. It is the logical evolution of NakedNews.com, the first Internet news company to present the news with naked newsreaders. The 50-minute program is produced weekly and features all eleven (11) webcasters appearing on the daily NakedNews.com program. Each new episode informs and entertains you with the lighter side of the news and the behind the scenes shenanigans of the Naked News anchors. It's pure fun from the program with nothing to hide.[20]

Undoubtedly, the most visible public benefit of the deregulatory era has been expanded consumer choice resulting from heightened competition and improved technology. But limitless choice and intense competition can also produce consequences that are a disservice to the public. In its most recent annual report on news media, the Project for Excellence in Journalism observes, with notable distress, that the new paradox of contemporary journalism is more outlets chasing fewer stories. The ramifications are plain and profound:

As the number of places delivering news proliferates, the audience for each tends to shrink and the number of journalists in each organization is reduced. [Not only do we get] more accounts of the same handful of stories each day . . . when big stories break, they are often covered in a similar fashion by general assignment reporters working with a limited list of sources and a tight time frame. Such concentration of personnel around a few stories, in turn, has aided the efforts of newsmakers to control what the public knows. One of the first things to happen is that the authorities quickly corral the growing throng of correspondents, crews and paparazzi into press areas away from the news.[21]

Not only do we now have more stations, networks, cable channels, and websites, all less accountable and more beholden to the bottom line, we have an intensely more competitive environment that affects the style, speed, and accuracy of mass media content. It is an environment created and sustained by several self-imposed pressures—the pressure of a nonstop news cycle, the pressure to produce the same or more news with fewer people, and the pressure to get the news out faster. This environment, these pressures, have led to more shortcuts, more errors, more blurring of the facts. In a few instances, it has led to the distortion or fabrication of the facts.[22]

Two of the most egregious errors of modern journalism were largely attributed to what has been called a "myopic zeal to be the first news organization" to report a particular story. The first was CNN's "Operation Tailwind" report in 1998 that, in a collaboration with commonly owned *Time* magazine, presented the story of a secret military mission inside Laos during the Vietnam War which dropped sarin, a lethal (and illegal) nerve gas, on an enemy village base camp. CNN and *Time* quickly acknowledged serious faults in the Tailwind story and retracted it, a major calamity for both members of the Time-Warner news family. In subsequent assessments, it was learned that although the story had been in preparation for months, in the end it was rushed into print and put on the air so as to coincide with the launching of a new prime-time television newsmagazine called "NewsStand: CNN and Time." Being first with a significant revelation had been thought to be critical to the success of the new program.

The second infamous instance involved a broadcast by CBS on 8 September 2004 about President George W. Bush's Vietnam War–era service in the Texas National Guard—a report that was aired during the height of the 2004 presidential election. When it became apparent that the documents supporting the report could not be authenticated, CBS was forced to make a number of embarrassing announcements about lapses in its reporting. A subsequent analysis by an independent review panel pinpointed one of the main problems:

Once the documents were obtained . . . there was a frantic effort to "crash" the segment, meaning to prepare the [news] segment for broadcast quickly. . . . Despite [an] enormous amount of work and the great sensitivity of the subject matter, it was decided to move up the date the story would air [by three weeks]. . . . This decision on timing was driven in significant part by competitive pressures.

The review panel also found that CBS's vetting process for the story was "seriously flawed," a result "caused in large part by the speed with which [the story] was produced."[23]

Competitive pressures can also lead to laxity of another sort. Instead of aggressively pursuing or developing stories in an effort to stand above the competition, many news organizations today, especially those in the electronic media, follow an easier, less expensive, less time-consuming route. They routinely accept government press releases or corporate handouts without challenge and without independent reporting. In many cases, if there is no government or corporate press release, there is no story. It is, at best, reactive journalism. It has even reached the point where some news reports seen on local television newscasts are prepackaged by others—including the government. This practice is usually problematic, but even more so when the story is closer to the news of the day and touches upon controversial public issues, like Medicare reform, school assistance programs, and regime change in foreign nations. Yet, in 2004 and 2005, it was revealed that the U.S. government was funding prepacked news reports on just such subjects for distribution to local television stations. Called "video news releases," they were prepared under the direction of different federal agencies but professionally produced to look like any other report in a daily newscast. Indeed, until the FCC warned TV stations in early 2005 that doing so might violate sponsorship identification rules, many stations apparently accepted and aired government-produced video news releases without any disclosure of their true source.

Prepackaged reports or "canned" interviews created to look like real news reports from various self-interested sources are not entirely new. For several years, willing broadcast stations (radio and TV) have been accepting and airing outside reports developed by public relations experts and freelance production houses on behalf of corporate clients. But they have become more prevalent in the deregulatory era because more stations, facing less regulatory accountability and greater competitive pressures, have been willing to accept them "as is"—without challenge and without full disclosure. Some of the most common are those disguised as "consumer tips" about a new electronic gadget or educational toy. Instead of being independent, objective reports, they are backed by vested interests and produced by outside professionals (typically in the form of a news interview made to look like any other report in a local station's newscast).

Inserts of this nature chip away at the credibility of news organizations that use them—even if the source of the externally produced material is fully revealed. Labeling alone cannot elevate a commercial plug to a legitimate presentation of consumer information. The role of mass media should be to provide citizens with information they need and opinion that is plainly identified.

In highlighting some of the pressures that consolidation and competition have forced on the changing ethics, style, and substance of today's journalism, it is well to remember the highly positive role mass media occasionally play in American life. Despite the slings and arrows of critics and the public's growing disenchantment with their performance, mass media are still the most significant watchdogs of wrongdoing. When, in June 1972, the *Washington Post* put two reporters on the trail of a seemingly innocuous break-in at the headquarters of the Democratic National Committee in the Watergate office building, a new benchmark for watchdog journalism was about to be established. For months, as a tangled web of political spying, dirty tricks, and secret funds was uncovered, the *Washington Post* stood as a lone beacon among major news organizations that failed or refused to take what would become the Watergate scandal seriously. Resisting tremendous political and business pressure to back off, the *Post* stayed with the story until, months later and following the presidential election in November 1972, government investigators and Congress joined the fray, eventually leading to impeachment proceedings and the toppling of Richard M. Nixon, the first president of the United States ever to resign from office. As characterized by Downie and Kaiser in their book, *The News About the News*, "Watergate became an example for the ages, a classic case when journalism made a difference."[24]

That, of course, was more than thirty years ago. In the summer of 2001, both the *Columbia Journalism Review* and the *American Journalism Review* published articles whose titles pose the more contemporary question, "Where Are the Watchdogs?" (*AJR*) and "Are Watchdogs an Endangered Species?" (*CJR*). Part of the problem today is that we have more news sources either chasing the same story or just any story to fill time. According to journalists Tom Rosenstiel and Bill Kovach, "We are reaching a moment of diminution by dilution." As explained in their *CJR* report, "In the nearly thirty years since Watergate and the rise of *60 Minutes*, the proliferation of outlets for news and information has been accompanied by a torrent of investigative reportage."[25] But many of these reports or programs focus on lifestyle, behavior, consumerism, health, or celebrity entertainment—a type of trivial pursuit that not only dilutes the watchdog function but, through overexposure and overreporting, undermines the credibility of mass media in uncovering abuses involving truly important issues such as corporate business practices, politics, national security, and social welfare. This penchant is graphically illustrated by another journalist, Neil Hickey, writing in the same journal:

> Investigative stories at networks and stations are not always acts of pure altruism and civic high-mindedness. The biggest and most eye-catching customarily go on the air during sweeps periods, preceded by a barrage of publicity and promotion in an effort to grab huge audiences and boost advertising rates. And what too often passes for investigative reporting is more properly consumer reporting or what some TV folk call "fear and loathing reporting"—exposes of crooked auto repairmen, diet-and-exercise fallacies, harmful cosmetics, sex shops, money scams, fortune tellers, tainted meat, faulty elevators—where the object is to scare viewers into watching.[26]

In the modern newsroom (print or broadcast), it is just much easier to produce a breezier story that requires less work, less money, and, yes, less commitment on the part of an attention-challenged audience. In contrast, in-depth investigations are usually more speculative in nature and, if done right, always expensive and time-consuming. As Mike Wallace of CBS News notes, "It's a question of time, money, and the ratings business." At the network level, fewer major investigations are initiated and the more entertainment-oriented newsmagazine shows that now predominate are "doing 'damned little' substantial investigation, and it's 'much softer than it used to be.'"[27] No doubt part of the change results from consolidation and competition. Reductions in staff, bureaus, and other facilities, combined with budgetary pressures forcing newsrooms to produce only that which sells, leaves little room for the serious, investigative piece that digs out and exposes aberrant conduct by the powerful.

Nevertheless, as Neil Hickey points out, some investigative journalism —whether bordering on the trivial or touching on the truly ominous—is still capable of "trigger[ing] new legislation, judicial action and regulatory alarm."[28] Among the several recent examples that he cites are the nine-month-long investigation by KHOU-TV in Houston that led to the federal investigation of faulty Firestone tires on Ford Explorers that had caused hundreds of injuries and fatalities, and an NBC report on "Dateline" that uncovered how some insurance companies were forging doctors' signatures and citing nonexistent databases in support of decisions to deny claims. Newspapers with strong management and stout ownership continue to challenge wrongdoing on behalf of their readers. In a classic example, the *Washington Post*, in a local four-part series published in 2001, uncovered a string of serious abuses by the police force in suburban Prince George's County, Maryland. These investigative reports brought needed public attention to a vital local issue affecting citizens, led to changes in some of the procedures followed by the Prince George's prosecutor's office, resulted in corrective measures being pursued by the Prince George's state delegation to the Maryland legislature, and caused a probe to be initiated by the Federal Bureau of Investigation. Although not exactly Watergate dimensions, to the citizens of this populous Washington, D.C., suburban county, the *Washington Post* performed a crucial public service where other elements of society failed. In 1999, the *Chicago Tribune* uncovered evidence that scores of men sentenced to death in Illinois who had been beaten by police into confessing crimes had either been convicted on questionable evidence or represented by incompetent trial counsel. In response, the governor of Illinois suspended all executions. In 2002, the *Boston Globe*, pursing a story that had been brewing for years, found internal documents demonstrating that officials of the Boston Archdiocese of the Catholic Church had been covering up the sexual abuse practices of prominent priests. The documents shed vital new light on an important issue that has since escalated into a national scandal.

—ᴡᴡ—

A final note on standards of the mass media. The proliferation of alternative sources using more sophisticated technology presents special problems for journalism and the role mass media play in an open society. Facing a complicated economy and faster-paced lifestyles, Americans continue to need editors to assimilate the mounds of information they confront and elucidate the sources they can rely on. I write not only of the Internet, where predators and others with no accountability lurk to spread misinformation or ribald fun, but of the increased potential for altering images in the digital era. Ethical questions stemming from how to use and shade visuals, hidden cameras, and other materials have long surrounded journalism. But today's digital technology ups the ante. In an era where different visual logos or images can be superimposed on outdoor signs or billboards (creating "virtual" signs and announcements) and digital technicians are able to create completely synthetic moving pictures or video (as well as sound), one can begin to appreciate the potential mischief that can be spread by unethical journalists or those intending to terrorize or propagandize. The problem, in fact, has already seeped into the traditional media newsroom. As John V. Pavlik, writing in *Journalism and New Media*, notes:

> In the old-fashioned analog television newsroom, it took an entire team of reporters, editors, and union technicians to gather, edit, and put on the air a single piece of video. Many pairs of eyes routinely viewed every video clip that made it on the air. In the digital newsroom, the number of eyes and concomitant amount of experience reviewing any given video is greatly reduced, not just for technical reasons but for reasons of cost cutting.[29]

As Pavlik points out, this not only reduces the likelihood of catching and correcting honest mistakes, "it will make it much easier for downright fakery to occur" in the newsroom but also, perhaps more important, in information coming into the newsroom.[30]

ELECTIONS AND POLITICS

The role of mass media in politics is paramount. Not only is knowledge of issues and participation by citizens essential to the success of democratic government, Americans rely heavily on mass media for news about candidates, campaigns, and elections. As Dautrich and Hartley found in studying the American elections of 1996, "For most voters [news organizations] are increasingly their primary source of information."[31] When voters were asked where they got most of their information during the 1996 presidential campaign, nearly 80

percent said they relied on the news media and only 7 percent identified interpersonal dialogue. "For better or worse, Americans experience campaigns mostly through the lens of the news camera, the pens
of the journalist, the mouths of radio talk show hosts, and, increasingly, the information superhighway."[32] As such, when mass media
perform this role poorly, democracy suffers.

It is especially distressing that substantive coverage of politics continues to abate even as the sheer volume of political news and information rises. This trend has been developing for years but probably
has been influenced, even accelerated, by changes in the deregulatory
era. Dautrich and Hartley highlight a string of media failings in covering presidential campaigns that could be applied to virtually all
elections: "a preoccupation with the horse-race [element of election
campaigns], an inclination to focus on personality stories, undue attention to campaign tactics and candidates' strategies, lack of attention to non-mainstream major party candidates, a dearth of news information about issues and candidate positions, and lack of coverage
that is meaningful to voters' decision-making."[33]

In *Democracy and the Media*, a collection of essays edited by Richard
Gunther and Anthony Mughan, the interface between mass media
and politics is examined in ten politically diverse countries. The following observations have stunning relevance to politics and media in
contemporary America:

> The first trend is a dilution of the substantive informational content of
> political communications disseminated by the media. The second is an
> increasingly rancorous relationship between journalists and politicians,
> ranging from struggle for control of the news agenda, as in Britain and
> the Netherlands, to pervasive negativity and cynicism about the actions
> and intentions of politicians, as in the United States. The first of these
> can be detrimental to the quality of democracy because its impact on the
> volume and content of political information reaching average citizens
> undermines their ability to assess the likely consequences for society of
> the electoral choices they make. The second can corrode both the ability
> and the desire of citizens to hold governments accountable for their
> (in)actions.[34]

With notable exceptions, most broadcast stations no longer initiate
any special news or public affairs programming in and around political campaigns. An increasing number no longer even broadcast candidate debates. And, in regularly scheduled newscasts, one is likely to

be exposed to more campaign advertising than campaign news. When thousands of the top-rated half-hour evening news broadcasts on 122 local TV stations in the top 50 markets were analyzed in the weeks leading up to the 2002 elections, it was found that only 44 percent of those broadcasts contained any local election coverage. Even newscasts that did provide some local election coverage did not provide much. The average campaign story carried by local stations was about 80 seconds long, and fewer than 30 percent of those stories included the candidates themselves speaking (such "sound bites" averaging 12 seconds).[35] At the same time, eight out of ten newscasts examined included at least one political advertisement, and the overall ratio of political ads to campaign news stories was approximately three-and-a-half to one.[36] In a similar study based on the 2004 elections, it was found that television stations in eleven major markets had devoted eight times as much airtime to car crashes and other accidents than to campaigns for the U.S. House of Representatives, state senate, city hall, and other local offices. Moreover, the amount of advertising sold to candidates seeking election to the U.S. House of Representatives during newscasts on those stations eclipsed any actual news coverage of the House election races at issue by a ratio of five to one.[37]

In short, in the deregulatory era, where accountability for public service has been supplanted by corporate priorities that force news departments to air only what can be sponsored, most broadcast stations do nothing extra to cover political races and issues. More typically, they carry large volumes of candidate advertising but only superficial snippets of the campaign, emphasizing strategy and who is leading or falling behind. Ironically, even as broadcast stations continue to play the most dominant media role in election politics, they contribute less journalistically to the process. For twenty years, the broadcast industry fought vigorously to repeal FCC rules that had formerly required stations to offer response time to any political candidate they editorially opposed. Although electronic editorializing might seem to connote a more substantive role in the electoral process, the final decision to repeal the rules in 2000 was largely symbolic. It was mostly for show because neither before nor following removal of those rules did broadcast stations routinely endorse or criticize specific candidates in elections. Rather, that role has been performed almost exclusively by print media, especially daily newspapers.

Mass media (print and electronic) undoubtedly still see their role as a "fourth branch" of government, with responsibility to act as a check on the executive, legislative, and judicial branches. But this role has become far more adversarial in recent years. Some of this is expected, even justified. It is kindled by the lingering effects of Watergate and the Vietnam War and stirred further by egregious examples of deception practiced by public officials, marked particularly by the Nixon and Johnson administrations during the 1960s and 1970s but given new impetus through the scandal-ridden years of the Clinton administration in the late 1990s. In addition, journalism, by its very nature, usually takes a negative slant regardless of the administration or politician involved. "Positive" coverage of news and politics is simply regarded as more boring. Controversy and confrontation are the normal stuff of politics. It makes for juicy stories and is also the way politicians often behave and campaigns are often conducted. Indeed, in today's election campaigning, the news and information agenda is driven as much by politicians as the media. This new style is described by Gunther and Mughan:

> Television is at its center, and politicians have called on the services of marketing experts, advertising agencies, actors, film directors, and other media professionals to cash in on its potential for the mobilization and conversion of popular support. Entertainment, not policy debate, is the hallmark of election campaigns. Rather than emphasizing their policies and promises, parties parade their leaders in a never-ending series of contrived settings, sound bites, and walkabouts. Sketchy policy pronouncements are made not at party meetings or in speeches before distinguished audiences, but in news conferences and "appropriate" settings on the road and in front of the television cameras—always in time to catch the evening news.[38]

Other efforts to manipulate campaign dialogue—particularly in national elections—occur more surreptitiously. Today, aggressive political organizations with the help of high-tech, savvy consultants not only set up rapid-response teams to defend their candidate and attack the opposition—instantly and incessantly—they actively seek out friendly media sources to better ventilate their views and help shape the campaign message. Today's abundance of media sources, in fact, makes it much easier for candidates to be fairly selective in who they embrace. It also makes it easier for politicians, once elected, to adopt similar methods of tightly controlling information while in public office.

With heightened commercial pressures, many more competitive outlets (including thousands of freelance bloggers operating in cyberspace), and a twenty-four-hour news cycle, is it any wonder that popular media have lost some of their capacity to produce news and information that is vital to making individual decisions in the political process? And, if campaigning politicians speak only sparingly—usually in witticisms, slogans, or sound bites—leading to media coverage that is correspondingly superficial, is it any wonder that many Americans express only superficial interest in elections and politics? Worse than that, many Americans have become cynical about politics, politicians, and news media. Instead of being turned on by political debate and involved in the political process in a way that enriches and propels a representative democracy, people are turned off. When the public at large comes to accept less of its officials and agents, it becomes desensitized to the process that is so critical to an open democracy.

These tendencies were brought into sharp relief during the 2000 presidential election when both the tactics and resources of electronic journalists were found sadly lacking. On that occasion, in their rush to be first and most breathless, all the major national networks (over-the-air and cable) prematurely called the election wrong—not once, but, effectively, four separate times, all within the course of an eight-hour time span. To briefly recap, at about 8:00 p.m. on election night, 7 November 2000, ABC, CBS, CNN, Fox News, NBC, and the Associated Press all called the election for Albert Gore of Tennessee, about an hour after the polls had closed in the pivotal state of Florida. At 9:55 p.m. that evening, all the television networks began retracting the Gore "call" as the results in Florida and elsewhere became shrouded in doubt. Then, in the middle of the night (just before 3:00 a.m. East Coast time), all the television networks changed course again and projected George W. Bush of Texas the "winner" in Florida and of the presidency. Dan Rather of CBS led the middle-of-the-morning network cheering with words that will surely linger in mass media infamy: "A hip-hip hurray and a big Texas howdy to the new president. . . . Sip it, savor it, press it in a book, put it in an album, hang it on the wall: George W. Bush is the next President of the United States."[39] Less than two hours later, the television networks started retracting the Bush "call," declaring the presidential race in limbo. Indeed, the results of the U.S. presidential election of 2000, conducted on 7 November, were not finally known until thirty-six days later, "making this election one of the most drawn-out, confusing, acrimonious and controversial elections in the nation's history."[40] Near total reliance on

vote projections by the television networks triggered an unprecedented chain of events. Candidate Gore first telephoned presumed
"winner" Bush with a concession statement which, shortly thereafter,
was retracted in a testy exchange between the two candidates.
Meanwhile, leading newspapers around the country—including the
*New York Times, New York Post, St. Louis Post–Dispatch, San Francisco
Chronicle, Miami Herald, USA Today, Boston Globe, Chicago Sun-Times,
Dallas Morning News,* and *Philadelphia Inquirer*—called the election
prematurely.[41]

An independent panel convened by CNN to investigate this debacle
concluded that the premature calls and retractions by the television
networks "constituted a news disaster that damaged democracy and
journalism." As described in the panel's report: "On Election Day
2000, television news organizations staged a collective drag race on
the crowded highway of democracy, recklessly endangering the electoral process, the political life of the country, and their own credibility."[42] The compounded failures of the electronic media in covering
election night 2000 have generally been attributed to a deadly combination of the competitive instinct to be first (if only by split seconds)
and undue reliance on a *single*, out-of-date voting tabulation and pro-
jection service—the Voter News Service (VNS), an organization jointly
owned by five television networks and the Associated Press. Before
1990, each of the major television networks had its own sample
precincts and conducted its own voter polling on which projections
were based. As a cost-cutting measure, VNS was established to pool
these activities. As described by Tom Wolzien, a former television
news executive, the "polling units [of network news divisions] came to
be seen as cost centers with no function that couldn't be handled by
a pool. The units became easy prey for a new breed of executives who
focused on the bottom line to please their new breed of corporate
owners."[43] In addition, the CNN report found serious flaws in the
polling methods used by VNS, including exit polling, outdated
polling models, and outdated technology. In fact, "There was a recognition well before the election that VNS technology was not up-to-
date, but the [network] partners [who owned VNS] did not upgrade
it,"[44] presumably owing to budgetary pressures.

So, the combination of a failed technical support system struggling
under budgetary constraints and a competitive compulsion to be the
first to deliver definitive news led to a monumental news failure.
When the same data and system is used by all "competing" news or-

ganizations, what the public gets is multiple sources breathlessly racing to announce the same substantive results. As Don Hewitt, the respected executive producer of "60 Minutes," recently conceded, "A lot of the screw-ups that happened election night [2000] were triggered because of competition. . . . If they weren't competing with each other and there were one broadcast, like when there's a debate and one network feeds everyone else, those mistakes wouldn't have been made."[45]

The embarrassment that journalism experienced election night 2000 was repeated several weeks later when the major television networks initially misreported the Supreme Court's decision which effectively ended the 2000 presidential election. Instead of allowing reporters and expert analysts sufficient time to read and decipher the court's opaque sixty-five-page decision, anxious Americans were treated to the live spectacle of correspondents rushing down the steps of the Supreme Court building on a cold winter's night gasping for breath to deliver nearly incoherent, conflicting views on what the court had decided. Only hours into the next morning did the true picture emerge. While the news fog that typically surrounds such tragic, confusing events as terrorist attacks or wartime battle is understandable and inevitable, the journalistic failures of the 2000 election were mostly self-imposed and avoidable.[46]

—m—

The perils of mass media described in this chapter may pale in significance to other ills threatening American society. But deficiencies in mass media performance are important nonetheless because they impact how all other issues are to be addressed. Environmental, economic, and terrorist threats cannot hope to be alleviated or reduced without a public and a government that is energized and connected via the power and presence of mass media. When decisions are made in a representative democracy they need to be enforced and supported by an informed citizenry. And you cannot have an informed citizenry without strong, responsible media.

Despite general agreement on the value and vital role of mass media in modern society, we entered the twenty-first century on the same worn policy track as we left the twentieth century. For nearly three decades, America's primary public policy has been to reduce government regulation in favor of reliance on the private marketplace. No policymaker, of course, was ever heard to say that service to the public was no longer important. Instead, the theme adopted by policymakers was that service to the public could be better achieved by marketplace forces—creating new outlets, new voices, and new services. But, as we have seen, unleashing mass media in this way, without more, has done little to enhance the quality of American democracy, much less the quality of American media.

Instead of more serious and frequent treatment of public issues by a greatly expanded media presence, we have nearly limitless media sources spreading information that is typically either greatly diluted or one-sided. Instead of more news and information relevant to citizenship in an open society, we have news and information presented like nonfiction entertainment. Instead of mass media demanding accountability in politics and business—in true watchdog fashion—we have bottom-line-oriented businesses increasingly limited in their capacity or willingness to perform this role. Instead of mass media providing a critical analysis and early warning of the defects and deficiencies of products and services, we all too often see and hear only a pro-advertiser flow of positive information. Although some commentators argue that the Watergate era produced a more contentious (and potentially dangerous) relationship between mass media and government,[47] the larger danger, I submit, is a weaker, more passive press that not only does not challenge government actions and officials but that, more often, retreats in the face of any orchestrated government pressure. We sometimes have a rancorous media. What we need but rarely get is an activist media.

To help counter some of the negative side effects of media performance discussed in this chapter, we need a broader-based public policy that is founded on more than blind faith in the marketplace. We need a policy that starts by identifying the most fundamental needs and interests of the American public that mass media can help satisfy—such as (1) free and easy access to essential information needed to make electoral and other choices, (2) exposure to the diversity of our multicultural society, and (3) sufficient faith and trust that our governments (local and national) and other bedrock institutions will be held accountable. Once basic goals are established, policymakers then need to decide how those goals can be guaranteed, given the irreversibility of mushrooming technology, evolving business practices, and changing lifestyles.

As described in the last two chapters, the near total dismantling of effective broadcast regulation, coming at a time when the commercial media marketplace was erupting in new techniques and technology, has brought us to a point where we can no longer expect results from the existing policy framework. The ritualistic biennial (now quadrennial) process by which Washington policymakers continue to tinker with what remains of broadcast ownership rules—in the unshakable belief that the commercial marketplace will somehow fill the gaping hole left by discarded policies (which previously laid down discrete public service benchmarks)—is more akin to an act of spinning wheels than weaving useful public policy Because ownership policies alone will not produce public service dividends, we must develop other, more realistic public policy remedies. Chapter 7 begins by exploring the underlying rationales for the existing system, describing how they are no longer relevant or viable. This leads to Chapter 8, which carries these thoughts forward, first by elaborating upon some of the specific failures under the existing regulatory system and then by laying out a proposal for an entirely new regulatory system.

7

The Making of
Mass Media Policy

Two historic events highlighted the need for public policy specifically tailored to electronic media. The first was the failure of communications during the sinking of the *Titanic* in 1912 and the second was the surge of electrical interference that threatened to jam America's airwaves in the early 1920s. The first response of policymakers—starting with the Radio Act of 1912 (which established the principle that no one could broadcast without a federal license) and culminating in the Communications Act of 1934—was to craft something that resembled regulatory schemes already in place. Indeed, the key words that have guided American mass media policy for nearly eighty years—"the public interest, convenience and necessity"—were lifted, in whole or part, directly from the Transportation Act of 1920, dealing with regulation of railway lines.[1]

The earliest broadcast legislation not only dealt with emergency communications and electrical interference, it addressed a growing concern over the possible monopoly control of radio. Without some restraint on the aggressive behavior that was beginning to characterize the radio business, many thought that power over this new medium would rest in too few hands. In the words of the Supreme Court, Congress acted "under the spur of a widespread fear that in the absence of governmental control the public interest might be subordinate to monopolistic domination of the broadcast field."[2] Accordingly, the 1934 act banned broadcasters from using their frequencies as common

carriers and rejected proposals to establish a system of "toll broadcasting" in which broadcast stations would be operated for hire like
railroads or telephones. Rather, pioneer policymakers sought to promote competition among broadcasters, hoping to avoid the monop-
olies that had already been formed in telephony and telegraphy.
While local broadcast stations have long bartered, sold, or contracted
their airtime to others, such as national networks, they, unlike common carriers, retain control over the content of what they broadcast,
even when the content is supplied by others.[3]

Instead of treating radio as a public utility, Congress favored a concept in which a distinct public service obligation would "attach" to the
otherwise private business interests of those holding a broadcast license. Under the "public interest" standard, broadcast stations are licensed to private commercial interests on a temporary, renewable basis. In return, stations are expected to operate as proxies or fiduciaries
for the public at large. This is referred to as the public trusteeship
model. While in some circles[4] debate persists over the failure of Congress to choose a different path, the legislative history reflects no serious consideration being given to government-sponsored broadcasting. In favoring private ownership, it is well to remember that even
before a broad legislative plan was agreed upon, the radio business
had become a budding popular medium with hundreds of stations
blanketing the nation.[5] Congress and Herbert Hoover, the secretary of
Commerce and Labor, had little interest in uprooting this preexisting
private industry structure.

While some parties actively lobbied for a more paternalistic, monopolistic system like those then emerging in Great Britain and Canada, such
discussions never generated widespread support. In fact, the only proposal of this nature gathering enough strength even for a vote was the
idea of setting aside 25 percent of available broadcast frequencies for use
by "educational, religious, labor, farm, fraternal, cooperative, and other
institutions dedicated to human welfare and higher education."[6] The
proposal was defeated and the general concept effectively tabled for
nearly two decades until Congress and the FCC eventually recognized
that certain frequencies should be reserved for "noncommercial" use, a
vital first step in framing our modern public broadcasting system.

Today, some critics continue to argue that the United States made a
fundamental mistake at the outset in allowing broadcasting to develop
and remain in the hands of private businesses. In their view, the shortcomings of contemporary broadcasting can be traced to this initial pol-

icy decision that virtually ensured the commercial excesses and other ills of modern mass media.[7] On the other hand, there are those who argue just as strenuously that the form of government regulation chosen has been an unnecessary, even destructive constraint on broadcasting. According to these critics, the American public is best served when media businesses are free to compete for "consumers" of news and entertainment in the same way other businesses compete for consumers of less ephemeral "products."[8] Others espouse a more libertarian position: that First Amendment principles bar any regulation of the content or other editorial functions of mass media, whether print or broadcast.[9]

If nothing else, such arguments reveal that mass media policy is undoubtedly a product of the society from which it arises.[10] Certainly, mass media are viewed and treated far differently in totalitarian societies than in free societies. But even among democratic countries of Western Europe and the Americas, there are significant differences in media policy based on significant differences in the form of democracy and type of commerce practiced. The United States, among all developed countries, has the strongest tradition of private capitalism and, owing to the First Amendment (a constitutional imperative unparalleled in Western culture), the greatest degree of separation between control of government and control of media. As Professor Starr reminds us, "Unlike the major European states, the United States privatized telecommunications, promoted communications development on a continental scale and resisted" the imposition of any special tax to support broadcasting. Given these conditions, "the press, and later other media in America, became more popularly oriented than their counterparts in Europe," requiring them "to find ways of appealing to audiences that cut across cultural boundaries."[11]

Building upon a radio structure already unfolding in the marketplace and reflecting America's unique blend of history, geography, business, culture, and political philosophy, policymakers chose to regulate broadcasting by licensing hundreds (eventually, thousands) of local stations to private interests. Instead of relying on government taxes or receiving public appropriations, the stations would support themselves by selling advertising. It is a scheme compatible with a political system that diffuses power among federal, state, and local governments, and with a Constitution that both encourages free enterprise and exalts freedom of expression. While roundly criticized by those who rail against commercialism and lowest-common-denominator programming, this approach has proven both durable and popular—not only in this country, but elsewhere. Even governmental systems that initially rejected broadcast advertising by private interests have come to accept it either on state-controlled stations or on separately authorized commercial stations.

SPECIFIC THEORIES UNDERLYING THE REGULATION OF AMERICAN BROADCASTING

Most broadcast stations in the United States are operated by commercial entities that have been granted an exclusive right to transmit signals over a discrete portion of the radio spectrum. Historically, the specific method of broadcast communication—electronic impulses sent through the air—has been regarded as uniquely implicating the public interest (if, for no other reason, than it produces a "product" that is highly accessible to a broad general audience). In addition, of course, certain physical or technical constraints limit who can broadcast with what type of apparatus in what locations. These simple, straightforward notions, however, have also led to a widely held but far less definitive notion that the airspace over which broadcast signals travel is publicly owned. Instead of thoughtful analysis on this point, one typically finds an implacable, ideologically driven assertion that because that airspace is presumed to be owned by "the public," it is not only proper but essential that the government regulate what passes through (via "airwaves" generated by broadcast equipment meeting certain specifications). But nothing in statutory law or legislative history definitively awards "ownership" of the air we breath and the space penetrated by broadcast signals to the government (as the people's representative)—at least in the normal sense of conveying irrefutable possession or total exclusivity. As former FCC commissioner and notable communications scholar Glen Robinson reminds us, even though the legislative history of the 1927 Act contains several references to "public ownership of the ether," such references were "merely quaint locutions denoting the power of the government to regulate the use of radio frequencies 'in the public interest'" (or as yet another "way of expressing the fact that stations did not have and could not gain vested rights in their licenses").[12] To be sure, the federal government, from the start, was entrusted with exclusive authority to manage the way in which broadcasters (and all others) use the electronic spectrum.[13] But it is quite another matter to construct and perpetuate a regulatory rationale based on the improbable notion that the federal government owns and possesses all the air stretching from the earth to the skies just like it owns and possesses park land or office buildings.

Under the system adopted, broadcast stations obtain a temporary but renewable license to operate by providing a service that must adhere to one, overriding standard: "the public interest, convenience [and/or][14] necessity." All regulation over the past eighty years, even contemporary deregulation, has been rationalized under this same test. A deceptively simple mandate, yet, as two prominent communications lawyers have observed, "Perhaps no single area of [mass media] policy has generated as much scholarly discourse, judicial analysis, and political debate . . . as has that simple directive to regulate in 'the public interest.'"[15]

Not only has the basic public interest injunction remained unsettled, offshoot theories of regulation rising from the same underpinning have likewise stirred debate and uncertainty. These include those based on scarcity, diversity (the rights of listeners and viewers), localism, intrusiveness, and the viability of the marketplace.

The "Public Interest" Standard:
The Root of All Broadcast Regulation

Sprinkled abundantly throughout the Communications Act, the public interest formula is the main ingredient of all mass media law and policy. Not so much a regulatory theory or rationale, standing alone, it is the starting point for all government action or inaction relative to the electronic media.

The Supreme Court more than sixty years ago described the public interest standard as a "supple instrument for the exercise of discretion by the expert body [FCC] which Congress has charged to carry out its legislative policy."[16] In practice, it is a "standardless" standard, little more than a general guidepost highly susceptible to different interpretations in the hands of different policymakers pursuing different political philosophies. In one sense, the meaning of the public interest *must* change periodically, if only to adapt to changes in technology, the economy, and general social environment. That the public interest concept has flourished for so many years is, in fact, a testament to the wisdom of the original drafters who chose extremely broad delegating language over detailed legislative standards. It is an intentionally flexible concept that contemplates a balancing of different interests, not the achievement of one single public interest, something especially important in a field as dynamic as communications.

For many years, the FCC interpreted the trusteeship model as requiring broadcast stations to follow a number of detailed programming and operational obligations. As we have seen, in more recent
years those "behavioral" requirements have been removed or relaxed
—under the same public interest mandate from which they arose.
What changed was not the legal standard but marketplace conditions
and the prevailing political philosophy. This turnabout is not particularly remarkable, given the Supreme Court's early observation that the
public interest concept was merely a "supple instrument for the exercise of discretion" by the FCC. What is remarkable is the crescendo of
voices today that attack the very idea of the "public interest" as a viable basis for any policy.[17] They say it is too difficult to interpret, too
imprecise, incapable of measurement, or just plain inefficient or irrelevant, forgetting, of course, that many concepts in our laws and
Constitution are essentially vague generalities that require interpretation and implementation as the nation and its institutions grow and
expand.[18]

Nevertheless, when the first FCC chairman to be appointed in the
twenty-first century was asked to supply a definition of that time-
honored phrase, he glibly responded that he "had no idea." Explaining further, Michael Powell said that the "public interest" concept is
like "an empty vessel in which people pour in . . . their [own] preconceived views or bias." Earlier, Powell regaled an audience of the
American Bar Association with these words: "The night before I was
sworn in [as an FCC commissioner], I waited for a visit from the an-
gel of the public interest. I waited all night, but she did not come."[19]
Criticizing Powell as "a blithe, postmodern sort of ideologue . . .just
perfect for the cool and snickering culture of TV" tends to emphasize
only the ideology of the critic.[20] Nevertheless, there is something unsettling and perhaps callous about a public official launching his policymaking duties with this frame of mind.

The reality is that Powell (who resigned in early 2005) and everyone else must deal with a purposely vague, flexible statutory directive
that is *intended* for policymakers to interpret and apply. No one ever
said that, because the phrase was simple of statement, it was easy to
apply or could always be applied with precision—which is what those
now mocking the standard seem to insist upon. Critics who proudly
declare that they do not know what the "public interest" means or
that the concept is unworkable not only ignore history—because the
concept has always been vulnerable to the same contention—they

usually take this position while advancing a political agenda. In other words, if one is comfortable in saying that the public interest phrase is not sufficiently clear to take any action, then it becomes easy to conclude that it means nothing. And, if it means nothing, government regulators should just get out of the way and let the marketplace meet public needs based entirely on economic considerations.

Public policy is rarely made and applied with mathematical precision—particularly when the "product" is news and information, not nuts and bolts. It is a judgment call that involves the careful balancing of values and general societal needs and objectives. Like most legislative action, it also contains a large element of predictive judgment. If policymakers now, after eight decades of doing so, contend this can no longer be done, what they really mean is that they are more motivated to follow a new path than stick with well-traveled routes of the past. Once the "public interest" concept is pushed to the sidelines because it no longer offers meaningful guidance, policymakers (and others) can more easily fill the vacuum with a rationale for action more to their liking.

The Scarcity Theory

The trusteeship model of broadcast regulation flows naturally from two threshold premises: (1) as a simple physical fact, there are only a limited group of frequencies that can efficiently carry radio waves,[21] and, because of the foregoing practical limitation, (2) not everyone who wants to broadcast can broadcast on any particular frequency. From these basic building blocks, the trusteeship model mandates that those who are awarded broadcast licenses must, in turn, operate their stations in a way that serves the varied interests of the public at large, not just their own private interests.

While other factors—such as avoiding monopoly control, promoting the fair and equitable distribution of broadcast stations among different states and communities, guarding against undue foreign influence, and reserving government power over electronic media in times of emergencies[22]—were all integral to the new regulatory scheme, the inherent scarcity of radio frequencies was perhaps the single most important initial factor. The Supreme Court explains:

> The plight into which radio fell prior to 1927 was attributable to certain basic facts about radio as a means of communication—its facilities are

limited; they are not available to all who wish to use them; the radio spectrum simply is not large enough to accommodate everybody. There is a fixed natural limitation upon the number of stations that can operate without interfering with one another. Regulation of radio was therefore as vital to its development as traffic control was to the development of the automobile.[23]

The electromagnetic spectrum, of course, is vastly larger than the small, valuable portion currently devoted to broadcasting. Available wavelengths along the spectrum support such diverse services or functions as radar; aeronautical navigation; x-rays; microwaves; satellites; cell phones; wireless Internet connections; military defense; mobile communication by police, fire, and rescue agencies; electronic news gathering; and weather tracking. Apart from the larger, continuing debate over the best method for accommodating all vital users, the issue most often raised in contemporary mass media policy discussions is whether spectrum scarcity remains a viable rationale on which to base any form of "content" regulation of broadcasting. The argument is generally framed as follows: if scarcity is no longer a reality in the new world of media plenty, can there be any justifiable basis for continuing to impose certain regulatory restraints on broadcast media that are not imposed on print media?[24] Some go further, arguing that since "numerical" scarcity is no longer sustainable, all forms of broadcast regulation must fall—not just what remains of content and behavioral regulation, but rules and policies affecting ownership as well.[25]

There is little doubt—indeed, the evidence is overwhelming—that even though no new radio frequencies have been created, technical and commercial advances have produced a plethora of new electronic media. Early AM radio begat FM that now dominates all radio broadcasting; radio begat television that now dominates all electronic media; early television service on a limited number of VHF channels begat expanded service on UHF channels; and television begat two distinct competitive video media, cable and satellite. These developments have been a triumph of both improved technology and free-market enterprise. Although the amount of spectrum used by broadcasting and related media services (cable, microwave, and satellite) has remained essentially unchanged, engineers and other scientists have, in recent years, greatly "expanded" the portion of the spectrum used for these services by innovative techniques such as digitalizing and compressing the signals used to transmit video and audio. Satellite services, for example, have become more viable because of our technical ability to compress available frequencies and literally squeeze more usable "space" out of the same discrete portion of spectrum. Television stations now converting their over-the-air signals from analog to digital will ultimately end up with the same six megahertz of spectrum. Yet, because of digital and compression technology, they will be able to simultaneously broadcast as many as six separate signals over the same slice of bandwidth. The amount of frequency space they use remains the same. No new spectrum was created for digital television, but, instead of one over-the-air signal—the current limit in analog mode—the same broadcast station will be able to disseminate multiple signals in digital mode. As a result, the number of audio and video outlets, already expanded beyond anyone's imagination, is likely to expand even more in the near future.[26]

As the number of electronic services—broadcasting, cable, satellite, and Internet—continues to rise, the basis for scarcity in the broadcast media begins to more closely resemble the basis for scarcity in print media (i.e., economic factors, not physical constraints). If, as some economists contend, broadcast spectrum differs little from any other economic good, one historical rationale for broadcast regulation begins to shatter.[27] It is a point of view enjoying increased currency in the deregulatory era.[28] Its logical extension is total replacement of the current government allocation system with a broad-based commercial market for spectrum.

But concrete proposals for any such massive transition are lacking, and some of the issues surrounding broadcast spectrum remain perplexing. It is one thing to declare scarcity dead or dying as a viable policy prescription; it is quite another to replace an eighty-year-old government allocation scheme with a free-market spectrum system. For example, if, in a fully deregulated marketplace, all frequencies were put up for bid, instead of being allocated and licensed for specific use, each spot on the radio and television dial would be sold to the highest bidder. Moreover, each successful bidder would be allowed to use its newly acquired frequency for any purpose, including a nonbroadcast purpose. In the world of economic theory this would be regarded as a public policy plus, merely ensuring that the highest bidder would make the "best" and "highest" use of the resource. More, however, is at stake. Despite recent policy decisions favoring marketplace solutions, mass media policymaking is not distillable into a single economic theory. What might work for other parts of the spectrum could lead to highly counterproductive results in broadcasting. Putting the frequencies currently used by twelve thousand or more broadcast stations up for bid would inevitably lead to more of the most desirable broadcast stations falling into the hands of the richest media companies and enormous numbers of other broadcast frequencies falling into the hands of parties who would convert them to nonbroadcast purposes.

Merely posing the quandary illustrates that more is involved than the numerical scarcity that economic theorists and deregulatory advocates usually rely on to support their positions. The scarcity concept in broadcast regulation has always had another dimension—one that is inherent to the medium. Until twenty-first-century technology produces a viable, practical means to avoid such consequences, a given frequency still cannot be used in the same area by more than one competing broadcast service or by one broadcast service and a totally different service, such as wireless telephone. In other words, just as in 1934, spectrum needs to be allocated to specific, discrete purposes. Unlike print, where there is no physical restraint to publishing, a choice must still be made as to who—or, at least, what type of service —should be favored on any particular frequency. Absent such choice, public service on any level would be deeply frustrated, if not totally impeded.

In the view of many experts, the key technical issue is not one of limited "airspace" but the unavailability of more sophisticated broadcast equipment. The point becomes clearer when one considers that the airwaves—what we usually think of as the scarce resource—only exist when electronic impulses are first created by a transmitting device made by a human being. The frequency spectrum typically characterized as being scarce is, in fact, neither natural nor a resource subject to depletion or damage in the manner of most natural resources. A radio or television station does not consume or damage the frequency it broadcasts on; rather, it occupies that space by the signals it transmits. In this sense, scarcity is seen more as an electronic compatibility issue in which interference could, feasibly, be greatly reduced or eventually eliminated by designing different and more efficient transmitting and receiving equipment—for example, equipment that would no longer be limited to sending or picking up single, distinct "channels" (defined by a specific frequency and power). In the future, broadcast equipment might be transformed into software-powered, computerlike devices, capable of scanning the spectrum to locate quiet bands for transmission, encoding digital information in new wave forms, and then analyzing incoming noise and picking out only the signal wanted.

However, even if contemporary technology had produced a fail-safe method to resolve this longstanding electronic compatibility problem —which it has not—key policy issues would remain. Mass media policy must not be driven exclusively by advancing technology or economic theory. In the first place, treating the spectrum used by broadcast stations like any other commodity by "allocating" it only to those willing to pay top dollar ignores the fundamental difference between a piece of real estate and a medium of communications. In the second place, given the special role mass media play in American society and the undeniable contribution they make to American democracy, the country's elected representatives and other key policymakers must continue making choices and reaching decisions that transcend both technical and economic factors.

For the immediate future, the most relevant scarcity issue is how the broadcast spectrum (along with all other spectrum) should be allocated or managed—not torn asunder and left to the vicissitudes of the marketplace. A steady evolution of administrative policy, not a radical retooling of the system, should be favored. Even if the best economic analysis or the greatest advances in technology allow broadcast spectrum to be regarded as less scarce, or no longer scarce at all, this hardly means that there is no remaining public policy rationale on which to base some continued regulation of the electronic media.

The Right of the Public to a Diversity of Viewpoints

The general concept of viewpoint diversity has been embedded in American society almost from the beginning, reflected most dramatically and permanently in the First Amendment which, as the Supreme Court has said, "rests on the assumption that the widest possible dissemination of information from diverse and antagonistic sources is essential to the welfare of the public."[29] The same fundamental postulate "has long been a basic tenet of national communications policy."[30] Indeed, in 1964, at a time when its broadcast ownership rules were being expanded instead of constricted, the FCC expounded upon this theme by declaring that "the greater the diversity of ownership in a particular area, the less chance there is that a single person or group can have an inordinate effect, in a political, editorial, or similar programming sense,

on public opinion at the regional level."[31] As the FCC explained, because broadcast stations must select, edit, and choose the method, manner, and emphasis of presenting stories in their news and information
programming, different owners of stations can be expected to bring different editorial viewpoints to their listeners or viewers.

Later, a string of significant judicial decisions helped elevate diversity to a more distinct regulatory rationale. In 1969, the Supreme
Court upheld the constitutionality of the now-defunct fairness doctrine in the seminal *Red Lion* case. In the process, it made clear that not
only did that policy (and certain related rules) not abridge the First
Amendment rights of broadcasters, they actually had the overall effect
of enhancing First Amendment values. In this sense, the court em-
broidered a new notion onto the preexisting theory that broadcast
regulation could be justified based on the limited nature of the spectrum. It said listeners and viewers have a unique right to receive ideas
and information, and regulation designed to promote that right
merely reinforces First Amendment principles.

> Because of the scarcity of radio frequencies, the government is permitted
> to put restraints on licensees in favor of others whose views should be
> expressed on this unique medium. But the people as a whole retain their
> interest in free speech by radio and their collective right to have the
> medium function consistently with the ends and purposes of the First
> Amendment. It is the right of the viewers and listeners, not the right of
> broadcasters, which is paramount. . . . It is the right of the public to re-
> ceive suitable access to social, political, esthetic, moral, and other ideas
> and experiences which is crucial here.[32]

A few years later, in two cases I participated in as a lawyer for ABC,
the Supreme Court sustained this regulatory rationale. In the first, the
court, while refusing to convert the foregoing *Red Lion* principle into
a general right of access to broadcasting—as the Democratic National
Committee and certain Vietnam War–era advocacy groups had urged
it to do—still pointed to the fairness doctrine as being adequate to
protect the public's First Amendment right of access to information.[33]
In the second, decided in the early stages of the deregulatory movement, the court once again affirmed the notion that the public has
First Amendment rights to be informed. The issue focused on the
proper interpretation of a provision Congress added to the Communications Act in 1972 affording federal candidates for public office
special access rights to the broadcast medium. The court found that

even if the provision inhibited the First Amendment rights of broadcast stations, it primarily advanced the paramount rights of the public to receive vital political information.[34] While the regulatory theory linking these three cases—*Red Lion*, the CBS general access decision, and the Carter-Mondale candidate access decision—is routinely questioned by some legal scholars and most proponents of further deregulation, the cases have not been overruled.

Although the FCC has frequently exalted diversity as a basic regulatory goal, it has not been consistent in explaining what the concept means. In my view, the only aspect of diversity that warrants special consideration as a regulatory rationale is *viewpoint* diversity—affording, as the Supreme Court has said, the general public with a range of divergent and antagonist voices. Nevertheless, the FCC has perceived the subject as being splintered into distinct parts. For example, as deregulation moved to the forefront, the emphasis has been on *outlet* diversity—a mere counting of the number of media outlets available to the public in the hands of different owners. The FCC has also periodically evaluated *source* diversity, or the number of content providers. Finally, the FCC sometimes looks at *program* diversity which, to be distinguished from viewpoint diversity, seems more oriented to assessing variety in program formats (typical of radio) or program genres (typical of TV)

With media services expanding like never before, the temptation to make policy decisions based on nothing but numbers becomes almost irresistible. It rests, however, on a very large assumption—that the multiplicity of outlets, standing alone, will produce the bustling marketplace of ideas that most scholars and policymakers acknowledge is vital to nurturing a representative democracy. In fairness, outlet counting is not only the easiest approach, it should be the preferred way to promote an array of viewpoints—because this form of policymaking is the most content neutral, ensuring the least impact on broadcasters' First Amendment rights. While sympathetic to this position, it must be said that neither the easiest nor most idealistic approach is always the best. A representative democracy needs not only an abundance of outlets but also a reasonable range of viewpoints to thrive, and the former does not ensure the latter—any more than an unfettered marketplace in the sale of certain drugs ensures equitable pricing or adequate consumer protection.

Researchers since P. O. Steiner in 1952 have posited various theories about how competition in broadcasting impacts diversity.[35] Steiner averred that a single monopolist would actually maximize "product" diversity in broadcasting, because that person or party would try to capture every possible listener or viewer by offering varied, not duplicative, programming. Although Steiner's theory has since been challenged on a number of economic grounds, echoes of his argument are still heard today. For example, many advocates of further broadcast deregulation contend that concentration and consolidation actually add to diversity, especially in radio program formats, because modern consolidators, holding multiple station licenses in the same market, will be less likely to want to compete against themselves with duplicative programming. In this view, bigger, more efficient companies will use their greater resources to create, not constrict, new services and content. Some industry supporters go further. They insist that the radio medium, with its myriad of music and talk formats, has already achieved "diversity nirvana," rendering viewpoint diversity moot as a policy rationale for limiting ownership in radio.[36] Indeed, one advocacy group candidly suggests that viewpoint diversity is not even relevant in today's radio marketplace:

> The problem of applying viewpoint diversity to radio is that radio has become a medium primarily of music and entertainment, rather than news and public affairs. News on the typical FM music station is limited to a few minutes per hour of headlines, sports, traffic and weather; the expression of political views is notably absent. Public affairs shows are typically consigned to low-audience time slots like Sunday morning. . . . Contemporary radio simply is not a "political" medium, if it ever was, so viewpoint diversity is hard to measure directly.[37]

Sadly, this commentary is valid. We have reached a point where the absence of meaningful viewpoint diversity in the marketplace can be used to justify policymaking intended to lift certain remaining restrictions premised, in part, on fostering diversity.

"Localism": Local Stations Serving Local Needs

The promotion of local stations to serve local interests has been a cornerstone of American mass media policy since the first days of regulation. Although there is no specific mention of "localism" in the Communications Act, the concept derives from the following statutory language: "In considering applications for [broadcast] licenses . . . the FCC shall make such distribution of licenses, frequencies, hours of operation, and of power among the several states and communities as to provide a fair, efficient, and equitable distribution of radio service to each of the same."[38] As recently as 1992, Congress affirmed that "[a] primary objective and benefit of our nation's system of regulation of broadcast television is the local origination of programming."[39]

Federal policy fostering local broadcast service parallels America's uniquely decentralized system of government. In contrast, most other nations, whether totalitarian (large or small) or just geographically limited (such as most European countries), have elected to organize electronic media on a national basis. Even the United Kingdom's storied BBC started life as a state-sponsored, nationwide monopoly. In the United States, localism historically also meant an obligation to present news and public affairs pegged, in part, to the particular needs and interests of local communities where broadcast licenses are assigned.[40] Although this obligation once entailed explicit programming guidelines—such as live shows, locally produced features using local talent, and specific program material addressing identifiable local issues—this type of specificity no longer exists.

In fact, years of deregulation have cast substantial doubt on the continued meaning and significance of localism. No one has yet proposed a change in the allocation system of local stations licensed to serve local communities, but many have questioned whether it remains necessary to have any rules fostering local ownership or promoting local service in commercial broadcasting. The argument usually contains two conjunctive elements. First, service to local communities can be achieved whether local stations are owned by local or national companies and, second, providing local service is just good business. Few would deny that most successful radio and television stations succeed, in part, by reflecting the local needs and interests of their audiences—something they are able to do whether they are owned by local or national interests. It is also clear, however, that a station owned by a vast media conglomerate, deemphasizing local management and demanding the airing of large amounts of programming from outside the market, can still achieve commercial success.

With longstanding uncertainty over what constitutes localism now matched by a growing uncertainty over what constitutes community in an increasingly interlaced media world, one finds less reason (or basis) for continuing to pretend that localism remains a guiding precept in commercial broadcasting—apart from its original formulation of ensuring that specific channels are assigned to specific localities. When the FCC removed accountability for local programming several years ago, it effectively rendered irrelevant any form of localism defined by the source or nature of content. What was always a vague policy goal is now nothing more than a highly illusive pursuit in a regulatory age focused almost exclusively on a few remaining structural standards.

Regulation Based on the Intrusiveness of Broadcast Signals

The fresh battle over broadcast indecency that erupted in 2004 highlights one of the lesser-known theories of broadcast regulation—a theory first recognized in a famous indecency case, *FCC v. Pacifica Foundation*. The case centered on a celebrated, off-color monologue by comedian George Carlin which had been broadcast by a New York radio station during a midday time period.

When it reached the Supreme Court in 1978, a new justification for broadcast regulation emerged—the so-called impact or intrusiveness theory. Under this theory, indecency can be regulated on broadcast stations even when the same content remains unregulated in other media, because broadcasting reaches directly into the home and is so easily accessible to children during most hours of the day. It is difficult to determine where this theory stands in light of subsequent developments. It may still buttress actions against broadcast indecency, but sweeping deregulation combined with vast changes in the media marketplace suggest limited future application in other areas—with or without comprehensive policy change. Certainly the expanded presence (in the home, on the job, and on the road) of the Internet, cable, satellite, and countless wireless devices make it increasingly difficult to suggest that the predicate for the impact theory remains unique to broadcasting.

A Market-Based Theory of Regulation

As mass media deregulation was first gaining momentum in the 1970s, alternative theories of public policy were beginning to permeate other parts of the nation's economic life. In banking, transportation, and telecommunications, policymakers were starting to question the "New Deal" thinking of the past that had enthusiastically extended government regulation to so many facets of American life.

Starting with the Depression-era presidency of Franklin D. Roosevelt in the 1930s and running through the Lyndon Johnson presidency of the 1960s, policymakers seemed to embrace an ever-expanding role for the federal government. Government, it was generally believed, could and should take affirmative measures in many areas to improve society. The Radio Act of 1927 and its successor, the Communications Act of 1934, reflected this approach. So too did early FCC and judicial decisions that fleshed out the new legislative framework. Government regulation, many thought, could make broadcasting (hence, society) better than if it were left uncontrolled. An opening regulatory act, where the government performed the relatively minor role of "traffic cop" directing electrical interference, quickly mushroomed into a much larger role. What was broadcast, by whom, and for what purpose became just as important as technical standards.

But the economic stagnation that swept over the country in the 1970s convinced politicians in both parties that the pendulum had swung too far. New notions were starting to appear that challenged the need to solve social problems with government regulation. Existing regulatory regimes like those in transportation and banking were questioned as being counterproductive, denying consumers the best service and prices. The distrust of the marketplace, so widespread in the 1930s and 1940s, started to be replaced in the 1970s with a new faith in the marketplace.

While the 1960s and 1970s generally remained a period of proactive mass media regulation, energized in no small part by a myriad of aggressive special interest groups given expanded status to participate in FCC proceedings, a few, light crosscurrents were beginning to blow over the regulatory landscape. One of these was a growing realization that certain FCC requirements had become so entwined in bureaucratic detail that both the government and the broadcast industry were suffering from regulatory overkill. Another was reflected in the debate that surfaced over the role the government should play in music formats on radio stations. The issue was prompted by a series of license transfer cases in which the federal court of appeals in Washington, D.C., reflecting its significant liberal bent at the time, developed a set of criteria for determining when the "public interest" standard required the FCC to hold a hearing to review proposed changes in the entertainment format of a local broadcast station—for example, changing from classical music to album rock. The FCC, under the more conservative Nixon/Ford administrations, resisted being thrust into this troublesome thicket. In a series of coordinated steps, the FCC announced that the public interest would be best served if diversity in entertainment formats was achieved through market forces and competition among broadcasters—not by administrative fiat. Not until this newly articulated policy underwent a further clash before a special en banc panel of the appeals court (resulting in defeat)[41] and a final decision by the U.S. Supreme Court (resulting in victory)[42]—cases I remember well as counsel in both—was the matter resolved. Significantly, the Supreme Court's ultimate decision expressly sanctioned the FCC's discretion to invoke market forces in carrying out its regulatory mission. With only a few sputtering detours, this approach has fueled much of the deregulatory movement ever since.

Other than a general consensus concerning some paperwork burdens, broadcast deregulation was not, it should be pointed out, propelled forward by any groundswell of public opinion. Quite the contrary; it derived most of its energy from a renewed ideological commitment to free-market economics. Starting with the Reagan administration in 1980, it "almost became an article of faith that the unimpeded private sector could carry on the affairs of society more economically, more efficiently, and more equitably than any public ownership or state-regulated alternative."[43]

This shift in broadcast regulatory policy from the traditional fiduciary approach to one more dependent on competition and the marketplace was perhaps inevitable.[44] Overregulation had reached a peak at about the same time technology was dramatically rearranging the broadcast economy (long dominated by just three TV networks). Mass media policy in a democracy should, most would agree, be directed toward maximizing the services the public desires and needs. Instead of attempting to define public needs and laying out discrete categories of programming to serve such needs, would it not be preferable for policymakers to rely on the ability of broadcasters to determine those needs through the normal mechanisms of the marketplace? In the ideal application of this theory, all minorities are served, young children are gratified, senior citizens are indulged, and all remaining, disparate demographic groups are satisfied, simply by having the opportunity to freely sample the veritable plethora of media sources put before them.

While consumer choice has reached unprecedented levels in recent years, the ideal media landscape painted by some to justify further deregulation hardly matches reality. First, not all media sources are available to all Americans—owing to factors of cost and geography. Not everyone in every town (small or large) has access to every media service offered over the air, at newsstands, or via cable, satellite, and the Internet. And not everyone living at the center of a media cornucopia can afford to purchase every service or device they would choose. Second, market forces alone, especially in an advertising-supported mass medium, often fail to serve all potentially worthy audiences. It is for this reason that both Congress and the FCC have singled out children's television as needing a special form of regulation.[45]

Third, the marketplace fundamentalism that echoed through the Reagan years, and found a statutory blessing in the Telecommunications Act of 1996, encourages a myth of omnipotent markets. The ascendant marketplace ideology claims to free us from government restraints. But when the marketplace is one of ideas, it tends to exalt only what is the most popular to the detriment of diversity and alternative choice. As Croteau and Hoynes remind us:

> The commercial marketplace operates on the basis of providing what is most popular to the greatest number. This approach may work reasonably well with consumer products, but when the "commodity" at hand is ideas, democracy is not likely to be well served by paying attention only to the popular and fashionable.[46]

A similar view is expressed by Professor Owen Fiss:

> A fully competitive market might produce a diversity of programs, formats, and reportage, but, to borrow an image of Renata Adler's, it will be the diversity of "a pack going essentially in one direction." [A] perfectly competitive market will produce shows or publications whose marginal cost equals marginal revenues. . . . But there is no necessary, or even probabilistic, relationship between making a profit (or allocating resources efficiently) and supplying the electorate with the information they need to make free and intelligent choices about government policy, the structure of government, or the nature of society. The point was well understood when we freed our educational systems and our universities from the grasp of the market, and it applies with equal force to the media.[47]

Policymaking in a democracy should be more than consumer polling, leaving the fulfillment of all needs and interests to a generic marketplace. It should consider not only what individuals want, such as widespread choice, but also what society needs, such as some public setting of priorities designed to serve the overall good. We know, as Owen Fiss reminds us, that markets do not work perfectly to the consumer's satisfaction in all areas of commerce, much less those affected with intellectual content. That is why we have regulation targeted to some businesses and antitrust laws applicable to all. We also know that in the media business, news and public service do not routinely produce adequate profits in the marketplace. That is why when regulatory reins are loosened or competition stiffens, cuts in news and public affairs almost always follow, especially at the local level.

MASS MEDIA POLICYMAKING
AT THE START OF THE TWENTY-FIRST CENTURY

The touchstone of post-1980 mass media policymaking has been that the federal government should regulate only where competition is not possible or adequate to achieve a vital, efficient, innovative marketplace. In the beginning, regulation had been imposed because of economic and technological factors thought to be unique to broadcasting. Over the years, it was also imposed to achieve specific social objectives, such as serving local community needs, fostering the discussion of public issues, and furthering the interest of children or minorities. The 1996 act, however, formally enshrined a policy goal that had been taking shape since the Reagan years. It is premised on the notion that the need for behavioral regulation has been diminished because we have now achieved a level of media abundance where marketplace forces can replace regulatory commands. Not only was this 1996 legislative message itself far-reaching, it was topped off with a new "procedural" mandate requiring the FCC to review—and repeal or modify, as necessary—every remaining rule affecting broadcast ownership every two years (changed to four years in 2004). With the influential federal appeals court in Washington, D.C., reading this requirement as constituting a presumption in favor of repealing or modifying all applicable ownership rules, little room is left for balanced policymaking. It fundamentally alters the way the FCC is permitted to look at its own rules and role. And it allows virtually no room for policy based on predictive judgment, past experience, or longstanding knowledge of the broadcast industry. Whereas the FCC might, in the past, have decided to wait a reasonable period of time to assess the impact of particular policy decisions, it is now instructed to forge ahead no matter what.[48]

These changes have caused major ripple effects. The "public interest" standard has been minimized, and engrained principles such as fostering diversity and localism have been relegated to subservient status. In the process, policymakers at the FCC and sitting on reviewing courts have become increasingly preoccupied with finding a handy empirical standard to better implement the new abiding regulatory rationale. As reported in early 2003, the chairman of the FCC was pushing the agency's staff to produce an "objective scientific formula" in order to "accurately measure the diversity of media voices in a local market."[49] While the "diversity index" actually adopted[50] was later criticized by a reviewing court (based on methodology not concept) and the current FCC appears unprepared to resuscitate the project, the effort itself was nothing less than a barely disguised search for the holy grail in policymaking—where tough decisions affecting citizens can be reduced to an easy, fill-in-the-numbers factual formula.

While empirical evidence can be vitally important, it should not be regarded as the ultimate cure-all for responsible policymaking. The crafting of public policy is never entirely or even primarily a scientific endeavor. It is more appropriately a political process that seeks to balance all public interests, weighing scientific and other verifiable evidence but also allowing for deliberation over other factors, some of them necessarily subjective, like the level of civic discourse and how the needs and interests of minorities and children can best be served. Although some argue that anything other than scientifically or economically based data allows political factors and personal ideology to seep into the debate, the same can be said of those who insist that we must only tolerate regulation that is scientifically based (to the exclusion of all factors other than the marketplace). The point is that mass media policymaking *should* be a political debate. It should not be restricted to empirical facts and expert proof but, instead, allow for opinion and political judgment as to what might best serve the public at large.

The major failure of public policy in recent years—by Congress and the FCC—can be attributed to an increasingly narrow view of what constitutes the public interest, combined with an overly broad calculation as to how public benefits can be achieved. Under this policy approach, the public interest standard is seen as commanding a single objective—stimulating a private commercial market that will, in some secondary, undefined way, ultimately lead to tangible public benefits.

The trouble with this ideal scenario is that it ignores history and basic common sense. It is an affront to American principles to cast the general public adrift in the belief that those who control commercial enterprises will necessarily reach out to underserved audiences or offer programs promoting civic discourse. Instead of serving diverse needs and strengthening democracy, recent media trends have likely weakened such goals. Sure, for the most affluent and elite segments of American society—those most motivated and able to explore all media options—the depth and breadth of news and information is unparalleled. Like the fertile fields of America's heartland, its newsstands and airwaves consistently yield a bountiful harvest—for those inclined to reap all that is sown. From great national newspapers like the *New York Times* and *Wall Street Journal*, serious periodicals covering everything from the arts to zero-based economics, and a legion of electronic services running the gamut from NPR, PBS, C-Span, CNN, or specialty offerings for children, women, golfers, gourmets, and history buffs to high-quality original entertainment on HBO that can equal the best in movies or live theater, American mass media produce an exceedingly large and diverse crop of ideas and information. But for most Americans who routinely elect or are able to choose only the most popular mass media, the experience is quite different. News and information they absorb is usually treated more like entertainment than a special form of intelligence relevant to people's lives. In fact, what constitutes "news" is often little more than an obsessive, repetitive cataloging of the trials (real or unreal) and tribulations of public figures, the unfolding agony of human events (large and small), and a relentless focus on stories with either a lighthearted or bizarre twist.

More serious news events or complicated issues are rarely allowed to intrude upon the more "entertaining" segments of one's local newspaper, broadcast station, or popular cable channel. Political news and issues, when offered, are typically presented as a contest among warring factions, narrated with polls and sound bites more focused on the personalities and foibles of candidates or public officials than the underlying substance. More Americans, especially younger Americans, are drifting away from mainstream mass media. At the same time, swift and profound advancements in the means of communication, coupled with significant changes in the ways people live—such as the growth of two-career families, the insulation-attendant urban sprawl, heightened time pressures affecting both business and personal pursuits, and a general decline in reflection—all contribute to a greater overall sense of disconnection. Where mass media might have once been thought to be a significant positive factor in developing a sense of community, recent developments in mass media and modern society point to a steady erosion of community.

Instead of greater participation by citizens, we find growing apathy, weaker voting levels, and widespread cynicism—a cynicism directed at politicians, government, and our popular media. In short, the very institutions and processes that are so crucial to a representative democracy are increasingly being viewed as either unresponsive or unpersuasive by the vast majority of Americans. While neither mass media performance nor mass media policymaking alone can be blamed for failing to better elevate American society, some steps are possible to help address these negative trends. There is no magic wand that, upon waving, would set us on an entirely new mass media course or reverse years of a broad societal drift. The best we can expect is a substantial shift in overall focus, accompanied by increased attention to preserving and protecting that which is manageable. It is impossible to start from scratch, and there is no time for pie in the sky.

The concluding chapter expands on the failures of mass media policy, demonstrating how the existing regulatory system has become dysfunctional, can no longer be repaired by applying standards and practices resurrected from the past, and, therefore, must be replaced. Charting an entirely new course for the twenty-first century, it calls for elimination of all remaining nontechnical regulation of commercial broadcasting, in exchange for better funding and improved regulation of public broadcasting, accompanied by more rigorous, regular, and expanded monitoring of commercial broadcasting under the antitrust laws.

8

A Mass Media Policy for the Twenty-First Century

This journey started by highlighting the vital role played by mass media in American society. Mass media took root in this country and began to flourish only when important social changes took place in the nineteenth century. Now, at the start of the twenty-first century, modern mass media are permanently linked with America's culture, business, and system of government in an intricate web that can't be untangled.

Because of their ubiquitous presence in our daily lives and because they often reflect some of the worst traits and trends in contemporary society, mass media have long been the target of scathing discourse by academics, grandstanding politicians, and advocacy groups brandishing many different banners. The criticism is understandable because mass media could, indeed, serve American society in the more ennobling manner envisioned by critics. Nevertheless, such criticism needs to be tempered by certain realities. First, mass media in an open society only succeed when they reflect and serve popular tastes. So, those who find fault with American media must also acknowledge that some of the underlying trends of contemporary society are neither solely generated nor exclusively spread by media. While mass media could better serve American society, the same can be said of our educational system, our government (at all levels), and American business. Second, mass media in America can be viewed much more favorably when they are considered as a whole—taking into account the output and quality of every broadcast station, every satellite or cable channel, every newspaper, every periodical, and every website available to every American—and when they are compared with any other media system in the world. Mass media in the United States, for all their warts and woeful faults, have been shaped by American social and political development. Just as America stands at the pinnacle of power in the world, American media is clearly the most powerful and responsive media in the world. Although it is tempting to glance back to a time when our media were different (tamer, if not better), it is difficult to argue that American mass media of any previous era was more diverse, free, and independent than mass media today. And, even if a higher trash quotient now infects a broader array of our most popular media, it is also undeniable that, for those willing to look beyond prime-time television, rant and rave radio, or sleazy periodicals, there are more high-quality and easily accessible media services available now than ever before. Simply put, American mass media today serve more diverse interests more widely with the least amount of government influence.

This is hardly a new debate. For virtually its entire history, broadcasting has been enthusiastically embraced by the masses while critics worried and complained that the medium was being controlled by too few owners whose sole motivation was profit. Forty years ago, after broadcasting had already been a fixture in American society for more than four decades, the radio and television scholar Harry J. Skornia wrote:

> Has the United States found the proper institutional framework and control mechanism for the essential communications functions which television and radio must provide if democracy is to prevail? Are vast and powerful business corporations, which centralize control each year in fewer hands, the best trustees for the nation's radio and television communications systems?[1]

Skornia's questions persist even as the conditions he observed have either worsened or produced new fault lines. Competition, long a highly envied hallmark of American media, has become so widespread and so intense that it is, in many cases, demeaning content, accelerating blatant commercialism, and fragmenting audiences so severely that the "mass" in mass media is in danger of becoming a misnomer. Recent policymaking related to electronic media has hastened these trends—pushing the deregulation wave to the point where we are literally awash in competition while drifting further and further away from the general public service role broadcast stations are expected to perform under a regulatory regime that, without fundamental change, has endured for almost eighty years. Evidence continues to mount that the current system is inadequate to ensure an ongoing public service dimension—something essential in an open democratic society but increasingly unobtainable by an unregulated, nonaccountable, commercially oriented media.

Unlike print media—which experienced government control only at the beginning—electronic media have grown from infancy to maturity under essentially the same comprehensive regulatory scheme. The question is whether that scheme remains relevant at the start of the twenty-first century. It must be remembered that, even in the beginning, nothing was preordained about the eventual blueprint for broadcast regulation. Congress, needing to cope with a technical crisis in the 1920s, chose to license broadcasting but permit its operation as a private enterprise. The exact regulatory system, like most legislation, evolved haphazardly. It required navigating numerous conflicting interests and, in the end, borrowing liberally from previous regulatory models. Congress could have favored, and, as we have seen, certain interests at the time proposed, a Canadian or British model involving far more government control. It might also have decided to treat broadcast licenses like patents, creating an intangible ownership right with a predetermined life span (e.g., twenty or thirty years) after which the privilege to use a particular frequency would revert back to the public domain. Or Congress could have chosen to auction frequencies to the highest bidder with the proceeds funneled into general revenue or earmarked to support a noncommercial system. The point is, in the beginning, these and many other variations were possible—ranging from much less to much more regulation.

It is doubtful, as a practical matter, whether the same variety of options remains today. With more than twelve thousand incumbent broadcast stations[2] now occupying assigned frequencies relied upon by the general public everyday in thousands of distinct local communities and the nonbroadcast media landscape resembling a vast untreated weed patch, the regulatory issues and alternatives are vastly different than in 1927 or 1934. We cannot start with a clean slate, and we should not continue to impose a policy framework that, increasingly, is both impractical and unenforceable. In short, we need a new policy better suited to the advanced state of deregulation now engulfing the electronic media—one that identifies and addresses the most basic media needs of modern society.

And events keep constricting the time for action. Free, over-the-air television, the indisputable norm for years, has already become a condition for only a distinct and dwindling minority of Americans. Today, most people pay for television, and many are also starting to pay for radio. Even as mass media policy remains stuck in neutral, commercial broadcasting is racing ahead with new, experimental business models—all of which center on pay or on-demand services. It is futile to remain focused on fixing a worn-out regulatory model when changed circumstances demand an entirely new one.

THE "PUBLIC TRUSTEESHIP" MODEL: A LITANY OF PUBLIC POLICY FAILURES

At the core of the current regulatory structure is the concept that local broadcast stations, in addition to operating profit-motivated businesses, must still act as public "trustees" for their local communities by presenting certain types of programming, whether profitable or not. As the Supreme Court once remarked, a broadcast station is "given the privilege of using scarce radio frequencies as proxies for the entire community, obligated to give suitable time and attention to matters of great concern."[3] This has been the basic legal or policy standard since 1927. Subject to free speech protections, the public trustee model has permitted (one might say commanded) the FCC to review the record of each broadcast station for the quantity, subject matter, and, until very recently, overall fairness of its nonentertainment programming.[4]

Every broadcast station license is temporary. It is awarded only for a set number of years and specifically carries no right of ownership in the frequency assigned.[5] The FCC can only grant or renew a broadcast license after finding that the grant is consistent with the public interest—in other words, only if the station will comply (initial grant) or has complied (renewal) with its public trusteeship obligations.[6] To ensure compliance, the FCC was given expansive powers and, aided by exceedingly broad statutory language, has often acted expansively. In order to add meaning to the public trusteeship concept, the FCC, from a very early stage, adopted and enforced a variety of standards by which a broadcast station's performance could be measured. That general approach was consistently followed for the first five decades of regulation. Then, beginning in the 1970s but especially propelled by political changes in the 1980s, the pendulum shifted. Many of the standards previously used to advance the public·trusteeship model were peeled away.

We have now had nearly eighty years of experience with the same regulatory scheme—spanning both a proregulatory phase lasting more than fifty years followed by a deregulatory phase that continues to resonate after more than twenty-five years. The question is whether it still works. While some might argue that the system has always been flawed and should have been jettisoned years ago, my focus is on whether it *can* work, given the substantial marketplace changes and massive deregulatory measures that have already occurred. How badly has our Humpty Dumpty broadcast system been shattered, and can it be put back together again? If not, what are the public policy alternatives?

After cataloging a few of the more prominent policy failures, I conclude that the current system is not only not working, it cannot be put back together again and it cannot be remedied by further revision. Instead, what we need is a more fundamental change in the basic system and regulatory mission.

Ineffective Regulation

The myth is that all broadcast stations provide beneficial public service to the local communities they are licensed to serve. The reality is that even when the FCC had more exacting standards, lax enforcement by the agency permitted stations to discount or disregard this basic obligation. Part of this stems from the inherent limitation of the regulatory scheme itself—one that calls upon the FCC to take actions based on the public trusteeship obligation but also prohibits the FCC from dictating (or censoring) any specific programming decisions made by broadcast stations. Historically, the FCC has been concerned that if it crafted standards for local and public service programming too explicitly or enforced such standards too aggressively, it would infringe on broadcasters' First Amendment rights. And, conversely, when guidelines have, in fact, been established they usually have either been highly generalized or loosely reflective of existing industry practices.

The best testament to the ineffective nature of the current regulatory system is the fact that virtually all broadcast renewal applications are granted. Not once in its entire history has the FCC denied renewal of a broadcast station license on the basis that the station failed to serve as an outlet for local or informational programming. Even in those exceedingly rare instances where the FCC has refused to renew a station license, the decision has centered on nonprogramming violations.

Probably the only broadcast station in history to lose its license as a result of a renewal challenge raising questions regarding programming was television station WLBT in Jackson, Mississippi. But even in that case it was not the FCC that took decisive action, it was the federal court of appeals in Washington, D.C. Despite evidence of blatant racism in WLBT's programming,[7] the FCC granted the station a conditional renewal. The court of appeals, however, overruled the FCC. It granted a local citizens group the right to challenge WLBT's programming, vacated the station's license, and issued an order requiring that WLBT be operated on an interim basis by someone else. Ultimately, in the wake of the court's mandate, a new license was awarded to an entirely new party.[8] It was not, however, the FCC's finest moment as caretaker of the public trusteeship model.

Although the WLBT case set off a brief period of regulatory activism, government supervision would eventually take a sharp turn in the opposite direction. When the deregulatory tide gathered strength and swept over many bedrock vestiges of the public trusteeship model in the 1980s and 1990s (see chapter 3), "effective regulation" became an oxymoron. An inherently difficult enforcement scheme was suddenly rendered weaker still. Longstanding standards and practices were swept aside, giving way to a new guiding light whose principal focus was now on the marketplace.

With many of the tools of regulation removed or relaxed, it was inevitable that enforcement attitudes would change as well. FCC officials who might have once expressed outrage at certain deceptive news practices, commercial excesses, or private management arrangements between broadcast competitors simply accepted such practices and arrangements as the new norm. In fact, by the dawn of the twenty-first century, vigorous regulatory enforcement was largely restricted to such narrow areas as technical violations—for example, broadcast towers threatening air navigation—or indecency complaints mainly fomented by America's defenders of morality.

Removal of Accountability

The WLBT case is also famous for giving birth to a consumers' movement in broadcasting. Previously, it was possible to intervene in a broadcast application case before the FCC only if you alleged electrical interference or could show some economic injury—in effect, only if you were a competing broadcaster. The WLBT case allowed members of the audience to intervene in FCC proceedings. As a consequence, during the 1970s and 1980s, numerous individuals and special interest groups participated in a wide variety of broadcast proceedings—directly challenging or testing the public trusteeship role of broadcast stations.[9] Although some abuses occurred, in general the presence of such groups set in motion a brief period during which broadcasters were goaded into more self-examination and the FCC was forced to exercise a higher degree of scrutiny. The result was a more palpable level of accountability on the part of all broadcast licensees. While no more licenses were lost, public activism combined with more detailed FCC standards, for a time, raised the general threat level and, presumably, the overall responsibility of broadcast licensees.

Other factors helped raise the level of accountability during this period. First, because broadcast licenses were renewed every three years, and the process was both slower and more cumbersome, oversight was nearly constant. Second, stations were not only examined more frequently, they were tested on regulations and policies involving specific station operations. These included (a) percentage guidelines for news and public affairs, (b) detailed procedures for surveying the general public and community leaders on important issues, (c) numerical guidelines on advertising, and (d) a policy requiring fairness in covering controversial issues. Third, ultimate accountability was written into the law by a statutory provision that made a broadcast station subject to competing applications every time it requested renewal. While challenges of this nature were relatively rare and almost always ended in victory for the incumbent broadcaster, they were a costly, time-consuming distraction that prudent stations sought to avoid.

Elaborate standards and procedures had the effect of making each broadcast station more accountable in fulfilling its public trusteeship role. Just the prospect of getting caught in a web of rules and rulings— often spun by aggressive special interest groups—usually caused stations to be more responsive. Now, almost everything has changed. The

deletion of standards and weakening of procedures has marginalized
the impact of anyone seeking to call into question the public trusteeship performance of broadcast stations. Not only are renewal and
transfer actions virtually automatic, there are scant methods to even
slow them down. When the FCC eliminated its three-year rule in
1982—which required a broadcaster to hold its license for a minimum of three years before selling—it became possible to buy and sell
stations as quickly as the FCC was able to process the paperwork.[10]
With no holding period, a broadcast station could be acquired—and
many were—simply for the purpose of being sold quickly for a profit.
In this environment, it became easy to subvert the concept of public
service to the bottom line. And, sitting as the efficacious fountainhead
of the broadcast deregulatory movement, the FCC and its professional
staff, always sensitive to prevailing political winds, became less and
less inclined to vigorously enforce what remained of public service
standards.

When the inherent ineffectiveness of the basic regulatory scheme is
combined with a diminished accountability, the myth of the public
trusteeship model is laid bare. With neither substance nor serious sur-
veillance to support it, this venerable regulatory model has become
more fable than fact.

Localism Lost

A cornerstone of the original Communications Act and a centerpiece of FCC policy ever since has been the notion that broadcast stations are licensed to serve local needs and interests. Even though, as a
physical fact, thousands of individual stations still operate within discrete localized areas, key decisions by Washington policymakers and
rapid consolidation by the industry have diminished *localism* as a viable concept. When local stations feature local news and information
today they do so because of market conditions, not FCC policy. While
continuing to pay homage to localism, most recent policy decisions
have not only failed to encourage more local programming, they have
produced the very opposite. Local ownership—which was once
thought to enhance chances for better local programming—has been
abandoned as a workable policy tool. This change, however, is probably the least significant, since it was never clear that favoring local residents as owners was directly relevant to achieving local service. On
the other hand, the steady relaxation of ownership rules permitting

greater consolidation has led to more centralized control of programming by vastly larger national chains. And the dismantling of FCC standards that previously permitted a periodic snapshot of a station's local program efforts under a system that encouraged more active participation by local groups has stripped the process of any meaningful enforcement mechanism.

The problem is compounded when one considers that the expanded media world created by satellite television, nonstop cable channels, and infinite websites—whose proliferation is repeatedly cited as the principal justification for such policy decisions—produces little, if any, local programming or information. Local communities still depend on traditional media outlets—local newspapers and local radio and television stations. Very little local news, information, or culture is beamed in from "new" media operating in cyberspace or outer space. Meanwhile, without any significant regulatory accountability and facing the mounting pressures of being part of a corporate media family whose instincts run toward centralization and standardization, it is increasingly difficult to find stations exercising substantial local autonomy or producing a service distinctly tailored to their own communities.

While localism is still regularly proclaimed by policymakers,[11] It has been lost in application. If there are no standards to define nor procedures to enforce localism, what purpose is served by still clinging to the concept? It just stands out as another symbol of a failed, ineffective policy. The promotion of local news, information, and entertainment can only be translated into a workable concept if such programming is clearly defined and regularly assessed—by type and quantity—and today's deregulatory commands preclude the adoption of such measures in commercial broadcasting.

The De Facto Replacement of the Public Trusteeship Model with a Market Model

One of most glaring failures of mass media public policy has been the de facto shift of the entire regulatory scheme from one premised on the public trusteeship model to one driven by, if not dependent upon, the marketplace. I use the phrase *de facto* because the basic law has never been altered. The provisions of the Communications Act and FCC rules that gave rise to the trusteeship model remain unchanged. And there has been no public debate over the removal or replacement of those provisions. Instead, policymakers—in Congress and at the FCC—have moved us from the trusteeship model to the market model on a de facto basis. Our policy focus and approach has changed without any change in the underlying law. Equally important, this fundamental shift has taken place without serious consideration of possible alternatives or likely consequences for some elements of American society. We have relegated the public trusteeship model to the scrapheap of antiquated regulatory thinking, supplanted by little more than a fervent belief that a vibrant marketplace with more and more media outlets will, in some overall, long-term fashion, satisfy most major segments of the audience. Ironically, those now insisting that the continued existence of any form of broadcast regulation must be supported by empirical proof have been eager to abandon the trusteeship model for a market model on little more than blind faith that a proliferation of media outlets will produce an enhanced marketplace of ideas. In this new policy postulate, commercial success is actually equated with public service. You promote one, you get the other. Where, one might ask, is the empirical proof for this flight of fancy? Why, in the face of perdurable, overwhelming evidence that commercial broadcasting only caters to audiences that advertisers will pay for, would policymakers suddenly adopt a new paradigm resting on a contrary assumption: that public service programming (which has never drawn sufficient advertiser support) will flow naturally from commercial success? It is a mystery the public record leaves unresolved.

For years, the FCC interpreted its regulatory mission as requiring the continued expansion of broadcast service—usually by authorizing more stations. There is no doubt that the public benefited directly and substantially from those enduring efforts, especially in the years before the advent of cable and satellite services. The policy began to fail, however, when the FCC continued to add new or to save failing stations in the 1980s and 1990s without also beginning to assess and weigh other factors crowding the regulatory agenda. This period was marked not only by a rising deregulatory tide carrying away many public service standards, it was accompanied by explosive growth in the number of broadcast stations. By 1970, just a few years before deregulation first took hold, the FCC had authorized 6,312 commercial radio stations and 683 commercial television stations. By 1996, the year deregulation was officially blessed by Congress (in the 1996 act), these numbers had ballooned to 10,215 commercial radio stations and 1,181 commercial television stations. By the start of 2005, the totals had "stabilized" at 10,992 and 1,366, respectively.[12]

Such dramatic growth might have been hailed as a triumph of public policy had it not been for several other key developments occurring simultaneously. For instance, even as policymakers were continuing to hand out more broadcast licenses, they were removing most of the standards that had helped ensure accountability for public service. Even if the FCC started down this road based entirely on the undocumented supposition that more competition would stir more vibrant public service, it should have been shaken almost immediately by one compelling example of its own making. In the early 1980s, the FCC revolutionized the FM radio band by creating new classes of stations and "dropping in" 700 new FM channel allocations. The action set off an immediate land rush in new station construction. If anything, the effort was too successful because, by the end of the decade, the commercial radio industry was clamoring for relief. It argued and the FCC agreed that increased competition and a sluggish economy were undermining the overall financial health of the radio business—producing stations not only incapable of providing exemplary public service but incapable of surviving. Accordingly, in a dramatic reversal, the FCC changed its radio ownership rules to permit substantially more stations under common ownership, nationally and in select local markets. Therefore, in rather short order, the FCC, in the 1980s, authorized hundreds of additional radio stations to stimulate service and, when the newly stimulated competition quickly led to economic distress in the 1990s, it changed its ownership rules to allow struggling stations to be combined with stronger stations. If there was a lesson in this scenario, it was not learned by policymakers. The ensuing years led to both further increases in the total number of authorized radio and television stations and a more relaxed attitude toward various station combinations. This took the form of allowing not only an increased number of competitive stations to be commonly owned but a more permissive attitude toward ways in which same-market stations could join forces, short of outright ownership. The latter included a hodgepodge of "local marketing," "brokerage," sales, and other operational arrangements entered into by competing radio and television stations that, beginning in the mid-1980s, were consistently sanctioned by the FCC.

While these actions may have muddled the FCC's regulatory mission, there was no denying that the general policy approach grew out of its longstanding urge to both expand and preserve broadcast service. If stations were faltering, public policy, it was thought, should be adjusted to save them from failure. Stations that might have, under normal marketplace conditions, gone out of business were actually spared by proactive government policy, even as government policy was transitioning to greater reliance on the marketplace. The long-embedded mindset of FCC officials was that the public benefited when any single station was saved from total failure.

Throwing a life preserver to failing stations might have been a legitimate policy prescription in an earlier era. But it became utterly implausible in the deregulatory era. Not only were stations being saved that were no longer accountable for public service, the broadcast marketplace was overflowing with new and old signals. Juxtaposed against these developments in broadcasting, evidence was growing that frequency space was badly needed for other services. Advancing technology and burgeoning public demand was creating a crisis in the availability of spectrum space for a new generation of wireless non-broadcast devices—equipment that could be used for personal, business, and, most important, emergency purposes. In sum, authorizing vast numbers of new stations while attempting to save others from becoming marketplace washouts was a colossal failure of public policy. The view that any privately owned, commercially operated station deserves to be rescued by government policy has always been suspect, but it became unfathomable in a deregulatory era stressing the primacy of marketplace competition.

The failure, nevertheless, has continued into the digital age. As noted, the number of commercial television stations doubled from 683 in 1970 to 1,366 at the end of 2004, mostly in the UHF band. While many of these stations provided the first or second nonnetwork service to some communities, there is little evidence they contributed to the growth or enhancement of nonentertainment programming. In fact, unless they became affiliated with a national network themselves —usually, one of the minor or specialty networks such as UPN, the WB, PaxNet, Telemundo, or Univision—or adopted a joint operating arrangement with a competitive station, they typically remained highly marginal operations.

In the end, how important was it to expand UHF television in this fashion under these conditions? The hundreds of new stations authorized by the FCC during this period provided very little public service, made it more difficult to free up valuable spectrum for emerging nonbroadcast services, and, ultimately, were unnecessary even as new sources of popular entertainment. The digital era has not only given us the two-hundred-plus channel universe—accessible to the vast majority of Americans who receive their television channels via cable or satellite—it has brought us to the point where all television stations have the capability of transmitting not one but three, four, or more separate signals with distinct streams of programming. A policy that seeks to save marginal stations amidst this set of circumstances is more wasteful than efficient. It has allowed many UHF television stations to be little more than pawns in a financial game, to be developed or held by private investors merely for a big payoff by either selling out to other broadcast interests or striking deals with those seeking to use the frequency for nonbroadcast services. Under a marketplace theory undiluted by regulatory instincts stuck in the past, these stations would never had been authorized and the frequencies they occupy would have long since been utilized for a more tangible public benefit.

The Creeping Commercialization of Public Broadcasting

Anyone tuning in to public broadcasting knows instinctively that the distinction between commercial and noncommercial broadcasting in this country is only a matter of degree. Corporate "sponsors" appear in both—they only differ in frequency and level of subtlety. Federal communications law specifically forbids noncommercial stations from accepting compensation for broadcasting messages that "promote any service, facility or product offered by any person who is engaged in such offering for profit." Yet, announcements that describe, display, and favorably advance the products and services of profit-making ventures conspicuously frame virtually all successful programs on public radio or public television. Short institutional announcements intended only to identify the company underwriting the cost of a program have, in recent years, given way to corporate messages plainly designed to promote products and services.

How did this happen, and who is responsible? In another deregulatory development, more a contortion than a confirmation of written law, the FCC, in 1984, "relaxed" its longstanding noncommercial policy to allow public broadcast stations to expand or "enhance" the scope of what had previously been called donor or underwriter "acknowledgements." Under this new interpretation, such announcements could mention "value-neutral descriptions of a product line or service" and include corporate logos or slogans that "identify but do not promote." In practice, this has allowed nonprogram announcements on public stations to spread vital commercial information, display commercial slogans, and describe commercial products—as long as they stop short of including price information or a specific call for consumer action. Given this new latitude, it was inevitable that perpetually needy public stations and their corporate underwriters or sponsors would find clever and aggressive ways to exploit this new opportunity. Today, a General Motors announcement on PBS may differ little from a General Motors commercial on CBS except for the explicit exhortation to buy GM products.

This episode is symptomatic of a broader failure of public policy directly traceable to the actions and inactions of Washington policymakers. Not only did Congress fail to establish a workable framework for public broadcasting until decades after it did so for commercial broadcasting, once it did allocate specific channels and authorize a national system, it failed to provide adequate funding. Instead of an enduring, insulated funding mechanism, it chose to keep federal funding for public broadcasting highly limited and totally dependent on the congressional appropriations process—effectively ensuring that it would always be susceptible to the wishes and whims of partisan politics. Given such an unreliable system, where not only the amount but the very fact of support could shift with the political winds, it is not surprising that the FCC would eventually feel compelled to relieve some of the persistent financial pressure on public broadcasting by allowing more commercial-like announcements. Without a steady, reliable stream of public funding, noncommercial broadcast stations have had little choice but to become more commercial, relying more heavily on corporate donations, foundation grants, and entrepreneurial ventures such as selling their own "branded" products.

Although commercial broadcasting has periodically sought to restrict the role and potential competitive threat of public broadcasting, the decisions that counted were in the hands of policymakers. From the beginning, Congress has repeatedly failed to help create or properly nourish a public broadcasting system that, despite such neglect, has grown, survived, and become a notable national treasure. This failure is only magnified when we consider that the longstanding campaign of Washington policymakers to deregulate commercial broadcasting has been carried out without any effort to make public broadcasting a less commercial, more accountable alternative. Instead of more enlightened policymaking that would have recognized that diminished accountability in commercial broadcasting required more attention to public broadcasting—to fill the obvious public service gaps—more often than not public broadcasting came under heightened partisan attack.

Congress Steps to the Plate and Strikes Out: The 1996 Telecom Act

The Telecommunications Competition and Deregulation Act of 1996,[13] a crowning symbol of the roaring 1990s, was primarily intended to deregulate the telecommunications industry. Hailed equally by conservative Republicans who controlled Congress and a Democratic administration that controlled the White House, this sweeping legislation was intended to promote competition and reduce regulation "in order to secure lower prices and higher quality services for American telecommunications consumers."[14] Swept up in the deregulatory zeal of the times and coaxed along by successful broadcast lobbying, the legislation advanced with no comparable policy goal for broadcasting. With Congress fixated on deregulating telecommunications in order to bring about more jobs for the economy as well as lower prices and enhanced services for consumers of telephone and computer services, broadcast deregulation proceeded with only a vague notion that it would somehow stir more competition, leading to enhanced diversity. The slogan of the movement was that it was time to throw off the shackles of an outdated regime by modernizing and updating all communications laws.[15] One enthusiastic legislator characterized his mission as reforming an "outmoded and antiquated, regulatory apartheid system in order to make exciting new information, telecommunications and entertainment services available for America."[16]

The 1996 act followed many unsuccessful efforts to rewrite federal communications law. Although various reform efforts were undertaken during the 1970s and 1980s, they produced only minor piecemeal measures. The 1996 act, however, came to fruition at a time when visions of the "information highway" inflamed the political rhetoric and partisans on both sides wanted to be viewed as responding to the technological and economic realities of the modern, information age. In addition, American telecommunications and media companies argued that relief from government restrictions in certain areas would unleash new technologies crucial to expanding their horizons and competing with foreign companies that often benefited from aggressive government support.

Finally, although the time was especially ripe for sweeping legislation, with or without a specific rationale for lumping broadcasting with the broadband world of telecommunications, it is doubtful whether anything as significant would have emerged without the heavy and steady influence of big telecommunications and media companies poised to get bigger as fast as the changing law would allow. John McCain, the mercurial Republican senator from Arizona, probably had it right when he commented that "it was clear to me all along that it was the . . . special interests that were driving this train"— pointing to the "wheeling and dealing that produced the final version of the measure."[17]

In sum, after many years of considering fundamental reform but doing little, Congress ultimately stepped to the plate in 1996 and enacted the most sweeping changes since 1934. It generally affirmed all previous deregulatory measures taken by the FCC, adopted a market-based approach nearly wholesale, and set the FCC on a mandatory course to review and drop additional regulations. In broadcasting, Congress, among other things, loosened the national television ownership cap, removed any remaining restriction on the total number of radio or TV stations one party could own, allowed for massive local consolidation, deleted key procedural standards designed to make broadcast stations more accountable, and, as icing on the proverbial cake, mandated that the FCC undertake a comprehensive review every two years looking toward further deregulation. If there was any doubt that the "public interest" would now be defined and advanced by merely stimulating economic competition, Congress actually told the FCC to delete all rules "no longer necessary in the public interest as the result of meaningful economic competition."[18] The change was sweeping and historic. "For the first time," exclaimed Congressman Bliley of Virginia, a key proponent, "communications policy will be based on competition rather than arbitrary regulation . . . [a] fundamental shift in philosophy."[19]

When critics lambaste the broadcast media for excessive concentration and increased emphasis on advertisers,[20] they need to also place substantial blame on the decisions of Washington policymakers that helped accelerate the changes they decry—decisions rooted in years of deregulation by the FCC and ultimately crowned by Congress in the 1996 act. With such a seismic shift in legislative direction, it was inevitable that a willing broadcast industry would take immediate advantage and that a more conservative federal judiciary, already in tune with the marketplace model, would push the FCC further down the deregulatory track. The legal burden had been shifted, and the broadcast industry should not be faulted for taking advantage. Broadcast stations and networks are private businesses whose principal purpose is to achieve commercial success. It should surprise no one, especially policymakers, that broadcasters, given new freedom to expand and operate, would concentrate on presenting programs that attract the largest audiences at the highest advertising rates and not on less commercially viable public service programs that attract smaller audiences at lower or zero advertising rates.

The 1996 act and its legislative history say little about promoting the marketplace of ideas. The focus is on the consumer, not the citizen. While this may be acceptable for the telecommunications industry, it fails to recognize the distinctly different role mass media play in America. By emphasizing markets as an economic issue and not as something crucial to fostering information and cultural awareness for a representative democracy, Washington policymakers struck out. Because they alone hold the power to shape such issues, they have failed mass media consumers every bit as much as the private businesses who operate broadcast stations.

—∰—

In the immediate aftermath of the 1996 act, several major broadcast transactions were proposed—even though they did not fully comply with applicable rules. But the deals were readily approved (and any inconvenient rules temporarily waived) because the applicants calculated and the FCC seemed to acquiesce in the premise that such rules were likely to be further relaxed in the next wave of deregulation that had been ordered by Congress. Major national networks such as CBS and Fox were permitted to acquire television stations even when their new holdings exceeded the new 35 percent national ownership cap just adopted in the 1996 act. Or they were allowed to own a second national network, or certain local stations before rules limiting such ownership were changed. Why worry? The deregulation train was moving and future rule changes could simply catch up with transactions that currently violated those rules. Congress had announced both a timetable and a clear-cut policy direction. The FCC was just marching in step.

One of the issues hotly debated in the 1996 act and reflected in various fragments of its legislative history was time brokerage among broadcast stations under what came to be known as local marketing agreements (LMAs). Under these arrangements, one station effectively operates a second station in the same local market—scheduling its programming, hiring its staff, and selling its advertising—even though, technically, ownership of the two stations remains separate. Starting in radio in the mid-1980s, LMAs flourished throughout the 1990s, expanding to include many television operations as well. With local ownership rules in flux but not yet legally loosened, LMAs were an effective means for aggressive groups to operate local stations they could not own. Although challenged at the outset as being violative of FCC rules and past policies, the FCC, without any formal rule making on the matter, issued a series of exceedingly timid ad hoc decisions that, in the years leading up to the 1996 act, effectively blessed such arrangements.

Nonetheless, because uncertainty continued to surround LMAs, Congress addressed the issue in the 1996 act. But it did so obliquely, delegating to the FCC the real task of deciding how to treat both pre-existing and future LMAs. Back at the FCC, the Media Bureau initially developed draft proposals not only discouraging the future use of LMAs but requiring many broadcasters to terminate such arrangements earlier than anticipated. When those proposals were leaked, however, broadcast industry lobbyists were able to convince certain key members of Congress that the FCC was being too rigid. When those members of Congress made their feelings known, the FCC listened. It backed off, adopting rules far more charitable than those originally proposed by its staff.[21]

How the FCC treated LMAs and the subsequent behind-the-scenes role played by influential members of Congress in the immediate aftermath of the 1996 act together illustrate additional failures of public policy. In the first place, the FCC never really took charge of these insidious practices. LMAs were not, as they were often billed, innocent arrangements that allowed two "independent" parties to join forces to preserve vital public service. They were expedient business arrangements where one aggressive party essentially took over the broadcast operations of another—in circumstances where such joint operations would normally not be allowed. The only rationale for allowing this circumvention of established rules and procedure was that, despite a near total vesting of operational authority in the party running both stations, "control" was thought to remain with the party technically still holding the FCC license. Based on personal experience representing parties on both sides of these arrangements, the reality rarely matched the rationale. Such deals and the FCC's laid-back approach, in fact, made a mockery of then existing ownership and transfer laws. In essence, policymakers looked the other way and allowed rules and procedures to be bent and stretched until the underlying laws were actually rewritten. A small matter, perhaps, in the overall scheme of things, but a strong backhanded deregulatory message nonetheless.

As noted, during the foregoing episode, certain key members of Congress personally intervened to orchestrate the FCC's resolution of the LMA issue. Meddling by individual members of Congress, especially by those sitting on critical oversight committees, is nothing new. But it has escalated to borderline chaos in recent years. In the post–1996 act period, when the FCC was beginning to conduct the "biennial" reviews of its media ownership rules mandated by Congress, influential members of Congress—some individually and some in gangs—bombarded the FCC with highly conflicting views on what deregulatory steps to take or not to take. It was as if Congress had forgotten what they had ordered in the 1996 act. The often heated colloquies were little more than a messy continuation of the deregulatory debate that was never satisfactorily concluded in the 1996 act. Again, instead of considering the impact of massive deregulation on American democracy and crafting a more appropriate overall policy, members of Congress seemed content to micromanage the FCC and influence policy on an ad hoc basis. Congressional involvement in this fashion—case by case or rule by rule—is, in fact, the worst possible way to develop critical policies. It results in the FCC being unduly pressured by various individual (not necessarily the most representative) voices coming from Congress and, in turn, invites members of Congress to succumb to the discrete influences of powerful industry representatives.

The same pattern of poor policymaking surfaced again following the FCC's 2003 decision to again alter its mass media ownership rules—an action taken in direct response to the "biennial" review process mandated by Congress. Among other things, the decision (a) increased the number of local markets in which a single party could own two TV stations (even three stations, in the nation's largest markets), (b) increased the percentage share of American TV households one owner could reach (the national "cap") from 35 percent to 45 percent, and (c) loosened the cross-media limits between broadcast stations and daily newspapers in local markets. During the course of this wide-ranging, nearly two-years-long proceeding, FCC deliberations attracted more than usual attention. A vast array of disparate groups filed written comments with the FCC. Others conducted well-organized public protests, on the streets of Washington, D.C., and on websites. This escalated level of activity generated greater media attention—in the trade press and over the Internet, if not in the daily press and over national networks. Not surprisingly, heavier media treatment seemed to attract greater interest by individual members of Congress. While engagement of the nation's legislative branch in a spirited, significant public debate might be presumed to be highly positive, the actual result was neither positive nor reassuring. Instead of real policy deliberations from Congress, the country witnessed little more than a cacophony of individual, competing voices. There were those who praised the FCC's actions, but the most vocal were those critical of such actions—on an issue-by-issue basis. Forgetting or ignoring, of course, that the FCC was merely carrying out the deregulatory imperative established by Congress itself, a host of different legislators ripped into different details of the FCC's decision, threatening to block or overturn one measure or another. A cynic might have characterized Congress's reaction as nothing more than the usual knee-jerk response when a highly visible public protest is mounted by a few influential groups. Indeed, an article in the *Economist* at the time observed that "Congressmen . . . are playing their own distasteful games, opening their pockets to donations from rival groups of big and small broadcasters, and pandering to a vocal minority of pressure groups, while carefully avoiding a direct vote on the [FCC] rules."[22] At best, it was a disjointed, discordant, even disingenuous, performance—consisting of a flurry of hastily convened, largely superficial hearings, resolutions of disapproval, and various attempts to use the appropriations process to block specific FCC actions, a backdoor method of preventing the FCC from using any of its congressionally authorized funds to enforce certain rules. At worst, it was not even legitimate policymaking. As a key staff assistant in the House of Representatives commented, "The leadership [of the House] recognizes that this [effort to undo FCC decisions that favored the broadcast industry] was more about settling old scores with network coverage than about setting a sound telecommunications policy for America."²³ The ostensible topic may have been media ownership regulation, but in the minds of many grandstanding members of Congress, it was more an opportunity to score points with the public by bashing the on-air performance of broadcasters—complaining about program content that the Constitution prevents government from controlling.

When the dust settled, the only concrete measure to come out of this ceremonial fist-pounding by Congress was a rider attached to the omnibus spending bill for fiscal 2004 that pushed back the TV national ownership cap adopted by the FCC from 45 percent to 39 percent. The "magic" figure of 39 percent was arrived at in closed-door bargaining sessions between representatives of the White House and the Republican leadership in Congress and, not coincidentally, was just high enough to allow media giants Viacom (owner of the CBS and UPN networks) and News Corporation (owner of Fox) to keep television stations that (as a result of earlier FCC waivers) had already exceeded the 35 percent limit established by the 1996 act.²⁴ As reported by the *Wall Street Journal*, Viacom and News Corporation spent a combined $5.5 million on lobbying between 1 January 2002 and 30 June 2003 and $2.3 million on campaign contributions for the 2002 and 2004 elections.²⁵

After pushing deregulation to a fare-thee-well in the 1996 act, many members of Congress quickly reversed course in 2003 when they faced some of the results of their own mandate. While some members reacted on principle and might have been willing to address the issues raised in a more responsible manner, most only spoke in sound bites about the corrosive effects of more media consolidation—when they were not delivering colloquies on extraneous issues. For these members of Congress, a chance to reap revenge on national media organizations whose integrity quotient with the voting public rivals that of the politicians they report on was just too appealing. Just as irresistible was the rare chance to get in bed with an extremely diverse set of special interest groups that had waged a highly effective campaign against the FCC actions—such as the National Rifle Association, children's advocacy groups, women's groups, educators, physicians, minorities, labor unions, and sundry church-affiliated groups. Finally, as a special signature to this particular fiasco, Congress employed backdoor parliamentary procedures derisive of sound public policymaking.

DISPELLING THE MYTH THAT CONTINUES TO
SUPPORT BROADCAST REGULATION

The deregulatory movement has ripped the heart out of the public trusteeship model. Standards on nonentertainment programming and commercialization no longer exist. Structural regulations designed to enhance diversity and localism have been eliminated or greatly weakened. A requirement that broadcast stations cover controversial issues of public importance by including representative and contrasting viewpoints was stripped from the books two decades ago. The one significant programming standard remaining—dealing with children's television—is not only minimally enforced but rendered largely irrelevant by industry practices and marketplace changes. While this deregulatory era anachronism still requires television stations to regularly report on the amount of children's programming they air, vague definitional standards and First Amendment considerations render the exercise highly ineffective. Stations can easily meet the minimum numerical requirement with virtually any "qualitative" selection, and the license renewal event where this would presumably be considered has been stretched to eight-year intervals. Equally significant, commercial networks and stations have effectively ceded their previously prominent role in serving children to public television and specialty channels widely available on cable and satellite systems.[26]

Ironically, the one aspect of public service that continues to be vigorously enforced is the obligation to present political programming. Not political programming designed to inform the electorate or to address controversial campaign issues. No, there are no rules and policies covering those topics. Rather, what exists are rules that (a) grant federal candidates—those seeking election or reelection to Congress and those running for president—special access rights to broadcast stations and (b) give all candidates for any public office special discount rates in purchasing broadcast time and the right to demand "equal opportunities" when their opponents use broadcast facilities. In sum, in an act of abject hypocrisy, Washington policymakers continue to pass laws that give themselves special access to the broadcast medium while, at the same time, taking other actions that effectively relieve broadcast stations of virtually all other forms of public service.

Despite general agreement on the value of mass media to modern society, we enter the twenty-first century on the same worn policy track as we left the twentieth century. For three decades our primary public policy has been to reduce government regulation in favor of reliance on the private marketplace. It has been a deceptively simple approach—at least in execution. Rules and standards originally intended to guide mass media in providing service to the public have been steadily dismantled in the name of deregulation. No policymaker, of course, was ever heard to say that service to the public was no longer important. Instead, the theme commonly heard was that service to the public could be better achieved by marketplace forces. The results have not been encouraging. The public trusteeship concept so central to the current regulatory system rests on the premise that local broadcast stations will (indeed, must) provide local audiences with programming tailored to their unique needs and interests without regard to achieving a profit. While many stations today continue to serve as significant outlets for their local communities, they only do so because they have found a way to make the presentation of news and information compatible with their overall commercial success. If they have not, and vast numbers have not, they simply ignore what has become a largely theoretical obligation. No broadcaster today lives in fear that not having a strong news presence in the community or not offering regularly scheduled public affairs programming will threaten his license to operate.

In other words, in the real world, the market model has already replaced the public trusteeship model. With the standards previously used to measure broadcaster performance largely removed and license renewal nearly automatic, the only real accountability broadcasters now face is in the commercial marketplace. Ignoring important local issues, dropping news, or failing to present any public affairs are factors no longer especially relevant to whether they retain their license. A process long diminished has become even more perfunctory and nonthreatening because the standards and procedures that could have, in the past, ensnared the truly poor performer have been deleted or drastically diminished. Even stations with 0 percent local informational programming can expect ready renewal.

The seeds of deregulation planted over two decades ago have produced a contemporary field of dreams for those who have long opposed the basic broadcast regime. Now, almost everywhere you look, regulatory oversight of the broadcast media is in retreat and few in Washington dare to suggest its return. It is time, therefore, to pronounce the "public trusteeship" model dead. It survives in name only and that merely underscores the overall failure of public policy.

DEVISING A PUBLIC POLICY MORE RESPONSIVE
TO CONTEMPORARY CONDITIONS

Waves of deregulation continue to batter a public policy levee constructed eighty years ago. Especially irksome is that policymakers persist in acting as if deregulation can be pursued without undermining the public trusteeship model. It cannot! We have long since passed the point when both the public trusteeship and market models can co-exist. It is time to recognize this and build a new policy framework more suited to the times and conditions.

Some of us, of course, might prefer a healthy dose of "reregulation" to counter the effects of nearly three decades of deregulation. Starting with reinstatement of the fairness doctrine, recycled standards for local public affairs programming, or redesigned guidelines on commercialism, one's reregulation wish list might also include shorter renewal terms and stiffer methods of enforcement. Others might covet a ban on all future media mergers coupled with rewritten rules forcing the breakup of existing combinations. For example, Ben Bagdikian, in the 2000 edition of his important and long-running critique of mass media, *The Media Monopoly*, argues that broadcasting ownership rules should be rolled all the way back to the 1940s when a single local owner could have only one AM radio station, one FM radio station, *or* one television station.[27] Still others might be satisfied with a rule change that no longer allowed two radio operators to control as many as sixteen stations and upwards of 80 to 90 percent of the audience and advertising revenue in a single local market. Or, a sweeping mandate barring a single giant conglomerate from no longer controlling vast, potentially conflicting interests in radio, television, cable, magazines, books, movies, daily newspapers, and the Internet. If only it were that simple.

We have traveled too far to put the genie back in the bottle. Years of deregulation have been accompanied by massive changes in the media marketplace. It is no longer feasible, even if it were constitutional, to impose the rigorous content restrictions of a bygone era on a commercial broadcasting system that has since lost its near-monopoly position. With so many more voices gushing from so many different sources, the American public has unalterably modified its media habits. Only a small (and dwindling) minority of TV viewers still watch video signals delivered over the air—reflecting the dominance of cable and satellite distribution systems. At the same time, a growing number of radio listeners "tune in" to music offered by satellite radio, Internet radio, or cyberspace podcasters (self-styled disc jockeys, hobbyists, and, increasingly, professionals who employ a new kind of software to create radio-type shows for easy downloading).[28] Younger adults, the long-time favorite demographic audience of broadcast stations and networks, spend less time with traditional, regulated mass media and more time with unregulated alternative media. Wherever one looks, the media experience is more personalized and fragmented—and likely to become more so. Finally, as we have learned, a more rigid, comprehensive regulatory scheme—even if one could be reconstituted—remains incapable of ensuring that an advertising-based medium will ever achieve anything near what its critics regard as its potential to serve American society. It is simply unrealistic to expect any private commercial business to act as a civic-minded, highbrow enterprise in the mold of the government-sponsored, publicly funded BBC. Certainly the structural regulations that remain—such as limiting common ownership of daily newspapers and broadcast stations or the number of competing local radio and TV outlets—are themselves incapable of producing improvements in public service. Indeed, all that can be said in support of their retention is that they may preserve a few more media voices in media markets that are not already heavily consolidated—a protection just as easily achieved by proper enforcement of the antitrust laws.

Given all of this, what is needed, I submit, is an entirely new approach to mass media policymaking. Instead of frenzied deregulation fueled only by marketplace theology, we need to build something that takes both marketplace changes and public needs into account. It is time to revisit how we look at mass media and its role in American society. Relying on rules and concepts forged in the early days of the twentieth century will not suffice at the start of the twenty-first century. If no opportunity reasonably exists to restore policies of the past, then we should look forward and craft new policies better suited to the present. If the public trusteeship model is no longer followed in any meaningful way, it should be discarded. Since commercial broadcasting already faces little real accountability, it should be set free of all operational, content, or across-the-board structural regulations. In effect, speed up and complete the process of deregulation. Instead of continuing to chip away at what is left of a deeply flawed system, call an end to the charade. Put the public trusteeship model on the shelf, where it belongs. Give commercial broadcasters a *permanent license* and freedom from all ongoing regulation—except what is essential to ensure technical operation without harmful interference to other broadcasters and other electromagnetic services. At the same time, revise the antitrust laws to better address the most egregious consequences of media combinations, and make public broadcasting a fully functioning public service "safety net" (propelled by a new funding mechanism and revised regulatory regime).

Mass media policy should be refocused in a way that ensures—not just promotes, in some indirect fashion—demonstrable benefits to the public at large. Just as public polices governing America's natural resources (forests, beaches, and navigable waters) have been designed to secure certain public benefits, governmental policy affecting broadcast transmissions sent over America's airwaves must be redesigned to secure public benefits of another sort. The maladies of mass media described in this text may pale in significance to other ailments threatening American society. But they are independently important nonetheless because they impact how all other issues and problems that threaten society are to be remedied. Environmental, economic, and terrorist threats cannot hope to be alleviated or reduced without a public and a government that are energized and connected by the power and presence of mass media. When decisions are made in a representative democracy, they need to be enforced and supported by an informed electorate and citizenry. And you cannot have an informed citizenry without strong, responsible media. As an increasingly urbanized society faces a more highly fragmented media environment, the glue of personal contact and shared experiences is inevitably weakened. If that is so, we need to strive harder to find ways to maintain common bonds and harbor more mutual understanding, acceptance, and respect of other people and ideas. This can and should be done by public institutions like schools, libraries, churches, community centers, and people-oriented public agencies. But it can and should also be assisted by private and publicly supported institutions like mass media.

Accordingly, after "experimenting" with a market-based model for more than two decades, it is time to complete the process. Give commercial broadcasting complete regulatory freedom but also provide a public service "safety net" over noncommercial broadcasting that preserves and protects the bedrock benefits of mass media: objective dissemination of vital information, diverse dialogue on public issues, and a steadfast sharing of cultural experiences. As deregulatory proponents argue, an unregulated commercial broadcast sector may eventually produce a flourishing marketplace of ideas, especially with a more vigorous, refocused enforcement of the antitrust laws. It might even bring forth a broadcast news service that, no longer sensitive to how regulatory decisions in Washington may help or hurt its corporate interests, is more likely to challenge errant public officials and expose bad legislative deal-making—the very essence of the media watchdog role. But responsible public policy cannot rest on unproven suppositions. The lifting of all remaining nontechnical regulations on commercial broadcasting must, therefore, also lead to a revised system for public broadcasting that would include better funding and greater accountability.

A NEW THREE-PART POLICY

My proposal is based on three essential steps, to be taken simultaneously: (1) giving commercial broadcasting permanent license status; (2) expanding antitrust enforcement; and (3) creating a public service safety net by reenergizing the public broadcast system. Before discussing each step in greater detail, I offer the following preliminary sketch to illustrate the many separate actions involved:

- The formal elimination of the public trusteeship model of regulation by amending or largely replacing all existing broadcast sections of the Communications Act.
- The complete deregulation of commercial broadcasting by new legislation that either directly or by delegation to the FCC would:
  - Lift all remaining rules and regulations governing the number, location, and types of broadcast stations a party may own, and all cross-ownership restrictions involving other, nonbroadcast media
  - Delete all remaining operational or content-related standards —for example, those dealing with advertising announcements, lotteries, contests, radio call-in show announcements, and the maintenance of public inspection files
  - Delete regulations that specifically target "indecency" on broadcast stations

- Delete regulations that require television stations to broadcast specific amounts and types of children's programming and that limit the advertising in such programs
  - Delete regulations that award political candidates special status and privileges in the use of commercial stations
  - Eliminate all remaining obligations to ascertain the general public concerning public issues and to present programming in response to such issues
  - Delete regulations that require commercial broadcast stations to follow FCC-prescribed EEO policies and standards
  - Eliminate all annual license fees and other fees intended to support the ongoing cost of government regulation
- The vesting of all qualifying commercial broadcast stations with a new *permanent license* no longer subject to either periodic renewal or restrictions on the sale or transfer.
- The adoption of new regulations requiring every commercial broadcast station to comply with or accept the following conditions before qualifying for a permanent license:
  - Pay a one-time fee to the federal government
  - Agree to use its assigned frequency only for over-the-air broadcasting to the general public
  - Agree to comply with all applicable technical rules imposed by the FCC to ensure the technical integrity of the American broadcast system
  - Agree to make its assigned frequency available at all times for government-originated emergency announcements
  - Agree to comply with any properly issued FCC cease and desist order to correct violations of technical standards
  - Acknowledge that a permanent license is ultimately subject to the eminent domain power of the federal government in the case of a national emergency or where there is a compelling public need for specific frequencies
- The creation of a new Public Broadcasting Service Trust, initially funded by the permanent license fees paid by commercial broadcasters.
- The enactment of new regulations for public broadcasting that would:
  - Retain the public trusteeship model for all public broadcast stations

- Install new political broadcasting obligations for all public broadcast stations
- Reinstate the fairness doctrine applicable to the coverage and treatment of important public issues by all public broadcast stations
- Impose new, specific, community-oriented public service programming obligations on all public broadcast stations to ensure that children, minorities, the less affluent, and the elderly are adequately served
- The expanded enforcement of the antitrust laws to specifically include the impact of proposed mass media transactions and, in special cases, existing combinations, on the marketplace of ideas, not just the economic marketplace.

Dream on, I hear you saying. Such sweeping changes are not only politically impossible, they would merely lead to more consolidation and poorer service by commercial broadcasting. If the electronic media are failing to serve the American public in ways that enhance democracy, do we not need more, not less, regulation? If years of deregulation have either hastened or actually contributed to broadcasting's poor performance, should we not reverse or at least halt those policy decisions? The answer to both questions would, of course, be yes—*if* we lived in simpler times, *if* technology were not advancing so rapidly, *if* the competitive environment in which all commercial media must operate had not changed so drastically, and, perhaps most important, *if* the prevailing political philosophy underlying the deregulatory movement was in decline or likely to be eclipsed in the foreseeable future by some powerful countervailing philosophy. But the stark reality is that none of these conditions will change in a way that would allow the sharp U-turn in mass media policy contemplated by both questions. As a result, any new public policy approach must be forged in recognition of these practical conditions. Having contributed, in no small part, to what commercial broadcasting has become, policymakers should set that sector completely free and concentrate, instead, on building a better public broadcasting system whose *primary* mission is the delivery of information, ideas, and varied social experiences essential to American culture and democracy.

At the moment, we have a frayed and failing policy. A venerable touchstone phrase still peppers the guiding statute promising public service from thousands of broadcast stations holding temporary licenses as public trustees but, in modern regulatory practice, acts more like a traffic light stuck on green. Turning back is impracticable and staying the course merely ensures a steady drift in the same direction we have been traveling—without safeguarding any level of public service. Policymakers may not have been wrong in moving toward a market model. Circumstances may, in fact, have dictated that course. But they failed in allowing this change to occur without assessing, in any serious way, the functions performed by mass media in a democratic society and the impact that a market-driven approach would inevitably have on such functions. If they had, they would have slowed the process or found alternatives to ensure continuing service to the *public's* varied interests. As we have seen, they did neither.

Theodore Roosevelt thought that a pivotal condition of his era was that economic power had become so centralized and dominant it could threaten democracy. The power of corporations, he said, had to be balanced in the interest of the general public. Big money and big business are now threatening the balance in our media system—if not our entire system. The "business" view of the world has overtaken much of our public policy—reflected in actions by the FCC, Congress, and, increasingly, the judiciary. What we have lost is the counterweight that used to be supplied by regulation. Regulation that had been designed to ensure a certain level of public service has been stripped away without establishing an adequate safety net. Congress and the FCC have simply not accounted for the possibility that corporate interests might not adopt a high-minded vision of what is good for American democracy instead of pursuing their normal commercial instincts. If advertising-supported broadcast stations have emphasized less public service while chasing more advertising dollars, they have only acted in the time-tested manner of virtually all commercial enterprises. The failure is not that a more unfettered commercial broadcast system is acting more like other profit-motivated businesses. It is that public policy formulated out of the deregulatory movement did not anticipate such conduct.

Media critics complain bitterly that mass media have not educated the public to the dangers of undue concentration—that they have, in effect, failed to report negatively upon themselves.[29] This notion is especially quixotic. Commercial media companies, whether controlled publicly or privately, all want to be more profitable, more powerful, and more influential by controlling larger market segments. That is not only understandable, it is the expectation of the capitalistic system. Critics who blame the media for not whistling this unhappy tune for the American public are pointing in the wrong direction. Under our system, the balance or counterweight to corporations acting purely in their commercial interests is regulation or public policy-making. If the general public needs to be better informed of problems arising from media consolidation, responsibility for satisfying that need rests with policymakers, not corporate media.

The economic motives that stir the marketplace are not the only motives that stimulate and influence human conduct in a free society. For this reason, commercial broadcasting must not be unleashed further without also finding specific ways to address the inevitable gaps in public service occasioned by profit-motivated media being relieved of regulatory accountability. A better-funded, reenergized public broadcasting system can and should fill those gaps. If technology and competitive developments in the commercial realm eventually provide even a small slice of the enriched diversity promised by deregulatory proponents, the American public will be the happy beneficiaries. But if those promises prove too optimistic, as seems likely, we will have set out a needed safety net in the form of a stronger, more local, more public service oriented, more accountable public broadcasting system.

When broken down into its component parts, this proposal seems anything but drastic or revolutionary. To begin with, the core recommendation—replacing the public trusteeship model and temporary licensing with a permanent license system for all commercial stations—mirrors trends already well under way. Little remains of rules and procedures previously intended to measure the performance of broadcast "trustees" on a periodic basis. Instead, the process for renewing "temporary" licenses has become both more perfunctory and more infrequent. Because the FCC has already eliminated standards and record-keeping requirements previously used to assess a station's public service programming or commercial practices, it would hardly be a major step to eliminate the remaining, less consequential behavioral or content-related rules. These include such minor regulations as those affecting station-conducted contests, lotteries, announcements in connection with radio call-in programs, sponsorship identification,[30] and a few other low-level regulatory matters.[31] Although some of these, especially the nature, amount, and source of advertising content, were once given studious attention by the FCC,[32] recent history has been more a story of neglect. In the end, it probably does not matter much, since the real danger posed by today's advertising—whether appearing in print or transmitted by electronic media—is fraud and deception, not inaccurate disclosure of the sponsor. If the public is to be afforded any protection from deceitful and fraudulent advertising claims in our oversaturated commercial world, it will have to come from agencies like the Federal Trade Commission, with expertise and authority in such areas, not from the FCC policing commercials that fail to include a proper sponsor name.

Other regulatory underbrush that could easily be swept away with little notice include those remaining policies that, technically, still require each broadcast station to ascertain the leading public issues in its local community, followed by programming reflective of those issues. A few rules, however, could not be eliminated without a likely outcry by affected groups. These include those that target broadcast "indecency," require television stations to air a certain amount of children's programming, and impose standards in two specific areas, candidate access and broadcast ownership.

Indecency

Many, if not most, Americans would, if given the chance, vote to cleanse broadcasting of material they (or their government representatives) define as indecent, and to require all television stations to serve only what *they* (or, again, their government representatives) consider a healthy diet of children's programs. The problem, of course, is defining *indecent* and *healthy*. If FCC regulators keep bobbing and weaving when these topics are before them, how could even the most conscientious member of the audience decide? Most Americans may say they favor decent programming for everyone and healthy programming for children, but achieving consensus on the particulars is impossible. Even if that were not the case, decisions on content should never be treated like an election. It is one thing to accept majority rule when voting on candidates. It would be quite another to apply it to broadcast content, where the tastes and interests of everyone not in the majority would not only be ignored but barred.

At present, we have a five-member, unelected commission unusually sensitive to elected members of Congress and the incumbent administration deciding what is inappropriate content carried by tens of thousands of stations serving thousands of local communities. To make matters worse, with virtually every other content-related standard having been eliminated or ignored, we are now treated to the unbecoming spectacle of an FCC demonstrating its regulatory toughness and lingering relevancy by clubbing broadcast companies with bigger and better publicized monetary fines for indecency.[33] This may command headlines and placate some seemingly indignant members of Congress, but it is not good public policy. Nor is it good public policy to require a politically sensitive government licensing agency to "vote" on whether companies over which it holds the ultimate power to operate have broken a criminal law.[34] It is time for a new approach.

Ideally, "indecency," however defined, should no longer be singled out as a form of content less offensive than "obscenity" but still banned during most hours on every over-the-air broadcast station in the nation—while it remains totally unrestricted in all other mass media, including other media using public facilities or space. While correcting this regulatory inequity may be more difficult than removing partisanship from politics, given the unique fusion of moral outrage and political grandstanding that usually accompanies the topic, at least a different enforcement approach should be adopted. In particular, even if "indecency" continues to be restricted only on broadcast stations and "obscenity" continues to be defined differently in different media (broadcasting, print, movies, cable, and cyberspace), there is no reason why these sensitive content restrictions should not be enforced in a more uniform manner. This can be achieved by entrusting future enforcement of broadcast indecency cases to federal district courts (sitting in the states where alleged violations occur). It simply makes no sense to continue to cast the FCC in the role of a federal indecency commission, enforcing a criminal statute and ruling on alleged criminal conduct on radio stations from Pocatello to Providence. If a station broadcasts something that shocks members of its audience and is potentially actionable under a criminal statute, it should be subject to the same legal procedures that apply to a local newspaper charged with violating obscenity laws in that community.[35] The specific laws and standard might still differ but the legal process and forum would be uniform.

Despite a prevailing sense that "anything goes" in today's broadcast media, the truth is far different—even if one includes radio "shock jocks." Because broadcasting relies on advertising, not paid subscriptions, most stations are far more likely to self-regulate in these areas than their nonbroadcast competition. If broadcast stations stray too far from popular or acceptable tastes, they will lose advertisers, endangering their sole financial support. In contrast, subscription (and some free) services offered over cable, satellite, wireless, or the Internet are effectively regulated by the choice people make when they affirmatively access or purchase such services. Satellite and cable television, motion pictures and print media (where far racier material is routinely tolerated) do not labor under the same restrictions imposed on the broadcast medium—even though two of those services, cable and satellite, also use public spaces and, typically, intrude directly into the home on the same distribution system as "over-the-air" television. As most readers will recognize, many standard broadcast programs are increasingly available over nonbroadcast delivery systems. How long can the federal government continue to dissect and decide the acceptable content of conventional radio and television programs while ignoring the same content when it appears on a satellite channel or webcast or is downloaded to an iPod, computer, or cell phone?

Children's Programming

In contrast to the passions stirred whenever broadcast indecency is discussed, it is unlikely that eliminating rules requiring all television stations to broadcast specific amounts and types of children's programs would generate widespread negative reaction among the general public. Undoubtedly, children's advocacy groups would protest vehemently, but even they must concede that without any real accountability most commercial stations currently bring little enthusiasm to children's programming. Rather, as many parents have already discovered, better children's programs can be found on public stations (where they are presented commercial-free) and specialized services available via cable or satellite. Whether or not this is regarded as sufficient, the situation is not helped by maintaining mandatory rules that are unenthusiastically received by over-the-air commercial television and weakly enforced by the FCC. The nation's children would be better served by (a) redirecting public policy toward enriching the capabilities of public television in this vitally important area, and (b) shifting regulatory attention from the amount of advertising to the misleading and potentially harmful nature of advertising in children's programming (a function better entrusted to the expertise of the Federal Trade Commission).

Candidate Access

Unquestionably, the most controversial and difficult individual step to take under this new regime would be the elimination of rules that award political candidates special privileges in the use of commercial stations. The reason, of course, is that those who benefit directly and exclusively from such rules are the only ones who hold the power to alter or delete them. In this unique case, the principal policymakers, members of Congress, are also the principal beneficiaries of the policy. It may be unrealistic to expect incumbent office holders, whose self-protection is almost always foremost, to ever acquiesce in any meaningful reform in this area. Nevertheless, I strongly believe that ending the public trusteeship model should include drastic revision, if not outright revocation, of the special privileges currently given political candidates. If Congress remains committed to broadcast deregulation and shows no interest in reversing course as to any other matter bearing upon content, it should accept the removal of rules that grant its members (and other candidates) special rights to use broadcast stations—rights they are constitutionally denied as to other mass media.

Certainly the public benefits little from the stream of slick advertising messages that political candidates purchase at heavily discounted rates during election campaigns. It would be a different matter, of course, if candidates routinely used these special rights to purchase larger segments of time to discuss public issues in a more expanded, informative format. But that is not the way broadcast media are used today. Indeed, even nonadvertising time by savvy political candidates and their handlers usually consists of carefully controlled sound bites timed for television newscasts.

The proposal I advance would not eliminate such uses. The only thing that would change is that political candidates for federal office would no longer have a favored right of access to commercial broadcasting, and political candidates for all public offices would no longer be entitled to receive highly discounted rates when purchasing broadcast time. Instead, if candidates wanted to use commercial broadcasting, they would have to pay the going rate applicable to other uses of the station or negotiate their own discount. On the other hand, if any medium—broadcast, cable, print, or Internet service—engaged in certain unfair practices, such as expressly charging political candidates exorbitant rates or offering to sell advertising in a competitive race only to the candidate of one political party, immediate injunctive relief should be available from either the Federal Trade Commission or a federal trial judge, under revised fair trade rules and procedures especially enacted for this purpose.

The American electorate is likely to applaud, not complain, if political candidates are no longer able to saturate the airwaves with heavily discounted political announcements.[36] Those who will complain, of course, are those most heavily vested in the current system: (1) politicians who are granted special legal rights to use broadcasting and (2) those commercial broadcasters who have long enjoyed and, in many cases, relied upon large "seasonal" advertising expenditures by political candidates. But even these vested interests must recognize that the system itself is beginning to change. As cable, digital broadcasting, and the Internet continue to fragment audiences, future political campaigns will continue to reduce their dependency on over-the-air commercial broadcast stations. Fifty million Americans go online for news everyday, according to a March 2006 survey by the Pew Research Center. By 2004, the last presidential election year, nearly 30 percent of Americans were obtaining election news online. Clearly, candidates and campaigns can no longer just buy television spots. If they want to get their message out, they must also infiltrate talk radio, buy ads on cable channels, and operate candidate or party blogs. They will also use e-mail and text-messaging to reach specific groups, target specific locations, and spur particular actions (fundraising, mobilizing support, announcing rallies, etc.). Instead of a near total dependency on the broad-brush approach of broadcast advertising, candidates and campaigns will increasingly adopt a multi-layered media approach, better targeted to discrete demographic groups and distinct geographic areas.

In sum, if we look beyond the shortsighted vision of the vested interests, this aspect of my proposal is relatively unremarkable. It would correct current inequities and correspond to developments already beginning to reshape how political campaigns are conducted. Nevertheless, to mollify the expected resistance of incumbent politicians, one possible modification to what I recommend would be to add a further "condition" to the permanent license of all commercial *television* stations. This would require each commercial station to set aside a designated amount of time during discrete election periods—for example, sixty days before the scheduled date of a general election—to be made available for priority, cost-free use by qualified political candidates in specified races. At the candidate's discretion, the time could be used for short programs and discrete announcements, or a combination of both. Since in the next few years, all television stations will be transmitting digital signals capable of broadcasting multiple "channels" simultaneously, stations should be allowed to satisfy this requirement by putting any mandated political access on any single channel they choose.

Ownership Rules

Finally, removing all remaining structural regulations concerning the number, location, and types of broadcast stations (and related nonbroadcast media) one party may own merely completes a process that has been under way for years. Many of these rules were dramatically relaxed by the FCC in the late 1980s and early 1990s. The process was then accelerated and permanently codified in the 1996 act. As such, the road map for this reform has already been drawn. However, even if this were not the case, there really is no longer any need for an agency like the FCC making and administering structural regulations essentially pegged to the economic marketplace. Given how far we have traveled on other deregulatory paths, it is more important than ever to entrust such matters to agencies like the Department of Justice and the Federal Trade Commission that are given direct responsibility for administering and enforcing the antitrust laws.[37]

—⚹—

Elimination of all remaining operational, content, and structural regulations of commercial broadcasting is justified only as part of a broader reform package that includes the following additional measures: (1) establishing specific parameters defining "permanent license" status for commercial broadcasting, (2) developing an expanded approach toward applying the antitrust laws to mass media businesses, and (3) creating a new Public Broadcasting Service Trust, accompanied by discrete "reregulation" of key aspects of public broadcasting.

Giving Commercial Broadcasting Permanent License Status

An issue periodically debated in mass media policy circles concerns the extent and nature of the rights that attach to a given broadcast license. While specific language in the Communications Act and longstanding FCC precedent support the conclusion that no current license confers ownership rights, the issue has remained the subject of sporadic FCC reexamination and intermittent court decision. At different times, the broadcast industry, investment community, and others have specifically advocated establishing such rights. Even though no formal change has resulted, years of deregulation have nevertheless moved us in that direction, at least implicitly. With renewal virtually automatic, and any real accountability long since removed, it is hard to deny that those who hold broadcast licenses today have not already effectively been given a more permanent status (or something akin to a vested ownership right). Even the way the federal government now decides who can use specific spectrum space better comports with a concept of permanent ownership than it does with the notion of temporary trusteeship. Whereas in the past applications for new broadcast stations (and some nonbroadcast facilities as well) were typically awarded only after extensive administrative hearings that carefully compared competing proposals, such stations (or other facilities) are now awarded based on competitive bids placed by private parties (with the winning applicant being the highest bidder).[38]

With this as background, it certainly seems more plausible and less drastic to grant all incumbent commercial broadcast stations a *permanent license*—that is, one no longer subject to periodic renewal and one that explicitly carries with it real attributes of ownership. Not only would a commercial broadcast station holding a permanent license no longer have to seek renewal, file any reports, or pay any ongoing regulatory fees, it would, like most other businesses (including most other media businesses), be able to sell or transfer its broadcast business—physical assets *and* the license—without advance regulatory approval.

However, because the broadcast business remains different than most other businesses (including most other media businesses), a permanent license to operate on an assigned broadcast frequency must remain subject to certain limitations—limitations not unlike those affecting other businesses using public property or facilities, such as airlines, trucking companies, and those engaged in oil drilling or cattle grazing on federal lands. The principal limitation would mirror the original justification for regulation—namely, the primacy of FCC technical rules to ensure that all holders of commercial permanent licenses continue to broadcast an acceptable technical signal that does not interfere with other signals (both broadcast and nonbroadcast). Such technical rules would also continue to require broadcast stations to (a) operate a minimum number of hours, (b) maintain limited records regarding technical compliance, (c) provide periodic on-air identification for the listening/viewing public, and (d) comply with federal guidelines and procedures for operation during national emergencies and natural disasters.[39]

Holders of permanent broadcast licenses would also be required to comply with a few newly established nontechnical rules and procedures. For instance, at the time a permanent broadcast license is awarded, the written authorization extending this right would specify certain conditions applicable to anyone holding the license, either the original grantee or any subsequent holder. In current FCC parlance, these conditions would "follow the license," under all circumstances. First among these would be a written certification promising compliance with FCC technical standards. Others are explained below:

- When the majority or controlling ownership interest of a broadcast license is sold in a private sale, the new controlling owner would be required to give the FCC written notice listing the name, address, and responsible officials of the new owner(s). In this way, the FCC would always have someone to look to for compliance with technical standards.
- The foregoing notice would be *after the fact*—for example, within thirty days of the consummation of a change in ownership. A separate but *prior* notice of the sale or purchase would be directed to antitrust authorities at the Department of Justice and Federal Trade Commission—for example, sixty days before the contemplated change of ownership. Under the current Hart-Scott-Rodino law, all business transactions (media and nonmedia related) that satisfy certain criteria[40] are subject to a notification and preclearance procedure administered by federal antitrust authorities. This requirement could easily be expanded to cover most, if not all, ownership changes in the broadcast industry.[41] Instead of the FCC applying highly arbitrary, predetermined, across-the-board ownership standards, antitrust authorities would be expected to review all significant transactions on a market-by-market basis without any preordained limits.
- Each permanent broadcast license would be issued only after a station paid its permanent license fee and agreed to use its assigned frequency only for broadcast purposes—that is, transmitting an over-the-air signal and supplying a service intended for the general public. If any station refused or was unable to pay, it

would be required to forfeit its license—by an established deadline. Any station that paid its permanent license fee but subsequently discontinued providing a broadcast service would likewise forfeit its license.

Because the privilege of broadcasting on specific frequencies remains a highly valuable asset, it should be awarded and protected by the government only in circumstances where those frequencies are used to supply an over-the-air program service for general public consumption. Once that function ceases, the license should be forfeited. At that point, the government can reallocate the frequency for other public purposes, ensuring that public, not private, interests benefit from the process. To the extent technically feasible, in given circumstances, the forfeited frequency should be reallocated to a nonbroadcast use and auctioned off to nonbroadcast interests.

- Anyone holding a permanent broadcast license would also be required to comply with any cease and desist order duly issued by the FCC to remedy any technical violation. Not only would the FCC continue to have authority to issue monetary fines for matters still under its authority, it would be vested with new, more effective, more expedient cease and desist powers. This would be necessary because, under a permanent license scheme, the FCC would no longer have the regulatory leverage it long maintained over broadcast stations holding temporary, renewable licenses.

- Anyone holding a permanent license would, as now, remain subject to the war powers of the president[42] and, in addition, the eminent domain power of the federal government.[43] If the federal government were, in the future, to determine that national security or some other compelling national interest required the use of specific frequencies subject to permanent licenses, it could institute procedures to reclaim those frequencies. However, as with all other eminent domain actions, the government would, in such circumstances, be required to offer the holder of the permanent license "reasonable compensation."

- Finally, special provisions would have to be established to guard against a permanent broadcast license falling into the hands of alien interests or those adjudged to be serious criminals. Just as current law[44] acts to deny other, specific government benefits to those convicted of serious crimes, a similar conviction by anyone holding a permanent broadcast license would lead to an automatic, streamlined revocation proceeding—one that would not only enjoin a sale to others but result in the loss of license.

Since current law restricts alien ownership of broadcast stations,[45] and such restrictions would no doubt be retained under a permanent license scheme, a few other procedural changes would be necessary. First, all permanent broadcast licenses would be conditioned on compliance with foreign ownership rules. Second, the Justice Department or other government agency with special expertise in dealing with issues relating to foreign influence would periodically monitor, investigate, and act on potential violations of the broadcast alien ownership restrictions. Finally, in situations where the holder of a permanent broadcast license contemplated an increase in foreign ownership over a specified benchmark—for example, in excess of 15 percent but still less than the 20 percent alien ownership allowed in the statute—it would be required to supply written notice to the reviewing government agency prior to completing the transaction. The transaction could only be consummated after the agency investigated and approved the change.

Expanding Antitrust Enforcement

In calling for expanded use of the antitrust laws in mass media matters, I recognize that similar refrains have been heard throughout the deregulatory movement. The reason is fairly obvious: "When de-regulation is based on assumptions about competitive benefits, antitrust laws—which protect that competitive environment—become surrogates for communications policy and increase in importance."[46] Thus, advocates for relaxation or removal of the remaining broadcast ownership rules usually argue that reliance on existing antitrust laws is the preferred way to limit undue consolidation or unfair competition in mass media services. In their view, broadcasting should be treated like any other business, where issues of bigness and undue market power are resolved exclusively under the antitrust laws. Even media scholars who favor more (not less) regulation of broadcasting usually include greater antitrust enforcement as one element of a media reform package.[47]

Egregious cases of media concentration can be controlled—by hard-hitting regulatory standards or vigorous antitrust enforcement. On the other hand, as recent history teaches, they can just as easily be

tolerated—by relaxed regulatory rules and tepid antitrust enforcement. What we need is aggressive decision making by decision makers, regardless of context. That being said, my argument is that if the
nation's policymakers eventually find sufficient backbone to explore
and act on the harmful effects of media concentration in given circumstances, they do so with expanded antitrust enforcement, not resurrected or rehashed broadcast ownership rules.

To date, the FCC's central role relative to competition has been to
monitor the media marketplace to preserve and stimulate ownership
diversity (in the hope of contributing to viewpoint diversity). On the
other hand, the Justice Department and FTC have perceived their role
under the Sherman Antitrust Act as evaluating media mergers solely
on the basis of economic factors. If, as I propose, FCC regulation of
commercial broadcasting is relegated to the original "traffic cop"
function—implementing and enforcing technical rules only—it will
not be enough to entrust media concentration and competition issues
to existing theories of antitrust enforcement. When Congress replaces
the public trusteeship model with a permanent license system, it
should also forge a new federal policy for applying the antitrust laws
to media businesses. Although the needed changes could conceivably
evolve out of Justice Department guidelines and ad hoc litigation,[48]
the course I recommend is a new antitrust policy written into a new
mass media law—one that broadens antitrust review of media matters
but also requires antitrust authorities to respect and protect First
Amendment rights (the same kind of balancing act entrusted to FCC
officials for the past eighty years). As now, the overriding focus would
be on structural conditions that impact media competition, not on activities that could be said to impact particular content.[49]

Historically, federal communications policy has been primarily focused on serving the interests of Americans as citizens, while federal
competition policy has primarily focused on serving or protecting the
interests of Americans as consumers. For years, communications law
emphasized the type and quality of information disseminated to the
general public. In contrast, the whole tradition of antitrust law has
centered on examining specific economic impact or economic behavior. Thus, Section 2 of the Sherman Act[50] prohibits the use of monopoly power in one market to gain advantage in a second, and Section 7
of the Clayton Act[51] addresses acquisitions that substantially lessen
competition or tend to create a monopoly.

Today, federal communications policy more nearly resembles federal competition policy. FCC rules and procedures that previously focused on listeners and viewers as citizens have been largely abandoned. Instead, the FCC's attention is on a few structural rules which it seeks to justify or modify by looking to antitrust concepts and formulas. In a wide-ranging reexamination of its remaining media ownership rules completed in 2003, the FCC openly embraced many of the tools of antitrust agencies. Before acting, it conducted or commissioned outside experts to conduct numerous economic studies of the broadcast and broader media marketplace. Some of these focused on the product or actual output of the media, but more focused on the habits of the audience or consumer public, such as defining the relevant product and geographic markets and determining the extent to which viewers and listeners (consumers) of broadcast stations use other media options—such as cable, DBS, DVDs, the Internet, and theater and concert venues—as substitutes for information and entertainment available on broadcast stations. Then, in the process of adopting new rules, the FCC constructed a diversity index which included a weighting factor based on the extent to which consumers rely on different communications technologies for news and current events. All of these approaches, of course, are classic tools used by antitrust authorities. Broadcast consumers are now being studied and treated by both the FCC and antitrust officials as essentially no different than consumers of all products.

This is the wrong course. A better course would start with policymakers acknowledging that, despite the pleas of deregulatory zealots and neoclassical economists, mass media are distinct from other businesses. The "product" they serve is not like any other commercial product offered to the American public. Yes, that "product" includes a lot of drivel, gross commercialism, and coarse entertainment (a form of protected speech nonetheless), but it also includes a basic diet of information, culture, and shared experiences essential to an open society and a representative democracy. Robert Pitofsky, a former chairman of the Federal Trade Commission, puts it this way:

> Antitrust is more than economics. . . . And I do believe if you have issues in the newspaper business, in book publishing, news generally, entertainment, I think you want to be more careful and thorough in your investigation than if the same problems arose in cosmetic fields. They're

going to take money out of consumers' pockets, but the implications for democratic values are zero. On the other hand, if they monopolize books, you're talking about implications that go way beyond what the wholesale price of books might be.[52]

This distinction between news and the typical commercial commodity is also captured in a famous opinion by Supreme Court Justice Felix Frankfurter:

> In addition to being a commercial enterprise, [the] Associated Press has a relation to the public interest unlike that of any other enterprise pursued for profit. A free press is indispensable to the workings of our democratic society. The business of the press, and therefore the business of the Associated Press, is the promotion of truth regarding public matters by furnishing the basis for an understanding of them. Truth and understanding are not wares like peanuts or potatoes. And so, the incidence of restraints upon the promotion of truth through denial of access to the basis of understanding calls into play considerations very different from comparable restraints in a cooperative enterprise having merely a commercial aspect.[53]

Because mass media create and disseminate a product of human intellect that helps bind American society and grease the wheels of American democracy, they should not be viewed through the same antitrust lens as all other business ventures. We depend upon mass media to provide a free flow of information, to facilitate public debate, and to hold public officials accountable. They are the only segment of American commerce whose "product" is given explicit constitutional protection. When commercial media are more uniformly deregulated—and broadcasting, finally, is able to stand in the same shoes as its print brethren—it will be critically important to not only reinvigorate antitrust enforcement but to recast antitrust policy when applied to mass media. In the future, antitrust authorities should have responsibility to protect American consumers not only in their purchase of commercial goods but in their access to information. The free flow of information must be dependent upon more than whether a proposed media merger or existing combination is economically efficient. Noneconomic factors such as reduced consumer access to a diversity of views and the potential for self-censorship should also be taken into account.

Although developing new standards would not be easy, it has never been easy to establish rules or procedures in this area. Certainly, the construction (and, more recently, the constant adjustment) of mostly formulaic, across-the-board FCC competition rules have failed the test of simplicity. Dangerous trends and harmful transactions in a multi-faceted modern media market are impossible to address with either precision or a one-size-fits-all approach. Inevitably, the enforcement agency—whether it is the FCC, the Competition Bureau of the FTC, or the Antitrust Division of the Department of Justice—must examine most situations on a case-by-case basis, weighing a number of inher-ently fluid factors that defy easy quantification or precise prediction. Because mass media policy as pursued by the FCC is now focused al-most exclusively on industry-wide competition rules, it would be bet-ter to entrust these responsibilities solely to antitrust officials who are not only the recognized competition experts, but also best positioned to consider diversity on a market-by-market basis. While the empha-sis in each case would still be primarily economic, it would, as needed, also include an assessment of the impact on diversity of view-points in the relevant market. In my view, entrusting such issues to an-titrust professionals or federal judges—neither of which has licensing authority over mass media—would be preferable to leaving them to politically appointed FCC officials acting under the undefined, un-quantified "public interest" standard, something we have done for the past eight decades.

To those who say demoting the FCC and promoting antitrust agen-cies represents the ultimate concession leading to a complete victory for corporate interests and defeat for the public's interests, I say one has to accept certain realities and move on. After nearly thirty years of deregulation, the public trusteeship model, at best, lies quivering on the floor, barely surviving. All that remains of consequence are struc-tural rules with less overall bite and a greater antitrust bent. Given the state of contemporary mass media policymaking and the evolution of mass media markets, it may make little ultimate difference whether responsibility for monitoring ownership of media properties is placed in the hands of the FCC, the FTC, or the Department of Justice. How-ever, since the latter two have superior antitrust expertise, they should begin monitoring activities and addressing ownership combinations in the broadcast media as they do now for media not regulated by the FCC. If the FCC has no remaining broad public interest mandate for broadcast stations, it should be relieved of any remaining competition regulation as well.

For those hoping for a return to ownership restrictions of the past—such as limiting control to only one local TV station with no cross-interests in radio, cable, or daily newspapers—it is well to remember that the antitrust laws have traditionally been enforced market by market, allowing authorities to pursue remedies that include not only the blocking of specific anticompetitive transactions but the breaking up of existing combinations. In addition, premerger advisory guidelines and similar enforcement tools such as the Department of Justice's Herfindahl-Hirschman Index could, if tailored to mass media, operate in much the same fashion as existing FCC ownership rules. For example, antitrust authorities could develop media-specific benchmarks in such areas as audience circulation and advertising dollars controlled, expressed as a nonbinding percentage guideline. Premised on market share and blind to particular content, the guidelines could establish different percentage limits in different competing media—broadcasting, cable, print, and the Internet—which, when applied to specific cases, could be assessed individually or cumulatively.

The FCC presently defines broadcast markets by either looking to the geographic area created by the overlapping signals of competing stations or by relying on widely used industry criteria (such as those published by Arbitron and Nielsen, based on audiences). It is anticipated that antitrust authorities would use similar definitional tools to establish relevant geographic markets. To date, courts, media managers, and media economists (including those typically retained by the Justice Department) have, in general, been unwilling to view media markets as multimedia markets—that is, markets in which diverse media compete for advertisers and audiences. However, because intermedia competition is now greater than it has ever been, this needs to change. It is no longer acceptable, for example, to view the distinct market that radio stations compete in as consisting only of other over-the-air *radio* stations. It may not be appropriate to include all local or regional media in the analysis for any given geographic market, but it would be appropriate, and necessary, to include all media (such as newspaper, cable, and some online services) that radio stations actually compete with for advertising revenue and, if applicable, the provision of any information services.

But more important than the transfer of function from one agency to another is the need to change the focus of antitrust enforcement. As noted, instead of concentrating solely on economic impact, it should also include an examination of any adverse impact on viewpoint diversity or what is often referred to as the "marketplace of ideas."[54] This is exactly what Maurice Stucke and Allen Grunes, two antitrust professionals in the Department of Justice, propose in a 2001 law review article.[55] Relying on amendments to the Clayton Act and a series of Supreme Court decisions upholding application of the antitrust laws to media companies,[56] they argue that, even without a change in the law, federal antitrust agencies could expand their scrutiny of media transactions to include the potential impact of such transactions on nonprice competition, including the marketplace of ideas. These authors and I do not enlist the marketplace of ideas metaphor to connote some lofty, unrealistic vision of media markets. Rather, the phrase is used merely to frame a general public policy goal that, while promoting openness and diversity in the provision of information services would, in practice, focus on avoiding or correcting the extremes (such as excessive control in a single voice).

Congress has already laid some groundwork for this approach. When it passed the Newspaper Preservation Act in 1970 it created an exception to the antitrust laws which allows two (or more) separately owned newspapers to form a joint operating agreement to relieve economic distress—as long as the editorial sides of the newspapers remain entirely independent. In effect, the act is said to serve First Amendment interests because it preserves editorial competition (separate voices) in situations where such competition is likely to disappear—a decidedly noneconomic policy determination. Moreover, when Congress passed the 1996 Telecommunications Act—speeding up the process of replacing years of behavioral regulation under the public trusteeship model with a form of structural regulation favoring the marketplace model—it also placed renewed emphasis on the antitrust laws. A provision was included stating that nothing in the legislation should "be construed to modify, impair, or supersede the applicability of any of the antitrust laws."[57] One member of Congress described this "savings" clause as "all-important" because it confirmed that "any and all telecommunications mergers and antitrust activities are fully subject to the antitrust laws. Teleco-cable mergers and all other broadcast, media, or telecommunications transactions will be fully subject to antitrust review, regardless of how they are treated under the bill or [by] the FCC."[58]

In closing this section, let it be said that the deregulatory actions chronicled in this text parallel a period in antitrust law also characterized by a strong belief in the ability of free markets to self-regulate. For example, in stark contrast to Pitofsky, Baker, and Stucke and Grunes, cited here, numerous other contemporary antitrust scholars have long maintained that political and social factors have no place in antitrust enforcement. Of course, some of the same scholars likewise argue that *any* FCC regulation of commercial broadcasting is an indefensible substitute for marketplace self-regulation. Putting scholarly discourse aside, history demonstrates that antitrust law is rarely conceived or executed in so pristine a fashion. Instead, it has always been subject to cyclical change and the periodic influence of political and social factors. It is time for Congress not only to chart an entirely new policy course for commercial broadcasting but to set us on a new cycle of antitrust enforcement—resulting in a new approach that, at least as to mass media, allows antitrust analysis to strike a balance between economic and sociopolitical concerns.

Creating a Public Service "Safety Net" and Reenergizing the Public Broadcast System

This section will develop in more detail two interrelated points: (a) the appropriate dollar amounts commercial broadcast stations should pay to receive their permanent government licenses (essential to establishing the new Public Broadcasting Service Trust) and (b) certain regulatory revisions to the public broadcasting scheme that should accompany adoption of this new funding mechanism.

Establishing a Public Broadcasting Service Trust from Permanent Broadcast Licensing Fees

Given the long history of public broadcasting's financial difficulties, the literature overflows with suggestions for finding better ways and means to fund it.[59] Most of these have involved some form of permanent tax on equipment sales (like the licensing scheme used to fund the BBC), a special fee imposed on certain broadcast transactions, or an annual "spectrum fee" assessed against commercial broadcasters for the continued use of their assigned frequencies. There have also been suggestions that a portion of future spectrum auctions be set aside to fund public broadcasting. Other suggestions have focused on allowing public broadcast stations to accept additional forms of advertising—beyond those already implicit in so-called underwriting announcements. On the other hand, most proposals have rejected a funding system entirely dependent on government appropriations or fees exclusively collected under government programs. Indeed, the last major study of public broadcasting by the highly respected Carnegie Commission concluded that while increased, more stable federal funding was crucial, "the freedom and integrity of public broadcasting would be best secured by drawing upon a range of income sources."[60] Twenty-five years later, it remains important that funding flow from different sources, especially those reflecting the region, state, and local community where public broadcasting performs its most vital role.

Federal grants or other distributions funneled through the Corporation for Public Broadcasting (CPB) to local public stations still account for only about 15 percent of the funds necessary to support public broadcasting.[61] The rest comes from state and local governments, university budgets, foundation grants, corporate underwriting, and private donations from on-air membership drives.[62] This range of funding, reflecting the strength and diversity of the country, should continue. But something more is badly needed to finally lift public broadcasting out of its perpetually precarious financial position. Moreover, with commercial broadcasting no longer accountable for public service, it is essential that the federal government play a more active, direct role in ensuring the stability and stimulating the development of public broadcasting. It should do this by institutionalizing increased federal financial support through the establishment of a Public Broadcasting Service Trust (PBST). Initial funding of the PBST would come from payments made by commercial broadcasters to obtain their permanent license. This would allow the PBST to become a workable, significant funding mechanism from the outset. However, to ensure long-term viability, additional steps should be taken to increase the initial "endowment" of the PBST. One of these would be to auction off all commercial broadcast frequencies not occupied by someone holding a permanent license and assigning the proceeds (or a portion thereof) to the PBST. This would include any frequency not subject to a permanent license at the beginning of the new system (because of a failure to qualify) or any frequency that was subsequently forfeited for some reason. Given the likely transformation of commercial broadcasting in coming years, placing an expanded number of marginal stations at risk, this method of providing future "investments" in the PBST seems likely to reap real rewards for public broadcasting—while also freeing up more frequencies for nonbroadcast purposes. Separately, PBST's "principal" could be greatly enriched by assigning the proceeds (or, again, just a portion thereof) that the government expects to receive when it auctions off the hundreds of TV channels that must be relinquished by public stations before February 2009, when those stations, like commercial stations, complete the conversion to digital broadcasting on a single, remaining channel. Each of these measures, it should be stressed, can be implemented without any need for direct public funding—such as congressional appropriations or a recurring tax or fee levied against equipment, profits, or use.

Past proposals to establish a special funding mechanism for public broadcasting have typically contemplated a very large federal contribution, or they have been advanced as a single, narrow policy change. My proposal is neither dependent on government appropriations nor narrowly tailored to a single, policy objective. These differences aside, it is nevertheless useful to examine other proposals—if only to assess the likely scope of the financial task at hand. Whether seeking to replace or merely supplement the current federal appropriation for public broadcasting, the dollar targets have ranged from $1 billion to several billion dollars.[63] Some call for direct government funding large enough to create interest income right at the beginning sufficient to support the annual operating expenses of public broadcasting. Others call for a 5 percent annual fee assessed on the gross advertising revenue of commercial stations, projected to yield yearly revenue of approximately $1.25 billion.[64]

Because I believe that funding for public broadcasting should continue to be mixed and, at the same time, seriously doubt the political feasibility of enacting a system of ongoing fees or creating a trust fund large enough to supplant most existing financial sources, the mechanism proposed here is best viewed as establishing an additional, significant financial pillar for public broadcasting. It will not replace existing funding, but it will give public broadcasting its first permanent funding source, a crucial step in building a public service safety net to ensure that all citizens, regardless of income and ability, have access to the information and experiences they need in a complex democratic society. While establishing the concept and getting the requisite structure in place is more important than the exact amount raised to fund PBST at the outset, some benchmark figures are needed. Accordingly, I suggest that the PBST be launched with a minimum $3 billion "endowment," which could generate annual income amounting to at least $120 to $180 million (based on conservative returns in a 4 to 6 percent range).

Raising this initial stake would involve no drain whatsoever on public treasuries and only a modest, one-time cost to private, commercial broadcasters. In 2003 there were approximately 4,800 commercial AM stations. If each was assessed an average $100,000 payment for its permanent license (with larger, more profitable stations paying more and smaller, less profitable stations paying less), this would yield $480 million. In 2003, there were approximately 6,180 FM stations. If each was assessed an average $200,000 payment for its permanent license (again, larger, more profitable stations paying more and smaller, less profitable stations paying less), this would yield $1.236 billion. Finally, there were approximately 1,340 commercial TV stations as of May 2003. If each was assessed an average $1 million for its permanent license (again, larger, more profitable stations paying more and smaller, less profitable ones paying less), this would yield $1.34 billion. Therefore, if, as expected, most stations paid the fee to obtain a permanent license, there would be more than $3 billion available to initially fund the PBST. Assuming a 5 percent return, this trust principal would earn nearly $153 million per year. If Congress chose to set the one-time permanent license payments at a higher level, yielding, for example, initial funding in the range of $5 to $10 billion, earnings alone from the PBST could easily match or exceed the current annual revenues public broadcasting receives from CPB. Moreover, once established, the PBST's endowment could be greatly increased, producing much higher earnings—by dedicating some spectrum auction proceeds to the PBST and by allowing future corporate, institutional, or private donations to be earmarked for the PBST.

My proposal, however, is premised on more modest initial levels, for several practical reasons. First, it is likely that, despite being promised total relief from all nontechnical regulation, commercial broadcasters will resist any payment that even begins to approximate the actual market value of the piece of spectrum they are allowed to occupy. Some will resist *any* payment whatsoever. Second, some policymakers and industry organizations will undoubtedly contend that the proposed payments for permanent commercial broadcast licenses would represent an unconstitutional, unfair, and discriminatory "tax" or spectrum fee. Third, long-festering partisan views concerning government support for public broadcasting will only be exacerbated if the proposal is seen as shifting too much funding and too much potential strength to public broadcasting. The more any reform measure fits rather than conflicts with these realities, the more likely something can be achieved to set us on a better course.

In this respect, it is noteworthy that the concept of commercial broadcast stations paying *annual* regulatory fees—for the general cost of ongoing regulation—and large *one-time* fees for specific transactions is well established. The current annual fees, moreover, are progressive in nature, escalating with the size of the broadcast market involved and the type and technical facilities at issue (with larger stations in bigger markets paying more and those with smaller facilities in smaller markets paying less). For example, among other periodic fees, a Class A commercial AM station in a medium-size city paid an annual regulatory fee of $2,700 in 2004. A Class B FM station in a major city paid nearly $7,000, and a VHF television station in one of the largest markets paid slightly over $60,000.[65] As such, the same AM station would pay the government at least $60,000 over the next twenty years (allowing for only modest increases), the same FM station would pay over $150,000, and the same TV station would pay about $1.5 million. These payments, it needs to be emphasized, represent only the basic ongoing regulatory expenses incurred by all broadcasters. They do not begin to cover the total expenses incurred by most broadcasters to comply with the current regulatory scheme. Certainly, viewed from that perspective, the level of fees I have suggested for permanent licenses is extremely modest.

Another rough measure of the value that might be attributed to a permanent commercial license—apart from recurring fees and associated operating costs that attend the current regulatory regime—is the amount other broadcasters are willing to pay to acquire operating stations in the open market and the amounts nonbroadcasters are willing to pay to acquire frequency space when spectrum auctions are held. As an example, in the ten-year period from 1992 to 2001, the average sale price of a radio station (AM and FM combined) was approximately $5.5 million (based on total radio sales of $40.5 billion, involving 7,384 stations) and the average sale price of a TV station was nearly $52 million (based on total TV station sales of $51.2 billion, involving 988 stations).[66] Many single radio station transactions have involved multimillion dollar price tags and a few recent single-station television transactions have topped one-half billion.[67] Although comparisons and projections are difficult, there is little doubt that if only the portion of the spectrum occupied by commercial broadcast stations were to be auctioned off—whether for future broadcast or nonbroadcast use—the total proceeds could easily approach a trillion dollars.[68]

To those who might argue that this still represents an unfair, inappropriate tax on broadcasters that, even if valid, must go into general treasury revenues instead of being dedicated to a special purpose such as public broadcasting, a clear answer is found in a long trail of precedent supporting this very concept. Of course, the largest social program in the nation, social security, is built on taxing individuals not to enhance general revenues but to support government-sponsored trust funds designed to provide retirement benefits. Similarly, the Unemployment Trust Fund is supported by an extra tax on wages and the Railroad Unemployment Insurance Account (incorporated within the federal Unemployment Trust Fund) as well as certain specific accounts of the Rail Industry Pension Fund are all supported by discrete taxes imposed on rail wages. Equally, if not more, pertinent is the federal Highway Trust Fund, in place since 1956, which receives revenue from special taxes levied on highway users, the most important being the fuel tax. Monies channeled through this fund are dedicated to the special purpose of providing federal assistance for the construction and repair of the nation's highways.

A number of other federal fundraising schemes are based on a similar model. For example, the federal Leaking Underground Storage Tank Trust Fund is funded by targeted excise taxes on gasoline, other motor fuels, and fuels used in inland waterways. The Aquatic Resources Trust Fund (Boating Safety and Sport Fishing Accounts) is supported by a dedicated tax on gasoline and special motor fuels used in noncommercial motorboats and a tax on certain sport fishing equipment. The Wildlife Restoration Account of the same fund is supported by special taxes on bows and arrows, plus certain firearms and ammunition. The Black Lung Disability Trust Fund is supported by a per-ton tax on coal taken from underground and surface mines. And the Vaccine Injury Compensation Trust Fund is supported by a special tax on each dose of specific vaccine sold by the manufacturer in the United States.[69] The federal government also sells or leases many of its natural resources—open lands for grazing, landlocked and off-shore water sites for mineral extraction, national parks and forests for various concessionaries (e.g., restaurants, lodges, ski resorts) to conduct business—with some of the revenues being set aside for continued improvement or maintenance of those resources (rather than being funneled into general revenues). For example, concession fees raised by the National Park Service are deposited in a special account, most of which are used for high-priority projects at the park unit where the fees are collected.[70]

If the federal government can target taxes and fees for such diverse dedicated purposes as outlined above, surely it can impose relatively modest one-time-only fees on all commercial broadcasters which would (a) pay for government relief from any remaining nontechnical regulation (including the future, permanent use of a valuable portion of the electronic spectrum) and (b) fund a new government-sponsored trust for public broadcasting. Equally relevant, the public policy goal—helping public broadcasting fill the ongoing role of a free, over-the air public service safety net—is equally worthy.

This proposal is offered with few delusions about the two most persistent problems plaguing public broadcasting: (1) the unreliability of all past and current means of financial support and (2) the continuing controversy over its essential role, usually touched off by partisan political debate. Despite these lingering difficulties, it is beyond question that the American public supports public broadcasting by overwhelming margins.[71] Even those who decry a perceived elitism or assume an abiding liberal bent in public broadcast programming must grudgingly acknowledge that this is an American institution that the American public wants protected and preserved. In an increasingly deregulated commercial media environment it is especially important that public policy focus more attention on public broadcasting. I leave to others who have studied these issues more thoroughly such questions as possible reform in the structure of public broadcasting, including how it is governed and how operational and programming funds are funneled from national sources to local stations. Just as the new Public Broadcasting Service Trust I propose would need both a mechanism to administer and a formula to allocate returns, adjustments to the overall governing structure may be needed as well.[72]

Adding Value to the Public Broadcast System

With commercial broadcasting relieved of all public trusteeship responsibilities and most competitive services available only by subscription, the American public must be able to look to public broadcasting as a constant, free, universally accessible source of information, diverse cultural experiences, and alternative entertainment forms. In this era of plenty, with mass media sources exploding and many Americans experiencing information overload, public policy should not be used to thrust public broadcasting into a more dominant role. Rather, what is needed is a more reliable public service safety net for the provision of programs that have never been well supported and are increasingly unlikely to be supported at all by the commercial system. Even though some of these program gaps are now filled by cable, satellite, or the Internet, those distribution technologies are not only subscription-based, they are largely nonlocal in source and content. What American mass media public policy should foster, therefore, is a noncommercial "public sphere" accessible to everyone regardless of socioeconomic class.

Any significant disparity in the quality of information and cultural experiences available to some citizens compared with others produces a corrosive effect on the democratic process, enlightening some but casting others to the sidelines of public discussion and communal experience. Public broadcasting—with expanded outlets and improved methods of distribution—supplies a free, over-the-air service to thousands of individual communities. Unlike cable, which reaches approximately 80 percent of American homes, and the Internet, which reaches approximately 75 percent of American homes, public broadcast stations reach virtually 100 percent of the American public, at home or on the road.

My proposal does not call for any fundamental change in the regulatory regime for public broadcasting. Only commercial broadcasting would be completely deregulated. Public broadcasting would remain subject to the public trusteeship model and public radio and TV stations would still be accountable through an ongoing license renewal process. To better monitor accountability, however, the renewal term for public stations should be cut in half, from eight years to four years. Other rules and regulations unique to noncommercial broadcasting would remain essentially unchanged, unless modified by new policy guidelines discussed below.

It is obvious that, from the beginning, public broadcasting has been cast as something vastly different than commercial broadcasting. Although its roots are as old as commercial broadcasting, public broadcasting was placed on a separate track more than sixty years ago when the federal government started setting aside specific frequencies for exclusive use by "noncommercial" or "educational" stations. Even though the line between programs aired by noncommercial and commercial stations is sometimes blurred, public and commercial broadcasting remain distinct, different services. As commercial broadcasting is further deregulated, public policy should place greater emphasis on the central strength and enduring mission of public broadcasting: providing a broadly oriented public service whose mix of information, entertainment, and diverse cultural experience enrich and assist citizens beyond what is available in more popular, mass appeal media.

This special role has long been crystallized in the mission statement of the Corporation for Public Broadcasting:

> The fundamental purpose of public telecommunications is to provide *programs and services which inform, enlighten and enrich the public.* While these programs and services are provided to *enhance the knowledge, and citizenship, and inspire the imagination of all Americans,* [CPB] has particular responsibility to encourage the development of *programming that involves creative risks and that addresses the needs of unserved and underserved audiences, particularly children and minorities.*
>
> [CPB] is accountable to the public for investing its funds in *programs and services which are educational,* innovative, *locally relevant,* and *reflective of America's common values and cultural diversity.*"[73]

CPB's mission statement derives from federal legislation which, among other things, explicitly directs CPB to interpret the "public interest" standard of the Communications Act as encouraging the growth and development of public radio and television "for instructional, educational and cultural purposes."[74] The statute also declares that the growth and "diversity" of "programming [offered by public broadcasting] depends on freedom, imagination, and initiative on both local and national levels."[75] Another key provision exhorts public broadcast programming to be "responsive to the interests of people . . . in particular localities," to "constitute an expression of diversity," and, finally, to stand as "a source of alternative . . . services for all citizens of the Nation."[76] And, if it were not otherwise apparent, congressional policy specifically calls on public broadcasting to address "the needs of unserved and underserved audiences, particularly children and minorities."[77]

Existing federal legislation also sets public broadcasting apart based on its coverage of certain public issues. Unlike commercial stations—

which have the right but rarely exercise it—public broadcasting stations are prohibited from supporting or opposing any candidate for public office.[78] Also, Congress requires CPB (not local public stations directly) to conduct its national operations in a way that better ensures that programs "obtained from diverse sources" are "made available to public entities with strict adherence to objectivity and balance in all program [material] of a controversial nature."[79]

While interested observers (partisan or nonpartisan) may read these provisions differently, it is clear that a system is already in place that explicitly seeks, through public policy, to achieve what is generally acknowledged to be the most vital roles played by media in general and over-the-air broadcasting in particular. These provisions boldly define the "public interest" standard in public broadcasting as calling upon mass media to instruct, educate, and serve the cultural needs of American citizens. Likewise, they constitute an unambiguous national policy requiring public broadcasting to reflect America's "diversity" and to serve as an "alternative" to mass appeal programming for "all citizens." Finally, they enjoin public stations to serve as "valuable local" outlets solving "local problems" through community-oriented programs.

What this shows is that the Public Broadcasting Act of 1967 long ago fleshed out a public trusteeship role for noncommercial broadcasting that far transcends anything ever developed for commercial broadcasting. What has been missing—to help public broadcasting fulfill this role—is a permanent source of funding and a proactive regulatory program to impose accountability. The suggestions that follow would raise the level of FCC oversight in this important area—helping ensure that public broadcasting everywhere better fills the public service gaps left by a deregulated commercial sector.

1. Enriched Localism. In today's confusing, vastly expanded media world—one that reaches from family rooms and neighborhood coffee shops to almost anywhere on the planet—the original mission of public broadcasting needs to be reenergized. A service created largely by local institutions—community colleges, state universities, community foundations, local school districts, or state-sponsored networks—needs to reinvigorate its "grassroots." More than ever, public broadcasting must have "a strong component of local and regional programming."[80]

With commercial broadcasting moving more completely to a marketplace model and the FCC more boldly assuming, incorrectly, that

localism (in the form of local service) can be achieved merely by preserving a few remaining structural regulations, it is increasingly evident
that our last great hope for any significant ongoing level of in-depth local public service rests with public broadcasting. Public broadcasting stations must become more involved in their local communities, teaming
up with local schools, universities, museums, and libraries. They must
provide not only a window to their communities but a forum for diverse
views and shared cultural experiences. Of course, many public broadcasting stations provide some of these services now. What is needed is a
new and broader emphasis on local programming that is made an explicit factor in the process by which every public station receives (a) federal funding and (b) a renewed license from the FCC. Whether established by the Corporation for Public Broadcasting or the FCC, there
should be clear guidelines defining what is an acceptable minimum
amount of local programming offered by each public broadcast station.
As with all previous FCC guidelines affecting programming, individual
stations should be afforded wide discretion for determining what constitutes local programming in their own communities. Certainly, local
service should include standard news and information programs (leading, it can be hoped, to more public stations adding local newscasts
whose goal and focus is distinctly different than that found on commercial stations). But it should also include programs featuring local arts and
culture, providing adult education or skills training for children and minorities or exploring any significant aspect of community life.

   *2. Required Service to Distinct Groups Underserved by Advertising-
Supported Media.*   Any formulation of a public service safety net
must include special programming aimed at children, minorities, the
elderly, and other underserved groups in the local community. While
most public stations presently serve some of these groups some of the
time, a more explicit, uniformly recognized system of accountability
should be established. This should start with a set of guidelines for
serving children and minorities that, hopefully, would be developed
and administered by leading self-regulatory associations, one for public radio stations and one for public television stations. General adherence to self-regulatory guidelines would then be taken into account when a public station asks the FCC to renew its license. A
similar method was effectively employed in the past when the FCC
looked to compliance with detailed codes of operation that had been
developed by the National Association of Broadcasters for its member
commercial stations.

Increasingly, commercial media (print and broadcast) produce shows and print articles catering to subgroups of society. If this trend continues, contributing to greater social isolation, the already under-served will be set even further adrift. It is, after all, the less educated, less affluent, less advantaged, as well as the youngest or newest Americans (immigrants), who most need a media experience that draws them into the cultural and social mainstream. "The News Hour with Jim Lehrer" on public television is generally considered one of the best sources of news and information, but it is also generally identi-fied as news and information for an elite or upscale audience. A bet-ter-funded public broadcast system with a reenergized mission could add special newscasts for the less advantaged in society, assisting them in becoming better-engaged citizens. Other programs could focus on job retraining or supplying meaningful, easily understood public health information. A revamped, broader-based public broadcasting system might also seek new ways to serve children and the less edu-cated with entertainment formats that also inform and uplift—for ex-ample, a "Sesame Street" for minority children and adults that, in ad-dition to using well-known celebrities from the minority community, employs graphics and techniques uniquely tailored to citizens with-out the language skills and cultural experiences of more advantaged citizens.

The *Washington Post*, in a series of articles in June 2002, reported that vast numbers of children of immigrants, who are U.S. citizens, are living impoverished, isolated lives mainly because of a lack of lan-guage skills—a condition that exists not only in traditionally poor neighborhoods but in pockets of some of our wealthiest suburbs.[81] More broadly, research increasingly shows that, for all children, brain development and acquisition of learning skills in the first five years of life largely determine later school achievement. And other research shows that quality preschool programs pay off, not just in better stu-dent performance but also in preventing dropouts, delinquency, and juvenile crime. In short, more emphasis on good preschool programs, whether in a classroom setting or supplemented by a well-designed media experience, can produce large dividends for American society.

3. Revised Role for Public Broadcasting in Providing Access to Politi-cal Candidates and Important Issues.   Although there is no reason to believe that the treatment of political news or controversial issues will diminish or change on commercial broadcasting following the re-moval of all remaining nontechnical regulations, certain adjustments will still be needed to promote public broadcasting's safety net role. For example, communications law should continue to impose an "equal opportunities" requirement on public stations—requiring them to afford any candidate, at any level of government, an equal opportunity to "use" their station if the station has been first "used" by his or her opponent.[82] Because candidate appearances on public stations are not allowed to be purchased, retaining the equal opportunities standard will give public stations a basis other than available campaign money—which still drives most candidate appearances on commercial stations—to allocate time equitably among competing candidates.

At present, federal candidates are granted the right to demand a certain amount of time (intentionally unspecified) on all licensed stations. In the future, federal candidates, as well as candidates for the highest elective office in a station's state and city of license, should be afforded a similar guarantee of time—but only on public broadcast stations. As now, individual candidate access decisions would be based on a standard of reasonableness, dependent on the circumstances of each political contest and negotiated by the specific parties involved.

The other major adjustment I propose is the reinstatement of the fairness doctrine for public stations. This is the FCC-developed and congressionally ratified policy that was enforced by the FCC for nearly forty years. Under it, all broadcasters had two affirmative responsibilities. First, they were expected to devote a "reasonable" amount of time to covering at least *some* controversial issues of public importance in their service areas. Second, once a broadcast station itself elected to cover a particular controversial issue, it was then obligated to provide a "reasonable opportunity" for significant opposing viewpoints on such issues. It is important to note that this policy never required a station to cover every controversial issue, include any or all conflicting views in a single program, or to achieve anything approaching overall balance on a given controversial issue. In fact, in practice, the FCC only once found a broadcast station deficient in failing to undertake coverage of a particular issue[83] and consistently tolerated unequal amounts of time being devoted to opposing views.

The FCC delivered the fatal blow ending the fairness doctrine in 1987. A few critical and timely court decisions, persistent pressure by some leading broadcasters, an executive branch ideologically committed to deregulation, and, ultimately, the inability of Congress to apply any effective counterweight, led to its demise. Although First Amendment interests were implicated, the doctrine was stricken without either the courts or the FCC finding it unconstitutional. It could, in fact, be reinstated by an act of Congress or mere reconsideration by the FCC.

Even though the blatant, persistent partisanship now practiced on many popular network and syndicated news and talk programs can be traced, in large part, to elimination of the fairness doctrine, I do not call for its general reinstatement. Rather, I think it should be revived to apply only to public broadcasting. First, public broadcasting, as a recipient of public funds, bears a special responsibility to be fair and balanced in its overall programming. Second, federal legislation and the guiding mission statement of the Corporation for Public Broadcasting have long demanded these traits of public broadcasting. Third, if public broadcasting is to assume a larger responsibility for serving a broader public interest under a new regulatory regime, it becomes especially critical that the only remaining regulated over-the-air medium strike the kind of balance the fairness doctrine was always intended to achieve. Public broadcasting needs to be a voice for groups that might not otherwise be heard and an ongoing source of alternative information and ideas. Reinstatement of the fairness doctrine will help foster those objectives.

It has long been fashionable in conservative circles to rant about the alleged liberal bias and general do-good attitude of public broadcasting.[84] Moreover, serious critics of all political persuasions have periodically complained about either the source of information or the creative leanings of entertainment on public stations. Whether the critics are right or wrong, there is no denying that public broadcasting is different than mainstream commercial broadcasting—focusing more frequently and more deeply on issues, problems, and cultural experiences in ways that most observers would regard as important to our society and our democracy. Attacking its "political" or artistic tendencies misses the central point. It is like saying that because the New York Times is a liberal-leaning newspaper and the Wall Street Journal is a conservative-leaning newspaper, neither is a valuable media source or social institution. Even if public broadcasting occasionally attracts views and features programs considered controversial in some quarters, it still stands, like our great public universities, as an essential pillar of community life in an open society. American representative democracy needs a multitude of reliable sources providing a variety of news, information, culture, and entertainment, especially in a non-commercial, more thoughtful, less hurried way. Our leading newspapers and newsmagazines are the bastions of serious journalism, and public broadcasting remains the most serious and diverse of our electronic media.

While some will argue it is unneeded or unwarranted, restoring the fairness doctrine for public broadcasting will help preserve that vital role—while also helping to quiet critics on both sides who want something else from public broadcasting. Properly applied and administered, a reinstated fairness doctrine for public stations will give public broadcasters a handy shield against both its critics and supporters while, at the same time, giving some needed comfort to partisans on both ends of the political spectrum.[85]

SAFEGUARDING THE PUBLIC'S INTEREST

The setting aside of specific broadcast frequencies for noncommercial use represented an important judgment by Washington policymakers that the American public is not fully served by the commercial marketplace. Decades later, policymakers must make another, equally consequential judgment. A marketplace dominated by the most popular media is literally awash in every conceivable form of commercialism and, correspondingly, less responsive to specialized needs and interests that do not normally attract the support of advertisers. While media alternatives abound, many of these, such as digital cable, personal recording devices, or Internet websites, require special equipment, fees, or a level of sophistication to access and use that is beyond the resources or abilities of those most in need—the very young, the elderly, minorities, immigrants, and those who, because of insufficient skills or endemic poverty, are trapped at the margins of American society. Over-the-air public broadcasting, despite its faults and difficulties, is the mass media outlet best positioned to serve these specialized needs while also serving as a broad-based safety net for the informational and cultural needs of all Americans.

The marketplace is a miraculous mechanism, but it is also a very unreliable one when it comes to filling the needs of citizens as opposed to consumers. Discrete segments of society with limited "buying power" remain unserved or unsatisfied in an environment totally dependent on economic factors. More broadly, the commercial marketplace has never been considered adequate to satisfy the diverse educational, cultural, and recreational needs of all Americans. If it had been, we would not have needed publicly supported schools and universities, symphonies, sports complexes, parks, museums, and theaters for the performing arts.

Advertising-supported commercial broadcasting is inherently geared to treating its target audience as consumers, not citizens. With diminished regulatory accountability, this tendency has become a preoccupation. Under heightened competitive pressure to gain and hold an audience, commercial broadcasting overflows with entertainment and information that is not only the most popular and appealing but immediately disposable. At the same time, the exploding choice of stations, channels, and websites continues to fragment the mass media audience, underscoring the difficulty—indeed, impossibility—of developing and sustaining commercially viable public affairs, cultural, and other nonentertainment programming. Narrowcast technologies and lifestyle patterns are pushing Americans into becoming more personalized media consumers fed by more special interest channels or sites. But, as Benjamin Barber warns:

> Democracy and participating institutions require exploration of common ground and are better served by a single widely-watched state network (or the three national networks), than by a thousand channels where citizens can find no common ground. Segmentation only undermines community, whether it is in a neighborhood, [or] a nation.[86]

The question posed is whether, as a nation, we have the political will to adopt and pursue measures that will make public broadcasting the kind of safety net that can help counter these trends. Both critics and advocates of deregulation have, in their own way, argued strenuously that our goal must be viable electronic media that enrich American democracy. But tinkering with what is left of broadcast ownership standards and chasing indecency violations more vigorously will do little to advance this goal. What is needed is fundamental policy change along the lines suggested here—starting with the creation of a new funding source for public broadcasting.

My proposals for public broadcasting both recognize and set out to accommodate certain crosscurrents that inevitably collide when this topic is raised. Because politicians have historically resisted anything approaching full funding but do not seem to want to lose control either, I offer a compromise that combines increased financial security for public broadcasting with continued dependency on existing funding sources. Because the United States faces large budget deficits that make government funding (from appropriations or new taxes) of a public broadcasting trust extremely unlikely, I propose to endow the new trust with fees collected exclusively from the private sector. Because periodic partisan bickering over public broadcasting is unlikely to ever totally abate, I propose reinstating the fairness doctrine for public broadcasting stations, providing political partisans of all stripes some cover when their viewpoint is not represented. And, because the powerful commercial broadcast lobby has always opposed (and effectively killed) proposals for new taxes or annual assessments on the broadcast industry (in the form of spectrum fees, equipment use taxes, transfer fees, or levies against advertising receipts), as a way to fund a public broadcasting trust, I propose a modest, one-time-only fee that directly benefits (instead of penalizes) commercial broadcast stations.

These changes are fundamental, not drastic. They build upon a long tradition of service already established by public broadcasting and a legal framework already in place. What I propose is a more concrete method for ensuring that these policies are carried out over the entire public broadcasting system. Implementing this new mission statement for the twenty-first century will be greatly assisted by twenty-first-century technology—digital operations that will, for example, allow one single public television station to program three, four, or five separate channels over the same frequency space it now uses to transmit a single analog channel. With expanded capacity, stations will be better able to provide wider access for political discussion and greater choices for underserved audiences such as preschool children.

While a somewhat larger federal role in funding could be perceived as increasing the risk of political interference or influence, that is a risk always present when government funds any editorial, cultural, or creative endeavor. Like other publicly funded institutions facing similar issues, public broadcasting is partially shielded from such influences because (a) it operates within a longstanding, independent structure; (b) it adheres to well-established traditions of public service; and (c) it faces a vigorous "competitive" commercial system that is far more dominant. Nevertheless, a new and improved funding mechanism may require new and improved methods for insulating government from the editorial process. While these are difficult, persistent problems and will never be resolved to everyone's satisfaction, it is important to point out that we have had sixty years of active government regulation of commercial and public broadcasting under the broad and highly supple "public interest" standard, which, in the past, gave birth to some fairly explicit content-related requirements. Yet, through it all, basic First Amendment principles survived. In form and function, nothing proposed here goes beyond anything that has not gone before.

Afterword

In an autocratic state, responsibility for the structure and performance of mass media rests with only one person or monopoly political party. In a mature, democratic, capitalistic society, responsibility is shared. It starts with those who own and operate media enterprises free of government censorship. It rests also with a general public that is given not only a choice of media but a voice to complain if dissatisfied. And, finally, it rests with policymakers—both elected and appointed—who are entrusted with the exclusive power to influence and direct certain mass media activities.

Even when responsibility is shared, criticism is almost always centered on those who own the broadcast stations, television networks, cable channels, and newspapers that deliver the "torrent of images and sounds" cascading over us every day.[1] That is probably inevitable, since the frequently subjective, often ephemeral nature of the product produced by mass media—information and entertainment—will always invite widespread, even passionate criticism. Only the most utopian would suggest that were information and entertainment to be delivered, instead, by government, academia, or any other alternative to private enterprise, would it be either free of criticism or universally revered.

This is not intended to deny or discount the validity of much of the criticism regularly heaped on contemporary mass media. Rather, we simply need to be reminded of two critical points. First, criticism is an

engrained part of the process, not unlike the highly personal judgments that are integral to the performing and creative arts. Second,
criticism of broadcasting—that it is too big, too commercial, too superficial, too risqué, or, in some circumstances, even harmful—is as
old as the medium.[2] Nearly fifty years ago, Wilbur Schramm, an early
mass media scholar, expressed a concern held by many in the late
1950s that "the mass communications system [was] getting out of
hand: . . . it is serving one political master rather than others . . . it is
moving away from the free marketplace of ideas . . . it is becoming
monopoly-ridden, plagued by bigness, or insensitive to minorities."[3]
Whether the current era of deregulation and massive consolidation
has brought commercial, over-the-air broadcasting to a new low in
quality entertainment and public service is probably beside the point.
All we really need to know is that similar pronouncements have been
made throughout broadcasting's history and all have been forgotten.
There can be little doubt, however, that the near total erosion of regulatory accountability, accompanied by an unprecedented frenzy for
advertising dollars in a more competitive, increasingly fragmented
media world, has resulted in less emphasis on public service and more
emphasis on cheaper forms of entertainment. Even if one assumes
that this trend has been counterbalanced by an explosion of media
alternatives, or will, over time, be remedied by more personalized, on-
demand services—or some other self-correcting mechanism of the
marketplace—the masters of media enterprises must bear a major
share of responsibility.

A smaller share should be borne by the general public—those who
actually choose to listen, view, or read particular media content. While
almost everyone is critical of prime-time television, local radio, news
reporters, or Hollywood movies, hardly anyone acts on those impulses. One reason, of course, is a certain sense of helplessness in being heard, a feeling undoubtedly magnified as media organizations
have become bigger and more powerful. But other factors may also be
at work. First, many who publicly criticize the media privately express
general satisfaction by their personal choices when using media. Popular media are obviously popular for a reason. Second, as more people opt for faster-paced lives, at work and at home, and face an escalating number of distractions and choices, they probably have come
to care less about the traditional mainstream mass media. Even
among the most educated and aware, there is no widespread, focused
activism. Instead of speaking up, most members of the general public

are inclined to tune out, move on, or just wash their hands of the offending medium. In the meantime, movie ratings, TV ratings, and technology now embedded in all TV sets (or available for computers and cable outlets) to filter out material unsuitable for children or offensive to some adults is largely ignored. Third, more technically proficient generations tend to view and use mass media differently than their parents and grandparents. Younger Americans will be the ones who lead the trend toward greater audience fragmentation, making media a more personalized and less mass experience. Fourth, an American public increasingly less involved in the general political process can hardly be expected to be more actively involved in media reform. In the end, it is nearly impossible, as a practical matter, to expect the general public—as opposed to organized, special interests—to participate in the process of media improvement or reform. One can only hope that, with the spread of media literacy programs[4] and greater use of the Internet for access and protest, the general public eventually will assume a more informed, active role.

In one sense, the American public—by the viewing, listening, and reading choices it makes, the political system it participates in or ignores, and the lifestyles it adopts—gets the mass media performance it deserves. Certainly, this is the answer that best comports with the view of deregulatory zealots who believe the mass media marketplace responds in an almost natural rhythm to the changing tastes and needs of the general public. The prevailing theme of this book, however, is that there is a responsibility that transcends the marketplace that can only be exercised by policymakers. That responsibility has been sorely missing during the last decades of the twentieth century. The decisions made throughout this period have done little more than dismantle policies of the past. There has been virtually no effort to forge a replacement policy for the future.

The movement to deregulate broadcasting started with the FCC. Propelled by an ascending belief that marketplace forces were just as effective as government regulation for instilling public service and achieving diversity, many FCC standards designed to promote those policy goals were gradually stripped away. When Congress finally got into the act, it did little more than jump on the deregulation bandwagon. Eschewing its earlier, failed efforts to write an entirely new law,[5] Congress merely expanded a series of deregulatory measures that had been started by the FCC or long championed by the broadcast industry. In contrast to telecommunications (telephone, wired, and wireless services), where Congress actually wrote new policy and adopted new concepts, when it turned to broadcasting, it acted with no foresight and no vision. In the end, it hatched a batch of piecemeal changes that, just a few years later, many of its members were quick to disavow. Instead of formulating policy in a more comprehensive fashion, it chose to take positions on narrow, very specific issues, such as the number of radio stations that could be owned by one party in markets of a particular size.

Scholars, critics, grandstanding politicians, even people on the street, blame mass media for failing to better serve the American public. A central premise of my text is that significant blame should also be placed on policymakers. Most of the changes discussed would not have been possible without the dramatic new course first chartered by appointed officials at the FCC and then enthusiastically pursued by elected ones in Congress and at the White House. While most legislators fail to acknowledge their own role in what transpired, one notable exception is the crusty, southern gentleman from South Carolina, Ernest F. ("Fritz") Hollings. Before his retirement in 2004, Senator Hollings had been at or near the center of most of the important debates swirling around mass media for twenty-five years. He embodied that rare policymaker who not only understands the natural instincts of the commercial world but candidly accepts his own special role. In the wake of the FCC's headline-grabbing decision to further weaken broadcast ownership standards in the summer of 2003, and while the Senate Commerce Committee (on which he served as the senior Democrat) was considering action to reverse the FCC, Senator Hollings said this: "I don't blame Sumner [referring to Sumner M. Redstone, chairman of Viacom-CBS] . . . I don't blame Rupert [referring to Rupert Murdoch, head of Fox Television and its News Corporation parent]. Heavens above, they are in a dog-eat-dog world." The media conglomerates, he continued, are "all fired up to buy and buy up and buy up, *and we're the culprits by allowing* [the FCC's deregulatory actions] to stand."[6] This remark could apply to virtually all actions or inactions of Congress over the past twenty-five years. Most of the prominent media developments that critics, including members of Congress, complain about today can be laid at the feet of Washington policymakers who either lifted specific rules that unleashed the changes we see or failed to act in a comprehensive way to balance such changes.

My approach—completing the deregulation of commercial broadcasting while reenergizing public broadcasting—is admittedly a prejudiced one, a very specific and critical point of view growing out of years of close observations of the policymaking process. The effort has been to find a new policy direction based on a new, viable foundation rather than continuing to patch an old one that no longer corresponds to current facts and challenges. The analysis and critique does not purport to present a balanced picture of contemporary broadcasting. Like a medical diagnosis that necessarily ignores the many parts of the body that are functioning properly, my specific prescription largely sidesteps other functioning parts of the mass media system and focuses on the parts that have failed but remain capable of being remedied. The public policy cure I am offering is not the only cure. But it is surely better than failing to medicate the problem at all or relying on little more than watchful waiting.

Indeed, if we do nothing, or worse still, if we continue to view commercial broadcasting as the same old business requiring the same old policy medicine, we risk losing a unique opportunity (maybe the last one) to use public policy in a way that will directly achieve concrete public service goals. At present, more than 85 percent of Americans receive television service by subscription via delivery systems that do not use broadcast spectrum. It is no longer idle speculation to suggest that, within the next ten or twenty years, commercial media may exist almost entirely online, over cable or by satellite—rendering "old-style" broadcast regulation premised on the temporary use of one form of public space even more obsolete, while underscoring further the necessity and value of a public broadcast safety net that is free, local, and oriented to serving Americans as citizens, not just consumers.

Finally, these proposals are not advanced without a deep appreciation of the political ramifications. After more than thirty years in Washington, I understand these realities. There are strong, vested interests that will resist virtually every element of any significant reform measure. Perhaps the strongest of these are key policymakers themselves—elected officials who accept large campaign contributions from mass media and, in turn, depend on mass media to help them remain in office. Members of Congress may never be willing to rip up the old and start down a new track. Or, more to the point, they may never be willing to loosen their tight oversight grip on commercial broadcasting (which remains so visible in the minds of their constituents) or to relinquish the special privileges that they have written into the law ensuring that, when seeking reelection, they receive access to broadcast stations in their districts at highly discounted rates.

But the question must be asked: how much longer can the world's leading democracy continue to pursue policies designed to stimulate the mass media marketplace without also considering some minimal preservation of the marketplace of ideas for all citizens? How much longer can the world's leading producer of mass media content and information technology continue to stand aside while millions of its citizens are still not connected to computers or able to buy the latest electronic gear or subscribe to the best services? As Gerald Sussman reminds us, "The cyber-community that some see as the 'global village' of the future has little meaning for the poorly paid classes, who are unlikely to interact within the better-educated and more mobile, affluent, and cosmopolitan networks"[7] inhabiting cyberspace. Mass media policy has failed to consider these issues, but it should consider them. Instead of focusing on the ability of the marketplace to produce more and different outlets—which policymakers now view as substitutes for traditional mass media—the crucial public policy question should be whether the public can be assured that it will always have access to affordable media outlets capable of (a) acting as a watchdog of government and other American institutions, (b) providing vital, ongoing information on public issues and the electoral process, and (c) offering different and diverse culture experiences to all major segments of American society. These issues are germane whether traditional broadcasting remains a media mainstay for years to come or is eventually transplanted, in whole or part, to the cyberspace world.

For the moment, "old-style" commercial radio and television remain vital beacons for a complex and hurried American society. As vehicles for mass entertainment they are unrivaled. They may be manipulative and sentimental, voyeuristic and vulgar, but they are still the most ubiquitous and practical means for informing, entertaining, and, occasionally, challenging Americans. No other institution in American life has the capacity to reach so many people with the events and stories that bind us as a nation. In an open society with flourishing technology and enhanced access, most significant views get through. Some observers may not like the balance at any given time, but that is the inevitable consequence of a free society. For these reasons, I am willing to trust the mass media—if not its individual parts, than at least its organic whole—on such matters. Indeed, since any meaningful reregulation of the commercial sector is both too late and wholly impracticable, I call for complete deregulation of commercial broadcasting. But, because markets are imperfect and fall short of filling all public needs, government policy must provide a public service safety net by better funding and reenergizing our public broadcast system.

Notes

PREFACE

1. According to a recent study by the Kaiser Family Foundation, "Generation M: Media in the Lives of 8–18 Year Olds" (March 2005), television is available in 68 percent of the bedrooms of children between the ages of eight and eighteen. A majority also have a CD/tape player, radio, or VCR/DVD in their bedrooms (86 percent, 84 percent, and 54 percent, respectively). Nearly as many (49 percent) have video game consoles in their rooms. A similar study conducted by Nickelodeon produced nearly identical results. As Nickelodeon's senior vice president of audience research observes, "Kids' rooms are becoming kind of like mini-media centers." Anne Becker, "Study Says More Kids' Rooms Have TVs," *Broadcasting and Cable*, 1 November 2005, www.freepress.net/news/print.php?id=12145.

2. Robert W. McChesney, *The Problem of the Media: U.S. Communication Politics in the 21st Century* (New York: Monthly Review Press, 2004), 252–97. While the public proceeding leading to the FCC's decision in 2003 did attract an unusually large and disparate collection of groups resisting different forms of further broadcast deregulation (McChesney characterizes what happened as "The Uprising of 2003"), this hardly constitutes an outpouring of historic proportions or even a clear reflection of widespread public sentiment on any media issue (especially any issue other than ownership). It does, however, demonstrate that agenda-driven groups now have better organizational tools (especially the Internet) to mount more effective protests of pending public policy decisions. For example, in 2004, a group called Parents Television

Council posted instructions on its website that offered members and friends direct assistance for filing electronic complaints with the FCC. *Wall Street Journal*, 8 April 2004, B-10. A subsequent Freedom of Information Act request to the FCC revealed that the Parents Television Council had been responsible for nearly 99 percent of all indecency complaints submitted to the FCC over the previous two years.

3. Paul Starr, *The Creation of the Media: Political Origins of Modern Communications* (New York: Basic Books, 2004), 339–46, 361–63, 392–402.

4. Any actual link between violence portrayed in mass media entertainment and the specific behavior of children remains a source of longstanding and heated debate. For instance, the Federal Trade Commission recently reviewed the body of scientific research in this area and found that most researchers agree that "exposure to media violence alone does not cause a child to commit a violent act" and that media violence "is not the sole, or even the most important, factor in contributing to youth aggression, anti-social attitudes, and violence." Federal Trade Commission report, "Marketing Violent Entertainment to Children: A Review of the Self-Regulation and Industry Practices in the Motion Picture, Music, Recording and Electronic Game Industries," Appendix A (2000). Others, of course, interpret the research differently. Indeed, on the heels of the foregoing FTC report, the American Medical Association issued a statement of its own asserting that "viewing entertainment violence can lead to increases in aggressive attitudes, values and behavior, particularly in children." "Joint Statement [of the AMA and certain other groups] on the Impact of Entertainment Violence on Children," 26 July 2000. In sum, after more than fifty years of study and controversy, there can be little question that the causes and consequences of violence, and the role of the entertainment media (which, today, include many different screens, not just the ones built into a TV set), remain extraordinarily multifaceted and complex.

5. In one recent example, FCC commissioner Michael Copps laid out the following personal laundry list of broadcasting's qualitative failures: "Too little news, too much baloney passed off as news. Too little quality entertainment, too many people eating bugs on reality TV. Too little local and regional music, too much brain-numbing national playlists. Too little of America, too much of Wall Street and Madison Avenue." See John Branston, "Reform Speakers Take on Big Media," *Nieman Watchdog*, 13 January 2007, www .freepress.net/news/print/20321 (16 January 2007). While such criticism may call to mind Newton Minow's famous (albeit more eloquent and restrained) "Vast Wasteland" speech (delivered by the former FCC chairman in 1961), Commissioner Copps speaks in vastly different times and faces dramatically different circumstances. Direct regulatory actions against the kind of media content he describes have never been tolerated and, in light of changed conditions, would be even more clearly violative of First Amendment protections today.

6. Although new data released by the FBI in late 2006 showed some incidents of violent crime starting to inch back up, throughout the 1990s and the first half of this decade crime fell significantly, especially among juveniles. For instance, juvenile murder, rape, robbery, and assault all decreased significantly over the past decade, and, overall, aggregate violent crime by juveniles fell 42 percent from 1995 to 2002. This is coupled with a steady decline in all serious crime throughout the 1990s. In 2000, the FBI reported that serious crime had decreased for eight consecutive years and that, in 2004, both five- and ten-year trend data indicated significant decreases in the overall volume of violent crime. See Department of Justice (FBI) press releases dated 15 October 2000 and 15 October 2004, respectively. On the other hand, there is no question that a culture of violence has been "writ large across the whole landscape of American history"—a part of life in America long before television became a part of life in America. James Gillian, MD, *Violence: Reflections on a National Epidemic* (New York: Vintage Books, 1996), 15. Think of frontier violence, civil war violence, probation-era gang violence, family violence long hidden from view, and blatant acts of violence based on discrimination or hatred.

7. Todd Gitlin, *Media Unlimited: How the Torrent of Images and Sounds Overwhelms Our Lives* (New York: Henry Holt & Co., 2001), 17 (emphasis in original).

8. "Further Notice of Proposed Rulemaking," released 24 July 2006 in Federal Communications Commission MB Docket No. 06-121, titled *2006 Quadriennial Regulatory Review of the Commission's Broadcast Ownership Rules Adopted Pursuant to Section 202 of the Telecommunications Act of 1996.*

CHAPTER 1

1. See Werner J. Severin and James W. Tankard Jr., *Communication Theories: Origins, Methods, and Uses in the Mass Media* (New York: Longman, 2001), 4; C. R. Wright, *Mass Communication: A Sociological Perspective* (New York: Random House, 1959), 15.

2. It is also noteworthy that "simultaneity" is no longer a constant in defining mass communication, given that sophisticated, widely available playback devices now allow many potential recipients of a "mass" presentation the ability to view it later or in a different mode. For a slightly expanded, decidedly updated explanation of the mass communication process, see Melvin L. DeFleur and Everette E. Dennis, *Understanding Mass Communication: A Liberal Arts Perspective*, 7th ed. (Boston: Houghton Mifflin, 2002), 16–23. As summarized by Professors DeFleur and Dennis, "Mass communication is a process in which professional communicators design and use media to disseminate messages widely, rapidly and continuously in order to arouse intended meanings in large, diverse, and selectively attending audiences in

attempts to influence them in a variety of ways" (18). DeFleur is also the coauthor of an earlier volume with Sandra Ball-Rokeach, titled *Theories of Mass Communication*, 5th ed. (White Plains, N.Y.: Longman, 1989), which, among other things, includes useful chapters on the early origins of mass communication, the emergence of the mass press, and the establishment of the broadcast media.

3. Irving Fang, *A History of Mass Communication* (Boston: Focal Press, 1997), 239.

4. Quoted in George Rodman, *Mass Media Issues*, 4th ed. (Dubuque, Iowa: Kendall/Hunt Publishing, 1992), 34.

5. The Alien and Sedition Acts of 1798 were not, however, the last effort to legislate governmental criticism. During World War I, Congress passed the Espionage Act of 1917, permitting censorship of ideas considered injurious to the war effort, and the Sedition Act of 1918, making any criticism of the Wilson administration illegal.

6. *Hoover v. Intercity Radio Co.*, 286 F. 1003 (D.C. Cir. 1923); *United States v. Zenith Radio Corp.*, 12 F.2d 614 (N.D. Ill. 1926). Shortly after the *Zenith* decision, in December 1926, President Calvin Coolidge sent the following message to Congress: "Due to decisions of the courts, the authority of [Secretary Hoover] under the law of 1912 has broken down; many more stations have been operating than can be accommodated . . . many stations have departed from the scheme of allocations . . . and the whole service of this most important public function has drifted into such chaos as seems likely, if not remedied, to destroy its great value" (H.R. Doc. No. 69-483 at 10 [1927]).

7. Francis Chase Jr., *Sound and Fury: An Informal History of Broadcasting* (New York: Harper, 1942), 21.

8. The word *ownership* and the issue of airwaves are linked at this point merely to underscore a distinction policymakers drew at the outset in fashioning regulation for the new broadcast medium. As discussed in chapters 7 and 8, the concept (i.e., what "ownership" actually means and how far it extends) is neither simple nor something definitively settled.

9. 65 Cong. Rec. 5735 (1924) (comments of Senator Howell).

10. Section 301 of the Radio Act of 1927 (emphasis added).

11. David Croteau and Williams Hoynes, *Media/Society: Industries, Images and Audiences*, 2nd ed. (Thousand Oaks, Calif.: Pine Forge Press, 2000), 69. For a broader perspective on the evolution of American newspapers from highly partisan oracles in the seventeenth and eighteenth centuries to less partisan voices for a wider public beginning in the nineteenth century, see James T. Hamilton, *All the News That's Fit to Sell* (Princeton, N.J.: Princeton University Press, 2004), 37–70. As Hamilton reminds us, half of our history "newspapers acknowledged and proclaimed that their judgments about news were influenced by partisan considerations" (37).

12. A series of four separate annual radio conferences immediately preceded passage of the 1927 Radio Act.

13. Quoted in "Public Service Responsibility of Broadcast Licensees," a report by the Federal Communications Commission, 7 March 1946, 41. Generally referred to as the "Blue Book," this well-known pamphlet governing broadcasters' conduct in a bygone era is available in *Documents of American Broadcasting*, 3rd ed. (Englewood Cliffs, N.J.: Prentice Hall, 1978), 132–216.

14. When World War I ended in 1918, the navy did not immediately relinquish control of the radio properties it had seized. Naval officials thought radio service might be too vital to maritime navigation to allow it to be placed in private hands. A bill proposing to effectively make radio a permanent government monopoly was, in fact, introduced in Congress in late 1918 but, despite the strong support of the navy, never made it out of committee.

15. The Radio Act of 1927 failed to address the advertising question largely because, at the time, the details and extent of commercialism were still in a state of flux. However, immediately after passage, one of the first topics attracting the attention of the Federal Radio Commission (FRC) was potential advertising abuse. The FRC announced that one of the "broad underlying principles" it would follow was that "the amount and character of advertising must be rigidly confined within the limits consistent with the public service expected of the station." *In re Great Lakes Broadcasting Co.*, 3 FRC Annual Report 32 (1929). Also, certain members of Congress thought that the FRC was being too lax in controlling advertising. In early 1932, the Senate passed Resolution 129 "authorizing and instruct[ing]" the FRC to (a) survey the feasibility of government ownership and operation of broadcasting facilities and (b) ascertain what plans might be adopted to "reduce, limit, control or, perhaps to eliminate" the use of radio for commercial purposes. See S. Doc. No. 137, 72nd Cong., 1st Sess. v (1932).

16. Discussing mass media, especially broadcasting, in relation to postmodernism is a way of analyzing how mass media, and the culture they serve and reflect, have changed. In a sense, the style and form of mass media and their place in contemporary society may have ushered in a new phase for both mass media and the culture.

17. Paul Starr, *The Creation of the Media: Political Origins of Modern Communication* (New York: Basic Books, 2004), 347. For those readers interested in going beyond the historical synopsis of chapter 1, the new Starr book would be a good place to begin. It presents a sweeping synthesis of the entire history of journalism and communications, including two chapters (327–85) specifically devoted to the origins of broadcasting and public policy bearing on the electronic media. Although the broad outline of historical events recounted in chapter 1 is both widely known and well reported—collected in numerous introductory texts, such as DeFleur and Dennis, *Understanding Mass Communication;* Joseph Straubhaar and Robert LaRose, *Media Now: Understanding Media,*

Culture, and Technology, 5th ed. (Belmont, Calif.: Thomson-Wadsworth, 2006); George Rodman, *Making Sense of Media: An Introduction to Mass Communications* (Boston: Allyn & Bacon, 2001); James R. Wilson and S. Roy Wilson, *Mass Media, Mass Culture: An Introduction*, 5th ed. (Boston: McGraw-Hill, 2001); and the classic survey text, first published in 1956, Sydney W. Head, Thomas Spann, and Michael A. McGregor, *Broadcasting in America: A Survey of Electronic Media*, 9th ed. (Boston: Houghton Mifflin, 2001)—there are several outstanding historical studies that predate the Starr book and concentrate exclusively on the history of broadcasting. One of these is Erik Barnouw's three-volume *History of Broadcasting in the United States*, especially volume 1, titled *A Tower in Babel* (New York: Oxford University Press, 1966) (covering the period up to 1933), and volume 2, titled *The Golden Web* (New York: Oxford University Press, 1968) (covering the years 1933 to 1953).

18. The depletion of what has been termed "social capital" has been a special topic of Harvard's Robert D. Putnam. See Robert D. Putman, *Bowling Alone: The Collapse and Revival of American Community* (New York: Simon & Schuster, 2000).

19. See, for example, David Von Drehle, "The Red and Blue States," *Washington Post*, 25–27 April 2004, a three-part series profiling an increasingly deep political divide throughout the nation. A few months later, in the midst of the 2004 presidential election, a public opinion poll by the Pew Research Center for the People and the Press found that "political polarization is increasingly reflected in the public's viewing habits."

20. See, for example, Ben H. Bagdikian, *The New Media Monopoly* (Boston: Beacon Press, 2004); David Croteau and William Hoynes, *The Business of Media: Corporate Media and the Public Interest* (Thousand Oaks, Calif.: Pine Forge Press, 2006); Elliot D. Cohen, ed., *News Incorporated: Corporate Media Ownership and Its Threat to Democracy* (Amherst, N.Y.: Prometheus Books, 2005); and Dean Alger, *Megamedia: How Giant Corporations Dominate Mass Media, Distort Competition, and Endanger Democracy* (Lanham, Md.: Rowman & Littlefield, 1998).

21. *Columbia Broadcasting System, Inc. v. Democratic National Committee*, 412 U.S. 94 (1973).

CHAPTER 2

1. The White House is also advised on communications by the National Telecommunications and Information Agency (NTIA), housed in the Commerce Department.

2. See FCC *News Release*, "Broadcast Station Totals as of March 31, 2005," 7 June 2005.

3. Judicial Improvements Act of 1990, Pub. L. 101-437, 104-Stat. 996.

4. Section 317; 47 U.S.C. § 317.

5. Sections 317 and 508-509; 47 U.S.C. §§ 508-509.

6. For example, Disney's ABC Radio Network serves thousands of local radio stations with several different types of full-service programs, centered on such formats as news/talk, adult contemporary, contemporary hit radio, urban, album-oriented rock, classic, and country. In addition, ABC's sports channel, ESPN, provides radio stations with sports news and play-by-play, and its Radio Disney network supplies programs for children.

7. Bill Carter, "A Struggle for Control," *New York Times*, 23 April 2001, C1.

8. A geostationary satellite orbits the earth at the same speed that the earth rotates on its axis, so it is essentially "parked" in space twenty-four hours a day.

9. Several years earlier the FCC had attempted to establish a new type of high-frequency noncommercial broadcast station that would have been licensed only to nonprofit educational institutions. See "Adoption of Rules Concerning Operation of 'Non-Commercial Educational' Broadcast Stations," 3 Fed. Reg. 312 (1938). While this effort proved unsuccessful, it probably represented the first official policy recognition of what we now call public broadcasting.

10. For those wondering about the math in this paragraph—82 total TV channels (twelve VHF plus seventy UHF) but 242 "reserved" for educational use—it should be noted that the same TV channel (e.g., channel 2 or 22) is allocated by the FCC for use in numerous different communities throughout the nation. As a result, eighty-two different channels allocated to distinct localities will yield thousands of stations.

11. John Witherspoon and Roselle Kovitz, *The History of Public Broadcasting*, a pamplet published by *Current* (a newspaper of public broadcasting), 1987, 33–34.

12. Witherspoon and Kovitz, *The History of Public* Broadcasting, 16.

13. Public stations, television and radio, are owned by a variety of state, county, and municipal governmental bodies, university trustees, and assorted other nonprofit foundations or organizations. Some entities own more than one station in an area or operate a state or regional network of public broadcast stations.

CHAPTER 3

1. As the U.S. Supreme Court famously declared in 1943, the Communications Act "gave the Commission not niggardly but expansive powers." *NBC v. U.S.*, 319 U.S. 190, 219 (1943).

2. For readers caught up in the twenty-first-century media reform movement—exemplified by new players such as Free Press, Center for Digital

Democracy, and the Prometheus Radio Project or older mainstays such as Common Cause, Media Access Project, and the Consumers Union—it is well to remember that this is but a new chapter in a very long-running story. Moreover, although contemporary activists sometimes speak of ushering in a new renaissance of public participation (see, e.g., writings of Robert McChensey, Eric Klinenberg, and Jerold Starr) the only real revolution in broadcast activism took place in the 1960s, immediately following the *WLBT* decision (*Office of Communication of the United Church of Christ v. FCC*, 359 F.2d 994, D.C. Cir., 1966) that gave public interest groups the right to participate in FCC proceedings. Armed with a new right of protest and exploiting an already impressive array of regulatory standards, several leading groups of that era—such as the aforementioned United Church of Christ, the National Citizens Committee for Broadcasting, the Citizens Communication Center, and Action for Children's Television—really made a difference. They filed numerous petitions, reached unprecedented settlement agreements with broadcasters, pursued innovative appeals, pushed existing standards in new directions, and proposed a host of entirely new standards. The pursuits of today's broadcast reformers pale in significance to those of earlier reformers. Their overall numbers may have increased (owing to better methods of connecting and rallying the troops) but their agenda and potential influence have been greatly restricted (owing to years of massive deregulation and vastly altered conditions).

3. See *Primer on Ascertainment of Community Problems by Broadcast Applicants*, 27 FCC 2d 650 (1971). In the years immediately preceding adoption of its *Ascertainment Primer*, the FCC adhered to a *Program Policy Statement* (25 Fed. Reg. 7291, 1960) that enumerated fourteen general areas of interest in reviewing broadcast performance: (1) opportunity for local self-expression; (2) use of local talent; (3) programs for children; (4) religious programs; (5) educational programs; (6) public affairs programs; (7) editorializing by stations; (8) political broadcasts; (9) agricultural programs; (10) news programs; (11) weather and market reports; (12) sports programs; (13) service to minorities; and (14) entertainment programming.

4. The "fairness doctrine" was developed by the FCC in the late 1940s and affirmed as constitutional by the U.S. Supreme Court twenty years later. *Red Lion Broadcasting Co. v. FCC*, 395 U.S. 367 (1969).

5. In 1976, for example, a full two decades before the landmark Telecommunications Act of 1996, the House Communications Subcommittee ambitiously announced its intention to rewrite the Communications Act of 1934 "from the basement to the attic." Two major legislative proposals ensued, the Communications Act of 1978 (H.R. 13015) and the Communications Act of 1979 (H.R. 3333, a rewrite of H.R. 13015), both championed by Lionel Van Deerlin, the subcommittee's chairman. Best described as before its time, H.R. 3333 actually foreshadowed the approach ultimately adopted years later in

the 1996 act, creating a presumption against regulation and in favor of reliance upon marketplace conditions. Despite extensive hearings over a two-year period, H.R. 3333 eventually died, leaving all significant deregulatory actions to the FCC, until 1996.

6. Many of the changes after 1980 (but before the 1996 act) were billed as money-saving measures to reduce unnecessary record keeping. In this spirit, Congress passed such things as the Paperwork Reduction Act of 1980 (Pub. L. 96-511, 11 December 1980), the Paperwork Reduction Act of 1995 (Pub. L. 104-13, 22 May 1995), and the Regulatory Flexibility Act (Pub. L. 96-354, 19 September 1980).

7. *Revisions of Programming and Commercialization Policies, Ascertainment Requirements, and Program Logs for Commercial Television Stations*, 98 FCC 2d 1076 (1984).

8. See *Elimination of Unnecessary Broadcast Regulations*, 57 RR 2d 913 (1985).

9. See *Application for Voluntary Assignments or Transfer of Control*, 55 RR 2d 1081 (1982).

10. The requirement for full documentation was replaced by a simple "certification" process, effectively permitting the applicant to judge its own financial qualifications—or, as was often the case in practice, the flexibility to work out the details later. The Communications Act requires that all broadcast applicants be judged on their financial, legal, and character qualifications.

11. It took more than forty years to get to seven, seven, or seven and less than twenty years to go from there to no limits whatsoever.

12. *Syracuse Peace Council*, 2 F.C.C. Rcd. 5043 (1987), upheld in *Syracuse Peace Council v. FCC*, 867 F. 2d 654 (D.C. Cir. 1989). While the question of the continued validity of the fairness doctrine was pending before the FCC in 1987, Congress passed a resolution intending to write it squarely into the Communications Act. On 19 June 1987, however, President Reagan vetoed the measure.

13. Children's Television Act of 1990, Pub. L. 101-437, 104 Stat. 996, approved 18 October 1990.

14. The 1996 Telecommunications Act included additional measures to protect the special interests of children. It mandated the inclusion of a V-chip in the manufacturing of TV sets to allow consumers to screen out violent and other harsh material, and it imposed a new requirement on TV stations seeking license renewal to submit a summary of written comments received from the public regarding allegedly violent programming by the licensee.

15. See House Rep. No. 104-204, 54-55, 118.

16. House Rep. 118.

17. See Joel Brinkley, *Defining Vision: The Battle for the Future of Television* (New York: Harcourt Brace & Co., 1997), 375–87.

18. For decades, the maximum license renewal term had been three years. Then, during the first wave of deregulation in the 1980s, Congress increased the term to five years for TV and seven years for radio. With the 1996 Telecommunications Act, the license renewal term was extended to eight years, for both radio and TV.

19. 1996 Telecommunications Act, Section 202(h), which reads: "The Commission shall review its rules adopted pursuant to this section and all of its ownership rules biennially as part of its regulatory reform review under Section 11 of the Communications Act of 1934 and shall determine whether any of such rules are necessary in the public interest as the result of competition. The Commission shall repeal or modify any regulation it determines to be no longer in the public interest." In 2004, Congress amended Section 202(h), changing the mandatory "biennial" (two-year) review to a "quadrennial" (four-year) review. See Consolidated Appropriations Act, Pub. L. 108-199, §629, 118 Stat. 3, 99 (2004).

20. "Parties in interest" is a term that, as a result of court and agency decisions, defines those persons or organizations directly affected by a given broadcast station or application—namely, a station's direct competitors, those who may experience electrical interference from the station in question, and members of the public who are viewers or listeners of the station.

21. 47 U.S.C. §309(k).

22. There are notable exceptions to the general proposition that the media industry abhors all regulation. For example, for many years the broadcast industry pushed aggressively for regulatory controls on the emerging cable industry. And, in more recent years, the cable industry fought just as vigorously to limit competition from telephone companies. Even today, some heavyweights in the broadcast industry find it in their self-interest to oppose and restrict the competitive activities of others. For example, in 2005, the National Association of Broadcasters (NAB) was pushing legislation in Congress to restrict satellite radio from providing local content to their customers. By the end of 2005, NAB's legislative solution, titled the "Local Emergency Radio Service Preservation Act of 2005" (H.R. 998) had attracted ninety cosponsors in the House of Representatives.

23. This includes two Nixon terms, one full and one partial (1969–1972 and 1973–1974); Ford's partial term (1974–1976); one Carter term (1977–1980); two Reagan terms (1981–1984 and 1985–1988); and one Bush I term (1989–1992). In just the first full decade of deregulation, President Reagan made nearly four hundred lifetime appointments to the federal courts. It has been said that "ideology trumped everything in the Reagan Administration's selection of judicial nominees." Joan Biskupic, "Mark on Judiciary to Endure for Years," *USA Today*, 10 June 2004, 6A, quoting political science professor Sheldon Goldman on the occasion of President Reagan's death. By 2005, the *Economist* reported that Republican appointees outnum-

bered Democratic appointees in ten of the country's thirteen federal circuit courts and accounted for 94 of the 162 active appeals court judges. "Judge Yourself: Conservatives v. the Judiciary," *Economist*, 23 April 2005, 31. When the entire federal judiciary is considered (i.e., all judges currently sitting on the Supreme Court, federal courts of appeals and federal district courts) more than 55 percent have been appointed by Republican presidents. Source: Alliance for Justice.

24. Even though the twenty-five-year period highlighted in the text was followed by two successive Clinton terms, the foundation for change had already been laid. Moreover, judicial appointments during the more proactive years of the Clinton administration were often tempered by a Congress that still favored a more limited government. And, of course, the twenty-first century began with a different Bush administration (Bush II), openly committed to appointing more conservative judges.

25. Ruel E. Schiller, "Rulemaking's Promise: Administrative Law and Legal Culture in the 1960s and 1970s," *Administrative Law Review* 53, no. 4 (2001): 1139.

26. Schiller, "Rulemaking's Promise," 1185.

27. Schiller, "Rulemaking's Promise," 1179.

28. *Office of Communication of United Church of Christ v. F.C.C.*, 359 F.2d 994 (D.C. Cir. 1966).

29. See *Petition for Rulemaking to Require Broadcast Licensees to Show Nondiscrimination in Their Employment Practices*, 13 F.C.C. 2d 766 (1968) and 23 F.C.C. 2d 430 (1970).

30. See *NAACP v. F.P.C.*, 425 U.S. 662 (1976).

31. *Bilingual Bicultural Coalition on Mass Media v. FCC*, 595 F.2d 621 (D.C. Circuit, 1978) (en banc).

32. *Beaumont Branch of the NAACP v. FCC*, 854 F.2d 501, 508 (D.C. Cir. 1988).

33. It is also relevant that, during this period, Congress extended the FCC's oversight responsibility in the EEO area to include the EEO practices of cable television operators and, a few years later, elevated the EEO obligations of television stations (first written by the FCC) into a statutory requirement. See Cable Communications Policy Act of 1984, Pub. L. 98-549, 98 Stat. 2779 (1984), and Cable Television Consumer Protection and Competition Act of 1992, Pub. L. 102-385, 106 Stat. 1460 (1992).

34. *Lutheran Church–Missouri Synod v. FCC*, 141 F.3d 344, 154 F.3d 494 (D.C. Cir. 1998).

35. See *MD/DC/DE Broadcasters Association v. FCC*, 236 F.3d 13 (D.C. Cir. 2001).

36. *Adarand Constructors, Inc. v. Pena*, 515 U.S. 200 (1995).

37. Stephen Labaton, "Media Companies Succeed in Easing Ownership Limits," *New York Times*, 16 April 2001, A1.

38. Labaton, "Media Companies Succeed," A1. While some readers might point out that another federal appellate court, the Third Circuit Court of Appeals in Philadelphia, took a slightly different approach in a 2004 decision questioning the FCC's most recent attempt to relax its ownership rules, the impact of that decision remains uncertain. *Prometheus Radio Project v. FCC*, 373 F.3d 372 (3rd Cir. 2004). While it did temporarily delay implementation of certain changes in FCC ownership standards (generally allowing further relaxation of such standards), the court's ruling focused on errors in the FCC's decision-making process, not on the FCC's basic authority to take the actions at issue.

39. *Time Warner Entertainment Co., L.P. v. FCC*, 240 F.3d 1126 (D.C. Cir. 2001).

40. *Fox Television Stations, Inc. v. FCC*, 280 F.3d 1027 (D.C. Cir. 2002).

41. *Fox Television Stations, Inc. v. FCC* at 1044.

42. The right to petition the government, of course, is guaranteed by the First Amendment to the U.S. Constitution.

43. Jeffrey Birnbaum, "The Road to Riches Is Called K Street: Lobbying Firms Hire More, Pay More, Charge More to Influence Government," *Washington Post*, 22 June 2005, A1. While the number of registered lobbyists in 2005 was nearly 33,000 (61 for every one of the 535 members of Congress), the total number is unknown but decidedly larger. Many persons who engage in lobbying do not register, because the rules are unclear and the penalties are slight.

44. Birnbaum, "The Road to Riches," A1.

45. The extent of the FCC's "independence" from the executive branch has always been in dispute. Not only does the White House appoint all FCC commissioners, it does so with a distinct political philosophy or approach in mind, especially in naming a chairperson for the agency. This obviously influences the FCC, if only in a nonovert manner. Sometimes, however, that influence becomes embarrassingly overt. For instance, it has been widely reported that the White House intruded rather directly in a major deregulatory battle waged in the 1980s when the FCC, at the insistence of the TV networks, sought to relax or eliminate its financial interest and syndication rules (known as "fin-syn" rules) that restricted the ability of the networks to take a financial interest in certain programs or to syndicate their own programs. The Hollywood community, from whence came the then sitting president, Ronald Reagan, was opposed to changing the rules and lobbied hard for their retention. But the Reagan administration, strongly committed to deregulation, was supporting the FCC's efforts to repeal the rules. Although Jack Valenti, the high-powered, high-visibility president of the Motion Picture Association of America, had lobbied the issue tirelessly, the movie industry ultimately decided to go straight to the White House. As chronicled in a 2001 profile of Valenti in the *New Yorker* by Connie Bruck, in the end "it was found necessary

to have [Lew] Wasserman [the head of MCA/Universal and the leader of the fight on behalf of the entire Hollywood community] himself talk to [President] Reagan. So there was this conversation between Lew and Reagan. Suddenly, the chairman of the FCC was summoned to the White House, lectured by Ed Meese [a presidential "counselor" at the time], and the rule was put back." Connie Bruck, "The Personal Touch," *New Yorker*, 13 August 2001, 52. To complete the loop, at "Reagan's behest, the Justice and Commerce Departments reversed their positions to favor retention of the rules. It was, of course, one thing for Reagan to have ordered his Cabinet officers to reverse themselves, and another to have interfered with the FCC, an independent agency." Bruck, "The Personal Touch," 53.

46. "What We'll Miss and What We Won't," *Time*, 29 November 2004, 32, an interview with four retiring U.S. senators, Democrats Ernest Hollings of South Carolina and John Breaux of Louisiana and Republicans Don Nickles of Oklahoma and Ben Nighthorse Campbell of Colorado. Political pressure backed by campaign contributions is also described in Leo Bogart's book on the commercial media system. In one particularly telling account, he describes how, in 1990 and 1991, Oregon senator Bob Packwood (a member of the Senate Commerce Committee) blocked bills to regulate cable rates at the behest of Ron Crawford, a lobbyist for the National Cable Television Association. An entry in Senator Packwood's diary found him ruminating about this cozy mutually dependent relationship: "The advantage Ron brings to me in the Washington PAC [political action committee] scene is that much of his income [from cable clients] is dependent upon his relationship with me. He has a vested interest in my staying in office." Quoted in Leo Bogart, *Commercial Culture: The Media System and the Public Interest* (New Brunswick, N.J.: Transaction Publishers, 2000), xxv.

47. Charles Layton, "Lobbying Juggernaut," *American Journalism Review* (October–November 2004): 26–27, quoting Joel Barkin, communications director for Vermont congressman Bernie Sanders.

48. From "The Fritts Years," *Broadcasting and Cable*, 21 March 2005, 32, 34. See also Neil Hickey, "TV's Big Stick: Why the Broadcast Industry Gets What It Wants in Washington," *Columbia Journalism Review* (September–October 2002): 50. As Hickey points out, the real source of NAB's influence is not its financing of free trips or even its copious political contributions, or its planting of Op-Ed pieces, or taking power brokers to lunch. "No, [m]ore important is its members' presence in virtually every Congressional district in the nation, and the perceived power of those television and radio stations to shape the news and control how issues that affect their own destiny get covered." Hickey, "TV's Big Stick," 51–52.

49. Stephen Labaton, "FCC's Rift with Industry Is Widening," *New York Times*, 16 October 2000, http://select.nytimes.com/search/restricted/article?res=F30710F93A5B0C758DDDA90994 (25 January 2007). Mark

Fowler, FCC chairman under President Reagan, succinctly summarizes the way the system now works: "[When] intense lobbying [of the FCC] from industry [is combined with] the 'soft corruption' [alluding to political donations] [it] often leads lawmakers to pressure the FCC. . . ." Quoted in *Broadcasting and Cable*, 26 May 2003, 17.

50. As one example of congressional intervention, the influential chairman of the House Commerce Committee and eight other members from the House and Senate wrote to the FCC on 19 September 2001 (only eight days after the 11 September 2001 terrorist attacks on New York and Washington), pressing the agency to lift the national TV ownership cap. In the letter, they issued this warning: "As the Commission undertakes careful, thoughtful review of the broadcast ownership rules—the national ownership cap specifically—we would stress that marketplace realities do not support the localism argument for retaining the national ownership cap." *Communications Daily*, 25 September 2000, 7. Preservation of localism was, of course, one of the principal contentions of those fighting for retention of the cap. If those words sprung from the independent, carefully researched thoughts of those nine members of Congress without the help or urging of a fundraising, campaign-donating broadcast lobbyist, it would be astounding.

51. See *Communications Daily*, 20 March 2002, 7.

52. See David Henry and Christopher H. Schmitt, "The Numbers Game," *Business Week*, 14 May 2001, 100.

53. Ted Turner, "My Beef with Big Media," *Washington Monthly* (July–August 2004), www.washingtonmonthly.com/features/2004/0407.turner.html (27 January 2007).

54. Quoted by Leonard Downie Jr. and Robert G. Kaiser in *The News About the News* (New York: Alfred A. Knopf, 2002), 84.

55. The deregulation movement has not been limited to the United States. Even in Europe, where state control of media has long been more deeply engrained, many countries—in response to marketplace changes similar to those in this country—have recently undertaken significant liberalization of their media ownership policies. See Gillian Doyle, *Media Ownership: The Economics and Politics of Convergence and Concentration in the UK and European Media* (London: Sage Publications, 2002); and Yaron Katz, *Media Policy for the 21st Century in the United States and Western Europe* (Cresskill, N.J.: Hampton Press, 2005).

56. The bias of such publications is hardly surprising since the advertising and subscription support they receive comes almost entirely from the industries they report on. In recent years, one of the leading radio trade papers (*M Street Daily*) was even acquired by the largest radio operator (Clear Channel) and later adopted the name of a competing paper, *Inside Radio* (following litigation that resulted in the merger of the two publications).

CHAPTER 4

1. The material cataloging the business interests of the new masters of mass media was assembled from many sources but principally from "Who Owns What," a running tabulation maintained by the *Columbia Journalism Review* on its website (www.cjr.org). At the beginning of 2006, Viacom-CBS divided itself into two separate public companies—Viacom and CBS. It was a transaction motivated to enhance equity value, not diffuse media control. Indeed, both before and after the transaction, both companies were controlled by the same man, Sumner Redstone, and his family.

2. The $134 billion revenue figure for 2003 is derived from GE's website.

3. Steve Rosenbush, "The Birth of Murdoch.com," *Business Week*, 16 August 2005, www.businessweek.com (20 August 2005).

4. In addition to the five domestic media giants treated in the main text, brief mention should be made of two powerful media conglomerates whose roots are in foreign soils; namely, Bertelsmann from Germany and Sony from Japan. While current U.S. communications laws restrict such companies from holding broadcast stations outright or taking a controlling interest in a broadcast or cable company using radio frequencies, each of these far-flung companies has found other ways of spreading their wings over domestic media. Sony owns Columbia Pictures, the giant Hollywood fixture, along with Screen Gems and related production facilities. It is also a major force in U.S. music sales, controlling such well-known labels as Columbia, Epic, and Sony. Bertelsmann, on the other hand, is heavily involved in both music production and publishing. It controls such influential labels as Arista, BMG Classics, RCA, and the Windham Hill Group. On the print side, Bertelsmann controls, among others, such renowned publishers as Random House, Knopf, Bantam, Doubleday, and Dell. It is also one of the largest magazine publishers in both Europe and the United States, in which capacity it is the current guardian of such popular symbols of American culture as *Family Circle*, *Parents*, and *Inc*. A third international company, Vivendi, of France, had also amassed a vast media empire by the start of the twenty-first century. However, after suffering serious financial and management problems, it all came tumbling down. Many of its assets, notably Universal Studios and several popular cable services, were sold to NBC in early 2004.

5. Steven H. Lee, "Clear Channel Builds Radio Empire from Single San Antonio Station," *Dallas Morning News*, 28 July 1996, 1H.

6. Stephanie Anderson Forest and Richard Siklos, "The Biggest Media Mogul You Never Heard Of," *Business Week*, 18 October 1999, 56.

7. 2001 *Broadcasting and Cable Yearbook*, D-639. See also *Radio Business Report*, 14 May 2001, 10.

8. Industry sources recognize as many as ninety different formats, from AAA (referring to adult album alternative) to Vietnamese. *Yearbook*,

D-617-638. A closer examination, however, reveals that only twenty or so would generally be regarded as major or significant formats. Otherwise, the list is peppered with such esoteric "favorites" as American Indian, Eskimo, hardcore, Hebrew, Korean, Polka, Portuguese, and underground. An industry report prepared in 2001 distilled the nominally different radio formats found on commercial stations into nineteen general groups. See Mark R. Fratrick, *State of the Radio Industry: What Is Going on with Radio Formats* (a report issued in 2001 by the BIA Financial Network), 6–7.

9. For more on format trends and the general recycling that goes on among the leading, longstanding brands, see *Radio Business Report*, 25 June 2001, 11; and Ben Sisario, "Jack and Bob and Hank and Ben: Meet Radio's Hottest Non-entities," *New York Times*, 17 July 2005, 23.

10. Fratrik, *State of the Radio Industry*, 10.

11. Compare *Investing in Radio 1996*, 1st ed. (listing Radio One, CBS, Infinity, Evergreen, Viacom, SFX, Greater Media, Colfax, Capital Broadcasting, and ABC as the major groups) with *Investing in Radio 2001*, 2nd ed. (listing just Infinity, Radio One, Bonneville, ABC, and Clear Channel as the major groups).

12. "Who Owns What," published by *Inside Radio*, 9 April 2001, 3.

13. Compare *Investing in Radio 1996* with *Investing in Radio 2001*.

14. See local listings of radio stations, *Washington Post*, 22 August 2001, C9.

15. A 2001 survey prepared by the Radio and Television News Directors Association and Ball State University reported that "in the last seven years, the size of the typical radio newsroom had fallen 56.7 percent." Published by RTNDA in the *Communicator* (September 2001): 6.

16. Marc Fisher, "Meeting the Challenge," *American Journalism Review* (October 2001), www.ajr.org/article_printable.asp?_ id=48 (4 September 2005).

17. Kathryn S. Wenner, "Bang, Bang, Bang," *American Journalism Review* (November 2002): 32, 34.

18. Wenner, "Bang, Bang, Bang," 34, quoting Bill Yeager, senior vice president of the Metro Networks news division.

19. Jack Hitt, "Talk-to-Yourself Radio," *New York Times Magazine*, 17 June 2001, 42.

20. Hitt, "Talk-to-Yourself Radio," 44.

21. For example, in Washington, D.C., the ninth-largest radio market, the only realistic alternatives to the tightly formatted and finely tuned products offered by the media conglomerates are a thin splattering of religious and nonprofit stations, such as those run by the Pacifica Foundation or public radio. See Samuel G. Freedman, "An Island of Idiosyncrasy on the AM Dial," *New York Times*, 12 August 2001, Section 2, 28, highlighting a station in Poughkeepsie, New York, that "combines the quaint mainstays of small-town radio—'Chamber of Commerce Chat,' 'Pet Talk,' 'The German Hour'—with music shows brimming with knowledge and taste."

22. Anna Wilde Mathews, "A Giant Radio Chain Is Perfecting the Art of Seeming Local," *Wall Street Journal*, 25 February 2002, A1.

23. After years of audience stability, radio listeners are switching off or turning away more quickly than previously. Radio listening has, in fact, slipped 11 percent since the early 1990s, according to Arbitron audits. Among listeners in the eighteen- to twenty-four-year-old bracket, one of radio's core groups, listening hours dropped almost 21 percent since 1996. Shelly Freierman, "The Youngsters Aren't Listening as Much," *New York Times*, 16 October 2006, C5. Some blame consolidation and the "sameness" it engenders while others point to changing lifestyles and the attraction of competing media, especially the Internet among newer generations of radio listeners.

24. "Consolidation Good for Public, Advertisers, Karmazin Tells TVB," *Communications Daily*, 27 March 2002, 2.

25. Ken Auletta, "How Much Bigger Can AOL Time Warner Get?" *New Yorker*, 29 October 2001, 50.

26. TV listings, *Washington Post*, 21 February 2002, C6.

27. See Dan Trigoboff, "KDNL's St. Louis News Blues," *Broadcasting and Cable*, 8 October 2001, 22, reporting on news being dropped on an ABC affiliate in St. Louis, Missouri, the twenty-second-largest television market in the country.

28. Thomas E. Patterson, "Doing Well and Doing Good: How Soft News and Critical Journalism Are Shrinking the News Audience and Weakening Democracy—And What News Outlets Can Do About It," a report published by the Shorenstein Center on the Press, Politics and Public Policy, Kennedy School of Government, Harvard University (December 2000), reprinted under the title "News You Can Lose," *Wilson Quarterly* (Summer 2001): 90–91.

29. Patterson, "News You Can Lose," 91. For additional evidence documenting the general softening of television news and how different audiences respond to news reporting, see James T. Hamilton, *All the News That's Fit to Sell* (Princeton, N.J.: Princeton University Press, 2004), 71–120, 137–89.

30. Study conducted by the Pew Research Center for the People and the Press, summarized in the monthly magazine of the Radio and Television News Directors Association, *Communicator* (September 2001): 28–39.

31. See, for example, Robert W. McChesney, *Rich Media, Poor Democracy: Communications Politics in Dubious Times* (New York: The New Press, 1999), 2. In McChesney's view, increased concentration of the electronic media merely "accentuates the core tendencies of a profit-driven, advertising-supported media system: hypercommercialism and denigration of journalism and public service," resulting in "a poison pill for democracy."

32. Apart from those that limit some forms of advertising designed to reach children, the FCC no longer has any policies concerning or mechanics for dealing with the quantity or quality of advertising on commercial broadcasting. In addition, industry self-regulatory codes have long since been

abandoned—spurred, ironically, by an antitrust lawsuit in the early 1980s against the broadcast industry by the Justice Department.

33. Jon Lafayette, "Clutter on Broadcast Rises: Three of Big Four Nets Surpass 15 Minutes Per Hour of Nonprogram Material," *Television Week*, 12 April 2004, 1. An earlier advertising industry study, cited by the FCC, found that the hourly commercial minutes in prime time on the big four TV networks had increased by 16.4 percent from 1991 to 2000. See "Broadcast Television: Survivor in a Sea of Competition" (a working paper of the FCC's Office of Plans and Policy, September 2002), 28. Of course, commercial clutter outside prime time (which includes the remaining twenty-one hours of the day) often runs much higher. Highly rated local newscasts and early-morning or late-night shows on national networks are among the worst.

34. See "Data Zone," *Electronic Media*, 25 February 2002, 6.

35. Steve McClellan, "Big Four in the Black: Fiscal 2000 Was a Profitable Year for ABC, CBS, Fox and NBC, with Decent Margins," *Broadcasting and Cable*, 28 May 2001, 36, reporting that "for the first time in years, in fiscal 2000, the four major TV networks made money." The network companies, in recent years, have complained loudly that they need relaxed ownership rules so they can acquire more properties, better compete, and save the network business. These results, as recently as 2000, belie that argument. In truth, as a group, the networks have rarely been profitable, even (or especially) back in the 1960s and 1970s when they still commanded more than 90 percent of the prime-time audience. At the same time, as this article also notes, the network companies have long been highly profitable, overall, when one takes into account their local station and other media ventures. For example, Viacom-CBS had pretax profits in 2000 for its electronic-media divisions that totaled $4.2 billion on $13.8 billion in revenue, producing a margin of 30 percent. McClellan, "Big Four in the Black," 30.

36. Section 201 of the 1996 act attempts to define "high definition television" as any "systems that offer approximately twice the vertical and horizontal resolution of receivers generally available on the date of enactment" of the 1996 law.

37. Stephen Labaton, "Most Commercial Broadcasters Will Miss Deadline for Digital Television," *New York Times*, 29 April 2002, C6.

38. "Snapshots," *USA Today*, 23 July 2002, 1A.

39. See Werner J. Severin and James W. Tankard Jr., *Communication Theories: Origins, Methods, and Uses of the Mass Media* (New York: Longman, 2001), 246–59. First proposed in 1970 by researchers Tichenor, Donohue, and Olien, the hypothesis was stated as follows: "As the infusion of mass media information into a social system increases, segments of the population with higher socioeconomic status tend to acquire this information at a faster rate than the lower-status segments, so that the gap in knowledge between these

segments tends to increase rather than decrease." Severin and Tankard, *Communication Theories,* 246–47.

40. Gerald Sussman, *Communication, Technology, and Politics in the Information Age* (Thousand Oaks, Calif.: Sage Publications, 1997), 17.

41. Quoted by Maureen Dowd in "Bloggers Double Down," *New York Times,* 10 June 2006, A27. A month later, on 19 July 2006, the Pew Internet and American Life Project released a survey report indicating that the vast majority of bloggers are "focused on describing their personal experiences to a relatively small audience of readers and that only a small proportion focus their coverage on politics, media, government or technology." Even the much smaller number of so-called higher-traffic A-list bloggers that receive most of the public and press attention rarely engage in original reporting. www .pewresearch.org/reports/?Report ID=36. (10 August 2006).

42. *New York Times,* 2 May 2005, C8 (chart listing websites/news organizations). See also Felicity Barringer, "Growing Audience Is Turning to Established News Media Online," *New York Times,* 27 August 2001, business section, 1.

43. Robert W. McChesney, *Rich Media, Poor Democracy* (New York: The New Press, 1999), 101.

44. The original formula for cultural imperialism was, in fact, articulated at least thirty years earlier by Herbert Schiller in *Mass Communications and American Empire* (New York: Augustus M. Kelly, 1969), a work that was updated by Schiller in 1992. See *Mass Communications and American Empire,* 2d ed. (Boulder, Colo.: Westview Press, 1992). An excellent critique of Schiller's work appears in John P. Thompson, *The Media and Modernity: A Social Theory of the Media* (Stanford, Calif.: Stanford University Press, 1995), 164–78.

45. James Lull, *Media, Communication and Culture,* 2d ed. (New York: Columbia University Press, 2000), 11.

46. See George Packer, "When Here Sees There," *New York Times Magazine,* 21 April 2002, 13.

47. Lull, *Media, Communication and Culture,* 229. For a further discussion of cultural imperialism, see Jonathan Bignell, *An Introduction to Television Studies* (London: Routledge, 2004), 62–84. In general, evidence of direct, lasting impact on other cultures from "imported" media content is, at best, tenuous and conflicting. A related development, however, is worth noting. America's experiment with mass media deregulation and its concomitant reliance on competitive services has seemingly taken hold in one form or another in a number of Western and developing countries—reflected in significant structural and organizational changes (including increased commercialization) of mass media in Europe, South America, and elsewhere. On this subject, see Lori A. Brainard, *Television: The Limits of De-regulation* (Boulder, Colo.: Lynne Rienner Publishers, 2004); and Gillian Doyle, *Media Ownership: The*

Economics and Politics of Convergence in the UK and European Media (London: Sage Publications, 2002).

48. See "U.S. Television Map," a pull-out supplement published jointly by *Broadcasting and Cable* and *Multichannel News* magazines, 18 July 2005.

49. Nielsen/NetRatings. Moreover, if we look beyond current events to the top web properties overall, similar results obtain. As of August 2005, the top ten web properties were maintained by the following entities (listed in order of ranking): Microsoft, Time Warner, Yahoo!, Google, eBay, the U.S. Government, Interactive Group, Amazon, Real Networks, and Viacom. www.nielsennetratings.com (15 November 2005).

50. "Poll Shows Broadband Growing Among U.S. Internet Users," *Wall Street Journal*, 12 May 2005, reporting the results of a recent Harris Interactive poll. onlinewsj.com/article_print/o,,SB111582078403930407,00.html (20 May 2005). See also Nielsen/NetRatings (February 2004).

51. Although much is made of the Internet's ascending role in providing news and information, the worldwide web remains a decidedly supplemental news source—according to a 2006 study of America's news consumption habits by the Pew Research Center for the People and the Press. For the moment, the Internet is seen more as a medium of convenience than as a primary medium of content. Despite the fact that almost one in three Americans now say they spend three or more days a week gathering news online, and despite dramatic reductions in audiences for newscasts offered by national television networks, online news has, essentially, "evolved as a supplemental source that is used along with traditional news media outlets." www.pewresearch.org /obdeck/?ObDeckID-42 (15 January 2007).

52. Some writers like Wilson Dizard Jr. define "new media" beyond the Internet, including such things as laser discs, advanced facsimile machines, handheld data banks, electronic books, videotext networks, intelligent multipurpose telephones, and a seemingly endless array of modern electronic gadgets capable of transmitting video, text, and sound.

CHAPTER 5

1. For other descriptions of the social functions of media, see Lawrence Grossberg, Ellen Wartella, and D. Charles Whitney, *Media Making: Mass Media in A Popular Culture* (Thousand Oaks, Calif.: Sage Publications, 1998), 244–50; William F. Baker and George Dessart, *Down the Tube: An Inside Account of the Failure of American Television* (New York: Basic Books/Perseus Books Group, 1998), 134–35; and Joseph Straubhaar and Robert LaRose, *Media Now: Understanding Media, Culture, and Technology*, 5th ed. (Belmont, Calif.: Thomson-Wadsworth, 2006), 46–48.

2. Richard Gunther and Anthony Mugham, eds., *Democracy and the Media* (Cambridge, U.K.: Cambridge University Press, 2000), 421.

3. Kenneth Dautrich and Thomas H. Hartley, *How the News Media Fail American Voters: Causes, Consequences and Remedies* (New York: Columbia University Press, 1999), 2.

4. Thomas Kunkel, "Our Hour of Need," *American Journalism Review* 24, no. 6 (July–August 2002): 4.

5. Straubhaar and LaRose, *Media Now*, 46.

6. For example, Robert W. McChesney opines that "the commercial basis of U.S. media has negative implications for the exercise of political democracy: it encourages a weak political structure that makes de-politicization, apathy and selfishness rational choices for the citizenry, and it permits the business and commercial interests that actually rule U.S. society to have inordinate influence over media content." Viewed this way, "the nature of the U.S. media system undermines all three of the meaningful criteria necessary for self-government." Robert W. McChesney, *Corporate Media and the Threat to Democracy* (New York: Seven Stories Press, 1997), 7.

7. For contemporary critics holding this view, see writings of Robert W. McChesney, Mark Crispin Miller, and Ben Bagdikian. For a broader historical perspective, see Theodore Peterson, Jay W. Jensen, and William L. Rivers, *The Mass Media and Modern Society* (New York: Holt, Rinehart and Winston, 1967), 227. Summarizing seven general themes popular among media critics at the time of their writing (1965), Peterson, Jensen, and Rivers put the following at the top of their list: "The media have used their great power to promote the interest of their owners. The owners have propagated their own views, especially in politics and economics. They have ignored or played down contrary views."

8. Despite the blame frequently and indiscriminately placed on mass media for various societal woes, most social scientists today reject the notion that media are an independent force directly shaping and molding social developments or conditions. See, for example, Marvin L. DeFleur and Sandra Ball-Rokeach, *Theories of Mass Communication*, 5th ed. (White Plains, N.Y.: Longman, 1989), 120–21.

9. Quoted in Irving Fang, *A History of Mass Communication* (Boston: Focal Press, 1997), 151, obtained from an essay found in the DeForest archives, originally reported by Stephen Green in an unpublished paper in 1991.

10. Quoted from the *Washington Post* of 28 July 1991 by Wilson Dizard Jr. in *Old Media, New Media: Mass Communications in the Information Age*, 3rd ed. (New York: Longman, 2000), 81.

11. David Croteau and William Hoynes, *Media/Society: Industries, Images and Audiences* (Thousand Oaks, Calif.: Pine Forge Press, 2000), 5.

12. See, for example, Donald Bogel, *Primetime Blues: African Americans on Network Television* (New York: Farrar, Straus & Giroux, 2001).

13. Susanne Ault, "ET: The Business Behind the Buzz," *Broadcasting and Cable*, 2 July 2001, 14.

14. Frank Rich, "The Best Years of Our Lives," *New York Times*, 26 May 2001, A 23.

15. See, for example, Daniel Boorstin, *The Image: A Guide to Pseudo-Events in America* (New York: Harper and Row, 1961), 57; James Monaco, *Celebrity: The Media as Image Makers* (New York: Delta Publishing, 1978), 5–6. Monaco distinguishes celebrities from heroes: "Before we had celebrities we had hero types. . . . What these hero types all share . . . are admirable qualities—qualities that somehow set them apart from the rest of us. They have done things, acted in the world: written, thought, understood, led. Celebrities, on the other hand, needn't have done—needn't do—anything special."

16. See Leo Braudy, *The Frenzy of Renown: Fame and Its History*, (New York: Oxford University Press, 1986).

17. Tom Shales, "Yakety Yak: Hosts Need to Let Celebs Talk Back," *Television Week*, 14 July 2003, 27.

18. Jack Hitt, "Talk-to-Yourself Radio," *New York Times Magazine*, 17 June 2001, 42.

19. See Kelley Heyboer, "Targeting Youth," *American Journalism Review* (December 2002): 14; Jacques Steinberg, "New Papers Hope Free and Brief Will Attract Younger Readers," *New York Times*, 13 October 2003, C1; Frank Ahrens, "Post Co. to Launch Free Tabloid," *Washington Post*, 11 July 2003, E1; Felicity Barringer, "An Old-Time Newspaper for Young Loyalties," *New York Times*, 31 October 2002, C1.

20. "Tabloiditis: Everywhere, Broadsheets Are Shrinking," *The Economist*, 29 May 2004, 65–66.

21. "Europe's Papers Shrink Pages to Boost Sales," *Wall Street Journal*, 22 December 2004, B1.

22. Joseph T. Hallinan, "Los Angeles Paper Bets on Softer News, Shorter Stories," *Wall Street Journal*, 3 October 2005, B1.

23. David Carr, "Rise of the Visual Puts Words on the Defensive," *New York Times*, 1 April 2002, C8.

24. Quoted by Michael Scherer, "Does Size Matter?" in *Columbia Journalism Review* (November–December 2002): 33.

25. Malcolm Jones, "Waiting for the Movie: Reading Is Going Out of Style, Even as Publishers Go Wild," *Time*, 29 July 2004, 58. See also Linton Weeks, "The No-Book Report: Skim It and Weep," *Washington Post*, 14 May 2001, C1.

26. Quoted by David Smith in "A Literary Lion Still Roaring," *Baltimore Sun*, 20 August 2001, E-1.

27. Neil Hickey, "Chicago Experiment—Why It Failed," *Columbia Journalism Review* (January–February 2001): 15. The Hickey article details the unhappy results when a Chicago television station tried to follow a no-frills, stripped-down form of journalism on its evening newscast that featured a

fifty-year-old anchorwoman and purposely avoided the familiar crime-and-mayhem, disaster, celebrity stories, and lifestyle features that typify most local newscasts.

28. In fact, a persuasive case can be made that, in recent years, good journalism has been steadily devalued not just by the companies that own and control electronic and print media but by a less engaged citizenry that fails to use or demand high-quality journalism. As political scientist Robert Entman laments, "Because most members of the public know and care relatively little about government, they neither seek nor understand high-quality political reporting and analysis. With limited demand for first-rate journalism, most news organizations cannot afford to supply it, and because they do not supply it, most Americans have no practical source of the information necessary to become politically sophisticated." Robert N. Entman, *Democracy without Citizens: Media and the Decay of American Politics* (New York: Oxford University Press, 1989), 17. If anything, this longstanding catch-22 has been exacerbated since 1989.

29. See Robert D. Putnam, *Bowling Alone: The Collapse and Revival of American Community* (New York: Simon & Schuster, 2000).

30. Michael E. Ruane, "An Instant Language, Packed with Meaning: Online Chatters Invent Shorthand for Fast Talk," *Washington Post*, 14 December 1999, A1.

31. According to a 2005 survey by the Kaiser Family Foundation, fifteen- to eighteen-year-olds average nearly six-and-a-half hours a day watching TV, playing video games, and surfing the Internet. About a quarter of the time (26 percent), they are multitasking. In the last few years the biggest increase has been computer use for activities such as social networking. Kaiser Family Foundation Study, "Generation M: Media in the Lives of 8–18 year Olds" (March 2005).

32. Quoted by Laura Sessions Stepp in "Point. Click. Think?" *Washington Post*, 16 July 2002, C1. Bernard Cooperman is a professor at the University of Maryland.

33. Edna Gunderson, "MTV Is a Many Splintered Thing: Mixed Reviews Greet 'Music' Channel's 20th," *USA Today*, 1 August 2001, D1.

34. Gunderson, "MTV."

35. Gunderson, "MTV."

36. Deborah Jannen, "Hey, Did You Catch That? Why They're Talking as Fast as They Can," *Washington Post*, 5 January 2003, B1.

37. Seth Margolis, "Back to the Present: A 1960s Show with Echoes of Today," *New York Times*, 2 January 2005, arts and entertainment section, 2.

38. Diane Brady, "Rethinking the Rat Race," *Business Week*, 26 August 2002, 142–43. This article not only confirms America's lead in working hours but underscores the point with the following poignant observation: "Americans take an almost masochistic pride in long hours. To be busy is a sign of

importance. The harder you work, the higher you rise. . . . In the U.S., it's all about what you do—not who you are. And those who sleep five hours a night or juggle two seemingly full-time pursuits evoke envy, not sympathy." See also Michael Mandel, "The Real Reasons You're Working So Hard . . .," *Business Week*, 3 October 2005, 60–73.

39. Quoted by J. Useem in "Dot-Com Ethics," *Fortune Magazine*, 20 March 2000, 86.

40. Alvin Toffler, *The Third Wave* (New York: William Morrow, 1980), 172.

41. Todd Gitlin, *Media Unlimited: How the Torrent of Images and Sounds Overwhelms Our Lives* (New York: Henry Holt &Co., 2001), 86.

42. Gitlin, *Media Unlimited*, 135.

43. Putnam, *Bowling Alone*.

44. Benjamin R. Barber, "The Uncertainty of Digital Politics: Democracy's Uneasy Relationship with Information Technology," *Harvard International Review* (Spring 2001): 42–47.

45. Barber, "The Uncertainty of Digital Politics," 46.

CHAPTER 6

1. In the early 1940s there were four national radio networks, one owned by CBS, one owned by Mutual, and two (the "Red" and "Blue" networks) owned by NBC.

2. Reported by Bill Moyers, "Journalism and Democracy," *The Nation*, 7 March 2001, 12, and by Bill Kovach and Tom Rosenstiel, "Are Watchdogs an Endangered Species?" *Columbia Journalism Review* (May/June 2001): 53.

3. In the fall of 2002, the Federal Trade Commission, in concert with the U.S. surgeon general, warned of a dramatic increase in the number of deceptive weight-loss ads appearing in all media. See Tom Taylor, "Too Good to Be True? The FTC Asks Broadcasters to Screen Weight Loss Ads," *Inside Radio*, 18 September 2002, 1.

4. James Poniewozik, "This Plug's for You," *Time*, 18 June 2001, 76–77.

5. Frank Ahrens, "The Spy Who Loved Nokia, and Other Next-Stage Ads: TV Plots Thicken with Real Brands," *Washington Post*, 28 September 2002, A1, A12.

6. Jeanne McDowell, "The Sponsor Moves In," *Time*, 23 August 2004, 41, reporting on a new drama appearing on ABC but owned by advertisers.

7. Neil Hickey, "Where TV Has Teeth," *Columbia Journalism Review* (May/June 2001): 42–46.

8. Hickey, "Where TV Has Teeth," 45.

9. Thomas Kunkel, "Go Slow on Cross-Ownership," *American Journalism Review* (March 2002): 4.

10. Sharyn Vane, "Taking Care of Business," *American Journalism Review* (March 2002): 60–61.

11. See Matthew Rose, "Wedding 'Church' and 'State' Works at Time, Inc. Unit," *Wall Street Journal*, 1 October 2002, A1 (describing how a lavish spread in *Southern Living* magazine featuring two new idea houses was carefully designed to please favored advertisers as much as readers).

12. "Radio and TV News Services: A Guide to Who Does What for Whom," a special report in *Broadcasting and Cable*, 13 August 2001, 38.

13. In one of the most celebrated recent failures of journalistic integrity, the venerable *Los Angeles Times*, in 1999, engaged in a cooperative venture with the Los Angeles Staples Center to produce a special section—without disclosing that the paper and the advertiser had a revenue-sharing arrangement for the extra section.

14. See, for example, Pamela McClintock, "Stodgy CNN Tries to Get Hip: Granddaddy of 24-Hour Newsies Takes on Younger Competition," *Variety*, 13 August 2001, 21; Alessandra Stanley, "How to Persuade the Young to Watch the News? Program It, News Executives Say," *New York Times*, 15 January 2002, C6. As the *Times* article notes, "The Buffy crowd, which had briefly tuned in during the immediate aftermath of September 11, 2001, has gone back to its old habits, much to the dismay of advertisers who are obsessed with youthful viewers."

15. Stanley, "How to Persuade," 16.

16. Paul Farhi, "Nightly News Blues," *American Journalism Review* (June 2001): 33–34. For daily newspapers, weekday readership among the adult population (age eighteen or over) has steady declined from 77.6 percent in 1920 to 55.1 percent in 2000. Moreover, whereas 61–72 percent of those over age forty-five still read a newspaper daily, only 40 percent of those in the eighteen- to twenty-four age group do so. "Facts About Newspapers, A Statistical Summary of the Newspaper Industry," published by Newspaper Association of America (2001), 6–7; Joseph T. Hallinan, "Newspaper Circulation Declines 1.9%," *Wall Street Journal*, 3 May 2005, B4, noting that figures available in early 2005 represented the biggest circulation tumble for newspapers in nearly a decade.

17. Quoted by Tad Friend in "Dead Air," a book review in the *New Yorker*, 7 May 2001, 90.

18. Friend, "Dead Air," 92.

19. Alessandra Stanley, "On Cable, a Fog of Words About Kerry's War Record," *New York Times*, 24 August 2004, A15.

20. Taken from www.nakednews.com (18 July 2002).

21. "The State of the News Media 2006," annual report of the Project for Excellence in Journalism (2006), Overview/Major Trends. www.stateofthenewsmedia.com/2006/printable_overview_eight.asp?media=1+cat=1.

22. See Rem Reider, "Sources of Despair," *American Journalism Review* (April/May 2004): 8.

23. Quoted material is from a Report of the Independent Review Panel, prepared for CBS by Dick Thornburgh and Louis D. Boccardi, 5 January 2005.

24. Leonard Downie Jr. and Robert G. Kaiser, *The News About the News* (New York: Alfred A. Knopf, 2002), 3.

25. Bill Kovach and Tom Rosenstiel, "Are Watchdogs an Endangered Species?" *Columbia Journalism Review* (May/June 2001): 50–53.

26. Neil Hickey, "Where TV Has Teeth," *Columbia Journalism Review* (May/June 2001): 42–46.

27. Hickey, "Where TV Has Teeth," 46.

28. Hickey, "Where TV Has Teeth," 43.

29. John V. Pavlik, *Journalism and New Media* (New York: Columbia University Press, 2001), 86.

30. Pavlik, *Journalism and New Media*, 86. The media world is being turned upside down by technology, including faster and more efficient means by which to gather and transmit news across traditional geographical barriers via the Internet. Compounding the threat to journalistic values such as objectivity and accuracy are the modern pressures of the never-ending news cycle and the demand for instant analysis. The dissemination of news is now instantaneous and global. A laptop is easily hooked to a satellite phone. Images from digital cameras are edited on a laptop and transmitted via the Internet within seconds from the site of a breaking story to a reporter's central office. This obviously broadens the opportunity for real-time news coverage but also carries new journalistic risks. For example, the advent of cheaper, lightweight video cameras has given birth to a new breed of freelance journalists who go into war zones and other dangerous places in search of marketable footage. When this is combined with the ease with which digital images can be manipulated, the risk for mischief becomes evident.

31. Kenneth Dautrich and Thomas H. Hartley, *How the News Media Fail American Voters: Causes, Consequences, and Remedies* (New York: Cambridge University Press, 1999), 2.

32. Dautrich and Hartley, *How the News Media Fail*, 6.

33. Dautrich and Hartley, *How the News Media Fail*, 113.

34. Richard Gunther and Anthony Mughan, eds., *Democracy and the Media* (Cambridge, U.K.: Cambridge University Press, 2000), 431–32.

35. Study conducted by the Lear Center Local News Archive, a collaboration between the Annenberg School at the University of Southern California and the political science department at the University of Wisconsin, titled "Local TV News Coverage of the 2002 General Election," 1, 4. www.local newsarchive.org/pdf/localTV2002.pdf (1 December 2004). See also Howard Kurtz, "Local TV News and the Elections: Ads Infinitum, but Few Stories," *Washington Post*, 5 November 2002, A7.

36. Lear Center Local News Archive, "Local TV News Coverage," 5.

37. "Local News Coverage of the 2004 Campaigns: An Analysis of Nightly Broadcasts in 11 Markets," a study conducted by researchers at the University of Wisconsin and Seton Hall University under the auspices of the Annenberg School for Communication at the University of Southern California.

38. Gunther and Mughan, *Democracy and the Media*, 23.

39. Neil Hickey, "Election Night: The Big Mistake," *Columbia Journalism Review* (January/February 2001): 32–35.

40. "Television's Performance on Election Night 2000: A Report for CNN," prepared by Joan Konner, James Risner, and Ben Wattenberg, 29 January 2001, 2.

41. Hickey, "Election Night," 32–33.

42. "Television's Performance," 1.

43. Tom Wolzien, "The Bottom Line: Election Night 2000," *Brill's Content* (February 2001): 97.

44. "Television's Performance," 3.

45. "CBS News President Promises Election Coverage Changes," *Communications Daily*, 26 July 2001, 6.

46. For a brief summary of an almost equally abysmal performance (albeit of a different sort) by mass media in the 1988 presidential election campaign, see Lawrence Grossman, *The Electronic Republic* (New York: Penguin Books, 1995), 220–21.

47. David Gergen, *Eyewitness to Power* (New York: Simon & Schuster, 2000), 335–37.

CHAPTER 7

1. The Transportation Act of 1920 is codified at 49 U.S.C. §10901. Other provisions of the Communications Act, notably those dealing with common carriers (telephone and telegraph), were derived from the Interstate Commerce Act of 1887, especially as amended in the Mann Elkins Act of 1910. Although the core phrase of communications law—"the public interest, convenience and necessity"—clearly originated from borrowed material, some researchers have pointed out that the phrase is actually an amalgamation, with the words "public interest" (used to connote service for the general public good) having been combined with "convenience and necessity," a concept long associated with public utility regulation. See Thomas W. Hazlett, "The Wireless Craze, The Unlimited Bandwidth Myth, The Spectrum Auction Faux Pas, and the Punchline to Ronald Coarse's 'Big Joke': An Essay on Airwave Allocation Policy," 14 *Harvard Journal of Law and Technology* 335, 362–63 (Spring 2001).

2. *FCC v. Pottsville Broadcasting Company*, 309 U.S. 134, 137 (1940).

3. See 47 U.S.C. §314 and 47 U.S.C. §313. Among other things, these provisions allow the FCC to revoke a broadcast license where the holder has

been found guilty under the antitrust laws. They also give an antitrust court the right to revoke a broadcast license as an additional remedy when violations of the antitrust laws are found.

4. See, for example, Robert W. McChesney, *Rich Media, Poor Democracy* (New York: The New Press, 1999), 189–225; William F. Baker and George Dessart, *Down the Tube* (New York: Basic Books, 1998), ix–xii, 32–42.

5. For example, there were already 536 stations and nearly 6 million radio sets in use by 1925. 67 Cong. Rec. 5498 (1926). Six years later, there were more than six hundred radio stations and the number of radio sets had doubled to twelve million. See *Report and Order and Notice of Proposed Rulemaking* issued by the FCC 2 July 2003 (FCC 03-127), 18 FCC Rec., No. 20, 13650 (paras. 92–93).

6. 78 Cong. Rec. 8828-37 (1934); See also McChesney, *Rich Media*, 226–80; Erick Barnouw, *The Golden Web: A History of Broadcasting in the United States, Vol. 2, 1937–1953* (New York: Oxford University Press, 1968), 23–26.

7. McChesney, *Rich Media*. In a Foreword to Baker and Dessart's *Down the Tube*, (journalist and critic) Bill Moyers offers this scathing indictment of television: "It was not by accident that we, almost alone among the nations of the world, delivered virtually the entire command of the public airwaves—and the public mind and heart and soul—directly and freely into the hands of the hucksters, the hustlers, and the hawkers." Baker and Dessart, *Down the Tube*, ix. Others criticize Congress's failure to provide explicitly for noncommercial radio at the outset. See Barnouw, *The Golden Web*.

8. See Ayn Rand, *Capitalism: The Unknown Ideal* (New York: The New American Library, 1966), 121 (the public interest "standard" amounted to a blank check on totalitarian power over the broadcasting industry, granted to whatever bureaucrats happened to be appointed to the [FCC])"; and Peter Huber, *Law and Disorder in Cyberspace: Abolish the FCC and Let the Common Law Rule the Telecosm* (New York: Oxford University Press, 1997), 4 ("A fateful choice was made: marketplace and common law were rejected. Central planning and the commission were embraced . . . to ration the scarcity and police the monopoly"). See also Bruce M. Owen, *Economics and Freedom of Expression* (Cambridge, Mass.: Bollinger, 1975); and Ithiel de Sola Pool, *Technologies of Freedom* (Cambridge, Mass.: Harvard University Press, 1983).

9. The libertarian view referenced here is one that argues that all mass media should be free of official government control in virtually all nontechnical activities. While it can be expressed differently and have different dimensions, one recurring theme is that the First Amendment allows no policy distinctions among media performing any kind of press function. In a 1973 opinion, in a case involving access to the broadcast media, Supreme Court Justice William O. Douglas put it this way: "What kind of First Amendment would best serve our needs as we approach the 21st century may be an open question. But the old-fashioned First Amendment that we have is the Court's only guideline;

and one hard and fast principle which it announces is that Government shall keep its hands off the press. . . . That means, as I view it, that TV and radio, as well as the more conventional methods of disseminating news, are all included in the concept of 'press' as used in the First Amendment and therefore are entitled to live under the laissez-faire regime which the First Amendment sanctions." *Columbia Broadcasting System v. Democratic National Committee,* 412 U.S. 94, 160-61 (1973). Traces of the argument can also be found in the positions sometimes taken by advocates of near-total freedom of access, expression, and association on the Internet.

10. Critics like Robert McChesney look at history and say that America made the wrong choice in the 1920s—that we should have placed broadcasting under a government charter like the BBC. Others, like Peter Huber, contend that the actual choice we made in 1927 and 1934 was "centralized planning" and law by "public edicts" from the FCC which reflected the more socialistic approach of the New Deal.

11. Paul Starr, *The Creation of the Media: Political Origins of Modern Communications* (New York: Basic Books, 2004), 394.

12. Glen O. Robinson, "The Federal Communications Act: An Essay on Origins and Regulatory Purpose," in *A Legislative History of the Communications Act,* ed. Max D. Paglin (New York: Oxford University Press, 1989), 3-24, 12, notes 39-41. Another perspective on this subject—with special relevance to contemporary media reformers who argue that America's failed mass media policy could easily be remedied if the "public" would just reclaim their rightful "ownership" of the airwaves—is found in the words of writer and philosopher Ayn Rand: "Since 'public property' is a collectivist fiction, since the public as a whole can neither use nor dispose of its 'property,' that 'property' will always be taken over by some political 'elite,' by a small clique which will then rule the public—a public of literal, dispossessed proletarians." Ayn Rand, *Capitalism: The Unknown Ideal* (New York: The New American Library, 1966) 124.

13. Near the end of the defining Senate debates on the Radio Act of 1927, its sponsor, Senator Clarence Dill, summarized the operable conceptual framework that he believed had been agreed upon: "The Government does not own the frequencies, as we call them, or the use of frequencies. It only possesses the right to regulate the apparatus, and that right is obtained from the provision of the Constitution which gives Congress the power to regulate interstate commerce." Bernard Schwartz, *The Economic Regulation of Business and Industry: A Legislative History of U.S. Regulatory Agencies,* vol. 3 (New York: Chelsea House Publishers/R.R. Bowker Co., 1973), 2079, 2297-98. At another point, Senator Dill said this: "The fact of the matter is that it makes no difference who owns the air or who claims to own channels in the air [which Senator Dill, in any event, thought to be impossible to possess in any ordinary sense]. The thing that is really controlling is the right to use apparatus which sends radio impulses into the air . . . When we talk about the

ownership of the air or ownership of channels in connection with radio, we only refer to . . . the right to use radio apparatus in a certain way." 68 Cong. Rec. 2871, 2873–74 (1927) (comments of Senator Dill).

14. The phrases "public interest, convenience and necessity," and "public interest, convenience, or necessity" appear throughout the Communications Act of 1934. One could search the act's remaining text and its legislative history endlessly without ever finding any significant differences seemingly intended by the conjunctive and disjunctive forms of these benchmark terms.

15. Erwin G. Krasnow and Jack Goodman, "The 'Public Interest' Standard: The Elusive Search for the Holy Grail," 50 *Federal Communications Law Journal* 605, 606 (1998).

16. *FCC v. Pottsville Broadcasting Co.*, 309 U.S. 134, 138 (1940).

17. See Randolph J. May, "The Public Interest Standard: Is It Too Indeterminate to Be Constitutional?" 53 *Federal Communications Law Journal* 427 (2001).

18. The right to "free speech," the promotion of the "general welfare," the "fair use" of copyrighted materials, and the exercise of "good faith" efforts in the performance of commercial contracts are similar, familiar concepts.

19. Quoted by Mark Crispin Miller in "What's Wrong with This Picture?" *The Nation*, 7/14 January 2002, 19–20.

20. Miller, "What's Wrong," 20.

21. The transmissions of radio and TV stations could, technically, occur on higher or different frequencies than those currently in use. But operating on the lower frequencies presently allocated to broadcasting has the distinct advantage of allowing broadcast signals to penetrate buildings and to cover greater distances at more efficient power levels.

22. From the beginning, Congress prohibited broadcast stations from being controlled by foreign interests (47 U.S.C. §310[b]), and made them subject to government control under emergency conditions. 47 U.S.C. §§308 and 606.

23. *National Broadcasting Co. v. United States*, 319 U.S. 190, 213, 215-17 (1943).

24. As expressed by Judge Bork in *Telecommunications Research and Action Center v. FCC*, 801 F.2d 501,508 (D.C. Cir. 1986), "It is unclear why [the mere excess of demand over supply in broadcast frequencies] justifies content regulation of broadcasting in a way that would be intolerable if applied to the editorial process of the print media."

25. See Mark S. Fowler and Daniel L. Brenner, "A Marketplace Approach to Broadcast Regulation," 60 *Texas Law Review* 207 (1982); Ithiel de Sola Pool, *Technologies of Freedom* (Cambridge, Mass.: Harvard University Press, 1983) 108–50; Peter Huber, *Law and Disorder in Cyberspace* (New York: Oxford University Press, 1997); Thomas W. Hazlett, "The Rationality of U.S. Regulation of the Broadcast Spectrum," 33 *Journal of Law and Economics* 133 (April, 1990); Glen O. Robinson, "The Electronic First Amendment: An Essay for the New Age," 47 *Duke Law Journal* 899 (1998); and *Action for Children's Television v. FCC*, 58 F.3d 654, 672-677 (D.C. Cir. 1995) (Edwards, C.J. dissenting).

26. See Peter Rojas, "Thinking of Radio as Smart Enough to Live without Rules," *New York Times*, 24 October 2002, E-5; Lee Gomes, "Visionaries See a Day When Radio Spectrum Isn't Scarce Commodity," *Wall Street Journal*, 30 September 2002, B1.

27. See Ronald H. Coase, "The Federal Communications Commission," 2 *Journal of Law and Economics* (October 1959): 1–40, an article that stirred academic debate in communications circles for years; Thomas W. Hazlett, "The Wireless Craze, the Unlimited Bandwidth Myth, the Spectrum Auction Faux Pas, and the Punchline to Ronald Coase's 'Big Joke': An Essay on Airwave Allocation Policy," 14 *Harvard Journal of Law and Technology* 335 (Spring 2001).

28. In a 1986 decision, well-known conservative judge Robert Bork wrote: "It is certainly true that broadcast frequencies are scarce [in the sense that demand would exceed supply if they were being offered free] but it is unclear why that fact justifies content regulation of broadcasting in a way that would be intolerable if applied to the editorial process of the print media. All economic goods are scarce, not least the newsprint, ink, delivery trucks, computers and other resources that go into the production and dissemination of print journalism. Not everyone who wishes to publish a newspaper, or even a pamphlet, may do so. Since scarcity is a universal fact, it can hardly explain regulation in one context and not another." *Telecommunications Research and Action Center v. FCC*, 801 F.2d 501, 508 (D.C. Cir. 1986).

29. *Associated Press v. U.S.*, 326 U.S. 1, 20 (1945).

30. *Turner Broadcasting System, Inc. v. FCC*, 512 U.S. 622, 663 (1994).

31. *In re Multiple Ownership of Broadcast Stations*, 45 FCC 1476, 1477 (1964).

32. *Red Lion Broadcasting Co. v. FCC*, 395 U.S. 367, 390 (1969).

33. *Columbia Broadcasting System, Inc. v. Democratic National Committee*, 412 U.S. 94 (1973).

34. *CBS, Inc. v. FCC*, 453 U.S. 367 (1981). Because the case centered on a political access complaint filed by the Carter-Mondale Presidential Committee, the case is often referred to as the "Carter-Mondale" decision.

35. P. O. Steiner, "Program Patterns and the Workability of Competition in Radio Broadcasting," *Quarterly Journal of Economics* 66(2), no. 1 (1952): 1, 194–223.

36. See, for example, "Reply Comments" of the Media Institute in MM Docket Nos. 01-and 00-244 (29 April 2002).

37. "Reply Comments," 4.

38. Communications Act, Section 307(b), 47 U.S.C. §307(b). This language was added in 1936. An earlier, more explicit effort to ensure local service had proven to be unworkable when matched with real-world engineering principles. This was the so-called Davis Amendment, enacted in 1928 out of concern for the paucity of stations in the South and West and a fear that radio was being monopolized by stations located in major cities. It required the Federal

Radio Commission to equalize, as nearly as possible, the number of stations, their power, and time of operation, among five zones into which the country had been divided. Further, the stations allocated to each zone were to be distributed evenly among the states in that zone. When it proved unworkable, the Davis Amendment was replaced by the current Section 307(b) in 1936.

39. Cable Television Consumer Protection and Competition Act of 1992, Pub. L. 102-385, 106 Stat. 1460 (October 5, 1992), §§2(a)(1).

40. Although the essence of "localism" is programming that serves a station's local community, the FCC, over the years, has developed a subset of standards designed to backstop the core concept. For example, a station must provide a signal of particular strength over its community of license; must maintain a "main studio" in or near its community of license; and must keep a special file with information on programming and other matters that is available for inspection by anyone from the local community. Other, formal requirements to help the public and the FCC measure broadcaster performance—such as written ascertainment and program processing guidelines—were early victims of the deregulatory movement.

41. *WNCN Listeners Guild v. FCC*, 610 F.2d 838 (D.C. Cir., 1979)(en banc).

42. *FCC v. WNCN Listeners Guild*, 450 U.S. 582 (1981).

43. Gerald Sussman, *Communication, Technology, and Politics in the Information Age* (Thousand Oaks, Calif.: Sage Publications, 1997), 179.

44. Competition was not always viewed by policymakers as a potential substitute for regulation. Indeed, in preregulatory days, unrestricted competition was sometimes seen as a vice that might undermine existing services. For example, at one time FCC policy (prompted by a federal court decision) actually took into account whether the introduction of an additional station into a particular marketplace might damage or destroy the level of public service provided by an existing station. See *Carroll Broadcasting Co. v. FCC*, 258 F. 2d 440 (D.C. Cir., 1958). A decade later, when advances in technology spawned new services that began to compete with mainline broadcasting, the FCC's initial reaction was to treat cable television, satellite, and similar distribution modes as secondary or "auxiliary" services that should not be allowed to undermine "free," over-the-air broadcasting. In furtherance of this policy approach, it adopted rules that not only mandated the carriage of local stations by cable systems but restricted the carriage of certain nonlocal signals.

45. Although these regulations have been on the books for nearly two decades, an argument can be made that what was enacted has failed and, in any event, has been overrun by marketplace developments. There is little doubt that regulation of some of the most offensive practices in children's television, introduced at a time when only three national networks dominated the mass media scene, changed the qualitative nature of such programming. On the other hand, there is also no doubt that in the ensuing years the marketplace has produced more children's programming in more formats—over-the-air television, cable, satellite, VCRs, DVDs, and computer discs—that,

in many instances, exceed the quality of offerings either before or since regulation began targeting only children's programming aired by over-the-air stations.

46. David Croteau and William Hoynes, *Media/Society: Industries, Images, and Audiences,* 2nd ed. (Thousand Oaks, Calif.: Pine Forge Press, 2000), 100.

47. Owen Fiss, "Why the State?" 100 *Harvard Law Review* (1987): 781, 787–88. See also John B. Thompson, *The Media and Modernity: A Social Theory of the Media* (Stanford, Calif.: Stanford University Press, 1995), 240. Professor Thompson capsulizes the same point as follows: "Left to itself, the market does not necessarily cultivate diversity and pluralism in the sphere of communication. Like other domains of industry, the media industries are driven primarily by the logic of profitability and capital accumulation, and there is no necessary correlation between the logic of profitability and the cultivation of diversity."

48. In 2004, Congress amended this perpetual review requirement by extending it from every two years to every four years.

49. Edmund Sanders, "FCC Eyes An Index for Media Mergers," *Los Angeles Times,* 10 February 2003, C. 1.

50. FCC *Report and Order* in MB Docket 02-277, released 2 July 2003 (paragraphs 391–481, Appendices C and D). The FCC's "diversity index" was inspired by the Herfindahl-Hirschman Index, long employed by the Antitrust Division of the Department of Justice. The FCC's media-only index accounts for television, radio, newspaper, and Internet outlets in local markets and also attempts to calculate the relative importance of these outlets as sources for local news and the concentration of ownership across different media.

CHAPTER 8

1. Harry J. Skornia, *Television and Society: An Inquest and Agenda for Improvement* (New York: McGraw-Hill, 1965), 7, 14. The issues identified by Skornia as plaguing broadcasting forty years ago have a familiar ring. They include: (1) excessive control by advertising interests; (2) a lack of courage in dealing with difficult public issues; (3) excessive concentration of station interests; (4) the exodus of creative talent from broadcasting; and (5) the failure to treat controversial issues and news inimical to big business. Interestingly, Skornia also lamented that TV executives in the mid-1960s were mostly "merchandisers and salesmen," arguing that broadcasting needed a new breed of leadership: "How is the nation to get a different kind of leadership to balance the views of the Sarnoffs, Paleys, Goldensons, Taishoffs . . .?" Now, of course, most observers look back at those early titans of the broadcasting business (respectively, the heads of NBC, CBS, ABC, and *Broadcasting* magazine) and the blended business and public service approach they followed as something sorely missing today.

2. See FCC *News Release,* 31 May 2003. The total of all *commercial* broadcast stations as of that date was 12, 323 (4,804 AM; 6,179 FM; and 1,340 TV). In addition, there were 2,400 educational FM and 381 educational TV stations.

3. *Red Lion Broadcasting Co v. FCC,* 395 U.S. 367, 394 (1969).

4. Although the fairness doctrine—which specifically required broadcast stations to present representative and contrasting viewpoints when treating controversial issues of public importance—was eliminated by an administrative decision of the FCC in 1987, the Communications Act still contains statutory language on which this policy was based. It says that broadcasters are under an "obligation . . . to operate in the public interest and to afford reasonable opportunity for the discussion of conflicting views on issues of public importance." 47 U.S.C. §315(a).

5. 47 U.S.C. §301.

6. 47 U.S.C. §§307–09.

7. Among other things, WLBT, despite having an audience that was nearly one-half African American, blocked programming feeds from its national network whenever the network scheduled a documentary about the civil rights movement or an interview with Dr. Martin Luther King. When it did so, it flippantly flashed on the screen the words, "Sorry, Cable Trouble."

8. See *Lamar Life Broadcasting Co.,* 38 FCC 1143 (1965), revised and remanded, *Office of Communication of United Church of Christ v. FCC,* 359 F.2d 994 (D.C. Cir. 1966).

9. See note 2, chapter 3. The leading groups at the time—such as the Citizens Communication Center, Action for Children's Television, the National Citizens Committee for Broadcasting, and the Office of Communication of United Church of Christ—simultaneously pushed for new standards and pressed for vigorous enforcement of existing standards. Among other things, this included expansions of the fairness doctrine to broadcast advertising, license renewal protests based on a station's failure to meet processing guidelines relating to public service programming or community ascertainment, and specific improvements in the areas of children's programming and minority hiring practices.

10. For many years the FCC maintained a three-year holding period on station licenses. It was called the "antitrafficking" rule and was intended to preclude profiteering in station licenses. Under the rule, anyone acquiring a broadcast property was required to actually operate the station in the "public interest" for a reasonable period of time. When this standard was unceremoniously dropped in the early deregulatory years, it became possible for parties to "flip" stations almost at will. Because the license renewal cycle has since been extended from three years to eight years, it is now possible for the ownership of a given station to change eight or more times during an eight-year *renewal* period.

11. In 2004, the FCC launched an official inquiry to explore, in very broad terms, where its localism policy stands at this late date. *In the Matter of Broadcast Localism*, "Notice of Inquiry" (MB Docket No. 04-233), released 1 July 2004.

12. See FCC *News Releases*, 10 February1970, 10 February 1992, 8 February 1996, and 10 February 2005, all titled "Broadcast Station Totals."

13. Public Law No. 104-104, 110 Stat. 56, 8 February 1996. Aptly named the Telecommunications Competition and Deregulation Act of 1996, it is referred to here as the "1996 act."

14. 1996 act; 1996 U.S. Code Congressional and Administrative News, Vol. 4, 11.

15. 142 Cong. Rec. S2207 (1996). Senator Pressler, chairman of the Senate Commerce Committee, emphasized among other things that "Congress had been so long about the business of updating the nation's antiquated communications laws . . ." 142 Cong. Reg. S686 (1996). "This is the first complete rewrite of the telecommunications law in our country. It is very much needed." 141 Cong Rec. S.7881 (1995). "We are in a situation today that our Nation very much needs to modernize its telecommunications laws." 141 Cong Reg. S.15144–45 (1995). "At stake is our ability to compete and win in an informational marketplace;" and, America is at a "historic turning point" where "the telecommunications and computer technology unleashed by [the 1996 act] will forever change our economy and society." 141 Cong. Rec. S. 7881 (1995).

16. 141 Cong. Rec. S7886 (1995). (Comments of Senator Pressler).

17. Quoted in Kirk Victor, "Here's a Train That Roared by Quietly," *National Journal*, 10 February 1996, 316.

18. Section 202(h) of the 1996 act.

19. 141 Cong. Rec., p. H. 8282(1995).

20. See, for example, Ben H. Bagdikian, *The New Media Monopoly* (Boston: Beacon Press, 7th ed., 2005); Elliot D. Cohen, "Corporate Media's Betrayal of America," in *News Incorporated: Corporate Media Ownership and Its Threat to Democracy*, ed. Elliot D. Cohen (Amherst, N.Y.: Prometheus Books, 2005), 17–32; Leo Bogart, *Commercial Culture: The Media System and the Public Interest* (New Brunswick, N.J.: Transaction Publishers, 2000); and Robert W. McChesney, *Rich Media, Poor Democracy* (New York: The New Press, 1999).

21. The story of how stiff LMA proposals drafted by the FCC's professional staff in 1998 quickly wilted in the face of intense congressional and broadcast industry pressure is captured in a set of trade press headlines at the time. See, for example, "LMA Threat Scares Broadcasters: NAB and Other Groups Mount Campaign to Head Off FCC Staff Proposals That Would Kill Most [LMA] Deals as Part of Major Revamp of the Commission's TV Ownership Rules," *Broadcasting and Cable*, 11 November 1998, 6 (quoting one source as saying that the broadcast "industry would hire every lobbyist in town to get Congress to crawl up the FCC's backside"); "LMA Battle Lines Being Drawn," *Broadcasting and*

Cable, 30 November 1998, 15 (reporting that key members of Congress were interested in stopping the contemplated action of the FCC); "Ownership Action on Hold at FCC," *Broadcasting and Cable,* 7 December 1998, 4; and " 'Bigwigs' Weigh in on Ownership: Wall Street Industry Executives Gain More Allies, Intensifying Pressure on the FCC," *Broadcasting and Cable,* 14 December 1998, 22 (reporting that the then speaker-elect of the House of Representatives, Bob Livingston, and various other members of Congress had written a letter "telling" the FCC to drop the proposal to eliminate LMAs).

22. "Media Madness," *Economist,* 13 September 2003, 14.

23. "Broadcasting's Split Sends Mixed Signals," *Broadcasting and Cable,* 21 July 2003, 48, quoting Ken Johnson, an influential aide to the then chairman of the House Commerce Committee, Billy Tauzin. Other members of Congress were quoted in the same article as having supported efforts to reverse the FCC's actions because of such matters as "NBC's . . . decision to run liquor ads . . . [and the TV] networks' lack of coverage of famine in Ethiopia, and the prevalence of such shows like 'The Bachelor,' 'The Bachelorette' and 'Joe Millionaire.'"

24. See "Legislation Increases Limit on Media Ownership to 39%," *Wall Street Journal,* online.wsj.com/article_print/o,,SB107481067953609343,00 .html.

25. Frank Ahrens, "Senate Adopts TV Station Limit," *Washington Post,* 23 January 2004, A.5.

26. On cable and satellite systems, for instance, services such as Nickelodeon, ABC Family Channel, Discovery Kids, the National Geographic Channel, and the History Channel offer parents and their children a wide variety and more conveniently scheduled array of prosocial programming than is typically found on commercial, over-the-air television channels.

27. Ben H. Bagdikian, *The Media Monopoly,* 5th ed. (Boston: Beacon Press, 1997), 228.

28. See "The New Radio Revolution," *Business Week,* 14 March 2005, 32–35.

29. See Bill Moyers, "Journalism & Democracy," *The Nation,* 7 May 2001, 11–17; Ryan Blethen, "Bashed, Thrashed and Encouraged,", *Seattle Times,* 19 January, 2007, www.freepress.net/news/print/20462 (January 20, 2007); William Safire, "Big Media's Silence," *New York Times,* 26 June 2003, A33; Ben H. Bagdikian, *The Media Monopoly,* 6th ed. (Boston: Beacon Press, 2000), xviii–xix.

30. These include rules and policies requiring sponsorship identification, banning subliminal advertising, and limiting any on-air "teaser" announcement (a specific type of inadequate sponsorship identification). Like separate laws that have long banned cigarette advertising on broadcast stations, any future problems in these other areas can be handled by other regulatory authorities under unfair trade laws.

31. Other rules of this nature to be eliminated include: (1) rules governing affiliation agreements between broadcast networks and their affiliated stations; (2) rules requiring stations to maintain a distinct main studio location; (3) rules requiring stations to maintain a public inspection file; (4) rules gov-

erning the broadcast of certain taped, filmed, or recorded material; (5) rules governing barter agreements and time brokerage; (6) rules governing agreements between broadcast stations and citizen groups; and (7) rules prohibiting broadcast hoaxes. In a separate category are statutory provisions that currently prohibit undisclosed payments or inducements to broadcast material ("payola" and "plugola") or the "rigging" of broadcast contests that involve "knowledge, skill or chance." If these latter provisions are retained, they should be enforced by other agencies of government such as the Federal Trade Commission or U.S. Department of Justice—both better able to investigate and prosecute this type of offense.

32. There is no doubt that, historically, the FCC looked to industry self-regulation to control broadcast advertising. But, it is also true that, until fairly recently, the FCC routinely monitored (and, thereby, effectively regulated) the overall quantity of broadcast advertising. Starting with its famous "Blue Book" in 1946, when the FCC announced that it would change its application forms to require each applicant to demonstrate how much time would be devoted to advertising in any one hour, and continuing with numerical processing guidelines employed throughout the 1960s and 1970s, the FCC has had a long history of focusing on the amount of broadcast advertising. The "Blue Book" is officially called "Public Service Responsibility of Broadcast Licenses" and can be found in *Documents of American Broadcasting*, 3rd ed. (Englewood Cliffs, N.J.: Prentice-Hall, 1978), 132–216. For more on the history of the FCC's regulation of broadcast advertising, see Carl R. Ramey, "The Federal Communications Commission and Broadcast Advertising: An Analytical Review," *Federal Communications Bar Journal* 20, no. 2 (1966): 71–116.

33. By early 2004, FCC fines had escalated to previously unheard of levels, reaching as much as $1.7 million in one network case. But that was only the beginning. In early 2006, under a new chairman, Kevin Martin, the FCC announced a batch of actions ensnaring several different broadcasters in new types of violations, including a record $3.6 million fine levied against more than one hundred station affiliates of the CBS television network that had aired an episode of the popular crime drama "Without A Trace," and a lesser but even more problematic fine against a documentary on public broadcasting depicting the history of jazz music. Then, in June 2006, Congress passed a new law raising the maximum fine for a single incident of indecency, from $32,500 to $325,000.

34. The federal provision that restricts broadcast obscene or indecent programming is not in the Communications Act but is part of the U.S. criminal code. See 18 U.S.C. §1464.

35. Technically, broadcasters who currently violate the indecency provision embedded in the criminal code can be punished directly by the Department of Justice, with such suits tried in federal courts and carrying the more serious risk of imprisonment. In practice, of course, virtually all infractions have been punished under the FCC's separate authority to assess forfeitures (fines). If the FCC were removed from this role, as urged in the main text, new standards

and remedies would have to be spelled out to not only put broadcasting in the same position as other media but to ensure that no media business faced the risk of jail time, except in cases involving the most egregious and highly repetitive conduct (e.g., where there had been a series of violations that followed explicit warnings).

36. Some might argue that political dialogue would suffer if the "equal opportunities" concept was eliminated from commercial broadcasting. That provision gives the opponent of a political candidate who has already purchased broadcast time an opportunity to purchase a similar amount of time on the same station. The argument would be that access would be denied (and hence, the public unable to hear or see) candidates who did not have sufficient funds to purchase such "equal time." But even now, such opposing candidates only obtain access if they have the funds to make a responsive purchase—since broadcast stations rarely afford political candidate's free, nonexempt program time. In short, under our system, candidates must first succeed in raising political funds before they can compete in the purchase of media advertising. This would not change under my proposal.

37. Other rules impacting local television stations but directed against local cable systems are the so-called must-carry rules which, when certain conditions are met, *require* certain cable systems to carry the signals of local TV stations. While such rules may have been justified in an earlier regulatory era and vastly different marketplace, they too must fall if commercial television is total deregulated—that is, finally, and completely, stripped of any public service responsibility or regulatory accountability. This is particularly relevant to the many secondary or marginal stations whose survival may have been sustained by carriage rights but who contribute virtually no public service benefits. If they are unable to survive without cable carriage rights or fail to pay the fee required for a permanent license, they *should* be allowed to fail. For stronger stations providing a more popular service, they should be able to negotiate their own private cable carriage arrangements—without the benefit of government rules. Such private arrangements would quickly become the norm if another essential step were taken. Specifically, deletion of the must-carry rules should be accompanied by a change in the copyright law which currently affords cable systems a special and highly beneficial "compulsory license" relating to certain television signals (resulting in favorable rates of payment for carriage of copyrighted program material). To the extent future abusive practices by either party adversely affected cable prices or the public's access to vital information, remedies would be available under the unfair trade or antitrust laws. Finally, since public television stations would, under my proposal, continue to operate under the public trusteeship model and, in fact, would assume new public service responsibilities, they should continue to receive basic cable carriage rights.

38. The use of competitive bidding was authorized in Pub. L. 105-33, Title III, §§3002(a)(1)–(3), 3003, 111 Stat. 258, 260, August 5, 1997. See 47 U.S.C. §309(j).

39. In my view, permanent license status should preclude any future change in technical facilities. A station obtaining a permanent license would acquire only that station's existing technical facilities, with no right to change facilities in order to improve or expand service. It would be necessary, however, to allow for some exceptions when specific technical changes were shown to be necessary to resolve a demonstrative conflict of a purely technical nature. On the other hand, permanent license status would also mean that the federal government could not take actions that would reduce a station's technical facilities—unless such actions were necessitated by a compelling national interest, in which case the station would receive an appropriate form of compensation.

40. Hart-Scott-Rodino Antitrust Improvements Act of 1976, Pub. L. 94-435, 90 Stat. 1383, 30 September 1976. This law makes companies or transactions meeting certain size requirements subject to reporting requirements and a waiting period, during which either the FTC or Department of Justice may investigate the proposed transaction and determine whether it raises any antitrust concerns.

41. As in all such matters, certain exemptions would undoubtedly be appropriate—such as excluding the very smallest transactions or exempting changes in ownership that are truly minor in nature.

42. See 47 U.S.C. §606, which gives the president authority to take possession and control of any radio system during time of war.

43. For the federal government, the power of eminent domain is found in the Fifth Amendment to the U.S. Constitution.

44. FCC application forms have long required broadcast applicants to inform the agency whether the applicant (or any party thereto) has been subject to any non-FCC proceedings, resulting in the denial of any specific government benefits, usually stemming from convictions under drug, fraud, and other criminal laws. Moreover, the Communications Act presently contains a provision giving any federal court hearing an antitrust case the additional power to revoke an FCC license when a licensed holder is found guilty under federal antitrust laws. 47 U.S.C. §313(a). Similar authority could easily be extended to federal courts hearing cases involving other crimes committed by the holder of a permanent FCC license.

45. Current law prohibits a broadcast license from being held by a company in which more than 20 percent of the capital stock is owned or voted by aliens, foreign governments, or their representatives, or in which more than 25 percent of a parent or controlling company is so held. See 47 U.S.C. §310.

46. Donald M. Gillmor, Jerome A. Barran, Todd F. Simon, and Herbert Terry, *Mass Communication Law: Cases and Comment*, 5th ed. (St. Paul, Minn.: West Publishing Company, 1990), 541.

47. Bagdikian, *New Media Monopoly*, 136–37; McChensey, *Rich Media*, 311–14.

48. See, for example, the proposal advanced by Maurice E. Stucke and Allen P. Grunes of the Antitrust Division of the Department of Justice in "Antitrust and

the Marketplace of Ideas," *Antitrust Law Journal* 62, no. 1 (2001): 249–302. Interestingly, one of the leading contemporary voices on antitrust, former FTC commissioner Robert Pitofsky, was emphasizing the same notion nearly twenty-five years ago. In his view, "It is bad history, bad policy, and bad law to exclude certain political values in interpreting the antitrust laws." Robert Pitofsky, "The Political Content of Antitrust," *University of Pennsylvania Law Review* 127 (1979): 1051. While stressing that "economic concerns would remain paramount," Petofsky also says that ignoring "non-economic factors would be to ignore the basis of antitrust legislation and the political consensus by which antitrust has been supported" (1075).

49. The risk of impairing First Amendment rights, always present when government regulates media, is not increased under my proposal. One might even argue that it is diminished, given the longstanding, highly politicized nature of the FCC. The "product" at issue may be information services, but neither the FCC, under existing law, nor antitrust officials, under a new law, can, or will be permitted to, engage in content regulation. Rather, they will need to focus on the number of owners, the number of competitive outlets (including their substitutability), the generalized kinds of information services provided, and overall market power, as reflected in such quantitative factors as audience and revenue share, or news and information resources (measured in terms of the levels of personnel, equipment, affiliations with others, etc.). And they should be able to examine other relevant objective criteria, such as the potential for conflicts of interest and the existence or absence of any self-regulating mechanisms.

50. 15 U.S.C. §2.

51. 15 U.S.C. §18.

52. Alec Klein, "A Hard Look at Media Mergers," *Washington Post*, 29 November 2000, E1 (available at WL29918451). A few years earlier, upon assuming the chairmanship of the Federal Trade Commission, Petofsky said: "You might take a tougher stance . . . in the media field [in contrast, say, with the shoe industry] because you are concerned that too much power in too few hands will impair freedom of expression." Quoted by Brian Gruley, "Petofsky Will Test Marketplace of Ideas Theory in FTC's Review of Time Warner-Turner Deal," *Wall Street Journal*, 9 October 1995, A14.

53. *Associated Press v. United States*, 326 U.S. 1, 27-28 (Frankfurter, J., concurring).

54. The "marketplace of ideas" is a term frequently heard in mass media policymaking discussions but rarely defined. The modern origin of the phrase is usually attributed to a famous dissenting opinion by the great Supreme Court jurist Oliver Wendell Holmes. In Justice Holmes's view, the First Amendment to the Constitution stands for the proposition that "the ultimate good desired is better reached by free trade in ideas [and] that the best test of truth is the power of the thought to get itself accepted in the competition of

the market. . . ." *Abrams v. United States*, 250 U.S. 616, 630 (1919) (Holmes, J., dissenting).

55. Stucke and Grunes, "Antitrust and the Marketplace of Ideas," 249. See also C. Edwin Baker, "Media Concentration: Giving Up on Democracy," *Florida Law Review* 54, no. 5 (December 2002): 839–919. Baker writes that "whether or not in other areas of the economy antitrust law should be largely restricted to economic efficiency concerns and monopolistic power over pricing, it should not be so limited in the media arena" (919).

56. Stucke and Grunes, "Antitrust and the Marketplace of Ideas"; *FCC v. National Citizens Committee for Broadcasting*, 436 U.S. 775, 800 n.18 (1978) ("this court has held that application of the antitrust laws to newspapers is not only consistent with, but is actually supportive of the values underlying, the First Amendment); and *Turner Broadcasting System v. FCC*, 512 U.S. 622 (1994). As Justice Black observed years earlier: "It would be strange indeed . . . if the grave concern for freedom of the press which prompted adoption of the First Amendment should be read as a command that the government was without power to protect that freedom. The First Amendment, far from providing an argument against application of the Sherman Act, here provides powerful reasons to the contrary." *Associated Press v. United States*, 326 U.S. 1, 20 (1945). Stucke and Grunes also believe that the legislative history of the Sherman and Clayton Acts lends further support for their proposal. The relevant points from that history are summarized as follows: "First, is the belief that, unless checked, industries may concentrate to such a degree that they could hamper our democracy. Second, if such concentration is not checked in its incipiency, more intrusive and undesirable governmental regulation may be required—which could be especially undesirable in the media industry. Third, the marketplace of ideas is subject to antitrust scrutiny. As a co-sponsor of the 1950 Clayton Act amendments stated, 'communities clearly benefit from this competing 'clash of opinion,' and the antitrust laws are intended to preserve this form of competition." Stucke and Grunes, "Antitrust and the Marketplace of Ideas," 258.

57. 47 U.S.C. §152(b)(1).

58. Statement of Representative John Conyers (D-Michigan), 142 Cong. Rec. H. (1996) 1171 (1996).

59. See, for example, Carnegie Commission on Educational Television, *Public Television: A Program for Action* (New York: Harper & Row, 1967) ("Carnegie I"); Carnegie Commission on the Future of Public Broadcasting, *A Public Trust: The Report of the Carnegie Commission on the Future of Public Broadcasting*, (New York: Bantam, 1979) ("Carnegie II"); William F. Baker and George Dessart, *Down the Tube: An Inside Account of the Failure of American Television* (New York: Basic Books, 1998); McChesney, *Rich Media*; and Jerold M. Starr, *Air Wars: The Fight to Reclaim Public Broadcasting* (Boston: Beacon Press, 2000). See also H.R. 3333, a comprehensive broadcast reform measure

considered by Congress in the late 1970s, and H.R. 2979, "The Public Broadcasting Self-Sufficiency Act of 1996," a measure that failed in the 104th Congress.

60. Carnegie II, as described in House hearings on H.R. 3333, 367.

61. See CPB's website at www.cpb.org under "Public Broadcasting Revenue." The exact figure has varied slightly from year to year but has always been less than 20 percent.

62. In addition to the nearly 16.39 percent received from CPB, public broadcasting in fiscal year 2005 received financial supported from the following sources: (1) membership (25.5 percent); (2) business (15.3 percent); (3) state governments (12.5 percent); (4) state colleges (7.8 percent); (5) foundations (6.8 percent); (6) local governments (3.4 percent); (7) federal grants and contracts (2.8 percent); (8) private colleges (1.6 percent); (9) other public colleges (0.9 percent); (10) auctions (0.5 percent); and (11) all other sources combined (5.37 percent). www.cpb.org (19 January 2007).

63. Carnegie II ($1.2 billion in 1979); Starr, *Air Wars*, 274–79.

64. See Henry Geller, "Promoting the Public Interest in the Digital Era," *Federal Communications Bar Journal* 55 (2003): 515, 518.

65. FCC "Notice of Proposed Rulemaking," FCC 04-66, 29 March 2004, Attachment D, "Schedule of FY 2004 Regulatory Fees."

66. Based on figures compiled by *Broadcasting and Cable Yearbook*, 2002–2003, A-90. See also FCC *Omnibus Order*, 2 July 2003 noting that over the past sixteen years, the average sale price of a radio station has been $5.74 million, while the average sale price of a TV station has been $43.14 million. 18 FCC Rec., No. 20, 13620, 13632 N. 58.

67. In 2000, Young Broadcasting Inc. purchased KRON-TV, a television station in San Francisco, for $823 million. In 2001, a secondary (nonleading) TV station in Los Angeles was sold for $239 million and a San Jose, California, station was sold for $230 million. And, in 2002, News Corporation (Fox) paid $425 million for a single TV station in Chicago. *TV and Cable Fax*, 17 July 2002, 2.

68. See "On the Same Wavelength," a special report on spectrum policy in the *Economist*, 14 August 2004, 61.

69. Information concerning various federal special purpose trust funds is based on consultations with Andrea Salinas, then a legislative specialist to Congressman Fortney Pete Stark, a senior member of the House Ways and Means Committee, and material supplied to Congressman Stark's office by the Congressional Research Service, May 2003.

70. See "Federal Sales of National Resources: Pricing and Allocation Mechanisms," a report prepared for Congress by the Congressional Research Service, 11 December 1998 (98-980 ENR).

71. A Roper survey in early 2005 showed that the American public trusts the PBS television service more than any other national institution. See John

Eggerton, "In PBS We Trust, According to PBS Survey," *Broadcasting & Cable*, 9 February 2005, 11. Even today, with hundreds of channels available, 82 million Americans tune in to PBS every single week, and in November 2004 (a month during which a national election was held), 140 million Americans watched PBS. Speech by Pat Mitchell, PBS president, before the Public Television Forum, University of Chicago, 2 December 2004. At the same time, weekly listenership to National Public Radio has soared, from around fifteen million in 2000 to twenty-five million in 2005. Arbitron.

72. See Carnegie I, Carnegie II; Baker and Dessart, *Down the* Tube, 214–63; Starr, *Air Wars*, 235–96; Hearings on H.R. 3333, 58–81 and 360–82.

73. CPB "Mission Statement," available at www.cpb.org (emphasis added).

74. The Public Broadcasting Act of 1967, as amended. See 47 U.S.C. §396(a)(1).

75. The Public Broadcasting Act of 1967, as amended. See 47 U.S.C. §396(a)(3).

76. The Public Broadcasting Act of 1967, as amended. See 47 U.S.C. §396(a)(5).

77. The Public Broadcasting Act of 1967, as amended. See 47 U.S.C. §396(a)(6). See also 47 U.S.C. §396(m) which requires CPB to assess periodically both "the needs of minority and diverse audiences" and the plans that public broadcasting has to address such needs.

78. The Public Broadcasting Act of 1967, as amended. See 47 U.S.C. §399.

79. The Public Broadcasting Act of 1967, as amended. See 47 U.S.C. §396(g).

80. Carnegie I (1967), p. 33.

81. See "Trapped Between 2 Languages: Poor and Isolated, Many Immigrant Children Lack English," *Washington Post*, 9 June 2002, A1.

82. The myriad exceptions and interpretations developed under the "equal opportunities" law largely for application to commercial broadcasters, could remain applicable to public broadcast stations. This would allow, for example, candidate debates and appearances on regularly scheduled news and interview programs to be carried without public stations being required to provide free time to every fringe candidate in every race.

83. In the *Matter* of *Representative Patsy Mink*, 59 F.C.C. 2d 987 (1976).

84. Ever since the public television system was established in 1967, it has had to dodge political bullets. During the early 1970s, the Nixon administration, reportedly unhappy with public television's heavy coverage of the Watergate hearings, initiated measures to curtail funding for the Corporation for Public Broadcasting. An even more frontal attack occurred in the mid-1990s when House Speaker Newt Gingrich famously declared war on Big Bird, a character on "Sesame Street," deriding PBS as a "little sandbox for the rich." Gingrich's offensive even sought to "zero out" federal subsidiaries for public television. In 2005, the political attacks took a more ominous tone,

with the focus shifting to the overall content and direction of public broadcasting. Instead of seeking to destroy or undermine the very existence of public broadcasting, these attacks seemed more determined to change its output, targeting individual talent and specific program material for their perceived partisan bias or cultural leanings.

85. Although focusing on improved content, the modified regulatory program for public broadcasting outlined in the text does not cross the line into impermissible content regulation. First, each of the standards flows naturally from existing congressional policy for public broadcasting and the long-standing mission statement of the CPB. Second, not one of the standards—focusing on local programming, public issue programming, and service to minorities and children—goes any further than policies once in place or continuing in place for commercial broadcasters. Over the years, special standards demanding the broadcast of certain kinds of political programming, children's programming, or controversial issue programming have all been upheld by courts when challenged on First Amendment or other grounds. Third, the procedures I have suggested to oversee ongoing performance in these areas—informal processing guidelines based on general standards first devised by industry groups—are exactly the sort of guidelines long used to oversee commercial broadcasters. Before being swept away in the deregulatory tide of the 1980s, such guidelines were used to examine the amount (expressed as a percentage of a typical week) of news, public affairs, and commercial matter that broadcast stations aired. Fourth, and finally, even if the foregoing were not the case, it is well to remember that public broadcasting has long operated under different constraints, starting with restrictions on advertising content and the prohibition against political endorsements. In short, the fact that public broadcasting receives public money puts it in a slightly different regulatory posture than commercial broadcasting. Content restrictions that might intrude on constitutional protections are no less important, but some of the standards and procedures historically employed to oversee public broadcasting have differed in some respects.

86. Benjamin R. Barber, "The Uncertainty of Digital Politics: Democracy's Uneasy Relationship with Information Technology," *Harvard International Review* (Spring 2001), 42, 47.

AFTERWORD

1. Todd Gitlin, *Media Unlimited: How the Torrent of Images and Sounds Overwhelms our Lives* (New York: Metropolitan Books, 2001), quotation taken from subtitle.

2. See, for example, Zecharia Chaffee Jr., *Government and Mass Communications: A Report from the Commission on Freedom of the Press* (Chicago: Univer-

sity of Chicago Press, 1947), 801–02; Wilbur Schramm, *Responsibility in Mass Communication* (New York: Harper & Brothers, 1957); Harry J. Skornia, *Television and Society: An Inquest and Agenda for Improvement"* (New York: McGraw-Hill, 1965); and John E. Coons, *Freedom and Responsibility in Broadcasting* (Evanston, Ill: Northwestern University Press, 1961).

    3. Schramm, *Responsibility,* 320–21.

    4. Robert W. McChesney, *Rich Media, Poor Democracy: Communication Politics in Dubious Times* (New York: The New Press, 2000), 300–02. "Media literacy" generally refers to education that teaches critical analysis skills so people can better understand how media interacts with and influences their lives. In some countries, like Canada, Australia, and England, a course in media literacy is often required to graduate from our equivalent of high school.

    5. See H.R. 13015 and H.R. 3333, introduced, respectively, in 1978 and 1979, by Lionel Van Deerlin, chairman of the House Communications Subcommittee. Among other things, H.R. 3333 (a revision of H.R. 13015) would have favored marketplace competition over behavioral regulation, given radio a near total exemption from public trusteeship obligations, relaxed certain television rules, and imposed a new, annual spectrum fee on commercial broadcasting.

    6. See Stephen Labaton, "Senators Take Steps to Reinstate Limits on Media Holdings," *New York Times,* 20 June 2003, A1 (emphasis added).

    7. Gerald Sussman, *Communication, Technology, and Politics in the Information Age* (Thousand Oaks, Calif.: Sage Publications, 1997), 282.

Bibliography

Alger, Dean. *Megamedia: How Giant Corporations Dominate Mass Media, Distort Competition, and Endanger Democracy*. Lanham, Md.: Rowman & Littlefield, 1998.

Bagdikian, Ben H. *The Media Monopoly*. 5th ed. Boston: Beacon Press, 1997.

———. *The Media Monopoly*. 6th ed. Boston: Beacon Press, 2000.

———. *The New Media Monopoly*. 7th ed. Boston: Beacon Press, 2004.

Baker, C. Edwin. "Media Concentration: Giving Up on Democracy." *Florida Law Review* 54, no. 5 (December 2002): 839–919.

Baker, William F., and George Dessart. *Down the Tube: An Inside Account of the Failure of American Television*. New York: Basic Books, 1998.

Barber, Benjamin R. "The Uncertainty of Digital Politics: Democracy's Uneasy Relationship with Information Technology." *Harvard International Review* (Spring 2001): 42–47.

Barnouw, Erik. *History of Broadcasting in the United States*. Vol. 1, *A Tower in Babel*. New York: Oxford University Press. 1966.

———. *History of Broadcasting in the United States*. Vol. 2, *The Golden Web*. New York: Oxford University Press, 1968.

Bignell, Jonathan. *An Introduction to Television Studies*. London: Routledge, 2004.

Bogart, Leo. *Commercial Culture: The Media System and the Public Interest*. New Brunswick, N.J.: Transaction Publishers, 2000.

Bogel, Donald. *Primetime Blues: African Americans on Network Television*. New York: Farrar, Straus & Giroux, 2001.

Boorstin, Daniel. *The Image: A Guide to Pseudo-Events in America*. New York: Harper & Row, 1961.

Brainard, Lori A. *Television: The Limits of De-regulation.* Boulder, Colo.: Lynne Rienner Publishers, 2004.

Brandy, Leo. *The Frenzy of Renown: Fame and Its History.* New York: Oxford University Press, 1986.

Brinkley, Joel. *Defining Vision: The Battle for the Future of Television.* New York: Harcourt Brace & Co., 1997.

Broadcasting and Cable. 11 November 1998–18 July 2005.

Business Week. 18 October 1999–3 October 2005.

Carnegie Commission. *Public Television: A Program for Action.* New York: Harper & Row, 1967.

———. *A Public Trust: The Report of the Carnegie Commission on the Future of Public Broadcasting.* New York: Bantam, 1979.

Chafee, Zecharia, Jr. *Government and Mass Communications: A Report from the Commission on Freedom of the Press.* Chicago: University of Chicago Press, 1947.

Chase, Francis, Jr. *Sound and Fury: An Informal History of Broadcasting.* New York: Harper, 1942.

Coase, Ronald H. "The Federal Communications Commission." *Journal of Law and Economics* 2 (October 1959).

Cohen, Elliot D., ed. *News Incorporated: Corporate Media Ownership and Its Threat to Democracy.* Amherst, N.Y.: Prometheus Books, 2005.

Communications Daily. 25 September 2000–27 April 2002.

Coors, John E. *Freedom and Responsibility in Broadcasting.* Evanston, Ill.: Northwestern University Press, 1961.

Croteau, David, and William Hoynes. *Media/Society: Industries, Images and Audiences.* 2nd ed. Thousand Oaks, Calif.: Pine Forge Press, 2000.

———. *The Business of Media: Corporate Media and the Public Interest.* 2nd ed. Thousand Oaks, Calif.: Pine Forge Press, 2006.

Dautrich, Kenneth, and Thomas H. Hartley. *How the News Media Fail American Voters: Causes, Consequences and Remedies.* New York: Columbia University Press, 1999.

DeFleur, Melvin L., and Sandra Ball-Rokeach. *Theories of Mass Communication.* 5th ed. White Plains, N.Y.: Longman, 1989.

DeFleur, Melvin L., and Everette E. Dennis. *Understanding Mass Communications: A Liberal Arts Perspective.* 7th ed. Boston: Houghton Mifflin, 2002.

Dizard, Wilson, Jr. *Old Media, New Media: Mass Communications in the Information Age.* 3rd ed. New York: Longman, 2000.

Downie, Leonard, Jr., and Robert G. Kaiser. *The News about the News.* New York: Alfred A. Knopf, 2002.

Doyle, Gillian. *Media Ownership: The Economics and Politics of Convergence and Concentration in the UK and European Media.* London: Sage Publications, 2002.

Economist. 13 September 2003–23 April 2005.

Entman, Robert N. *Democracy without Citizens: Media and the Decay of American Politics.* New York: Oxford University Press, 1989.

Fang, Irving. *A History of Mass Communication.* Boston: Focal Press, 1997.

Farhi, Paul. "Nightly News Blues." *American Journalism Review* (June 2001).

Federal Communications Commission. Adoption of Rules Concerning Operation of Non-Commercial Educational Stations. *Report,* 1938.

———. Public Service Responsibility of Broadcasting Licenses. *Report,* 1946.

———. Program Policy Statement. *Report,* 1960.

———. In Re Multiple Ownership of Broadcast Stations. *Report,* 1964.

———. Rulemaking to Require Broadcast Licensees to Show Nondiscrimination in Their Employment Practices. *Report,* 1968.

———. Primer on Ascertainment of Community Problems by Broadcast Applicants. *Report,* 1971.

———. Application for Voluntary Assignments or Transfer of Control. *Report,* 1982.

———. Revision of Programming and Commercialization Policies, Ascertainment Requirements, and Program Logs for Commercial Television Stations. *Report,* 1984.

———. Elimination of Unnecessary Broadcast Regulations. *Report,* 1985.

———. In the Matter of Broadcast Localism. *Notice,* 2004.

———. 2006 Quadrennial Regulatory Review of the Commission's Broadcast Ownership Rules and Other Rules Adopted Pursuant to Section 202 of the Telecommunications Act of 1996. *Notice,* 2006.

Geller, Henry. "Promoting the Public Interest in the Digital Era." *Federal Communications Law Journal* 55 (2003): 515.

Gergen, David. *Eyewitness to Power.* New York: Simon & Schuster, 2000.

Gillian, James. *Violence: Reflections on a National Epidemic.* New York: Vantage Books, 1996.

Gillmore, Donald M., Jerome A. Barron, Todd F. Simon, and Herbert Terry. *Mass Communication Law: Cases and Comment.* 5th ed. St. Paul, Minn.: West Publishing Company, 1990.

Ginsburg, Douglas H. *Regulation of the Electronic Mass Media.* 2nd ed. St. Paul, Minn.: West Publishing Company, 1991.

Gitlin, Todd. *Media Unlimited: How the Torrent of Images and Sounds Overwhelms Our Lives.* New York: Henry Holt & Co., 2001.

Grossberg, Lawrence, Ellen Wartella, and D. Charles Whitney. *Media Making: Mass Media in a Popular Culture.* Thousand Oaks, Calif.: Sage Publications, 1998.

Grossman, Lawrence. *The Electronic Republic.* New York: Penguin Books, 1995.

Gunther, Richard, and Anthony Mugham. *Democracy and the Media.* Cambridge, U.K.: Cambridge University Press, 2000.

Hamilton, James T. *All the News That's Fit to Sell.* Princeton, N.J.: Princeton University Press, 2004.

Hazlett, Thomas W. "The Rationality of U.S. Regulation of the Broadcast Spectrum." *Journal of Law and Economics* 33 (1990): 133.

——. "The Wireless Craze, the Unlimited Bandwidth Myth, the Spectrum Auction Faux Pas, and the Punchline to Ronald Coase's 'Big Joke': An Essay on Airwave Allocation Policy." *Harvard Journal of Law and Technology* 14 (2001): 335.

Head, Sydney W., Thomas Spann, and Michael A. McGregor. *Broadcasting in America: A Survey of Electronic Media.* 9th ed. Boston: Houghton Mifflin, 2001.

Heyboer, Kelley. "Targeting Youth." *American Journalism Review* (December 2002).

Hickey, Neal. "Chicago Experiment—Why It Failed." *Columbia Journalism Review* (January–February 2001).

——. "Election Night: The Big Mistake." *Columbia Journalism Review* (January–February 2001).

——. "Where TV Has Teeth." *Columbia Journalism Review* (May–June 2001).

——. "TV's Big Stick: Why the Broadcast Industry Gets What It Wants in Washington." *Columbia Journalism Review* (September–October 2002).

Huber, Peter. *Law and Disorder in Cyberspace: Abolish the FCC and Let the Common Law Rule the Telecosm.* New York: Oxford University Press, 1997.

Katz, Yaron. *Media Policy for the 21st Century in the United States and Western Europe.* Cresskill, N.J.: Hampton Press, 2005.

Kovach, Bill, and Tom Rosenstiel. "Are Watchdogs an Endangered Species?" *Columbia Journalism Review* (May–June 2001).

Krasnow, Erwin G., and Jack Goodman. "The 'Public Interest' Standard: The Elusive Search for the Holy Grail." *Federal Communications Law Journal* 50 (1998): 605.

Kunkel, Thomas. "Go Slow on Cross-Ownership." *American Journalism Review* (March 2002).

Layton, Charles. "Lobbying Juggernaut." *American Journalism Review* (October–November 2004).

Lull, James. *Media Communication and Culture.* 2nd ed. New York: Columbia University Press, 2000.

May, Randolph J. "The Public Interest Standard: Is It Too Indeterminate to Be Constitutional?" *Federal Communications Law Journal* 53 (2001): 427.

McChesney, Robert W. *Corporate Media and the Threat to Democracy.* New York: Seven Stories Press, 1997.

——. *Rich Media, Poor Democracy: Communication Politics in Dubious Times.* New York: The New Press, 1999.

——. *The Problem of the Media: U.S. Communication Politics in the 21st Century.* New York: Monthly Review Press, 2004.

Monaco, James. *Celebrity: The Media as Image Makers.* New York: Delta Publishing, 1978.

National Journal, 1 February 2007.

New Yorker. 7 May 2001–29 October 2001.

New York Times. 16 October 2000–16 October 2006.

Owen, Bruce M. *Economics and Freedom of Expression.* Cambridge, Mass.: Bollinger, 1975.

Patterson, Thomas E. "Doing Well and Doing Good: How Soft News and Critical Journalism Are Shrinking the News Audience and Weakening Democracy." *Wilson Quarterly* (Summer 2001).

Pavlik, John V. *Journalism and New Media.* New York: Columbia University Press, 2001.

Peterson, Theodore, Jay W. Jensen, and William L. Rivers. *The Mass Media and Modern Society.* New York: Holt, Rinehart & Winston, 1967.

Petofsky, Robert. "The Political Content of Antitrust." *University of Pennsylvania Law Review* 127 (1979): 1051.

Pool, Ithiel de Sola. *Technologies of Freedom.* Cambridge, Mass.: Harvard University Press, 1983.

Putnam, Robert D. *Bowling Alone: The Collapse and Revival of American Community.* New York: Simon & Schuster, 2000.

Ramey, Carl R. "The Federal Communications Commission and Broadcast Advertising: An Analytical Review." *Federal Communications Bar Journal* 20, no. 2 (1966): 71–116.

Rand, Ayn. *Capitalism: The Unknown Ideal.* New York: The New American Library, 1966.

Reider, Rem. "Sources of Despair." *American Journalism Review* (April–May 2004).

Robinson, Glen O. "The Federal Communications Act: An Essay on Origins and Regulatory Purpose." In *A Legislative History of the Communications Act,* edited by Max D. Paglin. New York: Oxford University Press, 1989.

———. "The Electronic First Amendment: An Essay for the New Age." *Duke Law Journal* 47 (1998): 899.

Rodman, George. *Making Sense of Media: An Introduction to Mass Communications.* Boston: Allyn & Bacon, 2001.

Scherer, Michael. "Does Size Matter?" *Columbia Journalism Review* (November–December 2002).

Schiller, Herbert. *Mass Communications and American Empire.* 2nd ed. Boulder, Colo.: Westview Press, 1992.

Schiller, Ruel E. "Rulemaking's Promise: Administrative Law and Legal Culture in the 1960s and 1970s." *Administrative Law Review* 53, no. 4 (2001): 1139–88.

Schramm, Wilbur. *Responsibility in Mass Communication.* New York: Harper & Brothers, 1957.

Schwartz, Bernard. *The Economic Regulation of Business and Industry: A Legislative History of U.S. Regulatory Agencies,* vol. 3. New York: Chelsea House Publishers/R. R. Bowker, 1973.

Severin, Werner J., and James W. Tankard Jr. *Communication Theories: Origins, Methods and Uses in the Mass Media.* New York: Longman, 2001.

Skornia, Harry J. *Television and Society: An Inquest and Agenda for Improvement.* New York: McGraw-Hill, 1965.

Starr, Jerold M. *Airwars: The Fight to Reclaim Public Broadcasting.* Boston: Beacon Press, 2000.

Starr, Paul. *The Creation of the Media: Political Origins of Modern Communications.* New York: Basic Books, 2004.

Steiner, P. O. "Program Patterns and the Workability of Competition in Radio Broadcasting." *Quarterly Journal of Economics* 66, no. 2 (1952).

Straubhaar, Joseph, and Robert LaRose. *Media Now: Understanding Media, Culture, and Technology.* 5th ed. Belmont, Calif.: Thomason-Wadsworth, 2006.

Stucke, Maurice E., and Allen P. Grunes. "Antitrust and the Marketplace of Ideas." *Antitrust Law Journal* 62, no. 1 (2001): 249–302.

Sussman, Gerald. *Communications, Technology, and Politics in the Information Age.* Thousand Oaks, Calif.: Sage Publications, 1997.

Thompson, John P. *The Media and Modernity: A Social Theory of the Media.* Stanford, Calif.: Stanford University Press, 1995.

Time. 18 June 2001–23 August 2004.

Toffler, Alvin. *The Third Wave.* New York: William Morrow, 1980.

USA Today. 1 August 2001–10 June 2004.

Vane, Sharyn. "Taking Care of Business." *American Journalism Review* (March 2002).

Wall Street Journal. 25 February 2002–3 October 2005.

Washington Post. 14 December 1999–22 June 2005.

Wenner, Kathryn S. "Bang, Bang, Bang." *American Journalism Review* (November 2002).

Wilson, James R., and S. Roy Wilson. *Mass Media, Mass Culture: An Introduction.* 5th ed. Boston: McGraw-Hill, 2001.

Witherspoon, John, and Roselle Kovitz. *The History of Public Broadcasting.* Pamphlet published by *Current,* 1987.

Wright, C. R. *Mass Communication: A Sociological Perspective.* New York: Random House, 1959.

Index

About the Author

Carl R. Ramey is a communications attorney and a thirty-year veteran of the Washington, D.C. policymaking process. Inspired by an adolescent fascination with broadcasting, he put himself through college working as a radio announcer and went to graduate school to pursue an academic career in mass communications. But an early course correction resulted in a JD, not a PhD. As a lawyer, he represented ABC and other leading media companies in several landmark Supreme Court cases and participated in virtually all important mass media issues coming before the FCC and Congress. Now living in North Carolina, he brings a unique and balanced perspective to the current Washington debates over the role and direction of mass media policy at the beginning of the twenty-first century.